Issues in Historiography

The Debate on the American Revolution

Manchester University Press

Issues in Historiography
General editor
R. C. RICHARDSON
University of Winchester

Already published

The Debate on the Norman Conquest
Marjorie Chibnall

The Debate on the French Revolution
Peter Davies

The Debate on the English Revolution
R. C. Richardson

The Debate on the American Civil War Era
H. A. Tulloch

The Debate on Black Civil Rights in America
Kevern Verney

The Debate on the Rise of the British Empire
Anthony Webster

Issues in Historiography

The Debate
on the American Revolution

GWENDA MORGAN

MANCHESTER
UNIVERSITY PRESS
MANCHESTER AND NEW YORK

distributed exclusively in the USA by Palgrave

Published by Manchester University Press
Oxford Road, Manchester M13 9NR, UK
and Room 400, 175 Fifth Avenue, New York, NY 10010, USA
www.manchesteruniversitypress.co.uk

Distributed exclusively in the USA by
Palgrave, 175 Fifth Avenue, New York,
NY 10010, USA

Distributed exclusively in Canada by
UBC Press, University of British Columbia, 2029 West Mall,
Vancouver, BC, Canada V6T 1Z2

British Library Cataloguing-in-Publication Data
A catalogue record for this book is available from the British Library

Library of Congress Cataloging-in-Publication Data applied for

ISBN 978 0 7190 5241 5 *hardback*
ISBN 978 0 7190 5242 2 *paperback*

First published 2007

16 15 14 13 12 11 10 09 08 07   10 9 8 7 6 5 4 3 2 1

Typeset by Action Publishing Technology Ltd, Gloucester
Printed in Great Britain by Biddles Ltd, King's Lynn, Norfolk

To Peter

CONTENTS

GENERAL EDITOR'S FOREWORD

History without historiography is a contradiction in terms. The study of the past cannot be separated from a linked study of its presenters. No historian writes in isolation from the work of his or her predecessors nor can the commentator – however clinically objective or professional – stand aloof from the insistent pressures, priorities and demands of the ever-changing present. In truth there are no self-contained 'ivory towers'. Historians' writings are an extension of who they are and where they are placed. Though historians address the past as their subject they always do so in ways that are shaped – consciously or unconsciously as the case may be – by the society, cultural ethos, and systems of their own day, and they communicate their findings in ways which are specifically intelligible and relevant to a reading public consisting initially of their own contemporaries. For these reasons the study of history is concerned most fundamentally not with dead facts and sterile, permanent verdicts but with highly charged dialogues, disagreements, controversies, and shifting centres of interest among its presenters, and with the changing methodologies and discourse of the subject over time. *Issues in Historiography* is a series designed to explore such matters by means of case studies of key moments in world history and the interpretations and reinterpretations they have engendered.

The American Revolution of the late eighteenth century, like the earlier mid-seventeenth-century English Revolution and the later French and Russian Revolutions – all featuring or about to feature in this series – were partly civil wars. All were divisive and dislodging at the time they happened. All had their radicals and conservatives, 'winners' and 'losers'. None of them was self-contained in time or place; all were directly impinged upon and shaped by their respective pasts and broader contemporary geograpical contexts. All decisively affected the future course of events. Crane Brinton's famous overview of all four revolutions *The Anatomy of Revolution* (New York, 1938, 1952), first written while the iron fist of Stalinism was still inflicting its terror, is probably the boldest attempt to portray their common denominators, structures, ideologies and impacts. Other historians, more recently and manageably, have explored the specific interconnectedness of the English and American Revolutions. (J. G. A. Pocock (ed.), *Three British Revolutions: 1641, 1688, 1776* (Princeton, NJ, 1980) and Margaret Jacob and James Jacob (eds), *The Origins of Anglo-American Radicalism* (London, 1984) are two major examples.) The American Revolution, it is clear, needs to be understood within the framework of the Atlantic World and British Imperialism of the time and in the light of a usable radical inheritance from the seventeenth-century English commonwealth and republic and its intermingling with the homespun ideas, beliefs and experience of the American colonists themselves. John Adams, writing in 1815, was pessimistic about the possibility of writing its complex, many-sided history. But a number of writers by that point had already taken up their pens, indulging their contrasting convictions about the significance of 1776 and the new nation which afterwards emerged. David Ramsay's insistence on the word *Revolution* in the title of his history, and Peter Oliver's contrasting loyalist preference for *Rebellion* in his, encapsulated some of the obvious dividing lines between those who had lived through the upheavals. Since then the teeming historiography of this subject has been unstoppable. Events and developments as varied as the American Civil War, the rise of Anglo-Saxonism, the First World War, the Civil Rights movement, feminism, the emergence of the New Left, and the bicentennial commemorations of 1976 have all left their mark on the ways in which the American Revolution has been presented and interpreted. Its relevance and capacity to arouse profound disagreement are no less today than they were originally, though the relevance and the nature of disagreement are now obviously very differently defined. That historians go on being drawn to the subject of the American Revolution is explained by its obvious defining centrality within the American experience. How they have written about it at particular times needs more careful and individual examination. (Major historian Charles Beard's formative experience in the disadvanged pre-1914 East End of London gives important clues in his case to the origins of his particular slant (far from worshipful) on the origins of the American constitution.)

Gwenda Morgan's helpfully structured and well-argued book charts a clear course through this densely difficult field and combines a broadly thematic treatment with an internal chronology in each of her chapters. Different past depictions of the causes and consequences of the Revolution are insightfully assessed and a whole chapter is given over to historians' verdicts on the working out of the Federal Constitution. The contributions of different 'party spirits' and 'schools' in the historiography of the American Revolution are carefully weighed as is the work of key individual writers such as George Bancroft (1800–1891) Charles Beard (1874–1948), Daniel Boorstin (1914–2004), Edmund Morgan (1916–), Bernard Bailyn (1922–) and Jack P. Greene (1931–). (Note the striking longevity of all these leading figures; this is clearly a healthy topic of study!) The impact from the late nineteenth century of the rise of the professional historian on American Revolutionary histiography is considered, as are the very different influences of British political historian Sir Lewis Namier (famous for his 'atomising' approach) and (much later) the new social history and 'History from Below' (English historiographical precedents were important here, too). Morgan also makes clear that the American Revolution, like other fields of study, is now no longer seen as exclusively a man's world in its making; nor are modern men its only historians. Mary Beth Norton's *Liberty's Daughters: The Revolutionary Experience of American Women 1750–1800* (Boston, 1980) and Linda K. Kerber's *Women of the Republic* (Chapel Hill, NC, 1980) are highlighted in Chapter 6 as two very significant examples (both published in the same year to boot) of a veritable 'new era in female history'. The 'disappeared' and the 'losers' – loyalists, women, African Americans and Native Americans – are all now receiving long-overdue scholarly attention. The debate on the American Revolution, as Morgan's book makes perfectly clear, is still hyperactive today. The appearance in 1991 of an encyclopaedia on the subject (edited by Jack P. Greene and J. R. Pole) testified to its burgeoning literature. This study by Gwenda Morgan, wide-ranging though not encyclopaedic, fills a real gap and students will recognize the obvious utility of a helpful survey which extends from William Gordon's *History of the Rise, Progress and Establishment of the Independence of the United*

States of America (1788) to historians such as Gary Nash writing at the beginning of the twenty-first century.

R. C. Richardson
October 2006

ACKNOWLEDGEMENTS

This project was made possible by generous financial support from the research committees of the Schools of Humanities and Social Science and of Arts, Design, Media and Culture of the University of Sunderland which granted me leave to pursue research in the United States on several occasions as well as in London. The British Library opened its new facilities shortly before I began work on this book and despite my regret at no longer being able to use the old reading room in the British Museum and walk through the King's Library, I have to admit it was a great place to work. Particular thanks are due to the staff of the Rare Books Room. As always I found the Institute of Historical Research of the University of London an essential resource. Local and regional libraries were also helpful and I thank the staff of the libraries of the Universities of Durham, Newcastle and Sunderland and especially Jane Moore, interlibrary loan librarian at the latter. This project could not have been completed had I not had access to the resources of the Library of Congress, the Boston Public Library and the New York Public Library as well as the opportunity to visit the Smithsonian National Museum of American History, and the National Museum of the American Indian, as well as the National Gallery of Art, Washington DC. The Omohundro Institute of Early American History and Culture provided me with a base in Williamsburg where I was able to exploit the resources of the Earl Gregg Swem library of the College of William and Mary, the Kellogg library of the Institute and the Rockefeller Library of Colonial Williamsburg. Among individuals I would like to thank Ron Hoffman for sharing his expertise with me and also Beverley Smith, Chris Grasso, Karin Wulf, Bob Gross, Jim Horn, Thad Tate, Woody Holton, Lorena Walsh, Lois Carr, Jack Greene, Tom Purvis, Karen Kupperman, Elizabeth Homsey, Pat Gibbs, Dorothy Rouse Bottom, Mary Beth Norton, Joan Hoff, Carmel Connelly, Laura Sandy, Jean Spence and Peter Rushton; also members of the British Group of Early American Historians, among them, Steve Sarson, Peter Thompson, Mike McDonnell, Matthew Ward and Rebecca Starr. Roger Richardson, editor of the series in which this book appears, and Alison Welsby of Manchester University Press, offered valuable advice and support over the years in this 'arduous but interesting task'. Alex Wadden, Jean Spence and Peter Rushton read some or all of the manuscript.

ABBREVIATIONS

AHR	*American Historical Review*
ANB	*American National Biography*
AQ	*American Quarterly*
AJLH	*American Journal of Legal History*
JAH	*Journal of American History*
JER	*Journal of the Early Republic*
JNH	*Journal of Negro History*
JSH	*Journal of Southern History*
PSQ	*Political Science Quarterly*
NEQ	*New England Quarterly*
ODNB	*Oxford Dictionary of National Biography*
SAQ	*South Atlantic Quarterly*
SQ	*Southern Quarterly*
WMQ	*William and Mary Quarterly*

INTRODUCTION

'To enter the domain of historiography,' writes Alfred Young 'one has to pass through the thorny thicket in which scholars are sorted out by "schools", the dangers of which have been persistently deplored by historians of almost all persuasions'.[1] Loyalist Jonathan Boucher made the first attempt to write an historiographical essay in 1797. He judged his fellow authors on the basis of 'party spirit', commercial motivation and objectivity, condemning the first two and extolling the third.[2] Carl Becker rejected this practice entirely. He regarded J. S. Bassett's use of the labels 'patriotic', 'literary' and 'scientific' to distinguish a number of nineteenth-century historians as useless for purposes of historical criticism. The labels told him little that he cared to know about and he reserved particular antipathy for the term 'scientific', a designation usually invoked to mark the bearer as a professional historian, trained in the graduate schools of Europe and the nation's reformed universities and committed to the quest for 'that noble dream', objectivity.[3] Charles Beard, on the other hand, had no such qualms. He identified three schools of interpretation that in his view had dominated 'American historical research and generalization': one was personified by George Bancroft, the second he termed 'teutonic', and the third made a point of having no hypotheses at all. Since none of these had proved satisfactory, Beard advocated a fourth, at least on a trial basis, one as yet untested in America though common enough in Europe, namely an economic approach.[4]

Writing in 1957 Edmund Morgan reasoned that neither imperialist, economic nor Namierite historians had inspired much research into English and American history over the past fifty years, thus failing to bring about a major re-examination of either the causes or character of the American Revolution. Though the works of the imperialists had 'necessarily squinted at the revolution in every sentence, the only direct confrontations have been brief and inconclusive'. The social and economic approach had addressed aspects of the Revolution, Morgan commented, but historians still had little grasp of the social and economic divisions in American society during the colonial and revolutionary periods. Unlike Beard whose comments were a prelude to a bold attempt to take American history forward, Morgan dared to suggest that the nineteenth-century Whig interpretation of the Revolution identified with George Bancroft – the idea of progress and the concept of America as 'the light of the world' – was worth another look. Morgan appears to have accepted the Namierite position that 'local interests were the keynote of British politics', but regarded Bancroft as asking the right questions in relation to the Revolution. Historians needed to break with the dominant approaches to early American history and the Revolution and seek out the origins of the Revolution in the American past.[5]

But if Edmund Morgan advocated looking backwards to George Bancroft, Page Smith proposed a return to David Ramsay's 1789 *History of the American Revolution* for the best interpretation of the causes of the Revolution. Despite advances in methodology, improved access to sources, specialization and a longer term perspective, later historians were prone to distortions imposed on them by their own *Zeitgeist*. Smith questioned whether subsequent generations of historians had actually improved on Ramsay's account. After all, Ramsay 'was there. He saw it happen, felt it, experienced it on many levels. It was part of the complex fabric of his life'.[6]

Certainly, to be fair, commentators on the work of the so-called imperialist historians such as Herbert L. Osgood, Charles M. Andrews and George L. Beer have made much of the Anglo-American rapprochment in the late nineteenth century tied on the one hand to a recognition of the problems of governing far-flung empires and a recollection of common origins, and, on the other, to the rise of Anglo-Saxonism, racism and mass immigration.[7] Sometimes the perception of change was identified with prodigious events. Writing in 1919, Arthur Schlesinger Sr argued that it was the entry of the United States into the First World War that caused Americans to seek 'a new orientation for the revolutionary struggle and to adopt a more objective point of view'.[8]

Advocating a temporal approach to historiography and without mentioning Page Smith by name, Bernard Bailyn brought the argument full circle. In the introduction to his study of the loyalist Thomas Hutchinson, *The Ordeal of Thomas Hutchinson* (1974) Bailyn identified three stages in historiography, applying this to his study of the Revolution. First, there were those who wrote too close to the event when its outcome and consequences were still in doubt; their writing was part of the event itself. Second, there was the long whig period which embraced a wide range of interpretations and third, there was the 'final turn' in which the relationship between 'viewer and event' was so far distant from the Revolution, that the historian 'is no longer a partisan'.[9] For Bailyn the losers, 'the real losers' were the American loyalists – 'those whose lives were disrupted, who suffered violence and vilification, who were driven out of the land and forced to resettle elsewhere in middle life and died grieving for the homes they had lost – these were not the English but the Americans who clung to them, who remained loyal'. Their history allows us to see the Revolution 'from the other side around and to grasp the wholeness of the struggle'.[10] Bailyn's description of the losers, however, excluded those who from the 1960s onwards began to assume a prominent place, some would argue *the* prominent place, in the historiography of the American Revolution. Though perceived on the margins by contemporaries and hardly at all by nineteenth- and twentieth-century historians before the final decades of the last century, women, African Americans and Native Americans are now in the frame if not fully integrated into the historiography of the Revolution. The terms adopted by Bailyn to depict the historiography of the Revolution as he saw it, were 'heroic', 'whig', and 'tragic', but his frame of reference did not include those whom we now recognize as the 'others'.

John Adams, one of the principal figures in the struggle against British colonial policy, a leading diplomat during the war years and during the Confederation, Washington's vice president and the second president of the United States, wrote in 1815 of the difficulties which would beset anyone attempting to write a history of the Revolution and fell out with Mercy Otis Warren when she accomplished it, finding her portrayal of him some kind of personal betrayal. 'Who shall write the history of the American Revolution? Who can write it?' he asked in a much quoted statement, adding with more precience than he could have ever imagined, 'Who will ever be able to write it?'[11] Almost two centuries later the process of answering Adams's rhetorical question continues, for as Michael Meranze writes, the American Revolution 'was not just any event in the nation's past. It was the founding moment'.[12]

Any attempt to review the historiography of the American Revolution over more than two centuries is by any estimate presumptuous, foolhardy and overly ambitious, especially when undertaken by a Welsh-born, English and American trained historian who has the privilege of teaching early American history in what was once termed 'one of the dark corners of the land'. Blame Philip Haffenden, Thad Tate, Gordon Wood and Jack Greene with whom I studied at different stages along this perilous and breathtaking path. I thank them all. And then there is the famous and infamous British universities' research exercise, the RAE, which makes cowards of us all but in its 'pigeonholing', 'dismissive labelling', 'distortion' and most of all counting, bears an uncanny resemblance to the 'pitfalls of bad historiography'. Yet 'there is still something to be said for it', writes Alfred Young, citing a comment by Edmund Morgan made in 1976, the year of the bicentennial of the Revolution, for 'it remains true', that 'historical understanding of the Revolution has proceeded in a series of reactions, one generation emphasizing problems and espousing views that the previous generation seemed to neglect or reject'.[13]

The historiography of the American Revolution is vast and any attempt to grapple with it requires tough choices to be made over what to put in rather than what consciously to leave out. In the end the choice is a personal one and there are vast swathes of material and areas of history which have not found their way into this book. Their exclusion in no way diminishes their importance and another historian would undoubtedly have chosen differently. In *The Debate on the American Revolution*, I have adopted a thematic structure which reflects the changing historiography of the Revolution. In Chapters 1 and 2 I have examined the historiography of the Revolution's causes and meaning, dividing them roughly into the period before and after professionalization. In Chapters 3 and 4 I have explored the consequences of the Revolution as they related to the creation of the Federal

Constitution, dividing these chapters into a consideration of those writing before the end of the Second World War and those writing in the post-war period taking the subject up to and including the debate over 'original intent'. The final three chapters of the book deal with the explosion of new work from the mid-1960s onwards but their starting point is the original historiography when the subjects of these chapters – African Americans, women and Native Americans – were first included in histories of the Revolution. This entails some overlap in the subject matter of some chapters but not in their historiographical treatment. Those who first wrote about the Revolution were conscious of their presence but lacked the historical apparatus to deal with them as autonomous subjects. Ironically or not, as the study of history developed as a discipline in the nineteenth century, these actors receded from view. For much of the twentieth century, they were 'the disappeared'. As late as 1976 Alfred Young's ground breaking collection of essays *The American Revolution: Explorations in the History of American Radicalism* – which included essays on African Americans, women and Native Americans – caused one reviewer to refer to their presence as 'incongruous'.[14] Yet their presence reflected not only the extent to which these actors had forced their way onto the political stage and into the history books but how the discipline of history, influenced by cross cultural developments, was greatly enriched in the process. Furthermore, the scholarship of the last two decades of the twentieth century is distinguished by a shift in perspective away from the preoccupation with the origins of the conflict to a concern over its consequences which for African Americans, women and Native Americans was little short of overwhelming. The recovery of these historical subjects and of others, not discussed in the present volume, presents historians with their greatest and as yet unresolved challenge, though Gary Nash has come closer than anyone else to resolving it: that is how to integrate the many peoples of the American Revolution into a master narrative. This structure entails the further reappraisal of some of the first generation of historians and their nineteenth-century successors in the chapters that follow.

Notes

1 Alfred F. Young, 'American Historians Confront "The Transforming Hand of Revolution"' in Ronald Hoffman and Peter J. Albert (eds), *The Transforming Hand of Revolution: Reconsidering the American Revolution as a Social Movement* (Charlottesville state and London; 1995), p. 371.

2 Jonathan Boucher, *A View of the Causes and Consequences of the American Revolution in Thirteen Discourses Preached in North America Between the Years 1763 and 1775* (London; 1797, reprinted New York; 1967), pp. i–v.

3 J. S. Bassett, *The Middle Group of American Historians* (New York; 1917); Carl L. Becker, 'Labelling the Historians' in Carl L. Becker, *Everyman His Own Historian: Essays on History and Politics* (New York; 1935), p. 135; on objectivity, see Peter Novick, *That Noble Dream: The 'Objectivity Question' and the American Historical Profession* (New York; 1988).

4 Charles A. Beard, *An Economic Interpretation of the Constitution of the United States* (New York; 1913), pp. 1–7.

5 Edmund S. Morgan, 'The American Revolution: Revisions in Need of Revising', *William and Mary Quarterly* (hereafter *WMQ*), 3rd ser., 14 (1957), pp. 3–15.

6 Page Smith, 'David Ramsay and the Causes of the American Revolution', *WMQ*, 3rd ser., 17 (1960), pp. 51–77, 76.

7 Novick, *That Noble Dream*, pp. 82–4.

8 A. M. Schlesinger Sr, 'The American Revolution Reconsidered', *Political Science Quarterly* 34 (1919), pp. 61–78, 61.

9 Bernard Bailyn, *The Ordeal of Thomas Hutchinson* (Cambridge, MA; 1974), pp. vii–xii.

10 Bailyn, *Thomas Hutchinson*, p. xi.

11 Douglass Adair and John A. Schutz (eds), *Peter Oliver's Origin and Progress of the American Revolution: A Tory View* (Stanford, CA; 1961), p. vii.

12 Michael Meranze, 'Even the Dead Will Not be Safe: an Ethics of Early American History', *WMQ*, 3rd ser., 50 (1993), pp. 367–78, 368.

13 Young, '"The Transforming Hand of Revolution"'; the quotation from Morgan appears on p. 371.

14 Alfred F. Young (ed.), *The American Revolution: Explorations in the History of American Radicalism* (DeKalb, IL; 1976), reviewed *WMQ*, 3rd ser., 35 (1978), pp. 168–71, 168.

1

The pioneers

In the preface to *The History of the Rise, Progress, and Establishment of the Independence of the United States of America* (1788), William Gordon (1728–1807), an English-born clergyman, set out his exemplary view of how and why history should be written.

> The instructions that events afford, are the soul of history, which doubtless ought to be a true relation of real facts during the period it respects. An essential requisite in an historian is the knowledge of the truth; and, as in order to perfection, he ought to be superior to every temptation to disguise it, some have said, that 'he should have neither country, nor particular religion'. The compiler of the present history can assure the public, that he has paid a sacred regard to truth, conscious of his being answerable to a more awful tribunal than that of the public; and has labored to divest himself of all undue attachment to every person, country, religious name or profession: whenever the reader is inclined to pronounce him partial, let him recollect, that he also is subject to the like human frailty. A regard to truth has often restrained him from the use of strong and florid expressions, that he might not impose upon the reader a pleasing delusion, and lead him into false conceptions of the events undertaken to be related.[1]

Born in Hitchin in Hertfordshire, Gordon was educated at a dissenting academy in London and began his career as an independent minister in Ipswich in 1752. In 1770 he emigrated to the American colonies, having become a partisan of the American cause. Two years later he became pastor of the Third Congregational Church in Roxbury, Massachusetts and following a sermon preached to the legislature was appointed chaplain to the Massachusetts Provincial Congress in 1775. The following year he began collecting materials to write a history of the colonial struggle against Britain. Gordon returned to England in 1786 where his four-volume history of the Revolution was printed in 1788. An American edition appeared the next year. Gordon quit the United States ostensibly because he feared that his attempt to write an impartial account of the Revolution would not meet with popular success or bring financial reward. The manuscript of the history circulated on both sides of the Atlantic and was revised in the light of critical comments. For over a hundred years, Gordon's history enjoyed a high reputation. His commitment to truth and impartiality were not only required of those consciously writing within an Enlightenment framework as most patriot historians were, but commended him to successive generations of historians. George Bancroft (1800–1891), who dominated the writing of American history for much of the nineteenth century, disliked Gordon's style but found his work 'invaluable'. Moses Coit Tyler (1835–1900), author of a pioneering literary history of the Revolution, wrote that despite the work of subsequent scholars, Gordon's account 'held its ground as one of the best yet produced'. Gordon's work also found praise among the new generation of professionally trained historians at the end of the century when Edward Channing (1856–1931) placed him alongside David Ramsay 'as an authority of the very first importance'. What made Gordon's work appealing was the fact that he had lived in two worlds and wrote authoritatively about both and he had a sound conviction of the justice of the American cause. In 1899, however, Orin Libby, in an article in the *American Historical Association Annual Report*, the forerunner of the *American Historical Review*, accused Gordon of plagiarizing material from the *Annual Register*.[2] Since the original manuscript of the book was no longer extant, it was impossible to estimate what proportion of it was re-written or by whom. Gordon's reputation never recovered and there are no modern editions of his work. Libby made a similar accusation against David Ramsay, the foremost patriot historian of his day, whose reputation was equally damaged.[3] Both men fell victim to the quest for objectivity in historical writing – 'that noble dream' – that accompanied the rise of history as a professional discipline at the end of the nineteenth century, a subject that will be discussed in the next chapter.[4] However, after a decent interval (six decades), Ramsay's reputation revived, not because he was innocent of the charge, but because how we conceive history as a discipline and whom we recognize as actors in history have been revolutionized since Gordon's day and also Libby's. The first historians of the American Revolution spoke to different audiences on each side of the Atlantic but Gordon attempted to speak to both. Possibly he paid a higher price for his professed impartiality than his flawed methodology. Yet in 1987, Gordon too was re-integrated into the community of revolutionary historians appearing in the essay by Lester Cohen (1944–) on the public role of historians in the early republic. Nationalists, these historians provided the new nation with a republican past, sought to present an example to the young and committed themselves to the pursuit of 'truth' and 'veracity' in the production of their narratives.[5] In the comprehensive history of the Revolution published by the distinguished historian Gary Nash (1933–) in 2005 Gordon features as a 'Massachusetts clergyman' who 'wanted young Americans to learn of both the ignoble and heroic aspects of the nation's birth' and who wrote to George Washington requesting access to his private papers declaring 'I am in search of genuine truth and not a fairy tale'.[6]

Removal and redemption

The first histories of the Revolution were written by those who, like Gordon, lived through the years of conflict and were witnesses to and often participants in the events they described. The loyalists among them were a diverse group, the most distinguished of whom was Thomas Hutchinson, one of the few Americans to rise to the position of colonial governor. Peter Oliver, another native-born New Englander and linked to Hutchinson by marriage, was chief justice of Massachusetts. Joseph Galloway, a native of Maryland who migrated to nearby Pennsylvania, became speaker of the Pennsylvania legislature and one-time ally of Benjamin Franklin. Born in northern England, Jonathan Boucher served as an Anglican minister in Virginia and Maryland while Alexander Hewat, a Scot, was minister at the leading dissenting church in Charleston, South Carolina. How these individuals viewed the origins of the Revolution will be explored in the chapter that follows. Some of their writings were self-serving, even satirical, others were more intimate, being closer to memoirs than histories, but regardless of their differences, there was a persistent theme that ran through their accounts: the existence of a deep-seated conspiracy on the part of the first New England settlers and their descendants, who, republican in character, wanted nothing less than independence from England.

Unlike the loyalist writers, patriot historians (or revolutionary historians as Cohen termed them), were engaged in a common enterprise to furnish the young republic with a usable past: a set of values and principles that would foster unity among the inhabitants of the separate states. They also saw themselves as presenting a model to the rest of the world that would be worthy of emulation.[7] They kept in touch with each other by correspondence and through membership of learned societies, exchanging information and encouraging each other in the arduous task of research, writing and publication, sometimes making their manuscripts available to one another. David Ramsay, Jeremy Belknap, Samuel Williams, John Lendrum and Mercy Otis Warren, who will be examined in this chapter, shared a number of characteristics. They were mostly New Englanders, and with one singular exception, white, male, Protestant dissenters and Federalists. Mercy Otis Warren (1728–1814), the sister of one activist and wife of another, was the exception not only on the grounds of gender but because she was not a Federalist.[8] This first generation of American historians wrote about the Revolution in decidedly conservative hues. They depicted the Revolution as a 'remarkably orderly contest over constitutional issues'. There was no hint, observed Arthur Shaffer, 'of an internal upheaval pitting class against class, and little to suggest that independence brought anything more within the country than a change of the forms of government'.[9] Cohen suggests 'that the historians' creation of a consensual, national past was a self-conscious ideological and literary effort, one fueled by the conviction that historical writing was valuable chiefly as an incitement to ethical and political action, rather than as a means of edification'.[10] New England was the only region that could be said to have a well developed intellectual tradition, though the revolutionary historians broke with this tradition by repudiating the providential theory of history which had dominated earlier writing because it could not furnish them with an adequate explanation for the Revolution: 'Providential history was God's history; revolutionary history was man's.'[11] Though Providence was not wholly absent from their accounts, human action largely replaced it as the principal cause of events.[12] They too believed in conspiracy though, in their case, it was the British government that had conspired against their liberties to reduce them to a state of 'slavery'.[13]

Loyalists

Lester Cohen, Arthur Shaffer and Page Smith have done much to restore the reputation of the first generation of historians of the Revolution but only those of a patriot persuasion. In this respect their work reflects the pattern of neglect that had befallen loyalists for much of American history. Cohen did not believe that there were any real 'tory' (loyalist) histories of the Revolution since none covered the entire period from 1763 to 1787: but this does not detract from the fact that it is the tories who provide us with some of the first histories of the coming of the Revolution – or rebellion as they were significantly inclined to call it. Cohen divided 'tory' writings into two groups, 'those written before the Revolution was over – indeed, even before the peace of 1783'; and those written after the Revolution, but which cover a period ending before 1763, 'the eve of the Revolutionary era', which he described as colonial histories.[14] Mary Beth Norton (1943–) refuted the notion of their scarcity. 'The exiles were not reluctant to express their views about the Revolution in print,' she wrote, 'so the historian has ample sources to draw upon for a study of their thought.' Some, however, wrote, but for a variety of reasons 'kept their writing private'.[15]

Thomas Hutchinson (1711–1780), fits into this latter category. Governor and de facto governor of Massachusetts Bay in the five years preceding the imposition of military government on the province, he had already published two volumes on the history of his 'native country' before his removal to England in

1774 where he died in exile six years later. But it is the manuscript of his third volume, unpublished during his lifetime,
detailing the years 1749 to 1774 that concerns us here.[16]
Hutchinson was hesitant about publishing the work lest it cause
embarrassment to the British government, but it was finally
published in 1828, edited by his grandson John Hutchinson, after
an approach from the Massachusetts Historical Society. [17] Scion
of an old New England family that had grown rich through
commerce, Thomas Hutchinson not only witnessed the demise of
British power in the colony, but in his public roles was one of the
principal players on the American scene and one of the
Revolution's principal victims. In his dedication, John
Hutchinson wrote of the price his grandfather paid for his loyalty
when 'during a long period of revolutionary excesses', he and
other leading figures 'maintained, at the frequent risk of their
lives, and with the final loss of their estates, an unshrinking allegiance to the Crown of which they were the delegated servants'.[18]
According to Bernard Bailyn (1922–), Hutchinson was also
'America's most accomplished historian'.[19] From the volume's
preface, one might suppose that he was an unabashed servant of
the Crown, steadfast in his loyalty and an apologist for imperial
policy, yet Hutchinson did not blindly support government
policy; in fact he opposed crucial aspects of it, though never in
public. His history of Massachusetts between 1744 and 1774 did
little to correct that public impression. Bailyn says of him that 'he
was a genuine if modest intellectual, with a true feeling for
history – any history ... above all, the history of his native
Massachusetts, which he knew better than any man alive; which
he chronicled in full, and whose historical documents he carefully
preserved, edited, and published'.[20] The final volume became an
account of the breakdown of relations between Britain and the
American colonies. It was written in the third person and with an
admirable stab at objectivity. Bailyn found Hutchinson's style,
like the man himself, curiously opaque. 'He wrote easily, abundantly, and logically', but his style was 'not only unaffected and
unadorned in the extreme, devoid of images, figures of speech,
thin even in adjectives, but so lacking in emphasis, so unpunctu-
ated, so *still*, as to seem at times inarticulate'. Hutchinson's style
was 'precise and elegant' wrote William Pencak, but it 'lacked

flair', a factor to which he attributed the neglect of Hutchinson as a political thinker.[21] But the criticism did not end there. 'His narratives, his arguments, his explanations are bland in content and blandly told. Personalities rarely come into focus.' But this was the character of the man for, as Bailyn described him, 'he was circumspect in everything he did. Caution, control, and prudence were the guiding principles of his life'. Hutchinson would probably have agreed with him. 'My temper,' he wrote, 'does not incline to enthusiasm.' But in a volume intended for posthumous publication, there were opportunities for 'self assertion' and 'personal opinion', and a disappointed Bailyn claimed that Hutchinson produced 'one of the most impersonal, bland, and circumspect accounts of revolutionary events ever written by a participant', and worse still, he worked hard to create this effect.[22]

Hutchinson's final volume contains a narrative within a narrative. There is the grand narrative – the breakdown in the colonial relationship – and the personal narrative – the ordeal of Thomas Hutchinson. In the grand narrative, Hutchinson traced the breakdown of the old colonial relationship; in the interior narrative he wrote his own obituary. Long before the end of the volume, unsurprisingly, the two narratives became intertwined. Hutchinson did not subscribe to the idea advanced by some loyalist historians that a deep-seated plan to overthrow the authority of the mother country could be traced back to the first New England settlers. Nor did he imagine that the events that unfolded around him were systematically planned. For him, the Revolution had its causes in immediate events that were the consequence of historical contingencies. Like other historians, whether patriot or loyalist, Hutchinson regarded the fall of Canada in 1760 and the expulsion of the French as a turning point in colonial history. But his emphasis on their consequences differed. British success not only marked the end of the French threat in North America but more importantly, it brought closer the prospect of an American empire. 'A new scene opened,' he wrote. 'The prospect was greatly enlarged.' In future nothing would 'obstruct a gradual progress of settlements, through a vast continent, from the Atlantic to the Pacific Ocean'. If population continued to grow at the same rate, 'the colonies would soon exceed the parent state'.

Hutchinson denied that these developments encouraged men to think 'immediately' about independence; there was no plan, at least not then, nor 'even a desire of independency'. Hutchinson tied this vision of America's future to a change of attitude towards the rights of colonials and the colonial relationship.[23]

The people of the colonies were whigs, wrote Hutchinson – 'ancient whigs', attached to the principles of the Glorious Revolution of 1688 which enshrined the rights of parliament alongside those of the monarchy in governing the country and upheld the succession of the monarchy in the house of Hanover. Party terms were uncommon; there was no 'special cause of disaffection' towards the administration at this time nor were there complaints about an invasion of the rights and liberties of the people. Yet 'Wilkes and liberty' could be heard on the streets of Boston as in London. Change came swiftly. 'All on a sudden', those officers of the crown who sought to maintain their authority were labelled tories – 'always a term of reproach' – while their opponents assumed the name of whigs 'because the common people, as far as they had been acquainted with the parties in England, all supposed the whigs to have been in the right, and the tories in the wrong'.[24]

It was against this background and linked to the 'amazing increase' in the size of the national debt that the colonies attracted closer attention: this was justification for England's attempt to tax the colonies.[25] Taxation by parliament was deemed 'incompatible with the rights of the people, unless represented'.[26] Although Robert Calhoun has demonstrated convincingly that Hutchinson opposed the Stamp Act (1765), there is little in the *History* to indicate this. 'Most people of judgment,' wrote Hutchinson, 'thought that it would force its way; but it did not.' The rejection of parliamentary authority in the colonies was a gradual process. 'At first, indeed, the supreme authority seemed to be admitted, the case of taxes only excepted'; but the exception gradually extended from one case to another, until it included all cases whatever. Hutchinson located the origin of the problem in the disappointments of those who belonged to the 'outs' rather than the 'ins'.

At all times there have been parties, *ins* and *outs*, in the colonies, as well as in the kingdom. In Massachusetts Bay, the exception to the constitutional authority of parliament was first taken, and principally supported, by men who were before discontented, and by them had been brought into the house of representatives, and there employed to strengthen the opposition to the governor in other points. The council, by degrees, had been brought to the same sentiments with the house.[27]

Hutchinson's account of his growing isolation in Massachusetts politics begins with his rivalry with James Otis Sr, soon joined by his son, the firebrand James Otis Jr, and is related by his unforgiving daughter Mercy Otis Warren in her history of the Revolution published twenty-five years after Hutchinson's death. Hutchinson attributed the enmity of the Otises to political rivalry arising from the failure of the elder Otis to obtain the position of chief justice, which went to Hutchinson. He viewed the Otises' advocacy of colonial rights not as a matter of principle but of political opportunism.[28] To Mercy Otis Warren, however, the monopolization of high office by Hutchinson and his cohort, a small group of interrelated families extending over two generations, was evidence of corruption in high places by self-serving men and thus inimical to public liberty. For a young man like John Adams, the then lieutenant governor's appointment also rankled because he was a merchant, not a lawyer. During the Stamp Act riots, Hutchinson and Oliver, the second and third most important crown officers in the colony, were among the principal victims, being forced out of some of their offices and losing their places on the Council. The families of both men were terrorized and their property destroyed. The *History* provides a graphic illustration of the choreography and effectiveness of 'mob action', as Hutchinson perceived it, and the role of ritual violence, the importance of print culture and the defencelessness of those targeted, however elevated their status.[29] Oliver and Hutchinson found themselves perilously isolated, members of the council, house of representatives, magistrates and militiamen being either unwilling or unable to defend them. When Hutchinson had assumed the position of lieutenant governor, the outlook was bleak. With no prospect of support 'from any of the executive powers of government under him', he was nonetheless bound by oath 'to support an authority to which the body of the people refused to submit'.[30] 'He stood absolutely alone.' After six to eight months Hutchinson questioned whether he could go on, whether he would have the 'firmness of body, or mind' for the job.[31]

It was little wonder that Hutchinson and his family were reluctant to publish the final instalment of his trilogy since he held the British political system and its ministers ultimately responsible for the collapse of British authority in the colonies. Highly critical of events in Britain and the frequent changes of administration, Hutchinson blamed party spirit for 'the feeble, ineffectual measures' of the government in supporting its own authority at home, let alone in the colonies.[32] The 'disorders in the colonies' had their origin in events in Britain where 'an open contempt and defiance of the legislative authority' prevailed and 'offenders escaped with impunity' due to the 'neglect of executive powers, or by the prejudice and bias of juries'.[33] For three to four years the people in the colonies were taught 'from England' that acts for taxing them were 'a mere nullity, and ought to be resisted', a doctrine 'countenanced by great men in both houses of parliament'.[34] Hutchinson believed that the future of the colonies lay with the powerful and imperial state that Britain had become and he could not envisage a future outside it. Edmund Morgan was not convinced by Hutchinson's position and had he been successful 'he would have left the colonists more vulnerable than before'. Submission to the demands of parliament carried with it precisely the dangers of which his opponents warned.[35]

Married to the sister of Hutchinson's wife was Peter Oliver (1713–1791), a successful businessman and political associate who, like Hutchinson, lived out his life in exile in England. His account *Peter Oliver's Origin & Progress of the American Rebellion* was probably completed at around the same time as Hutchinson's work but not published until as late as 1961.[36] Oliver's account of the 'Rebellion', was a work of a very different stamp. Oliver felt the impact of British policy because he was close to Hutchinson and because his brother and business partner was Andrew Oliver, the designated stamp master for the province of Massachusetts Bay. Both men found themselves under attack, their homes ransacked, their property destroyed and their families put in fear of their lives. Oliver's account was written in a spirit of anger, bitterness, fear and frustration. It conveys the real fear of its author and others similarly subjected to constant public scrutiny and less frequently, but more alarmingly, angry hostile crowds. For Oliver, the upheaval was the work of proud and ambitious men who, backed by a black regiment of New England clergy and the smuggling fraternity which infested the region, spread their poison among the common people, transforming them into a veritable hydra. In characterizing the 'people out of doors' in this way, Oliver invested them with an autonomy that distinguished them from the traditional image of the mob. He also laid some of the blame on the government in Britain which proved pusillanimous, and especially those members of parliament who rallied to the colonists' cause. Despite his suspicion of long-standing republicanism, Oliver could barely comprehend the changing political landscape except as the consequence of the subterfuge and duplicity of a set of men whose portraits he delighted in drawing as they entered and departed the scene and whom he contrasted with the noble figure of Hutchinson. They were jumped-up men, men of middling rank well removed from the colonial elite to which Oliver saw himself as belonging. They were ambitious men, anxious for status and hungry for profit. In this respect his interpretation of the causes of the Revolution was similar to Hutchinson's but, as we shall see in later chapters, there were aspects of his account which were more revealing than better-known works by patriots and loyalists.

An Historical Account of the Rise and Progress of the Colonies of South Carolina and Georgia which first appeared anonymously in London in 1779, falls into the first of Cohen's categories. Though not an exact fit, it merits inclusion in this study because its author, Alexander Hewat (*c*.1740–1824), included a brief account, 'a slight view' in his words, 'of the causes of that unhappy quarrel'. Moreover, he wrote from the perspective of events in the lower south.[37] Born in Scotland and educated at the University of Edinburgh, Alexander Hewat became a minister in Charleston until forced to abandon the colony because of his political views, his manuscript as yet unfinished.[38] At the end of the nineteenth century, it found favour among the so-called imperial historians who, recognizing its 'objectivity' and 'analytical approach', valued it 'as a primary source for social and intellectual history'.[39] Hewat, according to Geraldine Meroney, worked 'clearly within the Enlightenment tradition of historical writing and more precisely within the Scottish school represented by William Robertson'.[40] Hewat argued that the Stamp Act was both necessary for the security of the British colonies in America, and just, since the people of Great Britain already laboured under a heavy burden of taxation. Moreover, Britain sought to deal fairly with the colonies for shortly after the Act was signed into law, another was introduced intended to encourage the importation of wood into Britain from the colonies. Since the Stamp Act was estimated to bring in only £60,000 a year 'and timber was so plentiful over all the plantations, it was thought that the great advantage which the colonies must reap from the latter act, would be an ample recompense for the loss they might sustain from the former'.[41] Like Hutchinson and Oliver, Hewat assigned the English friends of the Americans a dynamic role in the breakup of the colonial relationship for, ever vigilant, they transmitted to the colonists 'the earliest intelligence of what was doing in parliament'. From them, the Americans also learnt of the opposition to the Stamp Act from a faction in the House of Commons. Yet Hewat divided the Americans into leaders and followers. Back home they thought that

> none deserved the blessing of liberty who had not courage to assert their right to it ... no means were neglected that could inflame and exasperate the populace. Bold and seditious speeches were made to stir up the people to resistance, by representing the act in the most odious light, and affirming that it would be attended with consequences subversive of all their invaluable rights and privileges.[42]

Submission to the Stamp Act 'would leave their liberties and properties entirely at the disposal of a British parliament'. Hewat located the heart of the resistance in the coastal towns.

> Having obtained a copy of the act, they publicly burnt it. The ships in the harbours hung out their colours half-mast high, in token of the deepest mourning; the bells in the churches were muffled, and set a ringing, to communicate the melancholy news from one parish to another. These flames, kindled in New England, soon spread through all the capital towns along the coast; so that there was scarcely a sea-port town in America in which combinations were not framed for opposing the introduction of stamp-paper.[43]

Pennsylvania lawyer and legislative leader, Joseph Galloway (1731–1803) was not one of those loyalist who chose to remain silent. In 1780 he published *Historical and Political Reflections on the Rise and Progress of the American Rebellion*, but according to John Ferling (1940–), the book failed to create a stir or influence historical accounts. Possibly the advertisement preceding the pamphlet which proclaimed that it was written 'in great Haste, amidst a multiplicity of other engagements and avocations' and 'published from the first draught, in a manner uncorrected' contributed to its reception. 'As the Author found the *American Question* coming forward in Parliament, he thought it his duty to throw what light he could on so important a Subject.'[44] Like other loyalist writers, Galloway dismissed the notion that the 'rebellion', this 'portentous event', was the result of 'the injustice and oppression of the present reign, – by a plan formed by Administration for enslaving the Colonies'. Despite 'the uniform language of the malcontents on both sides of the Atlantic', it was a fallacy. The rebellion in America sprang from very different causes, beginning as early as the sixteenth century and 'nourished and fed by those two fiends, Superstition and Ambition, the great enemies to religious and civil liberty'.[45] There could be no other explanation, because 'in almost every society, opposition to legal government has been a common event. In almost every instance which history affords, it has arisen from a continued series of extreme injustice and oppression in the rulers'. 'At the time it broke out,' he claimed, 'the people in the Colonies were more free, unencumbered and happy than any others on earth.'[46]

The Seven Years War was a turning point in perceptions of the colonies. Before 1763, 'America had been considered as an infant state, capable of contributing little towards the national defence'. As a result of the war, the circumstances of the colonies became better known, while the cession of Canada to Great Britain boosted 'the spirit of republicanism and independency, which had been awed by the neighbourhood of the French'.[47] After the Seven Years War, free from the French and the Indians, 'their numbers were greatly increased, which left them at leisure to execute their dark and insidious design of revolting from the parent state, under whose wing they had been tenderly nursed and protected'. Galloway claimed that the execution of the Stamp

Act was opposed by only a 'small faction' in America and he shared the conviction of most loyalist historians that they were 'vindicated and supported in Britain'.[48]

While Joseph Galloway was a leading figure in Pennsylvanian politics before the Revolution and a key loyalist in the state after the breach with Britain, Jonathan Boucher (1738–1804) was an outsider. A native of Cumberland whose family had all but lost its gentry status, Boucher sailed to Virginia in 1759 to become tutor to the children of planter Captain Edward Dixon, factor for the Whitehaven merchant John Younger, Boucher's patron.[49] He had ambitions to become a merchant but events conspired against him and he opted for a career as an Anglican minister instead.[50] Ordained in 1762, he spent ten years in Virginia serving in two parishes before removing to Maryland where salaries and prospects were better, taking up residence in Annapolis. Fleeing the colony in 1775, he resumed his ministerial career after an interval of nine years during which time he returned to teaching. While vicar of Epsom in Surrey, he published *A View of the Causes and Consequences of the American Revolution* in London in 1797 which he dedicated to George Washington, once his neighbour.[51] Boucher also wrote an autobiography *Reminiscences of an American Loyalist*, which, edited by his grandson, was not published until 1925 and was reprinted in 1967. Ralph Adams Brown, who was not one of Boucher's admirers, described the work as 'strongly prejudiced', 'extremely and probably unfairly critical' and written 'more than two decades after the events' it described.[52] Even so, Brown conceded that the memoirs had some value because Boucher knew many important people and historians might even find them interesting. Anne Zimmer's study *Jonathan Boucher* (1978) has done much to establish Boucher's true measure.[53]

Although allegedly given as a series of sermons between 1763 and 1775, these compositions, as Zimmer argues convincingly, were penned during Boucher's sojourn in England. Certainly, this is true of the lengthy introduction that preceded the sermons. It is from this that we learn about Boucher's ideas on history and how the American Revolution fitted into the larger scheme of things. At the time when Boucher was writing, the French Revolution threatened to eclipse the American Revolution, prompting

Boucher to describe it as 'already well nigh forgotten'. Boucher claimed that most attempts to write the history of the American Revolution had failed because their examination of the causes and consequences of the revolt was inadequate and their authors lacked the spirit of philosophical enquiry needed for the task.[54] The major problem was the prevalence of party spirit. While some bias was acceptable up to a point, and among 'political writers' was even desirable, the historian who was chiefly concerned with promoting party was 'negligent' or 'ignorant' of his vocation. James Murray's *Impartial History of the Present War in America* (1778) was 'extremely partial and inflammatory' and 'so very ordinary and mean' that it was unworthy of either criticism or note.[55] John Andrews's *History of the Late War* (1785) was condemned for its opportunism.[56] Boucher made a partial exception of David Ramsay's *History of the Revolution of South Carolina* (1785), and his later *History of the American Revolution* (1791) describing the former as 'a work of great merit in point of composition', but there was faint praise for its author, a doctor and member of congress, who despite being 'undoubtedly, a man of sense, and not illiterate' was 'by principle a puritan and a republican'. His worst failing, however, was that he was 'an avowed partisan of the revolt'. Boucher regarded William Gordon's *History of the Rise, Progress, and Establishment of the Independence of the United States of America* (1788) more highly. Though produced for commercial reasons, it was 'at least decently written' and a work of 'great profession and promise', more detailed and less biased than its predecessors. As for the Marquis de Chastellux's *Travels in North America*, this was not history at all but a work of 'shameless partiality'.[57] Boucher reserved his strongest criticism for the author, possibly Edmund Burke or someone connected with him, of the historical accounts appearing regularly in the *Annual Register*. 'Instead of obtaining an honourable niche in the temple of Fame', the writer was content 'to be classed with an ignoble herd, the party writers who abetted that revolt'. Stopping short of deliberately falsifying the facts, the writer nonetheless made use 'of everything that favoured the party he espoused and disregarding everything adverse to it'.[58]

Boucher attributed the American Revolution to manifold

causes. Although writing within the Enlightenment tradition, he vacillated over whether the American rebellion was unique, a curiosity that flew in the face of history, before rejecting the view. Like other loyalist writers, he found a partial explanation of the origins of the Revolution in the transplantation of republicanism from one side of the Atlantic to the other and in the support given by the British parliamentary opposition to American resistance.[59] Unlike most historians, he paid considerable attention to Virginia. Historically important, Virginia was strategically located and wielded influence over its southern neighbours. Boucher tied the state's role in the early stages of the Revolution to the appointment of Virginians to key positions in the emergent regime and to the problem of indebtedness among its planters. Americans owed an estimated £3 million to British merchants.[60] Added to these factors was the weakness of British authority in the colonies. 'Nothing was so naked,' wrote Boucher, 'as government in America.' Completing this list of 'first causes' was 'the loose principles of the time' which were still 'to be regarded as the *one great cause* of the American revolt'.[61] Taxation ranked only among subordinate issues. 'Irksome to mankind', it was submitted to only out of necessity, perhaps more so in North America than elsewhere where 'the people were studiously taught to regard all taxes as the arbitrary exactions of an oppressive Government'. Boucher shrewdly observed that the campaign against the Tea Act put the lower class, who drank little tea, on the same footing 'with their betters'.[62]

What is missing in Boucher's analysis of the causes of the Revolution, as in other loyalist accounts, is any serious assessment of British policy towards the colonies. What we get instead is an apologia for earlier British policies under which the colonies grew and prospered, and a sense of bewilderment at the outcome of events. Rather than the rebellious colonies, it is the friends of America in parliament who are assigned a major, if not the major, role in fomenting resistance to British policies among an emergent group of political figures. The latter were depicted as manipulating others, variously described as 'the populace', 'the common people' and the 'lower class'. From these comments, it would appear that the accounts of loyalists and patriots have little in common. Though to some extent true, an examination of a selected group of patriot historians suggests that the distance between them may not be quite so wide as anticipated.

The patriots

Revolutionary historiography 'had its brilliant beginning in the work of a Southerner', claimed Charles Sellers.[63] While he may have been overly enthusiastic in claiming David Ramsay (1749–1815) for the south – he was born in Pennsylvania of Scottish–Irish parentage, and educated at the College of New Jersey (later Princeton) – Sellers is not alone in allocating Ramsay a dominant, if not the dominant, role in early American historiography. Cohen described Ramsay's *History of the American Revolution* (1789) as one of the two best contemporary histories of the Revolution, while Shaffer goes one step further in crediting Ramsay with creating American history. Not only was his output formidable, but he was 'the first to compose histories addressed to the needs of the newly developing phenomenon of revolutionary nationalism'.[64] Highly respected in his own day, Ramsay's *History of the American Revolution* would stand 'unrivaled in American historiography until George Bancroft's great multivolume history reached the Revolutionary period in the 1850s'.[65] Thereafter Ramsay tended to fade from view, especially in the latter part of the nineteenth century but, as Libby's attack on him for plagiarism indicates, he was not entirely forgotten.[66] The process of rehabilitation began with a celebrated article by Page Smith in 1960 in which, paying scant attention to the issue of the *Annual Register*, he urged historians to take another look at Ramsay's interpretation of the Revolution. Ramsay, he declared, offered historians 'a wiser and better balanced interpretation than the most expert and "scientific" of his successors'. Smith praised Ramsay's 'generosity of mind and spirit' and 'critical sense' that tended to distinguish him from his contemporaries and was particularly evident in his treatment of the loyalists who remain somewhat neglected even today. Smith thought him worthy of an honourable place in the front rank of American historians.[67] Writing five years later Robert Brunhouse, editor of Ramsay's correspondence, still had reservations.[68] When *The History of the American Revolution* was republished in 1990, Lester Cohen, its editor, took a similar view. He dismissed Libby's judgement that Ramsay's *History* was 'well-nigh worthless' arguing that the plagiarism was minor in relation to the loose standards of citation common in the eighteenth century, besides which 'eighteenth-century American histories were performances, not proofs'; they were more like sermons than learned discourses. Furthermore Libby was speaking to a new generation of historians on a topic 'largely irrelevant to most modern readers'. We learn about 'the intellectual predilections of the eighteenth-century historian: the values, assumptions, principles, and expectations of one who lived and wrote amidst the events he narrated ... his use of language, his sense of the significance of people and events, his narrative style, his use of history as propaganda, as exhortation, and as fiction'. The value of Ramsay's *History of the American Revolution* lay not in its information, but 'the ways in which he reveals the sensibility through which the events of his era were filtered'.[69]

The History of the American Revolution was not Ramsay's first attempt to write a history of his time. Conceived when Ramsay was a prisoner of the British in St Augustine, Florida, *The History of the Revolution of South Carolina* was published in 1785. Although the work was well received and Thomas Jefferson negotiated a French edition on his behalf, sales were disappointing and Ramsay lost money on the venture. The book provides valuable insight into one state's participation in the Revolution. By the time British policy underwent significant change after the success in the Seven Years War, the people of South Carolina, according to Ramsay, had little to complain about; they had become 'more and more confident that the leading strings of the mother country were less necessary than in the days of their infancy'. When the war came, however, it plunged South Carolina into a bitter civil war.[70] Perceiving the importance of 'establishing a firm historiographical base for the Revolutionary tradition out of which a new nation was growing', Ramsay embarked on a broader study of the history of the Revolution.[71] Author of a superb study of Ramsay and his writings, Arthur Shaffer described *The History of the American Revolution* as his masterpiece.[72] The *History* was many things:

a narrative of the Revolution; a dissertation on order, virtue, and creativity in a republic; a textbook of revolutionary activism; a call for humanitarian reform; an exploration into the emergence of a new social being; a manifesto for a republican future. Above all, it was shaped by Ramsay's republican nationalism.[73]

Ramsay was very conscious of divisions between the states: 'We are too widely disseminated over an extensive country and too much diversified by different customs and forms of government to feel as one people', he wrote to one correspondent. Behind his notion of national identity lay two basic ideas: 'the republicanism of the national character' and the special destiny of the new nation 'to enlarge the happiness of mankind'. In these, ideology and environment combined.[74]

Ramsay invested the colonies with the 'spirit of liberty and independence'. From their first settlements, 'the English colonists' were 'devoted to liberty, on English ideas, and English principles. They not only conceived themselves to inherit the privileges of Englishmen, but though in a colonial situation, actually possessed them'.[75] The colonies were founded at a time when 'the dread of arbitrary power was the predominant passion of the nation'. The period between 1603 and 1688 witnessed 'a remarkable struggle between prerogative and privilege' and culminated in a revolution 'highly favourable to the liberties of the people'. Geographical isolation also played a part. 'In large governments the circulation of power is enfeebled at the extremities' so that colonists

> growing up to maturity, at such an immense distance from the seat of government, perceived the obligation of dependence much more feebly, than the inhabitants of the parent isle, who not only saw, but daily felt, the fangs of power. The wide extent and nature of the country contributed to the same effect. The natural seat of freedom is among high mountains, and pathless deserts, such as abound in the wilds of America.[76]

Their remoteness left them free from ministerial influence. Offices were too few and unprofitable to render them a source of patronage and corruption. The colonists themselves were for the most part 'strangers to luxury'.[77] All of one rank, wrote Ramsay: 'Kings, Nobles and Bishops, were unknown among them'. The

25

vast extent of 'vacant country' made it possible for every colonist to become a freeholder, settled on his own lands as 'both farmer and landlord'. He was free to hunt fish and fowl, unlike in Europe where harsh penal laws discriminated against the many in favour of the few.[78] By the time the Revolution began, some colonists were third and fourth (a few even fifth and sixth) generation settlers. 'The affection for the Mother Country, as far as it was a natural passion, wore away in successive generations, till at last it had scarcely any existence.'[79]

While Ramsay took a benign view of English colonial policy, what is distinctive about his account is that even after the passage of the Stamp Act, he had some sympathy for the British government facing the challenge of how to rule an extended empire in the aftermath of the Seven Years War. For 150 years England had employed a 'wise and liberal policy' towards the colonies.

> She gave them full liberty to govern themselves, by such laws as their local legislatures thought necessary, and left their trade open to every individual in her dominions. She also gave them the amplest permission to pursue their respective interests in such manner, as they thought proper, and reserved little for herself, but the benefit of their trade, and that of a political union under the same head.[80]

There was one other crucial factor which gave the colonies the capacity to advance 'nearly to the magnitude of a nation': it was institutional – the rise of the legislative assembly. Like Boucher, Ramsay recognized the weakness of British authority in the colonies. 'The King and government of Great-Britain' he observed, 'held no patronage in America, which could create a portion of attachment and influence, sufficient to counteract that spirit in popular assemblies.'[81]

Casting aside conspiratorial notions of French subterfuge and colonial ambitions of independence, Ramsay declared that no further explanation of the Revolution was necessary than 'the known selfishness of human nature'. He dated the 'sad story of colonial oppression' to 1764. The demands of one side and their refusal by the other 'occasioned the revolution'.

> It was natural for Great-Britain, to wish for an extension of her authority over the colonies, and equally so for them, on their approach to maturity, to be more impatient of subordination, and to

resist every innovation, for increasing the degree of their dependence.[82]

Had Britain proceeded no further than cramping colonial commerce, opposition might have evaporated. But while regulating trade was one thing, 'the novel claim of taxing them without their consent', was another, and based on exaggerated claims of their wealth. Left for 150 years to tax themselves, the demand was 'universally reprobated, as contrary to their natural, chartered, and constitutional rights'.[83]

Ramsay's work served as a model for other intellectuals who, in emphasizing the uniqueness of America, shaped a new history which diverged from Enlightenment historiography 'by subjugating scholarship to the service of nationalism'. Patriot historians did not repudiate the belief that human nature was everywhere the same, but exploited 'the relativistic strain in Enlightenment historical thought'. Though republics had failed in the past, what would save the American experiment and render it a beacon to the world was an adequate frame of government for a sovereign people and this was achieved with the creation of the Federal Constitution. Ramsay looked to education to complete the work of integration.[84]

Histories written to the standard achieved by Jeremy Belknap, whose *History of New-Hampshire* Ramsay much admired, would also serve to inform Americans in different parts of the new nation about one another.[85] Born in Boston, Jeremy Belknap (1744–1798) was the son of a leatherdresser and furrier. He attended Boston Latin School and entered Harvard in 1762. After graduation, like other young men, he began his career by teaching, in his case at a number of establishments, before entering the ministry. In 1767 he removed to New Hampshire and to the First Congregational Church of Dover.[86] Drawn towards the study of history when still a student, he wrote in his commonplace book that the qualities required in a historian were such that 'some have reckoned it one of the most difficult labours human nature is capable of', a view he retained throughout his life.[87] According to Kaplan, 'the providential theorizing of Puritan historiography Belknap had largely discarded; the partisanship of the Puritan historians he had not'.[88]

In his history Belknap could not refrain from adopting the first person: 'Though it may be accounted a deviation from the proper style of history, for the author to speak in the first person', he hoped he would be excused for expressing his feelings as an American, whilst relating 'the history of his own time, and his own country'. Belknap argued that from the earliest years of American settlement English authorities entertained a suspicion – Belknap called it 'a jealousy' – that the New England colonies sought their independence. He could not understand why this suspicion existed but, whatever its cause, it had grown stronger over time and 'became most evident, and began to produce its most pernicious effects, at a time when there was the least reason for indulging the idea'. The successful outcome of the Seven Years War had drawn the colonies closer to Britain than ever before: 'We were proud of our connexion with a nation whose flag was triumphant in every quarter of the globe; and by whose assistance, we had been delivered from the danger of our most formidable enemies, the French in Canada.' The accession of George III was celebrated in the colonies 'with as true zeal and loyalty, as in any part of his dominions'. Less convincing was Belknap's next claim, that had British policy remained limited to commercial regulation and continued 'the indulgencies' already allowed, then Britain could have easily 'drawn the whole profit of our labor and trade into the hands of British merchants and manufacturers'. This would have suppressed the rise of 'a spirit of enterprise in the Colonies, and kept us in as complete subjection and dependence, as the most sanguine friend of the British nation could have wished'.[89]

Unlike most revolutionary historians, Belknap identified sources of trouble within the colonies which contributed to the new direction of affairs. Citing the correspondence of Bernard and Oliver, Belknap maintained that there were those in America who aimed to enhance the status of their families by 'privately seeking the establishment of an *American Nobility*; out of which, an intermediate branch of legislation, between the royal and the democratic powers, should be appointed'. Indeed 'plans were drawn, and presented to the British ministry, for new modelling our governments, and reducing their powers; whilst the authority of Parliament should be rendered absolute and imperial'. In addition, military men, returning home after the war, reported on the wealth of the colonies, 'whilst the sons of our merchants and planters, who went to England for their education, exhibited specimens of prodigality which confirmed the idea' as did the quantity of goods imported from Britain at the conclusion of the war. Belknap tied the new direction of policy to the prevalence of corruption in Britain: 'In no age,' except perhaps when Rome forfeited its liberty, 'was the spirit of venality and corruption so prevalent as at this time, in Britain.' A new administration looked to America 'as a source of revenue', not for the purpose of defraying the expense of 'protecting, defending and securing it' or easing the tax burden on the people of Britain, but as a way of expanding the opportunities for corruption. 'Notwithstanding this pretext, it was our opinion, that the grand object was to provide for dependents, and to extend the corrupt and venal principle of crown influence, through every part of the British dominions.' If the ministry had been sincere, then surely the 'monopoly and control of our commerce' should have been sufficient?[90]

The first of the new measures restricted the commerce between the colonies and the islands of the West Indies which they had hitherto enjoyed, causing 'a general uneasiness and suspicion', but viewed as 'a regulation of trade', they submitted 'with reluctance' and protested in petitions and remonstrances. Rather than redressing colonial grievances, parliament passed the Stamp Act for the specific purpose of raising a revenue by means of a stamp duty on legal papers throughout the colonies.

> The true friends of constitutional liberty now saw their dearest interests in danger ... Even those who had been seeking alterations in the colonial governments, and an establishment of hereditary honors, plainly saw that the ministry were desirous of plucking the fruit, before they had grafted the stock on which it must grow.[91]

To have submitted 'was to rivet the shackles of slavery on ourselves and our posterity'. Yet 'to revolt, was to rend asunder the most endearing connexion, and hazard the resentment of a powerful nation'. Like Hutchinson, Belknap credited Virginia with raising the alarm when the house of burgesses passed a set of resolves, 'asserting the rights of their country, and denying the claim of parliamentary taxation'. Then in a much-quoted phrase he notes how 'the spirit of the Virginia resolves, like an electric spark, diffused itself instantly and universally'.[92] While Virginia raised the alarm, and Massachusetts called for united opposition, Boston confronted British policy 'by publicly exhibiting effigies of the enemies of America, and obliging the stamp-officer to resign his employment'. Though Belknap thought that 'the popular commotions' in Boston were carried to unjustifiable lengths, the spirit of opposition 'animated the body of the people in every Colony'. It is one of the virtues of Belknap's history that it offers us an insight into how the Stamp Act was resisted in one of the smaller colonies, of who participated, and how popular opposition was kept under control. The stamp distributor appointed for New Hampshire was George Messervè, whose father had died at Louisburg. Before landing in Boston, he was informed of the opposition to the Act and 'that it would be acceptable to the people if he would resign, which he readily did'. An exhibition of effigies had been prepared for him at Portsmouth 'and at his coming to town he made a second resignation, on the parade, before he went to his own house'. Everyone appeared satisfied.[93] Although New Hampshire sent no delegates to the Stamp Act Congress, their assembly adopted the same measures and sent similar petitions to Britain. Belknap was sensible of the role of the press, the newspapers being 'filled with essays, in which every plea for and against the new duties was amply discussed'. The printers had a direct interest in the outcome since they were liable for the duty. On the day before the Act was due to come into effect, 'the New-Hampshire Gazette appeared with a mourning border'.[94]

> The next day, the bells tolled, and a funeral procession was made for the Goddess of Liberty; but on depositing her in the grave, some signs of life were supposed to be discovered, and she was carried off in triumph. By such exhibitions, the spirit of the populace was kept up; though the minds of the most thoughtful persons were filled with anxiety ...
>
> The popular spirit was sufficiently roused to join in any measures which might be necessary for the defence of liberty. All fear of the consequence of proceeding in the public business without stamps, was gradually laid aside ... To provide for the worst, an association

was formed by the 'sons of liberty' in all the northern Colonies, to stand by each other, and unite their whole force, for the protection and relief of any who might be in danger, from the operation of this, or any other oppressive act.[95]

Belknap denied that there was any disaffection with royal government or any desire to 'shake off their allegiance' at this time. He was convinced that the professions of loyalty which suffused the many letters between members of the sons of liberty were genuine.[96] Belknap then laid out his view of the relationship of the colonies with Britain.

> The idea which we entertained of our political connexion [with the British empire] was that the King was its supreme head; that every branch of it was a perfect State, competent to its own internal legislation, but subject to the control and negative [veto] of the sovereign; that taxation and representation were correlative, and therefore that no part of the empire could be taxed, but by its own Representatives in Assembly.[97]

There was widespread support for resistance across the social spectrum: 'temporary expedients, if wisely applied, might have preserved the peace; but the most delicate and judicious management was necessary, to prevent irritation'. Belknap insisted that 'To the constitutional authority (as we understood it) of the King and Parliament, there had been no resistance; but to the assumed authority, of our fellow subjects in Britain, over our property, the resistance began, and was supported by the Representatives of the people, in their Assemblies.' Belknap identified members of the 'sons of liberty' chiefly as 'tradesmen of reputation, who were occasionally assisted by lawyers, clergymen, and other persons of literary abilities'. In support of 'the justice of our claims; they called on the writings of Sydney [sic] and Locke and the arguments that had been formerly used against the usurpations of the house of Stuart'.[98]

Looking back with amusement at one effect of independence Belknap recalled

> an aversion to every thing which bore the name and marks of royalty. Sign boards on which were painted the King's arms, or the crown and sceptre, or the portraits of any branches of the royal family, were pulled down or defaced. Pictures and escutcheons of

the same kind in private houses were inverted or concealed. The names of streets, which had been called after a King or Queen were altered; and the half-pence, which bore the name of George III, were either refused in payment, or degraded to farthings. These last have not yet recovered their value.[99]

Widely regarded for his scientific and scholarly achievements before his fall from grace, Samuel Williams (1743–1817), also a New England divine, served as minister of the First Church of Bradford in 1765, but according to Clifford Shipton his 'first love was science rather than theology'.[100] He became Professor of Natural and Experimental Philosophy at Harvard in 1779 only to resign under duress for financial malpractice in 1788. He identified himself as a member of the Meteorological Society of Germany, the Philosophical Society of Philadelphia and the Academy of Arts and Sciences in Massachusetts, was awarded an LL.D by the University of Edinburgh in 1785 and by Yale in 1786. His circle of correspondents was drawn from far and wide. In contrast to Belknap, Williams eschewed writing a detailed history of the Revolution in his *Natural and Civil History of Vermont* (1794), a work described by Shipton as 'of much more than regional interest'. As Williams explained in his preface, though the 'causes, operations [and] effects' of the war represented some of the 'most important events, which have taken place in modern times', he did not believe that they could be 'comprehended in the history of any particular state'. He would include only those details about the war which were necessary to explain the subject that he really wanted to write about.[101] The nature of man, declared Williams, remained unaltered but 'the state of society is perpetually changing'.

> To ascertain what there is thus peculiar and distinguishing in the state of society in the federal Union, to explain the causes which have lead [sic] to this state, to mark its effect upon human happiness, and to deduce improvement from the whole, are the most important objects, which civil history, can contemplate in America.[102]

The volume was dedicated to the citizens of Vermont in recognition of 'their many virtues', to promote 'a more particular acquaintance with their own affairs' and for 'their further improvement'.[103] Williams concentrated on conflict over land titles to the neglect of the conflict with Britain. In 1774, Vermont was engaged in a prolonged struggle with New York which claimed sovereignty over the region based on a contested grant of Charles II to his brother the Duke of York, the future James II. Vermont claimed that the grant reverted to the crown when James fled the kingdom. Vermont's uncertain status deterred the state from participation in the discussions of Congress, membership of the Confederation and later Federal Union.

Unlike Williams, John Lendrum sought a national market and wide reading public for his work *A Concise and Impartial History of the American Revolution*, first published in 1795, republished in 1811 in Trenton, New Jersey and in a revised and corrected pocket edition in 1836. The identity of John Lendrum is obscure and the name may have been a pseudonym, but his history of the Revolution was published in the first instance by Isaiah Thomas (1749–1831), the foremost printer in America who was also responsible for publishing the works of the better known Jeremy Belknap and Samuel Williams. Lendrum can hardly be said to have contributed anything to the development of the history of the American Revolution but he did popularize the history of the subject and he chose his sources well. Setting out his aim and method in the preface, he asserted 'It is of great importance to every citizen of the United States, in whatever station of life, to be acquainted with the history of his own country, and, in a secondary degree, with that of America in general.' Describing himself unashamedly as a 'compiler', his purpose was 'to comprise in small bulk and at a low price, from the best authorities, a general history of America, and an account of the United States from the discovery of North America, till the establishment of the federal government'. Endeavouring 'to unite brevity with perspicuity' he had 'accordingly abridged the matter from his authorities, as he judged necessary'. Frequently he had 'used the words as well as the ideas of the writers, without particularly apprizing the reader of it'. He had made a point of identifying his sources for American history before the revolutionary war because of 'the nature of the subject, and the remoteness of the period', but for more recent history, it was unnecessary 'to swell' the work 'with quotations'. Lendrum identified 'the Annual Register, Dr. Goldsmith's History of England, and the

Continuation of Hume's History' as his principal sources 'in describing foreign occurrences, connected with the Revolution'. For American affairs he had freely made use of 'the writings of Dr. Belknap, Dr. Ramsay, Dr. Gordon, and Dr. Morse'. He invited the public to decide whether he had executed the work with 'judgement and impartiality' but expected 'the candour of the learned ... to excuse any inaccuracies which may have possibly crept in'.[104]

Lendrum drew a sharp distinction between the nature of northern and southern societies, the former being made up largely of 'hardy, independent freeholders ... impressed with the opinions that all men are born entitled to equal rights' and where 'every town may be called a republic'. From their infancy, the inhabitants acquired 'the habit of discussing, deliberating, and judging, of public affairs; and where those sentiments are first formed, which influence their political conduct through life'.[105] While slavery disfigured the southern provinces, making the cultivation of the soil 'unfashionable', it had unexpected benefits for the planter class and the preservation of American liberty. Though Lendrum made his own antislavery sentiments abundantly clear, he relied on David Ramsay for an explanation of the relationship between liberty and slavery.[106] Slavery 'nurtured a spirit of liberty among the free inhabitants' and 'all masters of slaves' were 'proud and jealous of their freedom ... Nothing could more effectually animate the opposition of a planter to the claims of Great Britain, than a conviction that those claims, in their extent, degraded him to a degree of dependence on his fellow subjects, equally humiliating with that which existed between his slaves and himself'.[107]

Lendrum shared with other patriot historians a benign view of colonial development which he depicted along parallel lines with that of the mother country 'wherein ample provision was made for the liberties of the citizens'. Neither the Crown nor the government had more authority over the people of the colonies and their assemblies than they did over the people and parliament of England.[108] Colonies were allowed their own judgement 'in the management of their own interest' until 'at length the British parliament resolved to alter the system of colonial government by raising a revenue in America, by taxation'.[109] The colonists strenuously opposed the idea of taxation without representation, believing that it violated both the British constitution and their own charter privileges: 'These proceedings of the mother country gave rise to great disturbances in America.'[110] Unlike most revolutionary historians, Lendrum paid considerable attention to the internal politics of Britain which was much agitated by disputes during this period, and he treats the Wilkes riots at length. 'The spirit of party,' he observed, 'which was now so general as well as violent, was attended with one very great inconvenience. It was productive of such instability in public men, and consequently in public measures and counsels, that a new ministry and new measures commenced almost with every new year.' As a consequence, Great Britain was 'rent by internal dissensions, and factions, whilst succeeding administrations, with equal weakness and obstinacy, endeavoured to establish parliamentary supremacy over the colonies'.[111] As secondary causes of the Revolution Lendrum identified 'the turbulence of some North Americans, the blunders of some British statesmen, and the assistance of foreign nations'. These factors brought forward the Revolution but its source lay elsewhere. 'It was a love of liberty and a quick sense of injury which led the Americans to rise in arms against the mother country; at a time when there were very few who thought it their interest, or had any idea, to shake off their allegiance to Britain'.[106] In promoting the American cause, Lendrum recognized that the written and spoken word were vital:

> The cause of the Americans had received such powerful aid from many patriotic publications in their gazettes, and from the fervent exhortations of popular preachers, connecting the cause of liberty with the principles of religion, that it was determined to employ these two powerful instruments, printing and preaching, to operate on the minds of the Canadians. A complete apparatus for printing, together with a printer and a clergyman, were therefore sent into Canada ... These powerful auxiliaries ... were, however, of no avail.[113]

Of the two best contemporary histories of the Revolution, one was written by David Ramsay, the other by Mercy Otis Warren (1728–1814), whose *History of the Rise, Progress and Termination of the American Revolution* (1805) was certainly the most robust and forceful of the revolutionary histories.[114] Cohen described Warren as 'the most formidable female intellectual in eighteenth-century America' but placed her only among intellectuals of the second rank, yet she was excellently qualified to write the history of the Revolution and, for many years, had campaigned in support of the American cause across a number of literary genres.[115] Kate Davies described her as a 'well-educated well-placed woman' belonging to the Massachusetts elite. Born in Barnstable, Massachusetts, her father had been speaker of the House of Representatives and her brother was James Otis Jr who became the leading opponent of writs of assistance. Her husband James Warren was a justice of the peace, colonel of the militia, member of the Massachusetts Committee of Correspondence and a president of the Massachusetts Provincial Congress.[116] The Warrens' home was a meeting place for like-minded politicians in the 1760s and the more radical 1770s. John and Abigail Adams were close friends.[117] But Warren herself was also at the centre of a network of correspondents 'that connected republican women across Massachusetts' providing 'a forum for intellectual debate and the exchange of political opinion'. Warren's letters from this period ultimately formed the basis of her *History* as well as those that resulted from her 'epistolary friendship' with the English radical Catharine Macaulay, herself the author of a history of England.[118]

Warren's idealized portrait of the American colonists before the conflict with Britain was not unlike those of other patriot or for that matter loyalist historians. Shaped largely by assumptions about New England, Warren argued that the colonists appeared to have reached

> that just and happy medium between the ferocity of a state of nature, and those high stages of civilization and refinement, that at once corrupt the heart and sap the foundation of happiness. The sobriety of their manners and the purity of their morals were exemplary; their piety and hospitality engaging; and the equal and lenient administration of their government secured authority, subordination, justice, regularity and peace. A well-informed yeomanry and an enlightened peasantry evinced the early attention of the first settlers to domestic education. Public schools were established in every town, particularly in the eastern provinces, and as early as [1638], Harvard College was founded at Cambridge.[119]

In the southern colonies slavery and 'aristocratic principles' flourished. Warren was not convinced by those who argued that where slavery was encouraged, 'very high ideals of liberty' prevailed among the free inhabitants. If so, 'it was not so much from a sense of the common rights of man, as from their own feelings of superiority'.[120]

Unlike other revolutionary historians, Warren judged George III harshly, describing him as 'this misguided sovereign, dazzled with the acquisition of empire, in the morning of youth, and in the zenith of national prosperity; more obstinate than cruel, rather weak than remarkably wicked'. Through the machinations of Lord Bute, 'the preceptor of the prince in the years of pupilage' and then 'director of the monarch on the throne', the cooperation of the House of Commons. was secured. 'Thus the parliament of England became the mere creature of [the] administration, and appeared ready to leap the boundaries of justice, and to undermine the pillars of their own constitution, by adhering steadfastly for several years to a complicated system of tyranny, that threatened the new world with a yoke unknown to their fathers.'[121] It was essential for the preservation of English liberties, 'that no grants of monies should be made, by tolls, talliage, excise, or any other way, without the consent of the people by their representative voice'. The colonial reaction might have been anticipated but for the pride of a nation 'grown giddy with the lustre of their own power': 'Innovation in a point so interesting might well be expected to create a general ferment through the American provinces.' Colonial trade and manufacturing were already constrained by British policies and it was only to be expected that 'loud complaints should be made when heavy exactions were laid on the subject, who had not, and whose local situation rendered it impracticable that he should have, an equal representation in parliament'. Warren defended the colonists' record during military campaigns and especially during the previous war when they had not only supported their own government but contributed to 'every constitutional requisition' made by the parent state. Not satisfied with this, Britain had adopted 'weak, impolitic and unjust measures' that 'threw the whole empire into the most violent convulsions'.[122] The Stamp Act sounded the alarm throughout the continent and led to the calling of the 'first congress ever convened in America ... in order to justify their claims to the rights of Englishmen, and the privileges of the British constitution'. Their demands were moderate. The repeal of the Act was greeted with celebration: 'Bonfires, illuminations, and all the usual expressions of popular satisfaction, were displayed on the joyful occasion.'[123] Like Belknap before her, Warren located the blame for the mounting crisis in colonial relations to the corruption of the British government describing

> the accumulated swarms of hirelings, sent from Great Britain to ravish from the colonies the rights they claimed both by nature and by compact ... Peculation was generally the prime object of this class, and the oaths they administered, and the habits they encouraged, were favourable to every species of bribery and corruption.[124]

In stressing the unanimity of colonial opposition to British policies and denying that Americans deliberately sought independence, Warren differed little from other revolutionary historians.[125] Massachusetts assumed the leading role in opposing Britain because the colony was targeted by the British government who identified Boston as 'the seat of sedition'. When news reached the colonies in 1775 of Britain's decision to reinforce troop numbers and prosecute the 'coercive system', the alternatives were clear. Either the Americans could put up 'a bold and vigorous resistance', or make 'an abject submission to the ignoble terms demanded by [the] administration'.[126] After Lexington, there was little choice but to assume 'the precarious decision of the sword, against the mighty power of Britain'.[127]

Where Warren differed from her contemporaries was in her fear that the Revolution had lost direction once the war was over. Addressing her work to the younger generation, she sought as in all her literary endeavours 'to form the minds, to fix the principles, to correct the errors, and to beckon by the soft allurements of love, as well as the stronger voice of reason, the young members of society (peculiarly my charge), to tread the path of true glory'.[128] For Warren, history 'revealed a continual struggle against the blind pursuit of power, luxury and passion'. The virtuous American people had survived against a corrupt Britain but could they survive in a republic where symptoms of decay were already manifesting themselves?[129] In 1780, she wrote to John

Adams, then in Amsterdam, that 'the steady influence of all the old republicans' was needed 'to keep the principles of the Revolution in view'. By 1786, 'she believed the revolutionary venture might fail entirely'.[130] In Cohen's view, Warren exemplified Bolingbroke's conception of history as 'philosophy teaching by example', the proper task of which was 'to train people, especially young people in "public and private virtue"'. The exemplary theory of history matched Warren's aspirations and 'her understanding of her proper role' just as it had swept the revolutionary generation of historians.[131] Though forty years in the making, Warren's *History* sold poorly.[132] Judith Sargent Murray, editor of *The Gleaner*, wrote to Warren informing her that she was unable to raise many subscriptions because John Marshall's 'Life of Washington', 'it is said, forestalls, if not wholly precludes, the utility of this history, and very many urge the political principles attributed to the otherwise admired writer, as a reason for withholding their signatures'. It was reviewed only once in *The Panoplist*, a Boston magazine which was politically hostile. Whether gender was a factor in its poor sales is difficult to say.[133]

Warren died in 1814 and Ramsay a year later but it was the death of the latter rather than the former which marked the end of an era. The world was changing: 'romanticism and sectionalism were replacing Enlightenment ideals and the nationalists of his generation'. Despite continuities, 'independence necessitated a new political and intellectual agenda: to define an American identity, culture, political ideology, and institutions within the framework of something entirely new – an American nation-state'.[134]

The nineteenth century: the middle decades

Lester Cohen included Federalist Timothy Pitkin (1766–1847) among the revolutionary generation of historians though he was much younger than the others and his two-volume *Political and Civil History of the United States of America 1763–1797* was published in 1828, only six years before George Bancroft's first volume.[135] Pitkin, who served in the Connecticut legislature and in Congress, might be better seen as a transitional figure, who could look upon the Revolution dispassionately and was no longer exercised over Indian, Hessian and British atrocities, whether real or imaginary. Like the earlier generation of patriot historians, Pitkin sought to promote the union of the states through a better understanding of the development of the nation's institutions to which Americans owed their unique 'personal and political happiness' and which 'daily' were 'becoming more and more objects of peculiar interest and inquiry'. In this, Pitkin was also responding to the growing tensions generated by sectional conflict in his own day and reacting against the predominance of military history in revolutionary historiography.[136]

Pitkin's overview of the colonial period was influenced by the earlier generation of historians, especially Gordon and Belknap. Colonial history had been one long struggle between 'prerogative and power on the one hand, and freedom and the privilege of self-government on the other'. From the start, the government in England suspected that sooner or later the colonists would seek their independence and took every opportunity to extend the power and prerogative of the Crown and parliament 'at the expense of the best and dearest of rights of the colonists'. Yet despite these struggles, claimed Pitkin, the colonists still 'retained an affection for their parent country', recognizing that there were benefits to be derived from the relationship giving as an example the bounties offered for the production of certain types of goods.[137] Pitkin goes on to argue, not that the colonists were shaped by British institutions, but rather that the colonists shaped their own institutions. The character of the first colonists was distinctive and distinguished from 'the great mass of the people in Europe'. It was the passage of the Stamp Act and the 'insignificant duty' on tea that precipitated though did not cause the American Revolution. The origins of that 'great event' were to be found in 'powerful and efficient causes' deep in America's past. The united sentiments of two to three million people spread over a continent in opposition to the Stamp Act 'were not the work of a day or a year'. The rights claimed by the Americans were those their fathers had brought to America and passed on to their descendants.[138] But while the roots of the Revolution were to be found in the character of the American people, the final rupture was laid at the door of the British who provoked it by changes in policy.

Institutions were central to the work of George Bancroft (1800–1891), the dominant figure of nineteenth-century American history writing. Born in Worcester, Massachusetts, he was the son of Aaron Bancroft, a clergyman who once wrote a biography of George Washington which went into several editions in America and Europe. He attended Phillips Academy in Exeter, New Hampshire and then Harvard, after which he studied in Europe for four years, obtaining a doctorate in 1820. Having tutored in Greek at Harvard, he left to found a school on the German model at Round Hill in Northampton, Massachusetts in 1823 which he left in 1831.[139] Bancroft set new standards for research and writing in American history. He published the first volume of his history of the United States in 1834 and continued research and rewriting until the end of his life, publishing numerous editions of the *History* on both sides of the Atlantic. In the preface to volume one of the *History of the United States* Bancroft set out his conviction of how history should be written and 'the grandeur and vastness of the subject'.

> I have desired to give to the work the interest of authenticity. I have applied, as I have proceeded, the principles of historical skepticism, and, not allowing myself to grow weary in comparing witnesses, or consulting codes of laws, I have endeavored to impart originality to my narrative, by deriving it from writings and sources which were the contemporaries of the events that are described.[140]

Pursuing research in Europe, Bancroft obtained access to collections of papers, hitherto unknown or unavailable, and employed agents working full time on collecting materials on his behalf. Initially scrupulous in identifying sources, Bancroft did not maintain the practice in his later volumes. While professional historians today find his use of hyperbole excessive, his work is still the one that historians identify with the beginnings of professional practice.

According to Bancroft the origins of the conflict between England and her American colonies 'sprang necessarily out of the development of British institutions'. Parliament as the representative of 'English nationality' had resisted and overthrown the personal rule of the Stuarts and 'the supreme right of parliament' was 'the watch word of the revolution of 1688'. It had delivered the death-blow to 'monarchical absolutism' throughout the English dominions, and was 'the harbinger of constitutional liberty for the civilized world'. In transferring the succession to the house of Hanover, parliament again 'asserted its paramount authority over the crown'. But the supremacy of parliament, argued Bancroft, assumed 'an exaggerated form' and 'was claimed to extend without limit over Ireland and over the colonies' with the result that 'the theory which had first been used to rescue and secure the liberties of England became an instrument of despotism'. However there existed alongside this theory an earlier tradition of the rights of the individual and the liberties of organized communities. It was these two elements of British political life 'that were brought into collision by the American revolution'. It was provoked by the theory of parliamentary supremacy and the principle of liberty 'diffused through all the part of the commonwealth'. These two ideas 'struggled for the ascendancy in the mind of the British nation and in its legislature'.[141]

While in some respect Bancroft anticipated the research methods of the professional historian, in another he looked back to the past. According to one modern commentator, Dorothy Ross, what linked him most obviously to 'earlier modern modes of historical perception' was his retention of Providence as an active shaping force in history: 'Bancroft's work was pre-eminently a history of the millennial American republic, and in it the divine end required divine power. Providence was present in every chapter and incident that described the marvelous success of the American enterprise, arousing "amazement" and "astonishment" at what could only be God's guiding plan.' Bancroft was perfectly aware of the reality of human causation, and understood historical contingency. A different character at a different place or time would have altered the outcome. Weaving human causation and historical contingency into a fabric of Providential design, the result 'was to heighten our awareness of divine power rather than of human power in history'.[142] In the last analysis 'George Bancroft gave the American-centered grand narrative its most popular and compelling form. He cast it as a romance, the story of the achievement of America's divinely ordained identity.'[143]

The reputation of his contemporary Richard Hildreth, however, has fared rather better than Bancroft, his more illustrious rival.[144] Graduating from Harvard in 1826, Hildreth (1807–1865) served as editor of the Boston *Atlas* before publishing in 1849 his *History of the United States of America*.[145] There were already more than enough centennial and Fourth-of-July orations declared Hildreth, promising his readers 'plain facts in plain English' in a work on American history more extensive than anything that had yet been written:

> It is due to our fathers and ourselves ... to truth and philosophy, to present for once, on the historic stage, the founders of our American nation unbedaubed with patriotic rouge, wrapped up in no fine-spun cloaks of excuses and apology, without stilts, buskins, tinsel, or bedizenment, in their own proper persons, often rude, hard, narrow, superstitious, and mistaken, but always earnest, downright, manly and sincere. The result of their labors is eulogy enough; their best apology is to tell their story exactly as it was.[146]

The problem, as Hildreth saw it, was that the fathers and founders had been so enveloped by myths and distorted by eulogies that it was almost impossible to get at the truth despite the existence of 'copious contemporary records, such as the infancy of no other nation can show', and 'the labors of many diligent and conscientious inquirers'.[147]

Hildreth recognized the importance of the growth in power of the colonial assemblies at the expense of 'the royal and proprietary governors' during the Duke of Newcastle's long tenure in office but he detected no sentiment in favour of independence at that time, only a restlessness over restrictive British legislation, 'the fetters on their trade and industry'. 'The pretension of a greater regal authority in the colonies than at home, and a power of legislating for them by orders in council, had ceased to be countenanced. Even the crown lawyers now pointed to Parliament and the colonial Assemblies as the only rightful legislators.' But as the colonies advanced in wealth and commercial enterprise, 'few of the colonial merchants felt scruples at violating those restrictions, whenever they could without danger of detection'. The Molasses Act was virtually ignored.[148] Economic discrimination rather than political tyranny, Hildreth believed, was the mainspring of the Revolution. The response to his work must have been far from what Hildreth had wanted. The 'spirit of the author', declared one critic who had only managed to read the first volume, and that in 'a cursory manner', was that 'of a man fully satisfied that he is master of his subject'. The style was dry 'with occasionally a critical remark or a severe stricture', and so 'fearfully "earnest"' that it invited his readers to put it under a microscope to seek out its flaws. The critic protested at what he saw as the symptoms of 'simplicity and hardiness à la Carlyle'. 'Surely, grace and kindliness, a full and easy manner, are greater recommendations of a writer, than a course, insolent, frowning style, whose very force degenerates into impertinent quickness and hardness, and which seems more adapted for the torture and exasperation, rather than for the pleasure and consolation of readers.'[149]

While Bancroft's early volumes attracted criticism from some of the descendants of those who had participated in the Revolution – who felt he had slighted their contribution – and Hildreth was assailed by critics for his alleged lack of literary flare, the next generation of historians would be more concerned with their professional rather than their popular reception.

Notes

1 William Gordon, *The History of the Rise, Progress, and Establishment of the Independence of the United States of America*, 4 vols (London; 1788), preface.

2 Orin G. Libby, 'A Critical Examination of William Gordon's History of the American Revolution', *American Historical Association Annual Report* (1899), pp. 367–88, 369.

3 Orin G. Libby, 'Ramsay as a Plagiarist', *American Historical Review* (hereafter *AHR*), 7 (1901–1902), pp. 697–703.

4 Peter Novick, *That Noble Dream: The 'Objectivity Question' and the American Historical Profession* (Cambridge and New York; 1988).

5 Lester H. Cohen, 'Creating a Usable Future: The Revolutionary Historians and the National Past' in Jack P. Greene (ed.), *The American Revolution: Its Character and Limits* (New York; 1987), pp. 309–30, 313–14, 325–6.

6 Gary B. Nash, *The Unknown American Revolution: The Unruly Birth of Democracy and the Struggle to Create America* (New York; 2005), pp. xxi–xxii.

7 Lawrence J. Friedman and Arthur H. Shaffer, 'David Ramsay and the Quest for an American Historical Identity', *Southern Quarterly* (hereafter *SQ*), 14 (1976), pp. 351–71, 352–3.

8 Lester H. Cohen, *The Revolutionary Histories: Contemporary Narratives of the American Revolution* (Ithaca, NY and London; 1980), pp. 15–16; Arthur

H. Shaffer, *The Politics of History: Writing the History of the American Revolution, 1783–1815* (Chicago; 1975), pp. 104–5.

9 Shaffer, *Politics of History*, pp. 140–1.

10 Cohen, 'Creating a Usable Future', pp. 312–13.

11 Cohen, *Revolutionary Histories*, pp. 20–1.

12 Cohen, *Revolutionary Histories*, pp. 111, 115; Shaffer, *Politics of History*, pp. 140–1.

13 Shaffer, *Politics of History*, p. 113.

14 Cohen, *Revolutionary Histories*, p. 19.

15 Mary Beth Norton, *The British-Americans: The Loyalist Exiles in England 1774–1789* (Boston, MA; 1972), p. 264; Bernard Bailyn, *The Ordeal of Thomas Hutchinson* (Cambridge, MA; 1974), pp. 384, 386; John E. Ferling, *The Loyalist Mind: Joseph Galloway and the American Revolution* (University Park, PA and London; 1977), p. 101.

16 Thomas Hutchinson, *The History of the Province of Massachusetts Bay, from 1749–1774 Comprising a Detailed Narrative of the Origin and Early Stages of the American Revolution, edited from the author's MS, by his Grandson The Rev. John Hutchinson, MA* (London; 1828), pp. v–vi; all subsequent references are to this edition. (John Hutchinson edited only volume III of the original edition; all three volumes of the *History* were reprinted in 1936 edited by Lawrence Shaw Mayo: Thomas Hutchinson, *The History of the Colony and Province of Massachusetts Bay*, 3 vols (Cambridge, MA; 1936).)

17 Hutchinson, *History*, III, pp. vii–xi.

18 Hutchinson, *History*, III, p. iii.

19 Bailyn, *Hutchinson*, pp. xii, 1; for similar views of Hutchinson's importance, see William Pencak, *America's Burke: The Mind of Thomas Hutchinson* (Washington, DC; 1982), and Malcolm Freiberg, *Prelude to Purgatory: Thomas Hutchinson in Provincial Massachusetts Politics, 1760–1770* (New York and London; 1990); Michael Kraus, *A History of American History* (New York; 1937), pp. 113–20.

20 Bailyn, *Hutchinson*, p. 27; Pencak, *America's Burke*, on Hutchinson as a historian, pp. 62–4.

21 Bailyn, *Hutchinson*, p. 16; Pencak, *America's Burke*; Pencak, 'Thomas Hutchinson', *Oxford Dictionary of National Biography* (hereafter ODNB), pp. 33–5.

22 Bailyn, *Hutchinson*, pp. 17, 18.

23 Hutchinson, *History*, III, pp. 85–6.

24 Hutchinson, *History*, III, pp. 102–3.

25 Hutchinson, *History*, III, p. 103.

26 Cited in Hutchinson, *History*, III, p. 107.

27 Hutchinson, *History*, III, p. 257.

28 Hutchinson, *History*, III, p. 95.

29 Hutchinson, *History*, III, pp. 119–23.

30 Hutchinson, *History*, III, pp. 256–7.

31 Hutchinson, *History*, III, pp. 289–90.

31 Hutchinson, *History*, III, p. 223.

32 Hutchinson, *History*, III, pp. 324–6.

33 Hutchinson, *History*, III, pp. 263–4.

34 Edmund S. Morgan, *The Genuine Article: A Historian Looks at Early*

America (New York and London; 2004), pp. 147–55.

35 Edmund Morgan, *The Genuine Article: A Historian Looks at Early America* (New York and London; 2004), pp. 147–55.

36 Douglass Adair and John A. Schutz (eds), *Peter Oliver's Origin and Progress of the American Rebellion: A Tory View* (Stanford, CA; 1967).

37 [Alexander Hewat], *An Historical Account of the Rise and Progress of the Colonies of South Carolina and Georgia*, 2 vols (London; 1779, reprinted Spartenburg, SC, 1962).

38 Geraldine M. Meroney, 'Alexander Hewat, an Historical Account', in Lawrence H. Leder (ed.), *The Colonial Legacy*, 2 vols (New York; 1971), I, pp. 135–63.

39 Meroney, 'Alexander Hewat', pp. 139–40.

40 Meroney, 'Alexander Hewat', p. 137.

41 Hewat, *Rise and Progress of the Colonies*, II, p. 316.

42 Hewat, *Rise and Progress of the Colonies*, II, pp. 317–18.

43 Hewat, *Rise and Progress of the Colonies*, II, pp. 317–18.

44 Joseph Galloway, *Historical and Political Reflections on the Rise and Progress of the American Rebellion* (London; 1780), Advertisement; Ferling, *Loyalist Mind*, p. 101.

45 Galloway, *Historical and Political Reflections*, pp. 2–3.

46 Galloway, *Historical and Political Reflections*, pp. 3–4.

47 Galloway, *Historical and Political Reflections*, pp. 5–8, 47.

48 Galloway, *Historical and Political Reflections*, pp. 46–7, 9–12.

49 Anne Y. Zimmer, *Jonathan Boucher: Loyalist in Exile* (Detroit, MI; 1978), p. 37.

50 Zimmer, *Jonathan Boucher*, pp. 41–4.

51 Jonathan Boucher, *A View of the Causes and Consequences of the American Revolution in Thirteen Discourses Preached in North America Between the Years 1763 and 1775* (London; 1797, reprinted New York; 1967).

52 Jonathan Boucher, *Reminiscences of an American Loyalist, 1738–1789, Being the Autobiography of the Reverend Jonathan Boucher*, ed. Jonathan Bouchier (Boston, MA; 1925); and reprinted with a new introduction (Port Washington, NY; 1967); Boucher, *Reminiscences* (1967), p. v.

53 Zimmer, *Jonathan Boucher*, pp. 45, 48, 244–5.

54 Boucher, *Causes and Consequences*, pp. i–ii.

55 Boucher, *Causes and Consequences*, p. ii.

56 Boucher, *Causes and Consequences*, pp. ii–iii.

57 Boucher, *Causes and Consequences*, pp. iii–iv.

58 Boucher, *Causes and Consequences*, pp. iv–v.

59 Boucher, *Causes and Consequences*, p. xxix.

60 Boucher, *Causes and Consequences*, pp. xxxii–iii, xxxv, fn.

61 Boucher, *Causes and Consequences*, pp. xl–xlii, xliii–xliv.

62 Boucher, *Causes and Consequences*, pp. xlvi–xlvii.

63 C. G. Sellers Jr, 'The American Revolution: Southern Founders of a National Tradition' in A. S. Link and R. W. Patrick (eds), *Writing Southern History: Essays in Historiography in Honor of Fletcher M. Green* (Baton Rouge, LA; 1965), pp. 38–66, 38.

64 David Ramsay *The History of the American Revolution*, ed. Lester H. Cohen,

2 vols (Indianapolis, IN; 1990), originally published in Philadelphia in 1789, I, pp. xxv, xxxiv; Arthur H. Shaffer, 'David Ramsay and the Limits of Revolutionary Nationalism' in Michael O'Brien and David Moltke-Hansen (eds), *Intellectual Life in Antebellum Charleston* (Knoxville, TN; 1986), pp. 47–84, 48; Arthur H. Shaffer, *To be an American: David Ramsay and the Making of an American Consciousness* (Columbia, SC; 1991), p. 1; for the fullest details of Ramsay's publications and their reception, see 'David Ramsay, 1749–1815: Selections from His Writings', Robert L. Brunhouse (ed.), *Transactions of the American Philosophical Society*, New Series, vol. 55, Part 4 (1965), pp. 220–31; Friedman and Shaffer, 'David Ramsay'; all references to Ramsay's *History of the American Revolution* are from the Cohen edition.

65 Sellers, 'American Revolution', pp. 40–1.

66 Brunhouse,*David Ramsay*, p. 224.

67 Libby, 'Ramsay as Plagiarist', pp. 697–703; Page Smith, 'David Ramsay and the Causes of the American Revolution', *WMQ*, 3rd ser., 17 (1960), pp. 51–77, 73.

68 Brunhouse, *David Ramsay*, pp. 39, 224.

69 Ramsay, *American Revolution*, I, pp. xxxi–xxxii.

70 David Ramsay, *The History of the Revolution in South Carolina, from a British Province to an Independent State*, 2 vols (Trenton, NJ; 1785), I, pp. 66–7, 159; II, 275–6.

71 Sellers, 'American Revolution', pp. 40–1.

72 Shaffer, *To be an American*, p. 105.

73 Shaffer, *To be an American*, p. 107.

74 Shaffer, *To be an American*, p. 106.

75 Ramsay, *American Revolution*, I, pp. 25–7.

76 Ramsay, *American Revolution*, I, p. 28.

77 Ramsay, *American Revolution*, I, pp. 31–2.

78 Shaffer, *To be an American*, p. 117; Ramsay, *American Revolution*, I, pp. 30–1.

79 Ramsay, *American Revolution*, I, p. 27.

80 Ramsay, *American Revolution*, I, pp. 18–19.

81 Ramsay, *American Revolution*, I, pp. 32–3.

82 Ramsay, *American Revolution*, I, pp. 42–3.

83 Ramsay, *American Revolution*, I, pp. 46–7, 51.

84 Ramsay, *American Revolution*, II, pp. 665–7.

85 Jeremy Belknap, *History of New-Hampshire*, vol. 1 (Philadelphia; 1784), vol. 2 (Boston; 1791).

86 Clifford K. Shipton, 'Jeremy Belknap', Biographical sketches of those who attended Harvard College in the classes 1761–1763, *Sibley's Harvard Graduates*, XV, 1761–1763 (Boston; 1970), pp. 175–96, 175, 177; see also George B. Kirsch, *Jeremy Belknap: A Biography* (New York; 1982).

87 Shipton, 'Jeremy Belknap', p. 176; Sidney Kaplan, 'The History of New-Hampshire: Jeremy Belknap as Literary Craftsman', *WMQ*, 3rd ser., 21 (1) (1964), pp. 18–39, 30.

88 Kaplan, *History of New-Hampshire*, p. 31.

89 Belknap, *History of New-Hampshire*, II, pp. 317–19; italics added.

90 Belknap, *History of New-Hampshire*, II, pp. 319–22.
91 Belknap, *History of New-Hampshire*, II, p. 323.
92 Belknap, *History of New-Hampshire*, II, pp. 322–4.
93 Belknap, *History of New-Hampshire*, II, p. 325.
94 Belknap, *History of New-Hampshire*, II, p. 327.
95 Belknap, *History of New-Hampshire*, II, pp. 327–8, 330–1.
96 Belknap, *History of New-Hampshire*, II, p. 332, see fn.
97 Belknap, *History of New-Hampshire*, II, p. 332.
98 Belknap, *History of New-Hampshire*, II, pp. 332–4.
99 Belknap, *History of New-Hampshire*, II, p. 406.
100 Clifford K. Shipton, 'Samuel Williams', Biographical Sketches of Those Who Attended Harvard College in the Classes 1761–1763, *Sibley's Harvard Graduates*, XV, 1761–1763 (Boston; 1970), pp. 134–46.
101 Samuel Williams, *The Natural and Civil History of Vermont* (Walpole, NH; 1794), p. ix.
102 Williams, *Natural and Civil History*, pp. xi–xii.
103 Williams, *Natural and Civil History*, pp. 307–10.
104 John Lendrum, *A Concise and Impartial History of the American Revolution to which is Prefixed a General History of North and South America*, 2 vols (Boston; 1795), I, preface.
105 Lendrum, *History of the American Revolution*, pp. 223–6.
106 Lendrum, *History of the American Revolution*, I, pp. 230–6. Antislavery sentiments were dropped from the 1836 edition.
107 Lendrum, *History of the American Revolution*, I, pp. 234–5.
108 Lendrum, *History of the American Revolution*, I, pp. 220–1.
109 Lendrum, *History of the American Revolution*, I, pp. 257, 258.
110 Lendrum, *History of the American Revolution*, I, p. 266; Belknap, *History of New-Hampshire*, II, pp. 323–6.
111 Lendrum, *History of the American Revolution*, I, pp. 281–98, quotation pp. 290–1.
112 Lendrum, *History of the American Revolution*, I, p. 257.
113 Lendrum, *History of the American Revolution*, II, p. 73.
114 Lester H. Cohen, 'Introduction' in Mercy Otis Warren, *History of the Rise, Progress and Termination of the American Revolution*, ed. Lester H. Cohen, 2 vols (Indianapolis, IN; 1988), p. xvi. Kate Davies, *Catharine Macaulay and Mercy Otis Warren: the Revolutionary Atlantic and the Politics of Gender* (Oxford; 2005), pp. 3–8, 204; all references to Warren's *History* are to the Cohen edition.
115 Cohen in Warren, *History*, I, p. xvi.
116 Cohen in Warren, *History*, I, pp. xxii–iii.
117 Davies, *Catharine Macaulay and Mercy Otis Warren*, pp. 3–8, 204; William R. Smith, *History as Argument: Three Patriot Historians of the American Revolution* (The Hague and Paris; 1966), p. 36.
118 Davies, *Catharine Macaulay and Mercy Otis Warren*, pp. 2–3, 186–7.
119 Warren, *History*, I, p. 14.
120 Warren, *History*, I, p. 14.
121 Warren, *History*, I, p. 14–15.
122 Warren, *History*, I, pp. 15, 16.

123 Warren, *History*, I, pp. 17, 19–21.

124 Warren, *History*, I, p. 23.

125 Warren, *History*, I, pp. 24–5.

126 Warren, *History*, I, pp. 97, 98–9.

127 Warren, *History*, I, p. 104.

128 Cohen in Warren, *History*, I, pp. xvi–xvii.

129 Cohen in Warren, *History*, I, pp. xviii–xx.

130 Cohen in Warren, *History*, I, p. xx.

131 Cohen in Warren, *History*, I, p. xxi.

132 Cohen in Warren, *History*, I, pp. xxv–xxvi.

133 Smith, *History as Argument*, p. 38.

134 Shaffer, 'David Ramsay and the Limits of Revolutionary Nationalism', p. 48.

135 Timothy Pitkin, *A Political and Civil History of the United States of America from the Year 1763 to the Close of the Administration of President Washington, in March, 1797*, 2 vols (New Haven; 1828, reprinted New York; 1970). All references are to the 1828 original. Cohen, *Revolutionary Histories*, p. 16.

136 Pitkin, *Political and Civil History*, I, p. 3.

137 Pitkin, *Political and Civil History*, I, p. 137.

138 Pitkin, *Political and Civil History*, I, p. 4.

139 Kraus, *History of American History*, pp. 215–17.

140 George Bancroft, *History of the United States of America, from the Discovery of the Continent*, the author's last revision, IV (New York; 1888).

141 George Bancroft, *History of the United States*, IV (1866), pp. 262–4.

142 Dorothy Ross, 'Historical Consciousness in Nineteenth-Century America', *AHR*, 89 (1984), pp. 909–28, 915.

143 Dorothy Ross, 'Grand Narrative in American Historical Writing: From Romance to Uncertainty', *AHR*, 100 (1995), pp. 651–77, 653.

144 Russell B. Nye, *George Bancroft: Boston Brahmin* (New York; 1972), p. 186.

145 Richard Hildreth, *The History of the United States, from the Discovery of the Continent to the Organization of Government under the Federal Constitution 1492–1789*, 3 vols (1849). The version reprinted by Augustus M. Kelly in New York in 1969 is the revised version of 1877–1880.

146 Review of Hildreth in *The American Whig*, 10 (August, 1849), p. 220.

147 Richard Hildreth, *The History of the United States of America from the Adoption of the Federal Constitution to the End of the Sixteenth Congress 1788–1821*, 3 vols (New York; 1863), I, p. vi.

148 Richard Hildreth, *History of the United States of America*, Revised edition [1877–1880] (New York; 1969), II, p. 430.

149 Review of Hildreth, *American Whig*, 10 (August, 1849), p. 220.

2

'Noble ideals and ignoble interests'

Professionalization, imperialists and progressives

For all their achievements and their huge popular success, Bancroft and his fellow gentlemen amateurs were denounced by the next generation of historians who specialized in particular periods and subject matter and were professionally trained in the newly organized graduate schools pioneered by the Johns Hopkins University in Baltimore, and modelled on developments in nineteenth-century German institutions. Their ranks were made up of those who, unlike their predecessors, went on to careers in university teaching and were employed in institutions not only along the east coast but across the nation, and especially in the mid west. A professional association, the American Historical Association was founded in 1884 and its annual reports served as an outlet for its members until the creation of the *American Historical Review* in 1900. A Ph.D. in history became the highly desirable qualification for employment in the nation's universities. However, in his study of the rise of the historical profession, Peter Novick has disputed the assumption that the professionalization of history and historical writing was 'one of speedy and dramatic transformation'.[1] Citing one estimate, he observes that between 1890 and 1910, only twenty per cent of the membership of the American Historical Association was made up of college teachers, two thirds of its presidents between 1912 and 1927 lacked Ph.D.s and that distinguished work in the first decades of the twentieth century continued to be produced by those who lacked formal training.[2] The impact of the new scholarship, however, made an early and impressive impact on the historiography of the American Revolution. Putting nationalism to flight and cutting exceptionalism down to size, it crafted two contrasting approaches to the study of the Revolution, the imperial and the progressive, which despite the development of fresh theoretical perspectives, the creation of innovative methodologies and the opening up of new fields of enquiry, have dominated the historical landscape ever since – or at least until the advent of the linguistic turn and the fascination with material culture.

To perpetuate Bancroft's perception of the English colonial system, wrote Charles M. Andrews (1863–1943), his harshest critic, would be 'nothing less than a crime against historical truth'.[3] Andrews studied in the 1880s at Johns Hopkins University, under the guidance of Herbert Baxter Adams. A. S. Eisenstadt, author of a full-length study of Andrews, identified him with the new history's ideal of presenting the past 'as it actually was' as Ranke (1795–1886) had expressed it. While to Ranke, this had meant 'a philologist's ideal for using sources critically ... to the American historian of the late nineteenth century', it came to mean 'a scientist's ideal for recapturing the past'.[4] The first task of the historian, Andrews believed, 'was to reconstruct the past according to its own terms and materials' and draw only on the work of others, 'if this scholarship, too, was securely grounded in original research'.[5]

Andrews emerged as the leading figure among a group of historians who became known as the imperial school though, as Richard Johnson has pointed out, Andrews never employed this term in his publications and 'colonial' is a better fit.[6] This group of historians, the best known of whom were Andrews himself, Herbert Levi Osgood (1855–1918) and George L. Beer (1872–1920), the first two of whom enjoyed lengthy careers at Yale and Columbia respectively while the latter was a distinguished scholar and businessman, wrote about the American colonies in the context of the British empire. They asked questions that had rarely ever intruded into revolutionary historiography, which tended to leapfrog from the period of settlement to that of revolution.[7] They invented the colonial period. Though they seldom addressed the causes of the Revolution directly, the work of this group had profound implications for its interpretation. Osgood described the period from 1690 to 1763 as 'the unknown period' of American history, during which the colonies gradually coalesced into one system under the control of the British government. Osgood had previously studied the internal development of each of the continental colonies, their relations with one another, and the institutions and processes by which they were joined to the government of Britain. Through an analysis of the relationship between colonial assemblies – 'the embodiment of colonial self government' – and royal appointees, Osgood demonstrated the encroachment of the former on the putative powers of the latter and the steady erosion of royal authority.[8] Andrews declared that during the hundred years before the Revolution, the colonies passed through 'a silent revolution' and expounded the implications of this in *The Colonial Background of the American Revolution*, originally published in 1924. 'Self-absorbed and preoccupied with their domestic problems', the colonies 'were gradually and almost insensibly outgrowing their status as dependencies and becoming self-conscious independent communities'. They were

> fully competent to have a separate life of their own, even though they remained bound politically and legally to the mother country ... Their inhabitants knew very little of the world outside themselves or of the interests of the mother country across the sea, and among them were very few who understood at all the difficulties of Great Britain's position after 1763 or realized any better than did the Britons themselves the new status of the British empire.[9]

Whereas earlier historians had denounced British tyranny and oppression in the colonies, the imperialists demonstrated how large a degree of self government they enjoyed and the limited impact of British commercial policy on their economies. These historians wrote at a time of rapprochement between Britain and the United States when the latter was acquiring an empire of its own and the concept of Anglo-Saxonism was being promoted on both sides of the Atlantic.[10] Leonard Labaree (1897–1980), and Lawrence Henry Gipson (1880–1971) were the standard-bearers of a second generation of imperial historians. In his capacity as historian and editor, Labaree produced the first major study of royal government in America tracing the establishment, maintenance and ultimate decline of royal authority. He blamed the decline on the blindness of British authorities who never understood the causes that underlay it and 'never offered a workable solution for the problem before them'. He also edited *Royal Instructions to British Colonial Governors.* Gipson published the first volume of his life's work *The British Empire before the American Revolution* in 1936 and the final volume in 1967.[11]

If the vantage point of the imperialists was Whitehall and Westminster rather than the Atlantic seaboard, the inspiration of progressive historians was Paris and the events of the French Revolution. Writing at the beginning of the twentieth century and extending into second and third generations, the original progressives, Beard, Becker, Hacker and Jameson constituted one element of a broad reform movement during the Progressive Era in the years before the First World War. As rural Americans, migrants from Europe and elsewhere went to live in the city, historians recognized, Americans confronted the problems of urbanization, industrialization and immigration, and their experiences were not dissimilar to those of the peoples of Europe undergoing similar transformations. More closely concerned with the Revolution than the imperialists, the progressives sought the origins of the Revolution in internal conflict. They saw the Revolution as a social movement, broadly democratic, and viewed the Federal Constitution as a conservative reaction against it. Progressive historians introduced into American history the language of class and section but not of 'race'. Their approach to the Revolution will be examined in this chapter, their interpretation of the period of the Confederation and the making of the Federal Constitution in Chapter 3.

The concept of the Revolution as a dual contest was advanced by Carl Becker (1873–1945) in *The History of Political Parties in the Province of New York, 1760–1776* (1909). Born in Lincoln Township, Black Hawk County, Iowa, Becker studied with Frederick Jackson Turner (1861–1932) and Charles Haskins (1870–1937) at the University of Wisconsin and with James Harvey Robinson (1863–1936) at Columbia University.[12] Robinson in particular was identified with the 'new history' in its most presentist form. Becker was promoted to Professor of History at the University of Kansas in 1916 but spent the larger part of his academic life in New York state at Cornell University.

Becker was not the first historian to define the struggle with Britain in this fashion. Charles Lincoln had done so several years earlier in *The Revolutionary Movement in Pennsylvania 1760–1776* (1901) and in 1889, Charles Stillé published an article describing how the people of Pennsylvania had had to contend with two revolutions.[13] Arguing that Lincoln's study was superior to Becker's, Robert Gough attributed the relative neglect of the former to their different career paths though their books probably had a common origin in the influence of James Harvey Robinson who taught Lincoln at the University of Pennsylvania and Becker at Columbia.[14] Lincoln argued that

> no people in all America were more democratic than the dissatisfied communities in the Quaker colony, and it was because the provincial government would not grant them equal rights or equal opportunities that these dissatisfied people welcomed a national movement under cover of which they might revolutionize their own colonial conditions.[15]

He combined class and sectional factors to explain the combination of lower- and middle-class residents of Philadelphia and German and Scottish-Irish settlers in western Pennsylvania against 'a common exploiter', the city's merchant aristocracy, who 'maintained their power by disenfranchising all but a handful of Philadelphians and by gerrymandering assembly representation against the west'. It was the desire 'to change the control of the provincial government that motivated most Pennsylvanians to become involved in the Revolutionary struggle'. For Lincoln, 'the internal social revolution was the key element' in Pennsylvania's revolution whereas Becker equivocates, at one point asserting that the two components were 'about equally prominent', and at another that the internal revolution was 'fundamental'.[16]

Before 1765 the political history of New York was a contest between the governors and the assembly representing 'different interests and opposing principles'.[17] At this time, Carl Becker wrote, 'strictly speaking, there were no political parties [but] rather two centres of influence'. The only thing that was permanent about them was that those who were attached to the governor's interest were on one side and those who were opposed to him used the assembly to thwart him.[18] As the conflict with

Britain gathered momentum, extra-legal committees came to supersede the authority of the assembly.[19] 'The establishment of this extra-legal machinery', wrote Becker 'was the open door through which the common freeholder and the unfranchised mechanic and artisan pushed their way into the political arena' to the dismay of the land-owning and merchant aristocracy.

> The stamp act riots at once revealed the latent opposition of motives and interests between the privileged and the unprivileged, – an opposition which the war itself only half suppressed, and which was destined to reappear in the rivalry of Federalist and Republican. From 1765 to 1776, therefore, two questions, about equally prominent, determined party history. The first was whether essential colonial rights should be maintained: the second was by whom and by what methods they would be maintained. The first was the question of home rule: the second was the question, if we may so put it, of who should rule at home.[20]

Becker's initial analysis of the class structure of the colony of New York embraced all manner of people but he subsequently confined his attention to New York City. By ignoring urban–rural divisions as a factor in the coming of the Revolution, he implied that the city population alone played a conspicuous part in the struggle for home rule.[21]

Equally important in the progressive interpretation of the Revolution was Arthur Schlesinger's examination of the role played by colonial merchants, 'willingly and unwillingly', in the separation of the mainland American colonies from Britain. The problem was not, as John Adams had once put it, 'how to get the thirteen clocks to strike at the same time', because there really were only two, 'one functioning along characteristic lines in the northern provinces, and the other developing in a characteristic way in the southern provinces'.[22] This distinction drew on the work of one of the earliest and most influential of the progressives, Frederick Jackson Turner, a midwesterner who also studied for his doctorate at Johns Hopkins and whose identification of the existence of free land on the expanding frontier with the creation of American democracy, influenced the work not only of progressive historians but many others for at least two generations.[23] An assistant professor of American history at Ohio State University when *Colonial Merchants and the American Revolution*

1763–1776 was published, Schlesinger, a former student of Herbert Osgood at Columbia, identified merchants in the commercial colonies as 'the instigators of the first discontents in the colonies'.[24] Temporarily, they joined forces 'with their natural enemies in society – with the intelligent, hopeful radicals who dreamed of a semi-independent American nation or something better, and with the innumerable and nameless individuals whose brains were in their biceps, men who were useful as long as they could be held in leash'.[25] Mob action and the destruction of property which ensued caused merchants to recognize 'the growing power of the irresponsible elements and of the drift of events toward lawlessness'. Schlesinger argued that but for the ill-advised attempt of the British government to assist the failing East India Company which prompted the majority of the merchants to rejoin the radical opposition to defeat it, 'it is probable that the great influence of the trading class would have been thrown on the side of law and order at this time, and the separation of the colonies from the mother country postponed or prevented'.[26] In the last analysis, however, merchants believed that the maintenance of British authority would serve their interests better than the alternative. Tom Paine's appeal for independence in *Common Sense*, wrote Schlesinger, 'repelled the typical merchant while it carried ready conviction to the man of ordinary "'common sense'''.[27] In an article that appeared the following year, Schlesinger set out a framework for interpreting the Revolution in the context of the 'clashing of economic interests and the interplay of mutual prejudices, opposing ideas and personal antagonisms'. These were determined by conflicting economic interests within the empire and by sectional and class considerations within the colonies. Hard economic interests – the fear among merchants in the middle and northern colonies of new commercial regulation and the desire among the southern plantation aristocracy to repudiate their enormous debts – and not devotion to constitutional principles as such were what drove the colonial upper classes to oppose the new colonial policy. 'It was the union between the "interior democracyies" and the "democratic mechanical class" in the cities, a union promoted by men like Samuel Adams who epitomised a new breed of professional revolutionaries, that shaped the course of internal politics between 1763 and 1776'.[28] In 1926 John Franklin Jameson (1859–1937) published *The American Revolution Considered as a Social Movement* which, in focusing on the consequences of the Revolution, made explicit comparison between the American and French Revolutions.[29]

Consensus and exceptionalism

Though the work of the progressives had always attracted critics, in post-war America the attacks became more strident. Daniel Rodgers argues that the Second World War and the Cold War made it necessary to articulate 'a distinctive American way'. In the case of the American Revolution, post-war historians reformulated the event 'as an extraordinary historical anomaly'.[30] Rodgers made a distinction between difference and exceptionalism: 'Difference requires contrast; exceptionalism requires a rule.' Claims of difference 'feed on polarities and diversity; exceptionalist claims pin one's own nation's distinctiveness to every other people's sameness – to general laws and conditions governing everything but the special case in hand'.[31] Activated by contemporary events, exceptionalist assumptions were absorbed into new historical writing which challenged most of what the progressives had written about the origins, character and consequences of the American Revolution.

The first statement of the consensus idea is to be found in Richard Hofstadter's introduction to *The American Political Tradition and the Men Who Made It* (1948).[32] In what amounted to a repudiation of the progressive approach to American history, Hofstadter (1916–1970) declared that a new interpretation of America's political traditions was required in light of the existence of 'a common climate of opinion', one 'obscured by the tendency to place political conflict in the foreground of history'. Yet Hofstadter's own writings were not the most obvious place to look for this shift in perspective and it was not until 1959 that the new direction in historical writing acquired its own label.[33] When with a touch of unease John Higham defined the significant change that had overtaken the writing of American history during the 1940s and 1950s, he called it the cult of consensus. 'The great trio of yesterday (Turner, Beard and Parrington) ... have gone into eclipse'.[34] Instead of an America painted 'in the bold hues of conflict' invoking the clash of classes, sections and ideologies, there was a new-look America, one that was 'strikingly conservative', and defined by a 'remarkable homogeneity'. Taking conflict out of American history would lead 'to the creation of a homogeneous past' and transform the character of the Revolution into a unified conservative movement. Shorn of its revolutionary character, the Revolution again became 'what genteel historians had always said it was: a reluctant resistance of sober Englishmen to infringements on English liberties'. Higham sounded a similar warning note in 1962.[35]

Written in the first half of the 1950s, key texts in establishing the framework of consensus history and the parameters of the Revolution were Daniel Boorstin's *The Genius of American Politics* (1953) and Louis Hartz's *The Liberal Tradition in America* (1955).[36] While Boorstin (1914–2004) and Hartz (1919–1986) differed in significant ways – what Boorstin relished, Hartz found profoundly disturbing – both located the Revolution within a homogeneous past which Boorstin labelled conservative and Hartz called liberal. But they shared a common conviction of American distinctiveness, not just of difference but of exceptionalism. By the mid-1950s, the changes were becoming obvious.

> The new research was having a cumulative impact on the whole shape of American history. One after another, the great crises, which progressive historians had depicted as turning points in the battle between democracy and privilege, came under fresh examination. In each case the scale of conflict seemed to shrink. Sharp divisions between periods, sections, groups, and ideologies disappeared. Over all, the new digging amounted to a massive grading operation that smoothed and flattened the convulsive dialectic of progressive history.[37]

'Ours,' wrote Daniel Boorstin 'was one of the few conservative colonial rebellions of modern times ... it was hardly a revolution at all.'[38] Where historians had gone wrong was in putting the Revolution 'in the main current of European history'. They had concluded that Enlightenment ideas, assuming international significance, shaped American developments, that a social revolution did in fact take place, and that the American and

French Revolutions shared a common vocabulary and chronology. Thus, they transformed the Constitution of 1787 into a Thermidorian counter-revolution. Yet 'merely as a victory of constitutionalism', the American Revolution 'was significant enough as it was'. In failing to generate a distinct body of political theory, the American Revolution, 'our American Revolution' was a revolution without dogma. Boorstin's interest lay in seeking out 'those positive ideas and attitudes', which had done much to reinforce the American 'sense of "givenness"'. To identify the peculiarities 'which have affected the place of theory in our political life', he too turned to the French Revolution.[39] Three obvious factors distinguished the American Revolution, wrote Boorstin: 'First, and most important, the United States was born in a *colonial* rebellion. Our national birth certificate is a Declaration of Independence and not a Declaration of the Rights of Man.' This could be easily explained by a number of factors, the most important of which were the largely British origins of the colonial population, the similarities of climate and topography in many areas and the transplantation, pretty much wholesale, of British legal and political institutions. Unlike the case of the Spanish American colonies 'which were to rebel, at least in part, because they had had so little home rule, the British colonies in North America were to rebel because, among other reasons, they had so much'. Moreover the indigenous population was small and scattered. And there were no competing institutions to speak of. Second, 'the American Revolution was *not* the product of a nationalistic spirit. We had no Bismarck or Cavour or any nationalist philosophy. We were singularly free from most of the philosophical baggage of modern nationalism'. There was no great enthusiasm for the creation of the new nation. Old loyalties were only slowly overcome.[40] Third, was the fact that

> our Revolution was successful at the first try ... There was no long-drawn out agitation, no intellectual war of attrition, of the sort which breeds dogmas and intransigence ... More commonly in modern history (take, for example, the European revolutions of the nineteenth century) any particular revolt has been only one in a long series. Each episode, then, ends on a note of suspense which comes from the feeling that the story is 'to be continued'. [41]

According to Boorstin the true character of the constitution of the British Empire was the central issue and Charles McIlwain 'in his little book' had come closer to capturing it than anyone else. The institutions that Americans already had was what they regarded as 'normal' and what they regarded as normal, they sought to preserve.

Described by Higham as 'perhaps the most outstanding of the new interpretative books', Louis Hartz's *The Liberal Tradition in America* adopted a different perspective. Professor of Government at Harvard, Hartz maintained that 'after endlessly repeating that America was grounded in escape from the European past', American historians had singularly failed to interpret the country's past 'in the light of that fact'. The reason was not hard to find: it lay in the separation of the study of American history from that of Europe. The significance of the absence of feudalism in American history, Hartz's major contribution to consensus history, had thus eluded the nation's historians, yet the consequences that flowed from this fact were enormous.[42]

> One of the central characteristics of a nonfeudal society is that it lacks a genuine revolutionary tradition, the tradition which in Europe has been linked with the Puritan and French revolutions: that it is 'born equal', as Tocqueville said. And this being the case, it lacks also a tradition of reaction: lacking Robespierre it lacks Maistre, lacking Sidney it lacks Charles II. Its liberalism is ... a 'natural phenomenon'.[43]

Skipping feudalism, Hartz maintained, America was characterized by a liberal tradition sufficiently broad to embrace most Americans, so avoiding the sharp discontinuities that marked European history. The slave south alone lay outside this framework. The essence of the American Revolution, then, lay not in the quest for freedom through democratic revolution, but rather in the fact that there was no feudal structure that required demolition.[44] Thus it fell to the American revolutionaries of 1776 who, 'initially wore the appearance of outright conservatism', to mop up the changes that had been long under way, but America never really had nor did it develop a conservative tradition.[45]

The idea of 'givenness' is common to both Hartz and Boorstin, though they accounted for it in different ways. Hartz attributed the same political assumptions to revolutionaries, loyalists with the exception of Jonathan Boucher, and the English: 'When one's ultimate values are accepted wherever one turns,' he wrote, 'the language of self-evidence comes easily enough.'[46] Hartz, however, does not dismiss the concept of 'social revolution' inherited from the progressive generation but absorbs it within a general framework in which upheavals in America are perceived on a lesser scale than those experienced in Europe. Nor does he have difficulty in accepting the emergence of radicals. So enfeebled was the *ancien regime* in America, it was 'little wonder that the American radical liberal got out from under the moderate liberal so quickly and so successfully'. The Federalists were the ones who got it wrong. Lack of faith in America's future led to the rapid evaporation of their power.[47]

'In a world haunted by the destabilizing effects of revolution,' Daniel Rodgers writes, 'the American case seemed sui generis: a popular revolution which had remained within moderate, Lockean bounds, a revolution without its Jacobins or Bolsheviks, without its reign of terror, without its Lenin or Robespierre ... for American historians the upheavals of 1776 and 1789 were, symbolically and historically, worlds apart.' The idea of American exceptionalism had its roots deep in the American past, in the aspirations of early puritans and the secular dreams of the revolutionaries, but in its modern formulation and application, Rodgers maintains, 'it was an accidental by-product of the problems of the American Communist Party whose rationale for the failure of the United States to fit "the laws" of historical development was unacceptable to Stalin'.[48] In its modern reconceptualization 'as a given', exceptionalism was adopted by American historians in the 1940s not from any change in attitude towards America, but from a change in attitude towards Europe. Jack P. Greene takes a different view. He rejects the notion that American exceptionalism was the creation of nineteenth-century American historians (Bancroft is the obvious target here) whose ideas were then supplemented and distorted by post-war consensus writers. It was the American Revolution, Greene argues, that lifted Americans' 'own sense of self', sharpening the concept of America as an exceptional country in which land and resources were boundless.[49] Though Rodgers and Greene give the Revolution a central place in their discussion of exceptionalism, they differ over its meaning, longevity and legitimacy. In an interview with Bernard Bailyn, Roger Ekirch (1950–) drew a response similar to the position taken by Greene, probably one of the few things they would agree about.

Neo-whigs and counterprogressives

As specialist studies of the Revolution in the 1950s and early 1960s grew and multiplied becoming 'more political, legalistic, and constitutional', they acquired a new label: neo-whig. Dominant figures were Edmund Morgan (1916–), Bernard Bailyn (1922–) and Jack P. Greene (1931–) who had little in common except their opposition to the progressive interpretation of the Revolution. Because the neo-whigs rejected the ideas of the progressives, some scholars such as Alfred Young preferred to call them counterprogressives, while others favoured neo-conservatives. In a series of historiographical essays and in the incomparable introductory essay to *The Reinterpretation of the American Revolution 1763–1789* (1968), Greene discussed the sheer volume of new work, much of it concentrated on the twelve years between the end of the Seven Years War in 1763 and the outbreak of fighting in 1775, which dealt with aspects of colonial policy, the character of colonial politics and political thinking, and the structures of colonial society.[50] In summing up the neo-whig position in regard to the progressives, Greene wrote that 'some neo-Whig historians have implied not just that social and economic conditions were less important in bringing on the Revolution than we once thought, but rather that the social situation in the colonies had little or nothing to do with causing the Revolution'.[51] Looking back from the vantage point of 1981, however, Greene together with J. R. Pole, adopted a much more expansive view of the previous three decades. In the late 1940s, early American history had appeared to be in terminal decline, but within a period of less than twenty years it had been transformed into 'one of the most exciting and attractive areas of American historical study'. The editors identified three interrelated developments within the field of early American history that contributed to its rapid growth and expansion. One was the influence of Perry Miller whom Greene and Pole identify as the only

American historian who could be compared with 'the great European historians' of their and 'the previous generations of historians'. Second was the influence of the *William and Mary Quarterly* and its distinguished book publication programme. Third, they identified 'a well-situated group of unusually effective graduate teachers in several of the major graduate training centres' among whom they identified Edmund S. Morgan at Brown and Yale, Oscar Handlin and Bernard Bailyn at Harvard, Richard B. Morris at Columbia, Wesley Frank Craven at Princeton and Merrill Jensen at Wisconsin who attracted growing numbers of students into the field who subsequently sought an academic career. 'Within a decade, the students of these and other teachers were assuming posts at major universities and beginning to train students of their own.' During this period, not only was there a 'revived respect for ideas and values' evident in the work of Greene, Bailyn and Morgan but also a new interest 'in the economic, demographic, and social history of the colonies'. Partially this could be explained by the quest for suitable research topics among graduate students who pushed 'the boundaries of inquiry from one new area outward into another'. There were also two external stimuli to this phenomenal growth – the influence of the social sciences, which equipped historians with new concepts, and the European influences generated by the *Annales* school which was seeking to realize its aim of *histoire totale* embracing all the people at both macro and micro levels. In addition there were new techniques offered by historical demography epitomized by the Cambridge Group for the History of Population and Social Structure in England. New methodologies and broadened horizons equipped the next generation of scholars to tackle those areas of early American history which remained neglected and without which the history of early America and the Revolution remain incomplete.[52]

Undoubtedly the fiercest critic of the progressive interpretation of the Revolution was Robert E. Brown (b.1907), Professor of History at Michigan State University who devoted his career to this line of attack. Although Beard was his key target (see Chapter 3) – he devoted an entire book to one of Beard's books – Brown sought to demolish the dual revolution thesis associated with Becker in two other studies: *Middle-Class Democracy and the*

Revolution in Massachusetts, 1691–1780 (1955) and *Virginia: Democracy or Aristocracy, 1705–1786?* (1964), the latter written with his wife B. Katherine Brown. Brown sought to establish the democratic character of colonial Massachusetts and Virginia, which, he claimed, fifty years of modern scholarship had denied. This denial was based on two major assumptions:

> [1] 'that property qualifications for voting eliminated a large portion of the free adult male population from participation in political affairs [and 2] that inequitable representation heavily favored the older aristocratic commercial areas along the seacoast at the expense of the more recently settled inland agricultural areas. Hence it followed naturally that colonial political and economic life was dominated by the upper economic elite classes.[53]

In the earliest of these studies Brown found no evidence that Massachusetts was dominated by an upper-class elite. Rather it was a middle-class society where a majority of the population was made up of property-owning farmers. Nor was there a permanent class of landless labourers. The propertyless could acquire land or 'work for themselves as skilled artisans'. Economic opportunity opened the way for political democracy. Property qualifications for voting could be easily met. Moreover, representation favoured the farmer, not the merchant aristocrat.[54] But if the threat of an internal conflict was negligible, areas of conflict in British–American relations were real enough. Before 1760, though aware of the weaknesses in colonial administration, British officials were in no position to remedy them. They also recognized that colonial democracy was an impediment to the enforcement of colonial policy. To make the system work, the British needed to recover control over colonial officials too often under the thumb of the colonial legislatures. To pay them required a revenue under the control of the government but raised from local taxation. What this meant was only too clear to the members of the Massachusetts assembly. In the wake of the Tea Act and the Coercive Acts, 'there was no doubt whatever that the British intended to curtail colonial democracy as a necessary step toward recovery of British authority and the prevention of colonial independence'.[55]

We do not need a 'conservative counterrevolution' or a thermidorean reaction to explain either the Massachusetts Constitution of 1780 or the adoption of the federal Constitution in 1788. If there was no 'social revolution', there could hardly be a 'conservative counterrevolution'. Both constitutions must be explained in terms of a middle-class society in which most men could vote.[56]

In a slave society such as colonial Virginia one might think that the Browns would experience some difficulty in making the same argument stick, but nothing of the sort. In *Virginia: Democracy or Aristocracy?* (1964), the great bulk of the colonists were described as middle–lower-class slave-owning planters and artisans who found class lines fluid. Property qualifications were required for voting but ample economic opportunity existed which meant that few were excluded from the franchise. Sectional tensions between the tidewater and the piedmont were nominal.

Brown met his critics head on. He defended his equation of democracy with voting rights pointing out rightly that he had discussed other aspects of society such as education and church government which had democratic features and implications, but he had more trouble with the second criticism made of his work, namely that the right to vote and the existence of a broad franchise were not sufficient guards against aristocratic domination. His most effective critic was the distinguished British scholar J. R. Pole (1922–) who questioned the utility of Brown's concept of democracy. His undifferentiated and broad use of the term helped neither 'to describe the institutions or to explain the ideas'. Pole advocated an alternative view which saw 'the democratic elements in their proper perspective by adding a further dimension without which the rest is flat, incomplete, and for all its turbulence, essentially lifeless', what Cecelia Kenyon called 'institutional'.[57] Though there would be other scholars in the Fifties who repudiated Beard's legacy, among whom was Edmund Morgan, none were as exercised over the issue as Brown.

Born in Minneapolis, Minnesota, Morgan graduated from Harvard in 1937 and gained his Ph.D. from the same institution in 1942 where he studied with the great Perry Miller. Morgan taught for a number of years at Brown University before moving to Yale in 1955 where he remained until his retirement in 1986. His 1953 study, *The Stamp Act Crisis*, co-authored with his wife Helen Morgan, remains the definitive work on this critical juncture in colonial relations, despite the passage of time and revisionist work by other historians, some British, on the British political background.[58] A vivid and scholarly work, which seeks to recreate two of the most momentous years of American history, *The Stamp Act Crisis* became one of the main planks in the post-war revisionist case for a constitutional and political reinterpretation of the Revolution. Told partly from the perspective of some of the protagonists, including loyalists, it is part historical reconstruction, part textual analysis and part biography.

Before the Sugar and Stamp Acts, the rights of the colonists had never been examined because the British government always pulled back before they reached the brink.[59] This changed after 1763. The Morgans dismissed the notion that Grenville's putative offer to allow the colonists to devise their own scheme for raising taxes and so circumvent the need for parliamentary action was made in good faith. It was a ruse to manipulate them into a vulnerable position whereby their opposition to taxation by parliament would appear as a direct challenge to parliament's authority and ensure its hostile reception.[60] As petitions of protest poured in from the colonies, the issue ceased to be one of raising a revenue, 'but putting the Americans in their place'.[61] The financial consequences of the Stamp Act were not unduly heavy, but the implications of the Act were threatening: 'As they read the Stamp Act, then, the colonists would find themselves taxed without consent for purposes of revenue, their rights to common-law trial abridged, the authority of one prerogative court (admiralty) enlarged, and the establishment of another (ecclesiastical) hinted at.'[61] Americans dismissed the idea that parliament's right to tax the colonists was based on some spurious notion of virtual representation, later dropped by Grenville and his supporters in favour of parliament's sovereign power.[62]

In protests against the proposed Stamp Tax, in assembly resolves and the declaration of the Stamp Act Congress, through petitions and memorials to the Commons, the Lords, and the king, through the medium of newspaper articles and political pamphlets as well as in private correspondence, colonists made no distinction between internal and external taxes. 'The remarkable thing about these various remonstrances both against the

Sugar Act and the proposed Stamp Act is that except in Connecticut, their denial of Parliament's right to tax the colonies was wholesale and unqualified.'[64] In adopting this position, the Morgans specifically rejected the position taken by one of the leading progressive historians, Carl Becker, who in *The Declaration of Independence* (1922) had argued that only internal taxes were rejected at this time. Becker's argument, they declared

> presupposes that the first eight resolutions are based on constitutional principles and apply only to the Stamp Act and that resolutions 9–12 are based on economic considerations and apply only to the Sugar Act. By this reasoning there appears to be no constitutional objection in the resolutions to 'external' taxes levied by the Sugar Act.[65]

Most likely, this interpretation owed its origin to the 'supposition', then current in England, that the colonists had made such a distinction and did not oppose the latter. Morgan had examined this issue in two earlier articles which confirmed his view that the claim was 'unfounded'.[66] In *The Stamp Act Crisis* the Morgans reiterated the argument that the Stamp Act Congress 'was stating unqualified constitutional objections to all taxes and that in resolutions 9–12, it merely added the economic objections'. This view was consistent with the sentiments expressed in the petition to the House of Commons and the memorial to the House of Lords as well as that taken by John Dickinson who had written the resolves and who in the *Farmers Letters* (1767), denied any inconsistency in the American position.[67] In discussing 'the political thought surrounding the Stamp Act', Morgan was seeking to establish the 'intellectual consistency' of the colonists. 'In the last analysis,' wrote Morgan, 'the significance of the Stamp Act crisis lies in the emergence, not of leaders and methods and organizations, but of well-defined constitutional principles.'[68] In challenging Becker, the Morgans were in fact challenging the progressive preoccupation with economic and social factors to the exclusion of political principles. The implications were far reaching and, as Gordon Wood (1933–) pointed out, Morgan's preoccupation with 'intellectual consistency' was central to his attempt 'to bring down the entire interpretive framework of the socio-economic argument'.[69]

In a paper delivered at a meeting of the Mississippi Valley Historical Association, afterwards the Organization of American Historians, and published in the *William and Mary Quarterly*, Morgan produced one of those landmark statements which made explicit what was previously implied and threw out a challenge to fellow historians to seek new answers to the old and as yet unanswered questions. Morgan challenged not only the economic interpretation of the Revolution but also the imperialist and the Namierite. The imperialist historians, he charged, were too busy 'dissecting the workings of the empire as it existed before the Revolutionary troubles' to come to grips with the Revolution. Their only direct engagements with the latter were 'brief and inconclusive'. As for social and economic interpretations, these had been widely used but 'we still know very little about what the social and economic divisions actually were in most of the colonies and states at the time of the Revolution ... After thirty years we are only a little closer to the materials needed for such conclusions than J. Franklin Jameson was in 1926'.[70] The third approach was that of the Polish-born British scholar Sir Lewis Namier even though the technique of structural analysis associated with his name was confined largely to Britain and its impact on revolutionary historiography was limited.[71] Morgan pondered whether the Namierites had not raised the reputation of George III 'a little too high' and was sceptical of their position that 'virtually no one in British politics ... had any political principles that reached beyond local or factional interests'.[72] Doubtless surprising some of his audience, Morgan asserted that 'the Whig interpretation of the American Revolution may not be as dead as some historians would have us believe, that George Bancroft may not have been so far from the mark as we have often assumed' and was it not time

> to ask again a few of the old questions that he was trying to answer? How did the Americans, living on the edge of empire, develop the breadth of vision and the attachment to principle which they displayed in that remarkable period from 1763 to 1789? While English politics remained parochial and the empire was dissolving for lack of vision, how did the Americans generate the forces that carried them into a new nationality and a new human liberty?[73]

Morgan pointed historians towards the recently neglected field of American institutional history.

In 1956 Edmund Morgan's *The Birth of the Republic, 1763–89* was published.[74] A much used and reprinted text, this monograph has been in print for fifty years. The thoroughly whiggish *Birth of the Republic* and the quasi-Marxist *American Slavery, American Freedom* (1975) represent the range of Morgan's scholarship. His subsequent achievements have been *Inventing the People* (1988) which won the Bancroft prize and latterly *Benjamin Franklin: A Biography* (2002), not to mention the books and articles in between.[75] In the preface of *The Birth of the Republic*, Daniel Boorstin, editor of the Chicago History of American Civilization, the series in which the volume appeared, praised Morgan's rediscovery of 'the great issues of the Revolution': 'he sees the conflict as a struggle toward the clarification of these issues (political and constitutional), and he envisages the victory of the Americans as the triumph of a principle'. Morgan, it appears, was indeed restoring Bancroft to his pedestal. The struggle was after all about liberty and tyranny. The history of the American Revolution was the 'history of the Americans' search for principles'. It was a single continuous struggle culminating in the adoption of the Federal Constitution. Morgan himself described it as 'a noble search, a daring search, and by almost any standards a successful search'.[76]

Like Brown, Greene and Bailyn, Morgan believed that property ownership in the colonies was widespread. It was 'perhaps the most important single fact about the Americans of the Revolutionary period' because it meant that the colonies lacked the social divisions of the Old World: 'Ownership of property gave not only economic independence but also political independence to the average American.'[77] With its novel purpose of raising taxes, the Sugar Act was 'the first great challenge of the Revolutionary period'. Since 'liberty rested on property', it followed that 'whatever threatened the security of property threatened liberty'.[78] As in *The Stamp Act Crisis*, Morgan maintained that the position adopted by the Americans was consistent and described the notion of virtual representation as 'specious nonsense'.[79] How quickly the colonists organized to make the Stamp Act unworkable was testimony to their 'extraordinary conviction' that parliament had no business doing what it was trying to do.[80]

Some fifteen years Morgan's junior, Jack P. Greene goes some way towards answering Morgan's challenge in his book *The Quest for Power* (1963). Born in Indiana, Greene obtained his BA at the University of North Carolina and his Ph.D. from Duke University where he worked with John Alden. He became Professor of History at Johns Hopkins in 1966 where he remained until his retirement in 2005, during which time he supervised the dissertations of over eighty successful graduate students. In *The Quest for Power*, Greene examined the specific powers acquired by the lower houses of assembly in four southern colonies, and the extent of their authority at the end of the Seven Years War. This was not in itself a new theme but was one never previously studied in a systematic way (Greene used primitive technology in the form of a counter sorter). Without a clearer picture of the constitutional position, he maintained, it was not possible to understand what it was that the Americans were defending. Greene argues that 'the threat to assembly rights was of enormous importance in the coming of the Revolution and that the Declaration of Independence was a more realistic analysis of the causes of the Revolution than has generally been supposed'. The charges levied against George III were 'a fairly accurate state-ment of grievances as the signers saw them ... the crown and its ministers were an equal and perhaps even greater threat to American legislative power than was Parliament'.[81] Greene is above all an essayist. Unsurpassed as a historiographer tracking trends in colonial and revolutionary historiography, synthesizing vast numbers of publications and comprehending them within broad generalizations, there was nothing which could not be fitted into something. The monographs came later. In *Peripheries and Center* (1986), Greene moved towards the position taken by legal historians such as Barbara Black and John Phillip Reid and later adopted by Peter Hoffer, on the legitimacy of the colonial constitutional position. He argued that where authority and ideology at the centre were weak and local power and traditions were strong, 'local institutions and customs may be at least as important in determining existing legal and constitutional arrangements as those at the center'. The problem of where ultimate authority lay caused the dissolution of the early British empire, but separation from Britain was not to settle the question nor was it resolved by the creation of the Federal Constitution.[82] *Pursuits of Happiness* (1988) claimed that the Chesapeake colonies rather than those of New England set the pattern for the social and especially the cultural development of the American colonies in which the pursuit of individual happiness and material gain were the norms of society.[83]

In a forum on Revolutions in the Americas in 2000, Greene reiterated his view that the Revolution 'was not the result of internal tensions, social, religious, or political'; its origins did not lie in America but in Britain. Fearful that the growing strength of the colonies combined with the 'weakness of metropolitan authority and the extensive autonomy enjoyed by the colonies', royal officials were of the view that these factors 'might somehow lead to their loss'. Prompted by these concerns and 'developing a new sense of imperial order', government officials 'undertook a series of measures, the combined effects of which would have been to change the British Empire from the loose federal polity it had long been into a more unitary polity with authority more clearly fixed at the center'.[84] The American Revolution is best understood 'as a settler revolt, a direct response to metropolitan measures that seemed both to challenge settler control over local affairs and to deny settler claims to a British identity'.[85] The successor societies were much like those that had gone before: 'Like their colonial counterparts, these republican polities everywhere continued to be instruments of the predominant settler classes, principally concerned with the maintenance of orderly social relations, the dispensing of justice, and most important of all, the protection of private property.' The new republican regimes did not preside over a large-scale social reconstruction: 'The pursuit of individual happiness in the private realm remained the central cultural imperative.'[86] Greene returns to the progressive conception of revolution. Some historians have been too intent 'in assimilating the American Revolution to the great European revolutions, on emphasizing its revolutionary character and radical discontinuity with the American past' with the consequence that they have failed to 'explore the bearing of earlier American political and social experience on the events and developments of the American Revolution'. Yet doing so, Greene argues, 'suggests that the colonial and revolutionary eras were much of a piece'. The American Revolution was 'a profoundly conservative revolution'.[87]

Gordon Wood's major criticism of the neo-whigs was the polemic character of their work and their preoccupation with motivation. Wood argues that contemporary whig and tory interpretations were restricted by their preoccupation with men's purposes 'and it is still the weakness of the neo-Whig histories, and indeed of any interpretation which attempts to explain the events of the Revolution by discovering the calculations from which individuals supposed themselves to have acted'. Historians needed to 'dissolve the distinction between conscious and unconscious motives, between the revolutionaries' stated intentions and their supposedly hidden needs and desires, a dissolution that involves somehow relating beliefs and ideas to the social world in which they operate. If we are to understand the causes of the Revolution we must therefore ultimately transcend this problem of motivation'. This could not be achieved if historians tried to explain it as a result 'of the intentions of the participants'. Men's motives were many and complex and their interaction leads to unexpected results. 'It is this interaction and these results that recent historians are referring to when they speak so disparagingly of those "underlying determinants" and "impersonal and inexorable forces" bringing on the Revolution'.[88] This would be Bernard Bailyn's contribution to our understanding of the American Revolution.

In 1962, Harvard historian Bernard Bailyn wrote the final obituary of the socio-economic approach to early American history in an influential article that appeared in the *American Historical Review*, but it was not until five years later that his stunning work, *The Ideological Origins of the American Revolution* appeared. A New Englander, Bailyn's original academic interest was in literature. At Harvard he came under the influence of Oscar Handlin and later Perry Miller, the former a pioneer of modern social history, the latter a scholar who transformed our understanding of the New England puritans. Like Edmund Morgan, Bailyn's publications are broad-ranging and his graduate students number over sixty.[89] *The Ideological Origins of the American Revolution* began life somewhat inauspiciously as the introductory essay to the first volume of a projected multi-volume collection of revolutionary pamphlets (1965), but its impact was immediate, and the full-length monograph, which the subject richly deserved, followed two years later. Also in 1967, Bailyn published *The Origins of American Politics* in which he sought to answer the question of why the same set of political ideas should meet with such different responses on each side of the Atlantic.[90]

Ostensibly Bailyn's reading of over 400 pamphlets confirmed what he called his 'rather old fashioned view' of the character of the Revolution as 'above all else an ideological, constitutional and political struggle and not primarily a controversy between social groups undertaken to force changes in the organization of the society or the economy'.[91] This was a perspective on the Revolution which revisionist historians had been promoting since the 1950s and which Jack Greene termed neo-whig.[92] It would also have been familiar to patriot historians, themselves veterans of the Revolution, who were convinced that the British government was engaged in a conspiracy to destroy their liberties. Yet unlike the revisionists who tended to focus on developments immediately preceding the Revolution, Bailyn focused on ideas, in particular those which 'shed new light on the question of the sources and character of Revolutionary thought'. He did not dismiss ideas arising from the Enlightenment, religion, common law, and the classical world, which were present in the pamphlets, but another strand of ideas both surprised and interested him more.

> This distinctive influence had been transmitted most directly to the colonists by a group of early eighteenth-century radical publicists and opposition politicians in England who carried forward into the eighteenth century and applied to the politics of the age of Walpole the peculiar strain of anti-authoritarianism bred in the upheaval of the English Civil War.[93]

English radicals coalesced around the concept of the mixed or balanced constitution and its enemies, the struggle between power and liberty, the lessons of history, the role of standing armies, corruption and virtue. They advocated the need for constant vigilance, annual elections, rotation in office and other checks to restrain those who wielded power. This libertarian heritage which had gone underground in the early eighteenth century re-emerged in the colonial mainstream.

Bailyn cast the social and political experience of the colonies in a new light. He made it a central factor in the burst of constitution-making which took place between 1776 and 1787 at state and national level, thereby diminishing but by no means dismissing the significance of Enlightenment thought in this process. 'Major attributes of enlightened polities had developed naturally, spontaneously, early in the history of the American colonies, and they existed as simple matters of social and political fact on the eve of the Revolution,' he explained. There was the weakness of primogeniture and entail in landholding, the disestablishment of the church, the breadth and representative character of the franchise, the lack of placemen and pensioners and so on. But 'what had evolved spontaneously from the demands of place and time was not self-justifying, nor was it universally welcomed'. These were changes that many felt lacked legitimacy; in fact they 'represented deviance'. With the Revolution 'the grounds of legitimacy suddenly shifted' and 'precisely because so many social and institutional reforms had already taken place in America, the revolutionary movement there, more than elsewhere, was a matter of doctrine, ideas, and comprehension'. When rebellion occurred, it was a release; it 'called forth the full range of advanced ideas. Long-settled attitudes were jolted and loosened'.[94] The pamphlet literature argues Bailyn, confirmed his belief 'that intellectual developments in the decade before Independence led to a radical idealization and conceptualization of the previous century and a half of American experience'. It was 'this intimate relationship between revolutionary thought and the circumstances of life in eighteenth-century America that endowed the Revolution with its peculiar force and made it so profoundly a transforming event'. The radicalism the Americans conveyed to the world in 1776 was a transformed as well as transforming force.[95]

What distinguished Bailyn's work was not only his preoccupation with a particular set of ideas, those spelled out in detail by Caroline Robbins, a British-born, American-based scholar, most of whose career was spent at Bryn Mawr College, almost a decade before, or even his re-location of such ideas at the heart of American political culture, which she had only inferred. What gave his work its particular force was the dynamic character with which he invested ideas and the transcendent quality they assumed over the course of events. So pervasive were they that they pushed forward the Revolution. Bailyn's reading of this literature obliged him to reject the widely held notion that when Americans invoked the concepts of 'slavery', 'corruption' and 'conspiracy', these were at best rhetorical flourishes and at worst propaganda.

> In the end I was convinced that the fear of a comprehensive conspiracy against liberty throughout the English-speaking world – a conspiracy believed to have been nourished in corruption, and of which, it was felt, oppression in America was only the most immediately visible part – lay at the heart of the Revolutionary movement.[96]

Bailyn advised his readers to look again at the language of the revolutionaries. When they accused the British government of bribery and corruption and spoke of themselves as the victims of a ministerial conspiracy intent on reducing them to slavery, they meant what they said. Their denunciations were not exaggerations, nor were they tactical, least of all were they propaganda directed at mobilizing fellow colonists as John C. Miller and Philip Davidson once argued in the dark days of the 1930s and under the shadow of the Second World War.[97]

Gordon Wood, Bailyn's former student at Harvard, summed up his mentor's remarkable achievement after the publication of *Pamphlets of the American Revolution*. For Bailyn, ideas counted. They were dynamic, they drove the revolution forward but there was more to it than that. For Bailyn, argues Wood, the ideas of the revolutionaries took on 'an elusive and unmanageable quality' and 'by demonstrating how new beliefs and hence new actions were the responses not to desire but to the logic of developing situations, Bailyn had wrested the explanation of the Revolution out of the realm of motivation in which the neo-Whig historians had confined it'. Thus, matters of consistency and issues of motivation and responsibility over which historians disagree, were 'largely irrelevant': 'Action becomes not the product of rational and conscious calculation but of dimly perceived and rapidly changing thoughts and situations.'[98] Yet in seeking an explanation of Bailyn's paradigm, Wood took an unexpected turn. Bailyn's work, argues Wood, represented 'not only a point of fulfilment for the idealist approach to the Revolution, it [was] also a point of departure for a new look at the social sources of the Revolution'.[99] Bailyn's own explanation was forthcoming in *The Origins of American Politics* published the following year.[100]

Why should the ideas of the Commonwealthmen appeal so much more to the colonists than their compatriots in Britain? Bailyn's explanation for their currency in the colonies, expounded in *The Origins of American Politics*, was that they fitted American circumstances more closely than those of Britain. The writings of Trenchard and Gordon in *Cato's Letters* and *The Independent Whig* spoke to Americans much more powerfully in the light of British failures to give explicit recognition to the rights of American legislatures and the recurrent demands being made on them. There was no small irony in this for the swollen claims made by the British were very much at odds with their shrunken powers. Regardless of the fact that colonial politicians thwarted governors at every turn, British claims could be viewed alongside those of European regimes which had throttled the liberties once enjoyed by their own subjects. Liberty, for which the English had a peculiar affinity, was the natural victim of power. It could survive only where the people held firm to their virtue, but virtue was dependent on the maintenance of personal independence. Corruption destroyed virtue and without it there could be no independence. This was not an abstract issue. Parliament, for long the hope of the world, was according to its severest critics mired in corruption, its members, manipulated by 'influence', bought off by places and pensions in a ministerial conspiracy of aggrandisement, while voters were rendered complicit by bribery. As to why the British should forego their much-vaunted liberty, the rationale varied depending on which side of the political spectrum it came from. For the conservative Bolingbroke on the political right, when trade, commerce and especially finance replaced land and agriculture as the basis of the economy, the people were fatally damaged, their independence lost and their virtue forfeit. Independence was the property of an agrarian people. On the radical left, the failure of the people to remain vigilant and the conspiratorial tendencies of the ministry, especially that of Sir Robert Walpole, had augmented the power of a fourth estate unknown to the balanced constitution comprising king, lords, and commons in parliament. It fell then to Britain's American colonists to preserve that liberty which the British had lost so that in the last analysis, they rebelled because they were the only true Britons left.

In a political survey of the mainland American colonies in the half century before the Revolution, Bailyn found not harmony, the predicted outcome of a balanced constitution, but rather widespread factionalism and instability, the causes of which he attributed to the economic uncertainties and tensions generated by a political system that controlled access to resources but which, to all intents and purposes, was headless.[101] For the colonists who saw their forms of government as modelled on those of the mother country, 'appearances were deceptive': 'The similarities in government were superficial; the differences in politics profound'.[102] Except in the case of the corporate colonies of Rhode Island and Connecticut, ultimate authority resided in London where the government was responsible for the appointment of virtually all the chief officers of the colonies as well as membership of the upper houses of the legislature. Thither disgruntled colonists sent complaints to their friends in and out of government, in the mercantile houses of the capital and the outports, in the Anglican church and the dissenting sects as well as in the press, while hapless governors who survived on average for about five years, lacking the power of patronage and effective support from home, generally found themselves too weak to resist local factions, still less implement unpopular government policies.[103] Bailyn found that, as early as 1730, the language in which the character of colonial politics and society was discussed was that of the Commonwealthmen and the early eighteenth-century radical opposition. This literature furnished 'not merely the vocabulary but the grammar of thought, the apparatus by which the world was perceived'.[104] Its appeal was twofold. Not only was there its 'sheer availability and attractiveness', but also, and more significantly, 'the peculiar persuasiveness of these ideas in the context of American politics'. Political life in England and

America, though similar 'in important respects was yet significantly different in ways that would give a heightened meaning and a sharper relevance to ... the libertarian doctrines of coffeehouse radicals and the rancour of the "anti-Robinarchs"', the radical opponents of Sir Robert Walpole, effectively Britain's first prime minister.[105]

By juxtaposing the mismatch between the government's demands and its inability to enforce them with the effective power of colonial assemblies with their enlarged governmental role and the denial of colonial claims to the rights and privileges of Englishmen, Bailyn exposed the paradox at the heart of provincial politics.[106]

> American politics in the mid-eighteenth century was a thoroughgoing anomaly. Conflict was inevitable: conflict between a presumptuous prerogative and an overgreat democracy, conflict that had no easy resolution and that raised in minds steeped in the political culture of eighteenth-century Britain the specter of catastrophe.[107]

Legally, Bailyn points out, executive power in the colonies, with the exception of Rhode Island and Connecticut, was far stronger than in England, for colonial governors enjoyed a range of powers no longer available to the monarchy in England. Yet in some respects, the colonial constitutions 'were radically reformed' because 'influence', what the radicals called 'corruption', due to circumstances, was much reduced. Governors' freedom of action to engage in politics was in any case circumscribed by royal instructions. This was especially true of maritime affairs and paper money.[108] Moreover they lacked patronage. Though theoretically the governors enjoyed extensive powers over civil and military offices, they had to contend with the home government's desire to nominate men to the highest posts, but worse was the advance of local political powers. Control over the post of treasurer was a key loss to governors. Colonial legislators also adopted Place Acts. Governors were unable to influence elections. There were no rotten boroughs in the colonies as there were in England, and representation in colonial assemblies, already broader than in England, continuously expanded as boundaries were pushed westward. Further differences lay in the impermanence of governors and 'the lack of finality of their decisions'.[109] Commercial and religious links could also undermine the governors. 'Swollen claims and shrunken powers, especially when they occur together, are always sources of trouble, and the malaise that resulted from this combination can be traced through the history of eighteenth century politics.' But the sources of factionalism lay deeper than this – in 'the role of government in society'.[110] The remorseless logic with which he pursued his argument together with his ability to integrate thought and action in *The Ideological Origins of the American Revolution* proved well nigh irresistible to a generation of scholars tired of the endless squabbles surrounding the work of Charles Beard and bored by the carefully researched but generally unexciting work of the neo-whigs, even when enlivened by the odd outbreak of ill-tempered criticism. In the event, Bailyn was more admired than imitated for if what had gone before seemed prosaic by comparison, what lay ahead appeared to be a dead end. What was left for the intellectual historian of the Revolution after Bailyn, especially once Gordon Wood extended his analysis to the Confederation, the making of state constitutions and the Constitution of 1787 in *The Creation of the American Republic, 1776–1787* (1969) – still the best book on the making of the Federal Constitution after nearly four decades – which will be examined in Chapter 4.[111]

Not that the work of Bailyn and Wood lacked critics. Predictably, the neo-progressives – second and third generation social and economic historians in the progressive mould who to some extent overlapped with the New Left, found their work elitist and in the case of Bailyn, supported by a narrow research base. Staughton Lynd noted that there was no place in the 'commonwealth' tradition described by Bailyn (and Robbins and Colbourn) for the mid-century relativists, Blackstone, Montesquieu and Hume who rejected the natural rights apparatus of Locke and 'Cato'.[112] Harry Stout declared there was nothing wrong in how Bailyn portrayed ideology, 'the problem is pamphlets ... Although central to the rebellion and to the articulation of classical republican theory in the colonies', they alone could not explain 'the process of an egalitarian cultural transformation'.[113] Moreover, Trevor Colbourn in the *The Lamp of Experience* had demonstrated that a great many Americans were influenced by whig history. While Bailyn's research provided a more penetrating account of the unique frame of mind that existed in America, Colbourn's work was more valuable when looking beyond the revolutionary period. What stands out today in regard to both Bernard Bailyn and Edmund Morgan's work are their assumptions about the staid and static quality of contemporary British society and politics the character of which has been transformed by the work of historians such as John Brewer (1947–), Linda Colley (1949–), Kathleen Wilson (a former student of Brewer's at Yale) and others.[114]

The new social history: neo-progressives and New Left

What brought about the greater transformation of early American and revolutionary history was the rise and rise of the 'new social history'.

Historians in the 1960s opened old doors that the counter-progressives had tried to close, while the new social history 'opened doors to fields very few historians of any school had ever entered'.[115] Influenced by the work of historians such as Marc Bloch and Lucien Febvre in France and English Marxist historians, among them Christopher Hill George Rudé, Eric Hobsbawm and E. P. Thompson, American historians variously termed neo-progressive or New Left – terms sometimes used interchangeably though their origins were distinct – examined crowd actions, rural rebellions, slave conspiracies, urban radicalism and evangelical religion. Building on the work of the progressives, they analysed the structures of colonial society and reaffirmed the popular dimension of the Revolution.[116] *The American Revolution* edited by Alfred Young (1976) was essentially a report on work in progress.[117] In the aftermath of the Vietnam war and amid social conflict at home, historians approached the bicentennial of the Revolution not as the triumph of liberty over tyranny, as was the case one hundred years earlier, but with the recognition of its complexity, diversity and ambiguity, of the opportunities missed, aspirations ignored and the price some had to pay for American victory. The essays addressed issues of class, the allegiances of those at the bottom of society or on the margins, what role ordinary people played in shaping events, what ideas they entertained and 'the impact of radicalism, both in its achievements and in its failures'. What these essays demonstrated claimed Young, was 'the continued value of analysing the colonial and revolutionary eras in terms of class'. Class differences, class consciousness, and class antagonisms mattered. The aim of the collection, asserted Young, was 'to open up discussion'.[118] Some of the contributors to the volume were associated with what became known as 'the New Left'.

The New Left came to prominence in the early 1960s and sunk roots deep in the history of the American Revolution. Though its first identifiable practitioners in the revolutionary era had a background in an older tradition of labour and class struggle, the New Left appealed to a generation of students whose numbers had swelled as never before, and whose consciousness had been shaped by the civil rights and anti-war movements.[119] Yet when John Higham published the first edition of *History* in 1965, he failed to include the New Left, 'so inconsequential' did its impact seem to him at that time.[120] Peter Novick finds the label 'empty and misleading' because it lumped together individuals with very different approaches and linked them 'innocently or maliciously' to student extremism. Conscious of the deep cleavages in American society, historians of the New Left sought out those groups that were, as Young put it, 'blanks in the books of almost all historians'. He identifies two New Lefts, one group associated with William Appleman Williams, Fred Harvey Harrington and graduate students at the University of Wisconsin (and the latter's journal *Studies on the New Left* which ran from 1959 to 1967) and the other associated with Jesse Lemisch and Staughton Lynd and the concept of 'history from the bottom up'. In 1973 *Radical History Review* began publication as an outlet for this perspective.[121] Yet in what might be regarded as a manifesto published in 1968, Barton J. Bernstein, editor of *Towards a New Past,* did not repudiate the term. He accepted it as a broad designation of 'various "left" views' linking together a rising generation of historians whose essays not only broke decisively with the consensus past but in some cases sought 'explicitly to make the past speak to the present'. Understood in these terms, the designation was 'useful and meaningful'. Some of these essays also 'sought to explicitly to make the past speak to the present'.[122]

Rather than using the terms New Left and counter-progressive, the broader designation of 'new social history' has been chosen in order to discuss under a single heading some of the most brilliant and innovative work ever produced on the American Revolution, which appeared between the mid-1960s and the beginning of the 1980s.

Jesse Lemisch's essay helped to popularize the terms 'history of the inarticulate' and history 'from the bottom up' though their provenance was older and English in origin. Critical of the elite bias of much of the historiography of the Revolution, especially the tendency to generalize from conclusions pertaining to a 'minority at the top', Lemisch proposed a strategy for recovering 'the history of the inarticulate' and outlined its possible contours. It would begin by examining 'the place of the inarticulate in the political thought and practice of the elite and proceed to an examination of the thought and conduct of the inarticulate themselves'.[123] In a ground breaking article 'Jack Tar in the Streets', published in the same year, Lemisch demonstrated that, far from being the dupes of others who outstripped them in rank and status, seamen had reasons enough of their own for participating in the Revolution.[124]

Crowd action was another focus of the new work on the Revolution that began appearing in the later 1960s and 1970s, a subject all but ignored in the existing historiography, but one nonetheless recognized as instrumental in preventing the implementation of British innovations after 1763. The new body of work was much influenced by the ideas of Hill, Rudé, Hobsbawm and Thompson who rejected images of 'the mob' derived from the work of Gustav Le Bon. Instead of irrational, uncontrolled and inherently violent, crowd actions were described as purposeful, directed towards specific goals, organized and non-violent. In some circumstances and to some extent, they were legitimate within existing political systems. According to the definitive work by the German scholar Dirk Hoerder, *Crowd Action in Revolutionary Massachusetts 1765–1780* (1977):

> rioters are self-conscious and act according to concepts coming down by oral tradition rather than straight from the magistrates' law books. Much of the oral tradition had once been on the law books

or in the Bible but had been expunged by those in power. Riots are spontaneous in the sense that neither outside agitators nor police *agents provocateurs* nor influential men of the local community manipulate it [*sic*]. Of course, they may do so, but leadership is not a prerequisite for crowd action, though crowds may have spokesmen. In addition, crowd action, as opposed to repressive force, need not be violent. Symbolic action or the mere presence of large numbers of people is frequently sufficient to achieve the desired goal.[125]

Crowd actions could take different forms such as mock trials, processions, 'and nonviolent ritualistic imitations of legal punishments'. In his study, Hoerder defined crowds 'as groups of persons with common traditions intentionally acting together outside existing channels to achieve one or more specifically defined goals'. In his own work, he was less interested in the 'transfer of elements of class consciousness from England to America' than the processes of crowd action and their context in the colonies.[126]

An American, Edward Countryman, who has taught at universities in New Zealand, Britain and the United States, published *A People in Revolution*, a study of radicalism in New York, 'the province which in an earlier generation had sustained Becker's views', in 1981.[127] Identifying opposition to the Stamp Act as the first stage in the development of popular radicalism, Countryman maintained that the movement merited the description of 'radical' because in the first place, it generated discussion about British politics and was strong enough 'to frustrate those policies and make them unworkable'. Secondly, it 'brought to political consciousness large groups of people who previously had stayed out of public affairs' and thirdly, it gave rise to 'new political formations that were without precedent in colonial life'. As a result, the old institutions could no longer function. This radical opposition did not develop 'as a single united movement but rather as a series of coalitions'. Each stage of the Revolution was different, combining 'different groups, interests and individuals'. Its initial strength derived from two sources: 'the political elites' and the 'direct militant action of ordinary people'. Summing up the achievements of the latter between 1765 and 1775, Countryman argued that 'crowds nullified the Stamp Act, frustrated the American Customs Commissioners, brawled with redcoats and dumped tea into more than one harbour. They closed courts and tore down elegant houses. They broke jails open and stopped surveying parties and disrupted concerts'.[128]

Another aspect of colonial resistance which came under the spotlight was the growth of popular committees, a process traced in immaculate detail by Richard Ryerson in the city of Philadelphia. Committees were at the centre of the process of political mobilization which transformed the existing political structures of the colonies into effective organs of resistance. Between the adjournment of the First Continental Congress and the Declaration of Independence 'a new political world took shape' in Pennsylvania around 'a new extraconstitutional government':

> This government, a vigorous system of local committees of observa-
> tion, inspection, and correspondence, quickly became quasi-official;
> and with the severing of each remaining imperial bond, it grew
> mightily in authority, efficiency, and size. By the spring of 1775, all
> provincial commerce was under its control, by the fall, it was a
> power in Pennsylvania's defense establishment. By the spring of
> 1776, it had become an alternative source of authority coequal with
> the established government; in the summer, the committee move-
> ment seized control of the province from that establishment's vital
> core, the Assembly.[129]

But Pennsylvania's revolution was a revolution of the middle classes, as Ryerson acknowledges.

The urban character of resistance to British policy was examined by a number of historians. Though Countryman argues that rural disturbances in the late colonial period were more of a threat to the social order, it was in the towns that 'the Revolution was acted out'. From 1765 to 1774, urban interests were most threatened 'by the Sugar Act, the Stamp Act, the Townshend taxes, and the Tea Act. Townspeople, not farmers, had to deal with inquisitive customs men and with the constant harassment of redcoats among them. Except for the Virginia planters, it was town writers who worked out the rationale of American resistance'.[130] In his preface to *The Urban Crucible* (1979), Gary Nash, Professor of History at UCLA, posed the question of how urban people 'at a certain point in the pre-industrial era, upset the equilibrium of an older system of social relations and turned the seaport towns into crucibles of revolutionary agitation'. In doing so Nash sought to discover 'how people worked, lived, and perceived the changes going on about them, how class relationships shifted, and how political consciousness grew, especially among the laboring classes'.[131] In Boston, he found not only 'the commercial and intellectual center of New England Puritanism' with which historians are familiar, but also, by the 1740s, a 'center of mass indebtedness, widowhood, and poverty'. At the end of the Seven Years War, similar levels of poverty confronted urban leaders in New York and Philadelphia.[132]

Nash did not argue that by the end of the colonial period class formation and class consciousness 'were fully developed', but only that we can gain greater insight into the urban social process between 1690 and 1776 and can understand more fully the origins and meaning of the American Revolution if we analyze the changing relations among urban people of different ranks and examine the emergence of new modes of thought based on horizontal rather than vertical divisions in society. In Boston the patriot coalition remained unified during the course of the revolutionary war because the greater part of the merchant community remained committed to it thereby limiting opportunities for division. The situation differed in New York and was further complicated by the occupation of the British army. Philadelphia, on the other hand, saw the most marked advances.

Closely associated with Philadelphia was the English radical Thomas Paine who was the subject of an innovative study by Eric Foner (1943–) who conceived the book 'as a social history of ideas' in an early effort to counter mounting criticism of the fragmentation of the American past. Foner argued that Paine's importance lay

> in his role as the pioneer of a new political language and mode of political discourse. Paine played a pivotal role in the expansion of what scholars would soon call the 'public sphere' – the arena of political debate outside the direct control of government. In language carefully crafted to appeal to a mass audience of ordinary readers, Paine dismantled the traditional justifications for monarchy and hereditary privilege. He also articulated a vision of the world-wide historical significance of the American Revolution, identifying the new nation as an "asylum for mankind," a beacon of liberty in a world overrun with oppression.[133]

Foner links Paine's ideas and political language, especially his social egalitarianism and passion for economic improvement, to his experiences during the first half of his life, spent in England, and to the political struggle for independence. The book emphasizes Paine's 'modernity': 'At a time when many of his contemporaries were inspired by nostalgia for an imagined "ancient constitution" or pristine agrarian past, Paine's was a forward-looking vision that united natural rights, political democracy, and compassion for the poor with a belief in economic progress linked to expanding commerce.'[134]

How the Revolution and the war opened up the small town of Concord to change, and its impact on individuals, was the theme of Robert Gross's (1943–) compelling study *The Minute Men and their World* (1976).[135]

While most of these studies dealt with or were located in urban America, Rhys Isaac, a naturalized Australian who taught at La Trobe University, Melbourne, produced one of the most acclaimed monographs to emerge from the new social history, *The Transformation of Virginia 1740–1790* (1982) in which he adopted a methodology taken from ethnographic anthropology, in particular 'thick description'. Isaac believed that historians should go beyond the written record and could find meaning about social relations in the houses people built, the rituals they performed and the dramas they enacted. Over a fifty-year period Virginia was transformed, on the one hand by the conflict with Britain, and on the other hand by the rise of the evangelicals. In order to survive the years of turbulence, the gentry were obliged to make concessions to the evangelicals.[136]

Fragmentation and its remedies

Since 1975, revolutionary scholarship has continued to broaden and deepen, not only seeking out those areas of American life previously neglected or denied. Informed by black studies, women's studies, cultural studies and ethnohistory, to name only some of the influences on the writing of American history, the history of women, African Americans, Native Americans and non-English migrants has been conspicuous by its presence. Indeed, the proliferation of subfields in social history was so extensive, many becoming areas of specialization in their own right, that critics of the new social history charge, not without some justification, that this process has led to the fragmentation of the past, the eclipse of grand theory and the impossibility of creating coherent historical narratives. More so than other historians, and rather unfairly at that since some of their work has achieved considerable popular success, social historians have been accused of losing contact with the general reading public. Worse still they were accused of no longer talking to each other. The 1990s saw two very different attempts to craft a major reinterpretation of the Revolution which reflected the vast body of scholarship of the last two decades: Gordon Wood's *The Radicalism of the American Revolution,* published in 1992 to critical acclaim in some quarters and widespread scepticism in others; and Edward Countryman's article 'Indians, the Colonial Order, and the Social Significance of the American Revolution' which appeared in the *William and Mary Quarterly* in 1996 as the lead article in a forum 'Rethinking the American Revolution'. Wood, whose earlier study *The Creation of the American Republic* (1969), was one of the building blocks of the new 'republican synthesis' was accused by his critics of denying the existence of class and disregarding race (which was largely true) and supporting the claims of American exceptionalism at a time when they were largely discounted. Passing from monarchy through republicanism to democracy, Wood claimed that Americans created 'a new society unlike any that had ever existed anywhere in the world'. But instead of creating a new order of benevolence and selflessness, enlightened republicanism was breeding social competitiveness and individualism.[137]

In rejecting Wood's approach to the Revolution and its consequences as narrow and exclusive, it was incumbent upon social historians to advance an alternative. The problem, as Michael Zuckerman expressed it, was 'how to integrate our radically new understandings of early American race and gender relations with our modestly new understandings of the Revolution'.[138] In his brave, bold, complex and perhaps inevitably flawed essay Countryman, whose work has long been associated with neo-progressive and New Left historiography attempted to do precisely this. In searching for an 'understanding' that brought together all three racially defined groups of late colonial and early republican society, he tied new developments in commercial capitalism to the push westward which gave land to settlers at the expense of Native Americans and boosted the slave trade extending slavery into the south-west. But he also reached eastward to the Old World and linked 'what developed after Independence to a specifically American version of the eighteenth-century *ancien regime*'.[139] Countryman's book *Americans: A Collision of Histories* was also published in 1996. What, asked Countryman, was the significance of the American Revolution in defining American society and in releasing the nineteenth century's enormous burst of creative energy? What was the price and who paid it? His generation of historians, he claimed, had redefined the Revolution, 'seeing it as profoundly disruptive and transforming ... Our goal had been to understand the complexities of how the United States became a separate power and Americans a separate people in the world.' What the Revolution accomplished, wrote Countryman, was to turn the subjects of the British monarchy 'into citizens of the American Republic ... It fundamentally changed relationships of power, authority, obligation and subordination. The Revolution altered how every person and every group of the time lived their lives. All sorts of people affected the Revolution, and it affected them. The rising republic of George Washington was very different from the troubled colonies of George III. The Revolution was genuinely revolutionary.'[140]

Notes

1 Peter Novick, *That Noble Dream: The 'Objectivity Question' and the American Historical Profession* (Cambridge and New York; 1988), pp. 47–8.
2 Novick, *That Noble Dream*, pp. 49–50.
3 A. S. Eisenstadt, *Charles McLean Andrews: A Study in American Historical Writing* (New York; 1956), p. 165; Novick, *That Noble Dream*, pp. 46, 83.
4 Richard R. Johnson, 'Charles McLean Andrews and the Invention of American Colonial History', *WMQ*, 3rd ser., 43 (1986), pp. 519–41, 520; Eisenstadt, *Charles McLean Andrews*, p. xii.
5 Johnson, 'Charles McLean Andrews', p. 520.
6 Novick, *That Noble Dream*, p. 82; Johnson, 'Charles McLean Andrews', p. 529.
7 Leonard W. Labaree, Foreword to Charles M. Andrews, *The Colonial*

Background of the American Revolution: Four Essays in American Colonial History, revised edn (New Haven, CT and London; 1958, a reprint of the 1931 edition, first published in 1924), p. ix.

8 Gwenda Morgan, 'Herbert Levi Osgood', in Kelly Boyd (ed.), *Encyclopedia of Historians and Historical Writings*, 2 vols (London; 1999), II, p. 889.

9 Andrews, *Colonial Background of the American Revolution*, p. 183.

10 On Anglo-Saxonism, see Novick, *That Noble Dream*, pp. 80–4.

11 Leonard W. Labaree, *Royal Government in America: A Study of the British Colonial System Before 1783* (New York; 1930), pp. 447–8; Lawrence H. Gipson, *The British Empire before the American Revolution*, 13 vols (New York; 1967).

12 Carl Becker, *The History of Political Parties in the Province of New York, 1760–1776* (Madison, WI; 1909).

13 Charles H. Lincoln, *The Revolutionary Movement in Pennsylvania, 1760–1776*, University of Pennsylvania, Publications, History Ser., No 1 (Philadelphia; 1901, reprinted 1968); Robert Gough, 'Charles H. Lincoln, Carl Becker, and the Origins of the Dual-Revolution Thesis', *WMQ*, 3rd ser., 38 (1981), pp. 97–109, 100; Charles J. Stillé, 'Pennsylvania and the Declaration of Independence', *Pennsylvania Magazine of History and Biography*, 13 (1899), pp. 385–429.

14 Gough, 'Charles H. Lincoln', pp. 101, 104, 107, 109; Jack P. Greene is unusual in giving equal weight to both authors. Jack P. Greene (ed.), *The Reinterpretation of the American Revolution: 1763–1789* (New York and London; 1968), pp. 9–10.

15 Cited by Gough, 'Charles H. Lincoln', p. 98.

16 Cited by Gough, 'Charles H. Lincoln', p. 99; for other works in this tradition, see Charles H. Ambler, *Sectionalism in Virginia from 1776 to 1861* (1910, reprinted New York; 1964); H. J. Eckenrode, *The Revolution in Virginia* (Boston; 1916); R. D. W. Conner, *History of North Carolina* (Chicago; 1919).

17 Becker, *History of Political Parties*, p. 5.

18 Becker, *History of Political Parties*, p. 7.

19 Becker, *History of Political Parties*, p. 21.

20 Becker, *History of Political Parties*, p. 22.

21 Gough, 'Charles H. Lincoln', p. 99.

22 Arthur M. Schlesinger, *The Colonial Merchants and the American Revolution 1763–1776* (New York; 1918).

23 Frederick Jackson Turner, 'The Significance of the Frontier in American History' in *The Frontier in American History* (New York; 1940), pp. 1–38, originally given as a paper to the American Historical Association at the Columbian Exposition in Chicago in 1893.

24 Schlesinger, *Colonial Merchants*, p. 591.

25 Schlesinger cited in Morey Rothberg, 'John Franklin Jameson and the Creation of *The American Revolution Considered as a Social Movement*', in Ronald Hoffman and Peter J. Albert (eds), *The Transforming Hand of Revolution: Reconsidering the American Revolution as a Social Movement* (Charlottesville, VA, and London; 1996), pp. 1–26, 20.

26 Schlesinger, *Colonial Merchants*, p. 592.

27 Schlesinger, *Colonial Merchants*, p. 593.

28 Cited by Greene, *Reinterpretation of the American Revolution*, p. 11.

29 J. Franklin Jameson, *The American Revolution Considered as a Social Movement* (Princeton, NJ; 1926, reprinted Princeton; 1967); for recent explorations of this work, see Hoffman and Albert (eds), *The Transforming Hand of Revolution*.

30 Daniel T. Rodgers, 'Exceptionalism' in Anthony Molho and Gordon S. Wood (eds), *Imagined Histories: American Historians Interpret the Past* (Princeton, NJ; 1998), pp. 21–40, 28.

31 Rodgers, 'Exceptionalism', pp. 22–3.

32 Richard Hofstadter, *The American Political Tradition and the Men Who Made It* (New York; 1948), p. vii.

33 Michael Kraus and Davis D. Joyce, *The Writing of American History* (Norman, OK; 1985), pp. 311, 314–15; Richard Hofstadter, *The Progressive Historians: Turner, Beard and Parrington* (New York; 1968), pp. 440, 444, 450.

34 John Higham, 'The Cult of the "American Consensus": homogenizing our history', *Commentary*, 27 (1959), pp. 93–100, 93.

35 Higham, 'The Cult of the "American Consensus"', p. 94; John Higham, 'Beyond Consensus: The Historian as Moral Critic', *AHR*, 68 (1962), pp. 609–25.

36 Daniel J. Boorstin, *The Genius of American Politics* (Chicago; 1953); Louis Hartz, *The Liberal Tradition in America: An Interpretation of American Political Thought since the Revolution* (New York; 1955).

37 John Higham, *History: Professional Scholarship in America* (Baltimore, MD; 1983 [1965]), p. 214.

38 Boorstin, *Genius of American Politics*, p. 68.

39 Boorstin, *Genius of American Politics*, pp. 66–70.

40 Boorstin, *Genius of American Politics*, pp. 70–3.

41 Boorstin, *Genius of American Politics*, pp. 74–5.

42 Higham, 'The Cult of the "American Consensus"', p. 96; Hartz, *Liberal Tradition*, pp. 3–5.

43 Hartz, *Liberal Tradition*, pp. 5–6.

44 Hartz, *Liberal Tradition*, p. 35.

45 Hartz, *Liberal Tradition*, p. 47.

46 Hartz, *Liberal Tradition*, p. 57.

47 Hartz, *Liberal Tradition*, pp. 67–76, 78–86.

48 Rodgers, 'Exceptionalism', p. 28.

49 Jack P. Greene, *The Intellectual Construction of America: Exceptionalism and Identity from 1492 to 1800* (Chapel Hill, NC; 1993).

50 Jack P. Greene (ed.), *The Reinterpretation of the American Revolution 1763–1789* (New York; 1968).

51 Jack P. Greene, 'The Flight from Determinism: A Review of Recent Literature on the Coming of the Revolution', *South Atlantic Quarterly*, (hereafter *SAQ*), 61 (1962), pp. 237, 257; Gordon S. Wood, 'Rhetoric and Reality in the American Revolution', *WMQ*, 3rd ser., 23 (1966), pp. 3–32, 12.

52 Jack P. Greene and J. R. Pole, *Colonial British America: Essays in the New*

History of the Early Modern Era (Baltimore, MD and London; 1984), pp. 4–6.

53 Robert E. Brown, *Middle-Class Democracy and the Revolution in Massachusetts, 1691–1780* (Ithaca, NY; 1955), p. xi; Robert E. Brown and B. Katherine Brown, *Virginia 1705–1786: Democracy or Aristocracy?* (East Lansing, MI; 1964).

54 Brown, *Democracy in Massachusetts*, pp. 401, 402.

55 Brown, *Democracy in Massachusetts*, pp. 404–5

56 Brown, *Democracy in Massachusetts*, pp. 405–6.

57 J. R. Pole, 'Historians and the Problem of Early American Democracy', *AHR*, 63 (1962), pp. 626–46, 626, 628.

58 Edmund S. and Helen M. Morgan, *The Stamp Act Crisis: Prologue to Revolution* (Chapel Hill, NC; 1953); Peter D. G. Thomas, *British Politics and the Stamp Act Crisis* (Oxford; 1975).

59 Morgan and Morgan, *Stamp Act Crisis*, p. 5

60 Morgan and Morgan, *Stamp Act Crisis*, pp. 77–8, 82, 85–6, 91.

61 Morgan and Morgan, *Stamp Act Crisis*, p. 88.

62 Morgan and Morgan, *Stamp Act Crisis*, p. 98.

63 Morgan and Morgan, *Stamp Act Crisis*, pp. 106, 108.

64 Morgan and Morgan, *Stamp Act Crisis*, p. 57.

65 Morgan and Morgan, *Stamp Act Crisis*, p. 152.

66 Edmund S. Morgan, 'Colonial Ideas of Parliamentary Power, 1764–1766', *WMQ*, 3rd ser., 5 (1948), pp. 311–41 and 'The Postponement of the Stamp Act', *WMQ*, 3rd ser., 7 (1950), pp. 353–92.

67 Morgan and Morgan, *Stamp Act Crisis*, pp. 153–4.

68 Morgan and Morgan, *Stamp Act Crisis*, p. 369.

69 Gordon S. Wood, 'Rhetoric and Reality in the American Revolution', *WMQ*, 3rd ser., 23 (1966), pp. 3–32, 10–11.

70 Edmund S. Morgan, 'The American Revolution: Revisions in Need of Revising', *WMQ*, 3rd ser., 14 (1957), pp. 3–15, 6.

71 Morgan, 'American Revolution', pp. 6–7.

72 Morgan, 'American Revolution', pp. 12–13.

73 Morgan, 'American Revolution', p. 13.

74 Edmund S. Morgan, *The Birth of the Republic, 1763–1789* (Chicago; 1956).

75 Edmund S. Morgan, *Inventing the People: The Rise of Popular Sovereignty in England and America* (New York; 1988) and *Benjamin Franklin* (New Haven, CT; 2002).

76 Morgan, *Birth of the Republic*, p. 3.

77 Morgan, *Birth of the Republic*, pp. 7–8.

78 Morgan, *Birth of the Republic*, pp. 16–8.

79 Morgan, *Birth of the Republic*, pp. 19–20.

80 Morgan, *Birth of the Republic*, p. 23.

81 Jack P. Greene, *The Quest for Power: The Lower Houses of Assembly in the Southern Colonies, 1689–1776* (Chapel Hill, NC; 1963), p. x.

82 Jack P. Greene, *Peripheries and Center: Constitutional Development in the Extended Polities of the British Empire and the United States, 1607–1788* (Athens, GA; 1986).

83 Jack P. Greene, *Pursuits of Happiness: The Social Development of Early*

Modern British Colonies and the Formation of American Culture (Chapel Hill, NC and London; 1988).

84 Jack P. Greene, '*AHR Forum*: The American Revolution', *AHR* (2000), pp. 93–102, 99–100.

85 Greene, '*AHR Forum*: The American Revolution', p. 100.

86 Greene, '*AHR Forum*: The American Revolution', p. 101.

87 Greene, '*AHR Forum*: The American Revolution', p. 102.

88 Wood, 'Rhetoric and Reality, pp. 3–32, 16.

89 A. Roger Ekirch, 'Sometimes an Art, Never a Science, Always a Craft: A Conversation with Bernard Bailyn', *WMQ*, 3rd ser., 51 (1994), pp. 625–58, 626, 630.

90 Bernard Bailyn, 'Political Experience and Enlightenment Ideas in Eighteenth Century America', *AHR*, 62 (1962), pp. 339–51; Bernard Bailyn, *The Ideological Origins of the American Revolution* (Cambridge, MA; 1967); Bernard Bailyn (ed.), *Pamphlets of the American Revolution 1750–1776* (Cambridge, MA; 1965); Bernard Bailyn, *The Origins of American Politics* (New York; 1968), p. x.

91 Bailyn, *Ideological Origins*, p. vi.

92 Jack P. Greene, 'The Flight from Determinism: A Review of Recent Literature on the Coming of the Revolution', *SAQ*, 61 (1962), pp. 235–59, 237, 257.

93 Bailyn, *Ideological Origins*, pp. vii–viii.

94 Bernard Bailyn, 'Political Experience and Enlightenment Ideas in Eighteenth-Century America', *AHR*, 67 (1962), pp. 339–51, 349, 350–1.

95 Bailyn, *Ideological Origins*, pp. vi–vii, 61.

96 Bailyn, *Ideological Origins*, p. ix; Caroline Robbins, *The Eighteenth-Century Commonwealthman* (Cambridge, MA; 1959).

97 John C. Miller, *Sam Adams: Pioneer in Propaganda* (Boston; 1936); Philip Davidson, *Propaganda and the American Revolution* (Chapel Hill, NC; 1941).

98 Wood, 'Rhetoric and Reality', p. 23.

99 Wood, 'Rhetoric and Reality', pp. 24, 31–2; Wood raised the question in relation to the 1965 'General Introduction' to *Pamphlets of the American Revolution*.

100 Bailyn, *Origins of American Politics*.

101 Bailyn, *Origins of American Politics*, pp. 63–4; as a source of instability, the divorce between social and economic status on one hand and political authority on the other, was a theme developed by Bailyn in his essay 'Politics and Social Structure in Virginia' in J. M. Smith (ed.), *Seventeenth-Century America: Essays in Colonial History* (Chapel Hill, NC; 1959), pp. 90–115.

102 Bailyn, *Origins of American Politics*, p. 66.

103 Bailyn, *Origins of American Politics*, pp. 90, 92–5.

104 Bailyn, *Origins of American Politics*, p. 53.

105 Bailyn, *Origins of American Politics*, pp. 57–8.

106 Bailyn, *Origins of American Politics*, pp. 67–86.

107 Bailyn, *Origins of American Politics*, p. 106.

108 Bailyn, *Origins of American Politics*, pp. 70, 71.

109 Bailyn, *Origins of American Politics*, pp. 80, 81, 86, 88.
110 Bailyn, *Origins of American Politics*, pp. 92–5, 96, 101.
111 Gordon S. Wood, *The Creation of the American Republic, 1776–1787* (Chapel Hill, NC; 1969). See Ch. 4.
112 Review of *Ideological Origins*, *WMQ*, 3rd ser., 23 (1966), pp. 324–6.
113 Harry S. Stout, 'Religion, Communications, and the Ideological Origins of the American Revolution', *WMQ*, 3rd ser., 34 (1977), pp. 519–41, 536.
114 John Brewer, *The Sinews of Power: War, Money and the English State 1688–1783* (London: 1989); Linda Colley, *Britons: Forging the Nation, 1707–1837* (London; 1992), Kathleen Wilson, *A Sense of the People: Politics, Culture and Imperialism 1715–1785* (Cambridge; 1995).
115 Alfred F. Young (ed.), *Beyond the American Revolution: Explorations in the History of American Radicalism* (Dekalb, IL: 1993), p. 6.
116 George Rudé, *The Crowd in the French Revolution* (Oxford; 1959); E. J. Hobsbawm, *Primitive Rebels: Studies in Archaic Forms of Social Movement in the Nineteenth and Twentieth Centuries* (New York; 1965); E. P. Thompson, *The Making of the English Working Class* (New York; 1963).
117 Alfred F. Young (ed.), *The American Revolution: Explorations in the History of American Radicalism* (DeKalb, IL; 1976), p. 461.
118 Young (ed.), *American Revolution*, pp. 449–50.
119 Young, 'American Historians Confront "The Transforming Hand of Revolution"', in Hoffman and Albert (eds), *The Transforming Hand of Revolution*, pp. 346–492, 427.
120 Higham, *History*, p. 234.
121 Novick, *That Noble Dream*, pp. 417–18; Young, '"Transforming Hand of Revolution"', pp. 422–3.
122 Barton J. Bernstein (ed.), *Towards a New Past: Dissenting Essays in American History* (New York; 1968), p. x.
123 Jesse Lemisch, 'The American Revolution seen from the Bottom up', in Bernstein (ed.), *Towards A New Past*, pp. 3–45, 4, 6.
124 Jesse Lemisch, 'Jack Tar in the Streets: Merchant Seamen in the Politics of Revolutionary America', *WMQ*, 3rd ser., 25 (1968), pp. 371–407.
125 Dirk Hoerder, *Crowd Action in Revolutionary Massachusetts 1765–1780* (New York; 1977), p. 4.
126 Hoerder, *Crowd Action*, pp. 4, 19.
127 Edward Countryman, *A People in Revolution: The American Revolution and Political Society in New York, 1760–1790* (Baltimore, MD; 1981; reprinted New York; 1989).
128 Edward Countryman, *The American Revolution* (New York; 1985), pp. 17–18.
129 Richard Ryerson, *The Revolution Is Now Begun: The Radical Committees of Philadelphia, 1765–1776* (Philadelphia; 1978), p. 177.
130 Countryman, *American Revolution*, p. 87. See, for comparative purposes R. C. Richardson (ed.), *Town and Countryside in the English Revolution* (Manchester, 1992) which explores the question of how far the mid-seventeenth-century upheavals in England were urban-led.
131 Gary B. Nash, *The Urban Crucible: Social Change, Political Consciousness, and the Origins of the American Revolution* (Cambridge, MA and London; 1979), p. viii.

132 Nash, *Urban Crucible*, p. x.
133 Eric Foner, *Tom Paine and Revolutionary America* (New York; 1976, updated with a new preface 2005), pp. xiii–xiv.
134 Foner, *Tom Paine*, p. xiv.
135 Robert A. Gross, *The Minutemen and Their World* (New York; 1978), p. vii.
136 Rhys Isaac, *The Transformation of Virginia, 1740–1790* (Chapel Hill, NC; 1982).
137 Gordon S. Wood, *The Radicalism of the American Revolution* (New York; 1992), pp. 6, 210.
138 Michael Zuckerman, 'Through a Glass Darkly: Countryman's Radical American Revolution', *WMQ*, 3rd ser., 53 (1996), pp. 373–8, 377.
139 Edward Countryman, 'Indians, the Colonial Order, and the Social Significance of the American Revolution', *WMQ*, 3rd ser., 53 (1996), pp. 342–62, 344.
140 Edward Countryman, *Americans: A Collision of Histories* (London and New York; 1996), p. xii.

3

Present at the creation: the making of the Federal Constitution

The first hundred years

The men who gathered at Philadelphia in the summer of 1787 for the stated purpose of revising the Articles of Confederation agreed to keep their proceedings secret. This in itself was not exceptional but the fact that they remained silent so long has complicated the task of historians ever since. It was particularly galling for those constructing historical narratives in the early republic.[1] Yet these early writers, dismissed in some cases as scribblers 'long and justifiably forgotten', developed a number of themes which continue to engage historians in the twenty-first century.[2] Lacking material on the Constitution, they dwelt on the period of the Confederation. They were the original exponents of the 'critical period' thesis associated with the work of the great popularist John Fiske later in the nineteenth century.[3] While Daniel Shays, veteran of the revolutionary war and putative leader of the 1786 rebellion in Massachusetts which bears his name, became the embodiment of all that was wrong with the government of the Confederation and those of the states, the framers of the Constitution, re-cast as men of heroic stature, seized the initiative. Meeting in Philadelphia, with calm deliberation these men abandoned the Articles of Confederation in favour of a new form of republican government. In the work of historians in the early republic and later nineteenth-century historians, the Federal Constitution emerged as the culmination of the Revolution. The American Revolution 'was a work of thirteen years' declared John Quincy Adams: 'The Declaration of

Independence and the Constitution of the United States, are parts of one consistent whole, founded upon one and the same theory of government.'[4] Yet because the Convention met behind closed doors, it was the struggle over the ratification of the Constitution rather than the details of its creation that engaged historians. The campaign was conducted in pamphlet and newspaper, in legislature and convention; it was open, bitter and highly partisan with success for the Federalists by no means assured.

Beginning in 1819 and culminating in 1840 with the first edition of James Madison's notes on the 1787 Convention, records relating to the creation of the Federal Constitution and its ratification entered the public domain.[5] New sources did not change much. Noah Webster's *History of the United States* (1832) contained one sentence on the writing of the Constitution while Joseph Story's three-volume *Commentaries on the Constitution* (1833) managed only a few more, though he devoted a chapter to the opposition. On the other hand, Federalist Timothy Pitkin (1766–1847) made good use of newly released material in his two volume *Political and Civil History of the United States* (1828) producing 'a tolerable account' of 68 pages. Pitkin's work deserves to be better known; his coherent and well-balanced account was in advance of his contemporaries and can still be usefully read.[6] Pitkin recognized the importance of a range of factors in promoting the desire for constitutional change, such as the timing of New York's refusal to agree with other states on granting Congress the power to levy duties on imports and Washington's support for change, but none, perhaps, had greater influence than 'the insurrection in Massachusetts, in the year 1786', a crisis that not only imperilled the state but with 'partial risings' occurring elsewhere, the union itself.[7] Despite the measured tone, Pitkin regarded the gathering at Philadelphia as exceptional.

> The meeting of this august assembly marks a new era in the political annals of the United States. Men most eminent for talents and wisdom, had been selected and were met to form a system of government for a vast empire. Such an assemblage for such an object, the world had never before witnessed.[8]

'From the peculiar situation of the states,' wrote Pitkin, 'the difficulties in forming a new system of general government, were, indeed, of no ordinary magnitude.' Since the peace treaty in 1783, commerical and political jealousies had arisen between states which, added to the disparities in 'the habits, religion, and education of their inhabitants' presented apparently insurmountable obstacles. Yet like Bancroft a number of decades later, Pitkin depicted the debates within the Convention as conciliatory in nature. 'Nothing, indeed,' he wrote, 'but a spirit of mutual concession and compromise, could have overcome these obstacles and effected so fortunate a result.' Ratification was to prove more difficult and divisive. Pitkin's treatment of the anti-Federalists was conciliatory. Greeted with enthusiasm in some quarters, the radical change in the structure of government encountered distrust and hostility in others.

> It could not be supposed, that the same candid and calm deliberation, the same spirit of concession and mutual forbearance would prevail among the great body of the citizens, as among their enlightened representatives in the convention. State pride, state feelings, state interests, as well as state fears and jeolousies, would naturally have influence in deciding so important a question ... Preconceived opinions, long established prejudices, as well as interested views would govern the minds of many individuals.[9]

After the early successes, ratification stalled and for a while it appeared no further progress would be made without amendment to the Constitution. Although Pitkin did not invoke the vocabulary of the revolutionary generation, he depicted the struggle over ratification as a contest between power and liberty. Owing to the situation of the country however, 'without government, without funds, burdened with debt, and without the power or means of discharging it, despised abroad, and threatened with anarchy at home', he wrote, 'small majorities were at last induced to yield their assent, trusting to future amendments'.[10]

In 1838 Congress appointed Henry Dilworth Gilpin, solicitor of the United States Treasury and later Attorney General, to oversee the publication of papers belonging to James Madison, lately purchased from his widow for $30,000.[11] '[The] most significant event in the historiography of the Constitution' occurred when in 1840 *The Papers of James Madison* appeared in three volumes (reprinted three times in the next four years). Assisted by Jared Sparks, Gilpin contributed a foreword and footnotes, but the real work of editing the collection had already been performed by Madison himself. 'All, or almost all, the selections, revisions, and omissions had been determined by him or by members of his family working under his direction.'[12] In the 1950s the validity of Madison's notes was called into question by William Crosskey in his two-volume *Politics and the Constitution in the History of the United States* (1953).[13] As to whether Madison's editing was 'merely stylistic' or 'significantly altered what he or others had actually said or written during the Constitutional Convention of 1787', the editors of the definitive edition of his papers which began publication in 1962 refused to be drawn.[14] By failing to disclose events at the Federal Convention earlier, it has been argued, Madison contributed 'to the distortion of American constitutional history for a full half century'. Although Michael Kammen finds this charge excessive, he does not let Madison off the hook, maintaining that 'between 1787 and 1840 lay Americans as well as jurists did not know as much as they might have known, and perhaps should have known, about the activities and intentions of the framers'.[15] Nearly fifty years after ratification, there was no constitutional consensus.

While Madison's notes of the Federal Convention remained essential to all subsequent studies of the creation of the Constitution, the immediate impact of their publication was their appropriation by radical abolitionists. Seized upon by key figures such as Wendell Phillips and William Lloyd Garrison, they provided the basis for the denunciation of the Constitution as a slaveholders' compact. Combining Madison's statements on slavery with those of contemporaries, Phillips published *The Constitution a Pro-Slavery Compact: Selections from the Madison Papers* in 1843. Depicting the Constitution as an 'infamous bargain', a compromise between northern and southern states, Phillips accused its creators of forging a union with tyrants in order to 'share in the profits of their tyranny'.[16] Paul Finkelman, the foremost student on slavery and the Constitution, believes that Phillips 'both exaggerated and understated the nature of the relationship between slavery and the Constitution'. Some delegates who, he claimed, were party to the bargain, regarded it with severe misgivings while the implications of the bargain may not have been fully grasped by all delegates attending the state ratifying conventions.[17] Garrison went further than Phillips in denouncing the Constitution as 'A Covenant with Death and an Agreement with Hell' and called for 'its immediate annulment'. Under the slogan 'No Union with Slaveholders', Garrisonians called for the dissolution of the Union.[18] Moderate abolitionists took a different view.[19] Richard Hildreth (1807–1865) was the first historian to make explicit the link between the Constitution and slavery, which remained a staple ingredient of historical accounts for the next fifty years and was taken up again in the 1960s. Summarizing the abolitionist critique of the Constitution, New Left historian and activist Staughton Lynd argues that it saw slavery helping 'to shape the Constitution because slavery was the basis of conflict between North and South, and compromising that conflict was the main work of the Constitutional Convention'.[20]

Promising his readers a more realistic and substantial piece of work than anything hitherto available, Richard Hildreth published his three-volume *History of the United States of America, from the Discovery of the Continent to the Organization of Government under the Federal Constitution 1497–1789* in 1849, a work that has stood the test of time rather better than that of his rival George Bancroft.[21] Hildreth identified the distinguishing characteristic of the Revolution as 'the public recognition of the theory of the equal rights of man'. However, its progress was marred by widespread prejudice and institutional structures not only presented 'formidable obstacles to its general application', but gave rise to 'several striking political anomalies'. The most startling of these was domestic slavery. Slavery was inconsistent with the equal rights of man and the laws of England as decided in the Somersett case in 1772, 'an institution, therefore, which the colonial Legislatures and courts had no capacity to legalize, but which at the commencement of the struggle with the mother country, existed nevertheless as a matter of fact in every one of the United Colonies'. The continuing existence of slavery in half of the union 'more than all other causes' prevented the fulfilment of the principles of the Revolution.[22]

On the need for 'some extensive political change' under the Articles of Confederation Hildreth did not differ from earlier writers and his depiction of Shays's rebellion was not unsympathetic. The example of the Revolution 'suggested an appeal to arms and the overthrow of the existing state government as appropriate means for the remedy of social evils'.[23] Nor did he dispute that the men who gathered in Philadelphia in the summer of 1787 represented 'in a marked manner', the talent and intelligence of the country. What distinguished his analysis of the Federal Convention from those of earlier writers was his frank recognition of its class dimension and the primacy of property rights. Belonging 'almost exclusively' to the conservative class, members of the Federal Convention 'seemed to look upon property not so much as one right, to be secured like the rest, but as the great and chief right, of more importance than all others'.[24] 'The democracy', on the other hand,

> had no representatives, except so far as the universal American sentiment was imbued, to a certain degree with the democratic spirit. Jefferson, the ablest and most enthusiastic defender of the capacity of the people for self-government, was absent in Europe, and that theory, of late, had been thrown a little into the shade by the existing condition of affairs, both state and national.[25]

The 'great question' facing delegates at first appeared to be the proper relationship between the states and the new government, 'how far they were to control it, and how far they were to be controlled by it'. Discussion of representation in the first branch of the legislature, however, generated new questions 'leading to new combinations, and new conflicts of interest and opinion'. Debate over the three-fifths clause, whereby slaveholders could count a slave as three-fifths of a person for the purposes of representation, made it clear, however, that the conflict between the large and small states 'was in reality less radical and vital than that between slaveholding and non-slaveholding, planting and commercial, Atlantic and western states'.[26] Hildreth identified the extension of the slave trade for a further twenty years as the 'third great compromise of the Constitution'. It differed from the other two – the concession to smaller states of equal representation in the upper chamber and the three-fifths rule –

in that it was not only a political compromise but also 'a moral sacrifice'. As Hutson notes, implicit in Hildreth's depiction of the Founding Fathers was the image of a group of 'blemished political fixers'.[27]

Supporters and opponents of the Constitution divided largely along class lines. Apprehension was widespread that 'personal freedom should be sacrificed to the interests of property, and the welfare of the many to the convenience of the few'. Public creditors and merchants backed ratification but the outcome in Massachusetts, Virginia, New York and Pennsylvania, the largest and most populous of the states, was uncertain. Anti-Federalist leadership was weak in Massachusetts unlike in Virginia where, supported by many great planters and 'almost universally' by backwoods planters, it was strengthened by fears that the proposed new government would facilitate the payment of pre-war debts owed to British merchants. Able leadership among the anti-Federalists also distinguished New York, a state which according to Hildreth was more closely linked in political sympathy with Virginia and the southern states than with New England and where institutions and manners had a more aristocratic cast than were to be found elsewhere in the north.[28]

If Hildreth's position on the relationship between slavery and the Constitution was at one end of the political spectrum in antebellum America, George Ticknor Curtis (1812–1894) was at the other. A lawyer, historian and conservative Massachusetts whig, Kammen credits Curtis with writing the most authoritative history of the Constitution before the 1880s. Curtis himself maintained in the introduction to the first volume of his *History of the Origin, Formation and Adoption of the Constitution of the United States* (1854) that the events of the Revolution were well known, but the constitutional history of the United States had yet to be written.[29] As the contested issue of the expansion of slavery into the territories continued to rock the Union, Curtis's *History*, especially the second volume which appeared in 1858, offered nothing to those striving to limit the institution's growth, dismayed abolitionists and gave solace to the slaveholding south.

For Curtis, as for earlier historians, the case for a new structure of government in 1787 was overwhelming. With the return of peace, the American people discovered that their form of government, adopted for 'a mere federative union' was nothing 'but a rope of sand'.

> They were to learn this through a state of things verging upon anarchy; amid the decay of public virtue, the conflict of sectional interests, and the almost total dissolution of the bands by which society is held together. In this state of things was to be at last developed the fundamental idea on which the Constitution of the United States now rests – the political union of the *people* of the United States for certain limited purposes, as distinguished from a union of the *states* of which they are citizens.[30]

More so than previous historians, Curtis emphasized the consequences of Shays's rebellion should Americans fail to act.[31] The doctrines and purposes of the insurgents proved attractive not only to the disaffected of Massachusetts but to many in New England who were young, active and desperate. 'While thoughtful and considerate men were speculating upon the causes of diminished prosperity and the general feebleness of government, a gulf suddenly yawned beneath their feet, threatening ruin to the whole social fabric.' Achieving independence was 'but half of the great undertaking of liberty'. Order, security, power and great institutions were needed. Only the Federal Union could uphold liberty, but in order to accomplish this, 'it must become a government'.[32]

In order to create a government equal to the task, concessions to the slaveholding states were necessary. Of this Curtis was convinced and he appealed to the historian and the reader to judge the facts fairly.

> History should undoubtedly concern itself with the interests of man. But it is bound , as it makes up the record of events which involved the destinies and welfare of different races, to look at the aggregate of human happiness ... It is to arrive at results. It is to draw the wide deductions which will show whether human nature has lost or gained by the conditions and forms of national existence which it undertakes to describe.[33]

Thus, the true justification of existing institutions lay in 'the amount of positive good that has been gained for all, or the positive evil that has been averted from all'.[34] But, in prefacing his discussion of the concessions brokered in the Federal

Convention, Curtis loaded the dice by raising the spectre of failure.

> The imagination wanders over a dreary waste of seventy years, which it can only fill with strange images of desolation. That the administration of Washington should never have existed; that Marshall should never have adjudicated, or Jackson conquered; that the arts, the commerce, the letters of America should not have taken the place they hold in the affairs of the world; that instead of this great Union of prosperous and powerful republics, made one prosperous and powerful nation, history should have had nothing to show and nothing to record but border warfare and the conflicts of worn-out communities, the sport of the old clashing policies of Europe; that self-government should have become one of the exploded delusions with which mankind have successively deceived themselves, and republican institutions have been made only another name for anarchy and social order.[35]

Curtis dismissed as 'superficial' the criticism of those who protested that the Constitution of the United States, and the immense prosperity it generated, were obtained by concessions in favour of the institution of slavery.[36] He insisted that the failure to include men 'without political rights or social privileges' in the system of representative government was an 'unimportant anomaly'. Furthermore, it was sound policy to leave the question of emancipation in the hands of local authorities while the continuation of the slave trade for a few years brought about agreement on the commercial power of the United States yielding benefits so great for the American people that 'the patriot and the Christian can have no real cause for regret or complaint'.[37] Both races had benefited from these arrangements claimed Curtis – 'the whites by the superior refinement they have created' and 'the blacks by the gradual but certain amelioration of their condition'.[38]

Curtis knew only too well that since the Constitution had been ratified, nine slave states had joined the Union and the number of slaves had risen to over three million, but justifications could be found for these developments too. 'Wherever the institution of slavery has gone, there has gone with it the system of State government, the power and organization of a distinct community, and consequently a better civilization than could have been the lot of distant provinces of a great empire, or distant territories of a consolidated republic'.[39] The alternative would have been great concentrations of slaves in some regions, white flight and race war. Nor was the constitutional guarantee that fugitives would be returned from the free states merely a concession to secure the formation of the Union, but rather a means of securing 'the beneficent working of the Constitution after its acceptance had been obtained'. It was 'as important to the black race as it was to the whites'. The continued existence of the states and 'the firm maintenance of an exclusive local authority' over their internal domestic relations had been productive 'of a far higher civilization, and consequently of a far better condition of the subjugated race' than was attainable under a 'consolidated republic'. Where 'all legislative power, all the superintending care of government had been assumed by the central authority, men's pride in their separate state 'would have passed away' and 'vast tracts of wonderful fertility must have retained the African, and with him scarely any white man but the speculator, the overseer, and a solitary tradesman'. Government authority and the retraints of law would not have extended into communities 'so depopulated of freemen, so filled with slaves, and, so far removed from the seat of power'.[40]

Barely two years before the disruption of the Union and the beginning of the Civil War, Curtis concluded the second volume with a robust endorsement of the status quo. Ignoring domestic critics and the ongoing crisis of the Union, Curtis alleged there was no anomaly, no inconsistency, no 'matter of reproach' in the fact

> that a people who fought for political and personal freedom, who proclaimed in their most solemn papers the natural rights of man, and who proceeded to form a constitution of government that would best secure the blessings of liberty to themselves and their posterity, should have left in their borders certain men from whom those rights and blessings are withheld. But in truth the condition of the African slaves was neither forgotten nor disregarded by the generation who established the Constitution of the United States; and it was dealt with in the best and the only mode consistent with the facts and their welfare. The Constitution of the United States does not purport to secure the blessings of liberty to all men within

the limits of the Union, but to the people who established it, and their posterity. It could not have done more.[41]

Within a framework which tied acceptance of the Federal Constitution to the growth and prosperity of the United States, a commonplace of early histories of the young republic, Curtis constructed an argument based on counterfactual propositions in which enslaved 'Africans', though denied the equal rights of man, became the means of extending rights to others. In a way that Curtis would have found utterly repugnant, modern twentieth-century scholars Orlando Patterson and Edmund S. Morgan constructed white freedom out of the *creation* of black enslavement.[42] Curtis was engaged in revising his *History* when he died in 1894 but a second edition of this work edited by J. C. Clayton appeared in 1896 by which time its thesis which 'combined claims for national power with a desire for its prudent exercise' was outdated. This latter edition which in turn was reissued in 1965 assigned abolitionists a leading role in the coming of the Civil War, appeared to support states' rights and did not regard the Constitution as problematic.[43]

When George Bancroft published his two volume *History of the Formation of the Constitution of the United States of America* in 1882, it was unusual, not because it was the most thoroughly researched study to have appeared to date, but rather because, at a time when the pursuit of history was becoming the province of those trained in the graduate schools of prestigious universities organized on the German model, and serious scholarly interest in the origins and character of the Constitution was developing, its author still subscribed to an earlier popular view that the Constitution was 'the providential expression of American democracy'. Furthermore, there appeared on the title page of each volume, although dropped in subsequent editions, William Gladstone's panegyric to the British and American constitutions: 'As the British Constitution is the most subtile [*sic*] organism which has proceeded from progressive history, so the American Constitution is the most wonderful work ever struck off at a given time by the brain and purpose of man.' While such a view might accord with popular sentiment and reflect the Anglo-American rapprochement of the late nineteenth century, in these respects Bancroft's work looked backwards to the early part of the nineteenth century. Nonetheless, the work has some claim to be the first serious in-depth study of the Constitution: in the opinion of Gordon Wood, author of arguably the single most important study of the creation of the Constitution in the twentieth century, it 'still bears careful reading'.[44]

Bancroft's credentials as a whig historian were evident from his opening statement. 'However great may be the number of those who persuade themselves that there is in man nothing superior to himself,' he wrote, 'history interposes with evidence that tyranny and wrong lead inevitably to decay; that freedom and right, however hard may be the struggle, always prove resistless.'[45] He shared with an earlier generation of historians a sense of the Constitution as the culmination of the Revolution and its logical conclusion, though he was less inclined than they to inflate the significance of Shays's Rebellion in contributing to its formation.[46] With independence had come daunting new challenges. In order to ensure its future, the government needed to settle its vast domain, raise an adequate revenue, ensure domestic trade by prohibiting states from impairing the obligation of contracts and regulate foreign trade. Although each of these functions was vitally important, Bancroft argued that it was 'the necessity of regulating commerce [that] gave the immediate impulse to a more perfect constitution'.[47] Since the task of regenerating the union could not be accomplished by Congress the impetus had to come from outside.[48]

Theory played no significant role in the creation of the Constitution, argued Bancroft, still less abstract ideas. The men who framed the Constitution were not influenced by contemporary political thinkers or those of earlier generations.

> They harbored no desire of revolution, no craving after untried experiments. They wrought from the elements which were at hand, and shaped them to meet the new exigencies which had arisen. The least possible reference was made by them to abstract doctrines; they moulded their design by a creative power of their own, but nothing was introduced that did not already exist, or was not a natural development of a well-known principle.[49]

Bancroft shared with historians such as Pitkin a conception of the American people as uniquely favoured. He attributed the tenor of deliberations within the convention to their 'distinctive' character which enabled delegates by means of 'calm meditation and friendly councils' to provide 'a peaceful method for every needed reform'. Among them prevailed 'the principle of individuality ... as it had nowhere done before'. The Americans were 'a new people ... without king, or princes, or nobles'. They knew 'nothing of tithes and little of landlords, the plough being for the most part in the hands of free holders of the soil'. They were 'more sincerely religious, better educated, of serener minds, and of purer morals than the men of any former republic'.[50]

Bancroft's life spanned virtually the entire nineteenth century. A Democrat in a predominantly whig state (Massachusetts), he enjoyed a comfortable sinecure, rose to become Secretary of the Navy and subsequently served as ambassador to Britain and Prussia. Despite his zeal in seeking out sources, especially in Europe, Bancroft was less than assiduous in referencing his text. As politician, diplomat and historian, he had lived through the 'Age of Revolutions' and believed that the American constitution, based on the authority of the people and guided by the concept of justice, was indeed 'a government of the people by and for the people'. Unlike the forms of government elsewhere, in the United States 'all the branches of power – president, senators, and representatives – proceed directly or indirectly from the people'. With the people also lay the power to change the Constitution but not 'in haste', a feature attractive to Bancroft though not to later progressive critics. 'America,' concluded Bancroft, 'being charged with the preservation of liberty, has the most conservative polity in the world, both in its government and its people.' In making provision for peaceful change, it precluded the possibility of Revolution.[51]

Demythologising the Constitution

When Bancroft died in 1891, the professionalization of the discipline of history was well advanced though by no means complete. Bancroft's *oeuvre* received short shrift from the new generation of university-based historians who rejected not only his style but questioned his scholarship, his moral standpoint and his perspective.[52] By the time his *History of the Formation of the*

Constitution of the United States of America appeared in 1882, a major interpretive shift was already under way which rooted the Constitution firmly in American experience. James H. Robinson (1863–1936) laid out the new approach in 'The Original and Derived Features of the Constitution' published in *Annals*, the new journal of the American Academy of Political and Social Science which tied the outcome of deliberations in the Convention to long term, rather than short term, American experience. It was further developed by Sidney G. Fisher (1856–1927) in his 1897 work *The Evolution of the Constitution of the United States*. In *The Confederation and the Constitution* published in 1905 and long regarded as 'the best short survey of the period', Andrew C. McLaughlin (1861–1947) argued that the Articles of Confederation though not adequate 'to the social, political and industrial needs of the time' were in many respects models of their kind and much in advance of anything previously devised. As constitutional organs developed, 'administrative failures and experiments' pointed the way to 'a more effective and satisfactory system'. Conservatives led the movement for a new constitution in which the support of Washington was vital to the outcome.[53]

The experiential approach reached its culmination in 1913 with the publication of *The Framing of the Constitution of the United States* by Max Farrand (1869–1945), a study still admired and widely read.[54] Farrand disclaimed any intention of writing a definitive history of the Convention – in fact he doubted whether anyone could – he intended his work to be 'a brief presentation of the author's personal interpretation ... merely a sketch in outline'. He opened his first chapter with the statement that 'Democratic government was on trial before the world', a curious comment from a man who had spent ten years editing the Convention's records and contradicted by much of the content of his own book.[55] When discussing the membership of the Convention, he observed that 'in a time before manhood suffrage had been accepted, when social distinctions were taken for granted, and when privilege was the order of the day, it was but natural that men of the ruling class should be sent to this important convention'.[56] On the subject of the Articles of Confederation, Farrand took a middling position. He rejected as misleading the general assumption that the articles were unworkable and that the federal convention 'considering them hopeless of amendment, had started afresh to construct a new instrument of government': they were in the nature of an experiment, 'an attempt to solve the problem of a confederated republic'.[57] The task before the Convention 'was to remedy a series of perfectly definite defects, each of which had revealed itself in the experience of little more than ten years'.[58] There was 'practically nothing' in the Constitution that 'did not arise out of the correction' of specific defects in the confederation. In this, the framers of the Constitution drew on the constitutions of the states.[59] This was not to say that there were no compromises. In fact, Farrand had described the Constitution as 'a bundle of compromises' in an earlier article.[60]

> Compromises had been necessary at every point, and those compromises in some cases produced unforeseen results. With those two qualifications, it would seem to be a safe statement that the only new element in the constitution, that is, the only thing not originating in the correction of the defects noted, was the provision regarding impeachment.[61]

Farrand did not deny that delegates engaged in philosophical speculation and political theorizing but at the core of his argument lay the assertion that 'farmers and traders are practical people, and the compelling characteristic of the framers of the constitution was hard-headed common sense'. This sweeping generalization included Madison whose 'remedies for the unsatisfactory state of affairs under the confederation, were not founded on theoretical speculations, they were practical. They were in accord with the historical development of our country and in keeping with the genius of our institutions'.[62]

> However much the members of the federal convention may have prepared themselves by reading and study, and however learnedly they might discourse upon governments, ancient and modern, when it came to concrete action they relied almost entirely upon what they themselves had seen and done ... John Dickinson expressed this very succinctly in the course of the debates, when he said: 'Experience must be our only guide'.[63]

Farrand identified equal representation of states in the Senate as the key to 'the great compromise of the convention and of the constitution. 'None other is to be placed quite in comparison with it.' In his view, slavery was not an important issue at the Convention, and certainly 'not the moral issue it later became'. Its importance had become inflated as a consequence of the disclosure of the Convention's proceedings at a time when 'the slavery question had grown into the paramount issue of the day'. This had led 'to an overemphasis of the slavery question in the convention that has persisted to the present day'.[64] Farrand rejected the idea that the three-fifths rule was an important compromise or even a compromise at all, being embodied in 'the revenue amendment of 1783', the committee of the whole having added the amendment to the Virginia plan by nine votes to two. It was also part of the New Jersey plan. The three-fifths rule was 'a mere incident in that part of the great compromise which declared that "representation ought to be proportioned according to direct taxation"'.[65]

Farrand credited opponents of stronger government with being no 'mere obstructionists', and 'restraining the tendency of the majority to overrule the rights of states and individuals in endeavouring to establish a thoroughly strong government'.[66] He recognized that those responsible for calling the Philadelphia Convention were those who promoted ratification and that public opinion 'at least so far as it was represented in the state conventions', was divided.[67] Unlike J. Allen Smith, Professor of Government at the University of Washington, Farrand was quite sanguine about the status of the Constitution in his own day and its ability to adapt to changing circumstances. Describing it as 'a practical, workable document', he concluded that 'it has been adapted by an ingenious political people to meet the changing requirements of a century and a quarter', a view consistent with Farrand's closely reasoned arguments but quite at odds with contemporary events.[68]

Published six years earlier, *The Spirit of American Government: A Study of the Constitution* (1907) by J. Allen Smith (1860–1924), refuted any idea of the Constitution as a democratic document.[69] When the 1911 edition of Smith's book was republished in 1965, the editor Cushing Strout claimed that its chief value lay in the fact that it was 'one of the most characteristic and influential expressions of the Progressive temper'.[70] Other historians, among them Gordon Wood, have accorded *The Spirit of American Government* a more secure place in the historiography of the Constitution. It was Smith who gave legitimacy to the view then emerging that the Constitution was 'an aristocratic, reactionary document designed by its checks and balances, difficulty of amendment and judicial review to thwart the popular will and the democratic tendencies of the Revolution'.[71] Smith's career, according to Strout, with perhaps an echo of his own day, 'was that of the academic rebel, admired by the young, feared by the regents and trustees, and a worry for the college president'. Smith put the problem bluntly:

> It could hardly be expected that a political system set up for a community containing a large slave population and in which the suffrage was restricted, even among the free whites, should in any large measure embody the aims and ideas of present day democracy. In fact the American Constitution did not recognize the now more or less generally accepted principle of majority rule even as applying to the qualified voters.[72]

Smith made a distinction between 'the Revolution' – which he saw embodied in the new political ideas of the Declaration of Independence and the new state constitutions which swept away the executive veto, made governors subject to annual elections and centralized authority – and 'a conservative reaction' which followed.[73]

Smith believed that the Federal Constitution was modelled 'in a general way' on that of eighteenth-century England but 'while the English system of constitutional checks was a natural growth, the American system was a purely artificial contrivance'. The structure of the English government was designed to check monarchy and aristocracy: the American Constitution was supposed to limit the authority of government and render it responsible to the people. Believing that the democratic trend of the Revolution was carrying the country towards anarchy and ruin, members of the Convention 'restored the old order in a modified form'. It was in this context that Smith labelled the Constitution 'reactionary and retrogressive'.[74] The adoption of 'an elaborate system of constitutional checks', he argued, was 'the triumph of a skilfully directed reactionary movement'.[75] Though the Constitution as a whole was designed to curb the power of popular majorities, two features in particular stood out. Firstly, the framers made the amendment process so difficult that the prospect of change was remote. Democratic governments, Smith believed, were 'flexible and easy' to change. That the framers made the Constitution so difficult to amend was testimony to their intention to keep control of the machinery of government.[76] Not only was there no provision for amendments by direct popular vote which was 'a substantial check upon democracy', but success was contingent upon two-thirds support in both houses and in three-quarters of the state legislatures, an even more anti-democratic measure. This feature of the Constitution 'which nominally provides for amendments but really makes it an impossibility, is perhaps the best proof we could have that the Constitution as framed and adopted represented the views of a minority who intended by this means to perpetuate their influence'.[77] Secondly, the Constitution gave 'extraordinary powers' to the judiciary. The Federal judiciary was 'not only the most important of our constitutional checks on the people, but it is also the means of preserving and enforcing all the other checks'.[78] Life-tenure of a non-elective judiciary 'was designed as a check, not upon an irresponsible executive as was the case in England, but upon the people themselves'.[79] In America, 'the most important attribute of sovereignty, that of interpreting the Constitution for the purposes of law-making, which belonged to Parliament as a matter of course, was withheld from Congress and conferred upon the federal judiciary'. Judges were given powers which in England belonged to Parliament. 'This made our Supreme judges, though indirectly appointed, holding office for life and therefore independent of the people, the final interpreters of the Constitution, with power to enforce their interpretation by declaring legislation null and void.'[80] It would be hard to imagine a more powerful check on democratic innovation.

While Smith's swingeing attack on the undemocratic character of the Constitution was part of the broader progressive critique of American politics and society at the beginning of the twentieth century, it was Charles A. Beard (1874–1948), at that time Professor of Political Science at Columbia University, who published the work that finally 'penetrated the sacred penumbra' surrounding the Constitution. A mid-westerner, Beard received his BA from DePauw University and though he began graduate work at Columbia University, spent four years in England where he was active in the settlement movement in the downtrodden East End of London and in the organization of Ruskin College before returning to Columbia and completing his studies. Like R. H. Tawney in England he had first hand experience of the limitations of a modern demoracy. Described as 'the most influential book ever written in America', *An Economic Interpretation of the Constitution of the United States* which appeared in 1913, not only knocked the Founding Fathers off their pedestal, but 'laid out the agenda for a thorough revision of national history'.[81] According to Peter Novick, the book 'came to represent and dominate an entire generation's thinking about history and particularly the origins of the Constitution' and, despite virulent attacks on it from within the profession and outside it, Beard's study continues to cast a long shadow.[82]

Finding existing 'schools' of history wholly unsatisfactory, Beard resolved on an economic approach but his book did not emerge in a historical vacuum. A number of historians writing between 1881 and 1912 recognized the importance of economic issues identifying them as a significant factor in differentiating Federalists and anti-Federalists. Among these were John Bach McMaster, George Bancroft, John Fiske, Edward P. Smith, Orin G. Libby, Samuel B. Harding, Woodrow Wilson, Andrew C. McLaughlin and Edward Channing, none of whom would have quarrelled with Beard's conclusions on the clash of economic groups between 1787 and 1789.[83] As early as 1871 Henry B. Dawson, described by Hutson as 'the leading spirit of a group of iconoclastic and critical historians', had taken issue with the notion of the 'critical period' in response to John Lothrop Motley's description of it 'as a state of anarchy and general criminality, without Government and without shame'. On the contrary, the period from 1783 to 1787 demonstrated that 'every possible evidence of prosperity and peace ... prevailed throughout the Union'.[84] Acknowledging the influence of Frederick Jackson Turner and O. G. Libby on his thinking about American history and of E. R. A. Seligman on 'the theory of the economic interpretation of history', Beard rejected constitutional and legalistic approaches to the Constitution. Of constitutional histories he declared '[s]trictly speaking we have none', admitting the claims of Curtis and Bancroft only to dismiss them. As for the 'juristic view', its weakness lay in seeing the Constitution as 'the work of the whole people'. It thus bore 'no traces of the party conflict from which it emerged'; it reflected 'no group interests' and it recognized 'no economic antagonism'. Law, insisted Beard, did not 'grow'; it was 'made'. 'The concept of the Constitution as a piece of abstract legislation [was] entirely false.'[85] Attracted by the explanatory possibilities of an economic approach to the origins of the Constitution but conscious of the enormous amount of research required to pursue it, only some of which he had undertaken, Beard presented his work to the public as a half-finished project, suggestive rather than definitive. For his title he chose the indefinite rather than the definite article and citing William Cunningham, declared that the validity of any hypothesis could not be established 'until it has been worked to its utmost limits'.[86]

With the suggestion that it might only have been 'a phantom of the imagination' and a nod to Henry B. Dawson, Beard quickly disposed of 'the critical period'. No one, after all, had even identified what facts were necessary to prove that 'the bonds of the social order were dissolving'. Besides, most of the nation's history had been written by Federalists whose 'gloomy pictures of the social conditions' under the Articles of Confederation should be treated with scepticism. Of far greater significance were the exhaustive interests seeking protection.[87]

Beard began by advancing the seemingly innocent proposition that 'the Constitution was the creation of a certain number of men, and it was opposed by a certain number of men'. Assuming it were possible to construct economic biographies for the 160,000 or so men who played some part in its framing and adoption, and supposing it could be shown that there was no difference in property holding between those who supported and those who opposed the Constitution, then an explanation for their behaviour would have to be sought elsewhere. But if the reverse was true, and

substantially all of the merchants, money lenders, security holders,

manufacturers, shippers, capitalists, and financiers and their professional associates are to be found on one side in support of the
Constitution and that substantially all or the major portion of the
opposition came from the non-slaveholding farmers and the debtors
– would it not be pretty conclusively demonstrated that our fundamental law was not the product of an abstraction known as 'the
whole people,' but of a group of economic interests which must
have expected beneficial results from its adoption?[88]

Although it was not possible to recover all the desirable facts,
Beard maintained that the data presented in his subsequent chapters bore out the latter hypothesis thus creating 'a reasonable
presumption' in favour of an economic interpretation of the
Constitution.

Of the 'classes and groups' existing in the United States on
the eve of the Federal Convention, four would not be represented
in Philadelphia: slaves, indentured servants, the mass of men
without property qualifications for voting, and women. What
their numbers were Beard could not say. He claimed, however,
that working-class consciousness had not yet developed as 'a
separate interest' though he qualified this statement with reference to Becker's work on New York.[89] Holders of real property
categorised as small farmers, manorial lords and slaveholders and
those with personalty in the form of money, public securities,
manufacturing and shipping, and western lands interested Beard
most, especially those in the latter categories. Details relating to
ownership, size, value, and geographical distribution needed to be
recovered but the task was hard to accomplish and the result
'could only be approximate'.[90]

The pressure for political change came from those with interests in personalty which was adversely affected by the
government under the Articles of Confederation. 'It was receiving
attacks on all hands from the depreciators and it found the way to
profitable operations closed by governmental action or neglect.'
Within Congress, Beard discerned two distinct groups: 'those
working for the establishment of a revenue sufficient to discharge
the interest and principal of the public debt, and those working
for commercial regulations advantageous to personalty, operations in shipping and manufacturing and in western land
speculations'.[91] Furthermore,

it should be remembered also that personalty is usually more active than real property. It is centralized in the towns and can draw together for defence or aggression with greater facility. The expectation of profits from its manipulation was much larger in 1787 than from real property. It had a considerable portion of the professional classes attached to it; its influence over the press was tremendous, not only through ownership, but also through advertising and other patronage. It was, in short, the dynamic element in the movement for the new Constitution.[92]

The next question was to discover whether the property holdings of members of the Convention fell into one or more of these categories. 'In other words,' wrote Beard, 'did the men who formulated the fundamental law of the land possess the kinds of property which were immediately and directly increased in value or made more secure by the results of their labors at Philadelphia?' He disclaimed any intention of attempting to demonstrate that the Constitution was designed 'for the personal benefit of the members of the Convention'. The materials needed to pursue this issue were admittedly 'very scanty', but 'the rich unpublished records of the Treasury Department', never previously exploited, were available for scrutiny.[93] After surveying the economic interests of the individual members of the Convention, Beard concluded that 'at least five-sixths' of them were 'immediately, directly, and personally interested in the outcome of their labors at Philadelphia, and were to a greater or less extent economic beneficiaries from the adoption of the Constitution'.[94] The campaign for ratification was an ill-matched affair. 'Talent, wealth, and professional abilities', not to say money, were to be found on the side of the Constitutionalists.

> The opposition on the other hand suffered from the difficulties connected with getting a backwoods vote out to the town and county elections. This involved sometimes long journeys in bad weather, for it will be remembered that the elections were held in the late fall and winter. There were no such immediate personal gains to be made through the defeat of the Constitution, as were to be made by the security holders on the other side. It was true the debtors knew that they would probably have to settle their accounts in full and the small farmers were aware that taxes would have to be paid to discharge the national debt if the Constitution was adopted;

– and the debtors everywhere waged war against the Constitution –
of this there is plenty of evidence. But they had no money to carry
on their campaign; they were poor and uninfluential – the strongest
battalions were not on their side. The wonder is that they came so
near defeating the Constitution at the polls.[95]

A more detailed analysis of the state ratifying conventions
was eminently desirable but since too many of the delegates were
obscure men, it was difficult if not impossible to establish their
background and interests. Nonetheless, there was a body of work
by Libby, Harding and Ambler which, supplemented by new
materials, established 'certain general truths'. The conclusion was
inescapable.

> No one can pore for weeks over the letters, newspapers, and
> pamphlets of the years 1787–1789 without coming to the conclu-
> sion that there was a deep-seated conflict between a popular party
> based on paper money and agrarian interests and a conservative
> party centred in the towns and resting on financial, mercantile and
> personal property interests generally.[96]

In his final chapter Beard set out a series of conclusions
designed to show that a large proportion of the population had
no hand in the setting up, creation or ratification of the
Constitution; they were 'excluded from the outset'. The
Constitution began as a movement 'originated and carried
through principally by four groups of personalty interests which
had been adversely affected under the Articles of Confederation:
money, public securities, manufactures, and trade and shipping'.
With few exceptions those who drafted the Constitution were
'immediately, directly, and personally interested in, and derived
economic advantage from, the establishment of the new system'.
The Constitution 'was essentially an economic document based
upon the concept that the fundamental private rights of property
are anterior to government and morally beyond the reach of
popular majorities'.[97] Moreover, those who supported the
Constitution in the ratifying conventions 'represented the same
economic groups as the members of the Philadelphia
Convention', many of whom also stood to gain as a consequence
of their efforts. Small farmers and debtors stood on one side,
those with 'substantial personalty interests' on the other. Beard

rejected the claims of jurists who stated that the Constitution was created by 'the whole people' and of southern nullifiers who 'long contended' that it was created by 'the states'. The Constitution was created neither by 'the whole people' nor 'the states', argued Beard, but by 'a consolidated group whose interests knew no state boundaries and were truly national in their scope'.[98] Despite criticisms, *An Economic Interpretation of the Constitution of the United States* grew steadily in stature until it came to dominate the historical literature on the Constitution.

Writing in 1950 Richard Hofstadter (1920–1970) observed that 'although the book has not yet lost every vestige of its controversial urgency, it has entered calmly into history. It has become less and less a book to argue over, more and more a book that must be studied if we are to locate our own thinking in the stream of intellectual events'.[99] Methodologically it was 'a triumph' but while 'the general economic interpretation of history and Beard's specific version of the struggle over the Constitution' had been endlessly debated, his innovative use of career line analysis had attracted little comment.[100] A note of criticism entered Hofstadter's assessment, however, when he contrasted the carefully worked-out details relating to the Founders' property holdings with the treatment afforded their political ideas, the latter merely 'a literal compound of scattered quotes from the debates in the Convention'. There was no effort to place their ideas on democracy in the context of eighteenth-century thought. This 'rather casual treatment' of their political ideas 'seemed so much more representative of current political argument than of the intellectual climate of the late eighteenth century' because it appeared to be an insider story, an exposé that matched the politics of his own day.[101] But even as Hofstadter wrote, consensus history was emerging out of the shadows of the Second World War and into the icy blasts of the Cold War. Within ten years the pioneering methodology that Hofstadter had so much admired was being systematically taken apart by a generation of post-war historians, not all of whom were hostile to economic approaches to history, while other scholars, more concerned with the primacy of ideas, ignored or rejected the progressive paradigm. In 1962, Bernard Bailyn, the outstanding scholar of his generation, sounding the death knell of the socio-economic approach to early American history, issued a rallying cry for reconstruction. Historians, he wrote, had been chipping away piecemeal at the old architecture, 'here a beam destroyed, there a stone dislodged, the inner supports only weakened and the balance gradually thrown off'. Only habit and the force of inertia kept the edifice standing.[102] When Hofstadter published *The Progressive Historians* in 1968, Beard's work was reduced to 'an imposing ruin in the historical landscape of American histori-ography'.[103] The rise of consensus history in the 1950s presaged the rejection of his perspective, methodology and conclusions. Peter Novick (following Gene Wise) prefers the term 'counter-progressive' to describe the consensus historians because they targeted the central idea of progressive historians, that American history was the struggle between the interests and the people, between the haves and the have-nots, and identified 'the defense of freedom as the thread which wove American history together'.[104] Looking back on Beard and his legacy from the perspective of the bicentennial of the Constitution in 1987, Richard Beeman concluded in the introduction to *Beyond Confederation: Origins of the Constitution and American National Identity* (1987) that there was 'a scholarly consensus on two points':

> 1. That Beard's description of the *precise* configuration of economic interests both at the Philadelphia Convention and in the ratification process – a configuration revolving around the categories of 'person-alty' and 'realty' – was badly flawed.
> 2. That Beard's more general contention – that there was *some* sort of relationship between an individual's socio-economic position and political behavior on the matter of the Constitution – has some merit.

To these Beeman added a third, 'that most historians find the debate over economic interests and the Constitution, at least in its current form, increasingly uninteresting and unhelpful'.[105]

The anti-Federalist progressive view of the making of the Constitution was carried forward by Merrill Jensen (1905–1980) who, in a long career at the University of Wisconsin, supervised over 50 completed Ph.D. dissertations. In fact, 'the University of Wisconsin ... was something of a Progressive redoubt, holding out against postwar tendencies'. It overtook Columbia as 'the center of the second generation of Progressive historians and as the creator of a third', and while Jensen himself did not adopt this label, neither did he repudiate it.[106] In two very influential books, *The Articles of Confederation* (1940) and *The New Nation* (1950) Jensen anchored the period between the Declaration of Independence and the making of the Federal Constitution firmly in the progressive tradition. The Articles of Confederation, wrote Jensen, could only be understood 'in relation to the internal revolution in the American states: the individual and group interests, the social cleavages, and the interstate conflicts that existed at the outbreak of the Revolution'. An approach along these lines would yield a proper understanding of the Articles 'in terms of the concrete issues that Americans faced in 1776'. The challenge was considerable: acceptance required casting aside a century and a half of 'history-making and history-writing' during which historians had swallowed Federalist propaganda 'as historical fact', proclaiming not only the weakness and inadequacy of the Confederation government but the prospect of anarchy and the dissolution of society.[107] The rationale of the Federalist Party, Jensen told his readers, was the destruction of America's first constitution, 'a constitution embodying ideals of self-government and economic practice that were naturally abhorrent to those elements in American society of which that party was the political expression'.[108]

Jensen viewed the Revolution as a 'relatively' democratic movement whose 'significance for the political and constitutional history of the United States lay in its tendency to elevate the political and economic status of the majority of the people'. His assertion that 'the Articles of Confederation were the constitutional expression of this movement and the embodiment in governmental form of the philosophy of the Declaration of Independence' was much quoted and roundly attacked.[109] Responding to his critics, Jensen reaffirmed his belief in the democratic thrust of the Revolution in a 1957 article in which he surveyed changes in government in the states concluding:

> It seems clear, to me at least, that by 1776 there were people in America demanding the establishment of democratic state governments, by which they meant legislatures controlled by a majority of the voters, and with none of the checks upon their actions such as

had existed in the colonies. At the same time there were many Americans who were determined that there should be no changes except those made inevitable by separation from Great Britain.[110]

Jensen argued that social division and social conflict pre-dated the revolutionary period. In fact, they were present at the very founding of the colonies and became more pronounced with each passing decade. In politics they were marked by the curtailment of rights once widely enjoyed at least by adult white males, and in the increasing concentration of wealth and power in the hands of the few, generally the great planters in the south and wealthy merchants in the north. The upheavals of Bacon's Rebellion and the Regulator movement were the most dramatic and violent manifestations of that social unrest which in the eighteenth century came to be concentrated on the frontiers and in the towns. In the decade of the 1760s there emerged from the latter a radical leadership for whom opposition to British policy offered unparalleled opportunity. Jensen divided the opponents of British policy into radicals and conservatives; the latter were representative of the dominant ruling group which he termed both an 'aristocracy' and an 'oligarchy' while the former were drawn from the majority of the population, defined as 'the masses'.[111] Conservatives, recognizing that Britain was the only guarantor of social stability, resisted independence but, when their control of the situation was threatened in the first continental congress and lost in the second, some became loyalists. During the short-lived ascendancy of the radicals that ensued, there was an attempt 'to write democratic ideals and theories of government into the laws and constitutions of the American states'. Though weakened by the Revolution, 'the continued presence of groups of conservatives ... is of profound importance in the constitutional history of the United States'.

> When forced to accept independence, they demanded the creation of a central government which would be a bulwark against internal revolution, which would aid the merchant classes, which would control Western lands, which would, in short, be a 'national' government. In this they were opposed by the radicals who created a 'federal' government in the Articles of Confederation and who resisted the efforts of the conservatives to shape the character of those Articles while they were in process of writing and ratification.[112]

Thus in Jensen's analysis, the radicals became the true 'Federalists' and the conservatives became the 'Nationalists'. The Articles of Confederation, he argued, were created to preserve state sovereignty in which democracy could prevail. From 1776 to 1780 the democratic-Federalists prevailed. In 1781, however, they succumbed to an aristocratic counter-revolution that brought the nationalists to power until 1784, when power swung back to the Federalists. Since most historians accepted Jensen's account of the Confederation, the question arises, was the Constitution really necessary?

The anti-Federalists

Before the second half of the twentieth century, the anti-Federalists aroused little interest among historians. Their reputation was particularly poor in the decades after the Civil War when, because of their opposition to centralized government, their ideas were linked to those of southern secessionists and they shouldered some of the burden of guilt for the trauma of the war. Moreover, as supporters of paper money, they were also identified with contemporary advocates of radical changes in monetary policy, which did nothing to enhance their image. With the reputation of the Confederation period at an all-time low thanks to the popularity of the work of John Fiske, the opposition of the anti-Federalists appeared not only misguided but something worse. With popular esteem for the Constitution riding high and buttressed by accolades from overseas, there seemed little prospect of a re-evaluation of the anti-Federalists and their ideas.[113]

Cecelia M. Kenyon claimed that what opponents of the Constitution wanted was not unfettered majority rule but more checks and balances and separation of powers, but without these features a national government 'was politically unfeasible'. To assume otherwise was 'unrealistic and unhistorical'.

> Perhaps because theirs was the losing side, the political thought of the Anti-Federalists has received much less attention than that of the Founding Fathers. Since they fought the adoption of a Constitution which they thought to be aristocratic in origin and intent, and which by Beardian criteria was inherently anti-democratic in structure,

there has been some tendency to characterize them as spokesmen of eighteenth-century democracy. But their theory of republican government has never been closely analyzed, nor have the areas of agreement and disagreement between them and the Federalists been carefully defined.[114]

Kenyon concluded that Beard's view of the system of separation of powers and checks and balances as undemocratic owed more to the ideas of the populists and progressives of his own time than to the study of the political beliefs current in 1787.

Central to anti-Federalist opposition, according to Kenyon, was the belief that republican government could only prevail in a small area where the population was limited in size and homogeneous in character. But the states were a thousand miles from north to south and eight hundred miles across, differentiated from each other by economics, politics and culture. The provision for 65 representatives was thus inadequate; moreover, it was likely to exclude 'democratic' and 'middling' elements because the upper class could be expected to dominate the voting system. Anti-Federalist expectations were low because they viewed human nature as weak and fallible. Like their opponents, they believed that behaviour was based on the pursuit of self interest, and 'found its most extreme political expression in an insatiable lust for power'. Their opponents' 'excessive confidence in the future virtue of elected officials' was misplaced and too little had been done to contain man's lust for power. The absence of a bill of rights 'caused genuine fear' especially over the failure to secure such common law procedures as trial by jury, the right to trial in the vicinity, the right to counsel and guarantees against cruel and unusual punishment. The very vagueness of the Constitution was a major problem for the anti-Federalists; 'its brevity, its generality, its freedom from minutiae' were qualities that the anti-Federalists feared. Critics 'wanted everything down in black and white, with no latitude of discretion or interpretation left to their representatives in Congress'. They did not assume, as had the framers of the Constitution, 'that the "genius" of the country was republican, and that the behavior of the men to be placed in office would in general be republican also'.[115]

'The Anti-Federalists wanted a more rigid system of separation of powers, more numerous and more effective checks and

balances, than the Founding Fathers had provided', wrote
Kenyon. Most of the anti-Federalists were more afraid of the
Senate than the President, 'but all feared the two in combination
and wanted some checks against them'. They were not 'latter-day
democrats', wrote Kenyon:

> [they] 'may have followed democratic principles within the sphere
> of state government and possibly provided the impetus for the
> extension of power and privilege among the mass of the people,
> though it is significant that they did not advocate a broadening of
> the suffrage in 1787–1788 or the direct election of the Senate or the
> President. But they lacked both the faith and the vision to extend
> their principles nation-wide. It was the Federalists of 1787–1788
> who created a national framework which would accommodate the
> later rise of democracy.[116]

A student of Merrill Jensen, Jackson Turner Main published
the first major study of the anti-Federalist viewpoint in 1961.[117]
Main defined anti-Federalism not as 'a single, simple, unified
philosophy of government' but 'rather a combination, a mixture
of two somewhat different points of view adhered to by two
different groups of men'. First, it was 'the doctrine of those who
preferred a weak central government'.

> This concept attracted many well-to-do thinkers, most frequently from
> the agricultural interest, and these men provided the Antifederalists
> with their ablest and best-educated leaders. The origins of this body of
> thought lay far back in colonial and English political history, and it
> became especially relevant during the last years before independence
> and the period of constitution-making, when fundamental principles of
> government had to be defined and applied. From the broadest point of
> view, the issue was whether authority or liberty should be emphasized.
> Once the authority of the British government had been overthrown,
> many were satisfied with the degree of liberty thus achieved and were
> willing to retain or reconstruct a strong central government at home;
> but others continued the struggle for local self-rule and individual
> freedom from restraint. In an equally general way, the former view was
> defended by those who desired a political system which would protect
> property and maintain order in society, while the latter was held by
> those who feared oppression: the former wished to exert power, the
> latter feared the effects of it.[118]

Second, there was the idea of government by the many rather

than the few which was favoured by small property owners and especially small farmers.

> All of the socio-economic groups had their peculiar, often conflicting interests, which they attempted to further by political action. Because the small property holders were a majority in Revolutionary times, they wanted a government dominated by the many rather than the few, and they therefore favored democratic ideas. Thus the Antifederalists included two major elements: those who emphasized the desirability of a weak central government, and those who encouraged democratic control. The democrats at this time accepted the doctrine of weak government, but the advocates of weak government did not always believe in democracy.[119]

Main argued that 'the mercantile interest' broadly understood to include 'shipowners, seamen and other persons in maritime industries, the "mechanics and artisans," the apprentices and other hired employees in almost every town' and those depending on them, 'was the key to the political history of the period'. It stood in juxtaposition to the interests of the subsistence farmer, but included those farmers engaged in production for market in urban centres or overseas. 'This is a socio-economic division based on a geographical location and sustains a class as well as a sectional interpretation of the struggle over the Constitution.' Main concluded that the ratification struggle 'was primarily a contest between the commercial and non-commercial elements in the population. This is the most significant fact, to which all else is elaboration, amplification, or exception'.[120]

Some twenty years later James Hutson, in contrast to Main, sought 'to offer a more servicable definition of anti-Federalism' and show how anti-Federalism could be 'more intelligibly differentiated from Federalism'. To this end he applied the contemporary British terms, 'Country and Court', to the problem.[121] The difficulty was essentially historiographical, since 'an uneasy coexistence of Progressive and consensus historiography' existed. While progressivism has identified two discrete socio-economic groups, consensus historiography has wiped out much of what once were seen as ideological differences between them. 'The problem for historians has been to capture the essence of those differences with appropriate terminology' while taking into account 'their social dimension', specifically 'their relation to social conflict arising from the opposition of men living in agrarian and commercial milieus.' 'A relative newcomer to the vocabulary of American historians' though long a staple among British, the word was 'COUNTRY'. Its antonym was 'COURT'. For two centuries, it signified 'opposition to the exercise of power by government', writes Hutson. The latter term was attached to the tories following the Restoration but the Glorious Revolution 'reversed these roles and also produced a closer identification of the Court and Country with contrasting socio-economic groups than had previously existed'. Hutson extended the conceptualization of earlier American opposition to British policies which Bernard Bailyn had popularised as 'country' ideas to the struggle over ratification. He labelled the opponents as 'country' and the promoters as 'court'. Lance Banning and others had already identified the contests of the 1790s in these terms; Hutson argues that it can be applied earlier and to the anti-Federalists.[122] Subsequent work has differentiated the anti-Federalists even further into a multiplicity of different groups according to social status and particular issues. Each group had distinctive interests they wanted represented in government, favoured contrasting methods of action, and identified in different ways with locality and state.[123]

Notes

1 David D. Van Tassel, *Recording America's Past: An Interpretation of the Development of Historical Studies in America 1607–1884* (Chicago; 1960), p. 32.
2 James H. Hutson, 'The Creation of the Constitution: Scholarship at a Standstill', *Reviews in American History*, 12 (1984), pp. 463–77, 464. This essay has been of great value in the preparation of this chapter.
3 John Fiske, *The Critical Period of American History, 1783–1789* (Boston; 1888); Michael Kammen describes this volume as 'probably the most widely read book ever published on the formation of the U. S. Constitution' and 'the most influential'; Michael Kammen, *A Machine that Would Go of Itself: The Constitution in American Culture* (New York; 1986), pp. 25, 128.
4 Cited in Kammen, *A Machine That Would Go of Itself*, p. 21.
5 John Quincy Adams (ed.), *Journal, Acts, and Proceedings of the Convention ... which formed the Constitution of the United States* (1819); Edmund C. Genet (ed.), *Secret Proceedings and Debates of the Convention Assembled at Philadelphia, in the Year 1787 ... From Notes taken by the late Robert Yates,*

Esq ... (1821); Jonathan Elliot (ed.), *The Debates, Resolutions, and other Proceedings in Convention on Adoption of the Federal Constitution*, 4 vols (1827–1830); H. D. Gilpin (ed.), *The Papers of James Madison*, 3 vols (1840).

6 Hutson, 'The Creation of the Constitution', p. 464; Michael Kraus, *A History of American History* (New York; 1937), pp. 187–90.

7 Timothy Pitkin, *A Political and Civil History of the United States of America from the Year 1763 to the Close of the Administration of President Washington, in March, 1797*, 2 vols (new Haven; 1828, reprinted New York; 1970), II, pp. 220–2.

8 Pitkin, *Political and Civil History*, II, p. 225.

9 Pitkin, *Political and Civil History*, II, pp. 225, 264.

10 Pitkin, *Political and Civil History*, II, p. 265.

11 They comprised 'the original and one copy of Madison's notes taken in the Constitutional Convention of 1787, together with his notes made on the debates "in the Congress of the Confederation in 1782, '83, & '87 ... and selections made by himself & prepared under his eye from his letters, narrating the proceedings of that Body during the periods of his service in it"'. William T. Hutchinson and William M. E. Rachal (eds), *The Papers of James Madison* (Chicago; 1962–), I, pp. xvii–xviii.

12 Hutson, 'Scholarship at a Standstill', p. 464.

13 William W. Crosskey, *Politics and the Constitution in the History of the United States*, 3 vols (Chicago; 1953–80); James H. Hutson, 'Riddles of the Federal Constitutional Convention', *WMQ*, 3rd ser., 44 (1989), pp. 411–23.

14 Hutchinson and Rachal, *Papers of James Madison*, I, p. xviii.

15 Kammen, *A Machine that Would Go of Itself*, pp. 88–90, 453, fn. 52.

16 Kammen, *A Machine that Would Go of Itself*, pp. 96–8; Hutson, 'The Creation of the Constitution', pp. 464–5.

17 Paul Finkelman, *Slavery and the Founders: Race and Liberty in the Age of Jefferson* (Armonk, NY and London; 1996), p. 2.

18 Paul Finkelman, 'Garrison's Constitution: The Covenant with Death and How it was Made', *Prologue*, 32 (2000), pp. 230–45.

19 Kammen, *A Machine That Would Go of Itself*, p. 98. Hutson, 'The Creation of the Constitution', p. 465.

20 Staughton Lynd, 'The Abolitionist Critique of the Constitution', in Staughton Lynd (ed.), *Class Conflict, Slavery and the United States Constitution: Ten Essays* (Indianapolis, IN and New York; 1967), pp. 154–83, 158.

21 Russell B. Nye, *George Bancroft: Boston Brahmin* (New York; 1972 [1944]), pp. 186–7; Kraus, *History of American History*, pp. 244–5; A. M. Schlesigner Jr, 'The Problem of Richard Hildreth', *New England Quarterly* (hereafter *NEQ*), 13 (1940), pp. 223–45.

22 Richard Hildreth, *History of the United States*, revised edition, 3 vols (New York; 1863) [1849]), pp. 390–1.

23 Hildreth, *History*, pp. 472–7.

24 Hildreth, *History*, pp. 484, 534.

25 Hildreth, *History*, p. 484.

26 Hildreth, *History*, pp. 486–7, 495–6, 501.

27 Hildreth, *History*, p. 520; Hutson, 'The Creation of the Constitution', p. 465.
28 Hildreth, *History*, II, pp. 35, 37, 38–9.
29 George Ticknor Curtis, *History of the Origin, Formation and Adoption of the Constitution of the United States*, 2 vols (New York, 1854–1858), p. x; Kammen, *A Machine that Would Go of Itself*, p. 110.
30 Curtis, *History*, I, pp. 121–3.
31 Curtis, *History*, II, p. 234.
32 Curtis, *History*, I, pp. 273–4.
33 Curtis, *History*, II, pp. 22–3.
34 Curtis, *History*, II, pp. 22–3
35 Curtis, *History*, II, p. 313.
36 Curtis, *History*, II, p. 313.
37 Curtis, *History*, II, p. 371.
38 Curtis, *History*, II, pp. 316–17.
39 Curtis, *History*, II, p. 465.
40 Curtis, *History*, II, pp. 462–3.
41 Curtis, *History*, II, p. 467.
42 Orlando Patterson, 'Slavery: The Underside of Freedom', *Slavery and Abolition*, 5 (1984), pp. 87–104; Edmund S. Morgan, *American Slavery American Freedom: The Ordeal of Colonial Virginia* (New York; 1975).
43 Mark V. Tushnet, 'George Ticknor Curtis', *American National Biography* (hereafter *ANB*), V (1999), pp. 894–5.
44 George Bancroft, *History of the Formation of the Constitution of the United States of America*, 2 vols (New York; 1882, reissued in 1983 and 2000); Gordon S. Wood (ed.), *The Confederation and Constitution: The Critical Issues* (Lanham, MD; 1979 [1973]), p. 181.
45 Bancroft, *Formation of the Constitution*, I, pp. 5–6.
46 Bancroft, *Formation of the Constitution*, II, p. 86.
47 Bancroft, *Formation of the Constitution*, I, p. 146.
48 Bancroft, *Formation of the Constitution*, I, pp. 209, 265–6.
49 Bancroft, *Formation of the Constitution*, II, p. 322.
50 Bancroft, *Formation of the Constitution*, II, pp. 323, 366–7.
51 Bancroft, *Formation of the Constitution*, II, pp. 329–30.
52 M. A. DeWolfe Howe, *The Life and Letters of George Bancroft*, 2 vols (London; 1908), pp. 318–27; Kraus, *The History of American History*, pp. 237–9; Peter Novick, *That Noble Dream: The 'Objectivity Question' and the American Historical Profession* (Cambridge and New York; 1988), pp. 43–6; Nye, *George Bancroft*, pp. 191–2.
53 J. H. Robinson, 'The Original and Derived Features of the Constitution', *Annals*, 1 (1890), pp. 203–43; Sidney G. Fisher, *The Evolution of the Constitution of the United States, Showing that it is a Development of Progressive History and not an Isolated Document Struck Off at a Given Time or an Imitation of English or Dutch Forms of Government* (Philadelphia; 1897); Andrew C. McLaughlin, *The Confederation and the Constitution* (New York; 1962 [1905]), pp. 44–5, 47; Wood, *The Confederation and the Constitution*.
54 Max Farrand, *The Framing of the Constitution of the United States* (New Haven, CT; 1913, reprinted 1962).

55 Max Farrand (ed.), *The Records of the Federal Convention*, 3 vols (New Haven; 1911; supplementary volume, 1937; rev. 4 vols, 1966); the publication was based almost exclusively on Madison's notes and the few other extant accounts of the Convention by insiders; James H. Hutson with the assistance of Leonard Rapport, supplementary volume, 1987.

56 Farrand, *Framing of the Constitution*, p. 39.

57 Farrand, *Framing of the Constitution*, pp. 42, 43.

58 Farrand, *Framing of the Constitution*, p. 52.

59 Farrand, *Formation of the Constitution*, pp. 202–3.

60 Max Farrand, 'Compromises of the Constitution', *AHR*, 9 (1904), pp. 479–89, 484.

61 Farrand, *Framing of the Constitution*, p. 203.

62 Farrand, *Framing of the Constitution*, pp. 196–7.

63 Farrand, *Framing of the Constitution*, pp. 203–4.

64 Farrand, *Framing of the Constitution*, pp. 105, 110.

65 Farrand, *Framing of the Constitution*, pp. 107–8.

66 Farrand, *Framing of the Constitution,* p. 200.

67 Farrand, *Framing of the Constitution*, p. 207.

68 Farrand, *Framing of the Constitution*, p. 210.

69 J. Allen Smith, *The Spirit of American Government: A Study of the Constitution: Its Origins, Influences and Relation to Democracy* (New York; 1907).

70 When republished in 1965, the subtitle was dropped and an introductory essay by Cushing Strout was added. J. Allen Smith, *The Spirit of American Government*, ed. Cushing Strout (Cambridge, MA; 1965), p. lxvi.

71 Wood *Confederation and Constitution*, p. 182.

72 Smith, *Spirit of American Government*, Preface, unpaginated.

73 Smith, *Spirit of American Government*, pp. 86–7.

74 Smith, *Spirit of American Government*, pp. 125–30.

75 Smith, *Spirit of American Government*, p. 37.

76 Smith, *Spirit of American Government*, pp. 40–1.

77 Smith, *Spirit of American Government*, pp. 43–4, 48–9.

78 Smith, *Spirit of American Government*, p. 65.

79 Smith, *Spirit of American Government*, p. 69.

80 Smith, *Spirit of American Government*, pp. 70, 98.

81 Charles A. Beard, *An Economic Interpretation of the Constitution of the United States* (New York; 1913); Joyce Appelby, Margaret Hunt and Margaret Jacob, *Telling the Truth about History* (New York and London; 1994), pp. 137–8; Wood *The Confederation and the Constitution*, p. ix.

82 Novick, *That Noble Dream*, pp. 95, 96–7; Wood *Confederation and the Constitution*, p. x; T. C. Clark, 'The Writing of American History in America, from 1884 to 1934', *AHR*, 50 (1935), pp. 439–49, 447–9.

83 Beard, *Economic Interpretation*, pp. 1–4; James H. Hutson, 'Country, Court and Constitution: Antifederalism and the Historians', *WMQ*, 3rd ser., 38 (1982), pp. 337–68, 339.

84 Henry B. Dawson, 'The Motley Letter', *The Historical Magazine*, 2nd ser., 9 (March 1871), pp. 171, 200, 166, cited in Hutson, 'The Creation of the Constitution', p. 466.

85 Beard, *Economic Interpretation*, pp. 10–13, 15, fn. 1, p. 188.
86 Beard, *Economic Interpretation*, pp. 6–7, 24.
87 Beard, *Economic Interpretation*, p. 48.
88 Beard, *Economic Interpretation*, pp. 16–17.
89 Beard, *Economic Interpretation*, pp. 24, 25, fn. 1.
90 Beard, *Economic Interpretation*, pp. 19–20, 26.
91 Beard, *Economic Interpretation*, p. 50.
92 Beard, *Economic Interpretation*, pp. 50–1.
93 Beard, *Economic Interpretation*, pp. 73–4.
94 Beard, *Economic Interpretation*, p. 149.
95 Beard, *Economic Interpretation*, pp. 251–2.
96 Beard, *Economic Interpretation*, p. 292.
97 Beard, *Economic Interpretation*, pp. 32–4.
98 Beard, *Economic Interpretation*, p. 325.
99 Richard Hofstadter, 'Beard and the Constitution: the History of an Idea,' *American Quarterly* (hereafter *AQ*), 2 (1950), pp. 195–213, 195.
100 Hofstadter, 'Beard and the Constitution', pp. 203–4.
101 Hofstadter, 'Beard and the Constitution', p. 208.
102 Bernard Bailyn, 'Political Experience and Enlightenment Ideas in Eighteenth Century America', *AHR*, 72 (2) (1962), pp. 339–51.
103 Richard Hofstadter, *The Progressive Historians: Turner, Beard, Parrington* (New York; 1968), p. 344; Hutson, 'Creation of the Constitution', pp. 468–9.
104 Novick, *That Noble Dream*, pp. 332–5.
105 Richard Beeman, Stephen Botein and Edward C. Carter II (eds), *Beyond Confederation: Origins of the Constitution and American National Identity* (Chapel Hill, NC; 1987), Introduction, pp. 13–14.
106 Novick, *That Noble Dream*, pp. 345–6; Young, 'American Historians Confront "the Transforming Hand of Revolution"' in Ronald Hoffman and Peter J. Albert (eds), *The Transforming Hand of Revolution: Reconsidering the American Revolution as a Social Movement* (Charlottesville, VA, and London, 1996), p. 379.
107 Merrill Jensen, *The Articles of Confederation: An Interpretation of the Social-Constitutional History of the American Revolution, 1774–1781* (Madison, WI; 1940), pp. v, 5.
108 Jensen, *Articles of Confederation*, pp. 4–5; Jensen cites George Ticknor Curtis as one of the principal offenders; George Ticknor Curtis, *History* 2nd edn, p. 85.
109 Jensen, *Articles of Confederation*, pp. 15, 239.
110 Merrill Jensen, 'Democracy and the American Revolution' in Esmond Wright (ed.), *Causes and Consequences of the American Revolution* (Chicago; 1966), p. 281.
111 Jensen, *Articles of Confederation*, pp. 7–10.
112 Jensen, *Articles of Confederation*, pp. 11, 14.
113 Hutson, 'Creation of the Constitution', pp. 341–2; Fiske, *Critical Period*.
114 Cecelia M. Kenyon, 'Men of Little Faith: The Anti-Federalists on the Nature of Representative Government', *WMQ*, 3rd. ser., 12 (1955), pp. 3–43, 5.
115 Kenyon, 'Men of Little Faith', pp. 6, 13–15, 18–19, 21–2.

116 Kenyon, 'Men of Little Faith', pp. 23, 42–3.
117 Jackson Turner Main, *The Antifederalists*: *Critics of the Constitution 1781–1788* (Chapel Hill, NC; 1961).
118 Main, *The Antifederalists*, pp. x–xi.
119 Main, *The Antifederalists*, p. xi.
120 Main, *The Antifederalists*, pp. xiii–xiv, 270–1, 280.
121 James H. Hutson, 'Country, Court, and Constitution: Antifederalism and the Historians', *WMQ*, 3rd ser., 38 (1981), pp. 337–68, 338.
122 Hutson, 'Country, Court, and Constitution', pp. 356–7.
123 Saul Cornell, *The Other Founders: Anti-Federalism and the Dissenting Traditions in America 1788–1828* (Chapel Hill, NC; 1999); review by Robert E. Shalhope, 'The Anti-Federalists: America's Other Founders', *Reviews in American History*, 28 (2000), pp. 201–7, 'a brilliant study which will stand as the definitive study of the subject for years to come'.

4

Ideology, slavery and original intent

Ideology

The recurrent characterization of its framers as 'practical men' long obscured the role of ideas in the making of the Constitution while the emphasis of the progressives on the clash of interests and their palpable distrust of ideas further contributed to their neglect. This situation changed in the latter half of the 1960s when, building on the work of Caroline Robbins, Douglass Adair and Trevor Colbourn, first Bernard Bailyn and then Gordon Wood, his former student at Harvard, re-orientated a generation of students towards the study of early American history and the role of ideas.[1] As Jack P. Greene observed in 1968, ideas now came to play 'a dual role in the coming of the Revolution' providing 'a framework within which Americans could explain British and their own behavior' and determining 'in significant and fundamental ways their responses to the developing situation'.[2] When Gordon Wood published his sweeping account of the making of the Federal Constitution in 1969, he completed the reconsideration of the role of ideas in early American history which had begun some twenty years earlier.[3] The collective impact of this body of scholarship was to alter dramatically how historians viewed the Revolution. It was not that ideas had been wholly ignored by earlier historians, but never before had they assumed so radical a character or the power to determine behaviour.[4]

In *The Creation of the American Republic, 1776–1789*, Wood extended and elaborated Bailyn's work but went further in contending that 'Americans of the Revolutionary generation' constructed not only new forms of government, 'but an entirely new conception of politics, a conception that took them out of an essentially classical and medieval world of political discussion into one that was recognizably modern'. Out went the mixed constitution, to be replaced by the separation of powers; in place of the representation of estates, there was the sovereignty of the people. And more so than Bailyn, Wood 'was instrumental in turning the attention of intellectual historians to "*ideology* as a cultural system"'.[5]

Originally, Wood conceived his book as a study of constitution-making in the revolutionary era but found he could make little progress until he understood the assumptions from which the constitution-makers proceeded and for this he needed to immerse himself in contemporary political literature.

> The approach of many historians to the American Revolution, it seemed, had too often been deeply ahistorical; there had been too little sense of the irretrievability and differentness of the eighteenth-century world. Although the vocabulary of the period was familiar ... I learned that words such as 'liberty', 'democracy', 'virtue', or 'republicanism' did not possess a timeless application. Indeed, even within the very brief span of years I was studying, it soon became clear that the terms and categories of political thought were under-going rapid change, beset by the strongest kinds of polemical and experiential pressures.[6]

Comparing the debates of 1776 with those of 1787, Wood concluded that a fundamental transformation of political culture had taken place.

Wood was 'the first author both to clearly recognize the dynamic qualities of republicanism and effectively define and analyse these qualities'.[7] 'Republicanism,' wrote Wood, 'meant more for Americans than simply the elimination of a king and the institution of an elective system.' It added a moral dimension, a utopian depth, to the political separation from England:

> The Americans had come to believe that the Revolution would mean nothing less than a reordering of eighteenth-century society and politics as they had known and despised them – a reordering that was summed up by the conception of republicanism.[8]

Crucial to republicanism were three basic elements: the concept of the public good, the need for virtue and the doctrine of equality. The first of these required the sacrifice of individual interests for the good of the whole.[9] The second, 'the life blood of the republic', was essential for its maintenance and survival. 'Every state in which the people participated needed a degree of virtue; but a republic which rested solely on the people absolutely required it.'[10] Equality, on the other hand, was 'a beautiful but ambiguous ideal'. For Wood, American society in the mid-eighteenth century was quite extraordinary. It was both one thing and another, 'remarkably equal yet simultaneously unequal', '... so contradictory in its nature that it left contemporaries puzzled and later historians divided'.[11]

During the course of the revolutionary struggle Americans experimented with a series of state governments and found that they too were lacking in the virtue which alone could provide for the continuity of the new republic. The drive to change the Articles of Confederation, declared Wood, was a reaction against the excesses of democracy manifested in the separate state legislatures, but the struggle over ratification highlighted 'a clear economic divide' between supporters and opponents. By the time Wood reached the conclusion that the Constitution 'was intrinsically an aristocratic document designed to check the democratic tendencies of the period', he appeared to have moved away from the neo-whigs and into the progressive camp.[12]

The concept of republicanism took on additional layers of meaning and complexity in the work of J. G. A. Pocock who in a lengthy, erudite and somewhat forbidding study, *The Machiavellian Moment* (1975), examined its origins in the classical world in which the idea of pure forms of government – monarchy, aristocracy and democracy – was formulated and history defined as a cyclical process whereby these forms of government degenerated respectively into tyranny, oligarchy and anarchy. Only a mixed or balanced constitution held out the promise of breaking the cycle. The idea of the mixed or balanced constitution combining the best elements of all three was revived during the Renaissance among Florentine humanists, but this, wrote Pocock, was slow to reach England and it was not until the middle of the seventeenth century that James Harrington, who regarded Machiavelli as 'the greatest of post-classical political theorists', fitted his writings 'into English political, legal, and historical terms'. The cluster of ideas revolving around virtue and corruption, independence and servility, agriculture and commerce, history and society, developed further by the neo-Harringtonians, became identified with both court and country factions in early eighteenth-century Britain. Though opposition writers and politicians identified Sir Robert Walpole's administration with corruption, the very antithesis of virtue, government in eighteenth-century Britain was widely seen both at home and on the continent as the epitome of the mixed, balanced constitution. Oppositionist thought, however, crossed the Atlantic where it moulded the thinking of the American revolutionaries and the framers of the Federal Constitution. There, too, something approximating a 'court' position developed in the 1790s becoming associated with the economic policies of Alexander Hamilton.[13]

Given the strength of republican ideas, Pocock questioned whether 'the end of classical politics' had indeed come about as a consequence of the making of the Constitution and the Federalist–Republican debate as Wood claimed.[14] Rather than the whole web, it was just 'one guiding thread in a complex tissue' that had dropped from view. The rhetoric of virtue and corruption, of balance and separation of powers and fears of a standing army, was still much in vogue. Yet Pocock may have overstated his case for he had placed 'civic humanism' (after Machiavelli), in which the virtuous man as an active citizen sought out the public good, at the core of republicanism. The Federal Constitution, on the other hand, marked a retreat from the concept of virtue, albeit implicit, and broke the link with active citizenship, yet it is difficult to see the creation of the Federal Constitution as a cry against modernity and the last gasp of the Renaissance.[15] Pocock summarized Wood's position as follows: 'Wood's "end of classical politics" is at bottom predicated upon an abandonment of the closely related paradigms of deference and virtue.'[16] A key figure in Pocock's case for the persistence of republicanism in its classical form was Alexander Hamilton who appeared to his republican and Jeffersonian adversaries in the 1790s as 'a figure defined in ominous outline by every tradition in which corruption threatened the republic'. Hamilton saw himself as 'a modern whig', and looked to Britain as a model for emulation in his financial policies. 'To a quite remarkable degree,' wrote Pocock, 'the great debates on his policies in the 1790s were a replay of Court-Country debates' that had taken place in Britain 'seventy and a hundred years earlier'.[17]

Published in 1978 and 1980, two monographs originating as dissertations at the Universities of Washington (St Louis) and Virginia stressed the continuity of republican values into the 1790s and beyond. Lance Banning, a student of Pocock at Washington University, found it central to the creation of the first party system, thus contradicting Wood's claim about 'an entirely new conception of politics' in the 1780s. Historians had failed to recognize that the influences identified by Bailyn, Pocock and Wood had also shaped the early national experience. In *The Jeffersonian Persuasion* (1978), Banning sought to demonstrate how 'a constellation of inherited concerns gave rise to the Republican party and its foes ... that the Republican persuasion was a great deal more coherent than has formerly been thought, and that it exercised a greater influence on the party's growth and conduct than has yet been recognized.'[18] He approached the republicans as the heirs of the 'country' tradition rather than as promulgators of the early republic's first party system.

> Throughout the 1790s, a Republican revision of British opposition thought served as the most important justification for the existence of the party and as the general framework for specific criticisms of administration plans ... When the party came to power, the ideology of opposition days played a larger role in shaping policy than has usually been seen.[19]

Ideology did not tell the whole story, Banning admitted, but it did help to explain why Americans divided into parties so rapidly despite 'sharing a constitutional consensus'. While suspicion about Federalist motives, concern over the structure of the new government and fear over prospects for the future were expressed in newspaper articles, private correspondence and legislative assemblies by the end of 1789, reminiscent of earlier Anglo-American thought, it would be wrong to exaggerate their importance.[20] What spread alarm across the country, brought the government into disrepute and put republicanism under threat, was Hamilton's financial schemes in which he proposed to have the federal government fund the revolutionary war debt, assume state obligations, create a national bank, and encourage the growth of American manufacturing.[21] Banning followed Gerald Stourzh in arguing that Hamilton saw 'the enormous burden of revolutionary debt as a great instrument for nation-building, a tool for binding an important class of citizens to the nationalist cause' (and not for the 'personal benefit of monied men' as his critics claimed).[22] As accusations of conspiracy and corruption were raised by Madison and Jefferson, the political mood of the country shifted in the late summer of 1791.[23] The result was the transformation of a congressional opposition into a political party and the creation of the first American party system. The victory of the Jeffersonian Republicans in 1800 marked a return to first principles.[24]

Unlike Banning, who stressed continuities between American political thinking and earlier English commonwealth and country influences, Drew McCoy viewed republicanism as 'an ideology in transition'. In his elegantly written though not entirely convincing study, *The Elusive Republic* (1980), he sought to chart how republican thinkers attempted 'to cling to the traditional republican spirit of classical antiquity without disregarding the new imperatives of a more modern commercial society', and still remain resistant 'to the decay and corruption that had overtaken so much of the Old World'.[25] 'Simply stated,' wrote McCoy, 'the problem was this: in a predominantly agricultural society like America, where subsistence was so easily procured, what would sustain industry, and hence virtue among the people?' The Scottish philosopher David Hume, a major influence on Madison, was an advocate of commerce but that way led to urban growth, division of labour, and dependency. Opening up markets overseas to American surpluses was to be preferred.[26] While Madison was committed to free trade and envisaged 'a new, more open international commercial order', westward expansion 'developing across space rather than through time' was central to his outlook. That way, 'the United States would remain a nation of industrious farmers who marketed their surpluses abroad and purchased the "finer" manufactures they desired in return'.[27] What stymied Madison's aspirations, however, were the failure of the United States to acquire access to the desired markets and the burgeoning growth of manufacturing. Associated with an increase in the land-less poor on the one hand and luxury on the other, this posed a dilemma for Madison, wrote McCoy, that he was unable to resolve.[28]

Challenges to the preoccupation of historians with republi-canism as the prevailing ideology of the Revolution were relatively slow to appear. An early but isolated attempt was that of German scholar Willi Paul Adams (1940–) who, regarding republicanism as multifaceted rather than one dimensional, contested Bailyn's and Wood's use of the term in *The First American Constitutions* (1980).[29] The most serious challenge came from Joyce Appleby whose *Capitalism and a New Social Order* (1984), prefigured in a series of articles and essays from the early 1970s onwards, appeared in 1984.[30] Questioning the primacy of republicanism, Appleby sought to broaden the quest for the ideological origins of the American Revolution in order to make sense of what happened next. The neo-whigs had 'come up with a colonial past ill-adapted to serve as the story of the begin-nings of what was to come' she observed, for

> if a classical republicanism imbued with traditional notions of politi-cal authority dominated colonial thinking, where are the roots of that liberalism which flowered so quickly after independence? If the Revolution was fought in a frenzy over corruption, out of fear of tyranny, and with hopes for redemption through civic virtue, where and when are scholars to find the sources for the aggressive individ-ualism, the optimistic materialism, and the pragmatic interest-group politics that became so salient so early in the life of the new nation?[31]

The conundrum could be resolved, Appleby believed, by refer-ence to the considerable body of seventeenth-century economic literature which, like that on republicanism, had also crossed the Atlantic. These writings which Appleby explored in her 1978 study *Economic Thought and Ideology in Seventeenth-Century England*, 'nurtured a very different attitude toward human nature and the terms of social stability' than that of the republican liber-tarian tradition.[32] The roots of liberal social thought did not lie in past politics or classical theories of government, but rather in the first writings on the free market economy in the seventeenth century.[33]

The debate between those who identified republicanism as 'the defining mode of thought in the early republic' and those who identified liberalism was bitter.[34] Appleby's argument received considerable support from the continuing work of Isaac Kramnick whose 1968 study of Bolingbroke and his circle 'provided a crucial link in this intellectual chain by associating corruption with social and political themes, a critical concept in the language of eighteenth-century politics'.[35] By questioning the validity of extending civic humanism to encompass the entire eighteenth century in his 1982 article 'Republicanism Revisionism Revisited' Kramnick plunged into 'the thick of battle for historiographical control of the late eighteenth century'.[36] 'In seeking to free the entire eighteenth century of Locke, of socioeconomic radicalism, and of bourgeois liberalism', Kramnick maintained, that republican revisionists such as Pocock, Murrin and Banning had gone too far.[37] The 'model of court versus country' or 'the dialectic of virtue and commerce' were of dubious validity in the last three decades of the eighteenth century when radicals embraced the market, adopted the language of class and the very concepts of virtue and corruption assumed new meanings. 'As Burgh, Price, Priestley, and all the dissenting middle-class reformers eventually did, Locke divided society into an industrious, enterprising middle beset by two idle extremes.'[38]

James Kloppenberg offered a way forward. 'In place of the sterile juxtaposition of liberalism and republicanism', he urged historians 'to see how eighteenth- and nineteenth-century Americans worked to balance their commitments to individual rights against their equally firm commitments to personal and civic virtue'.[39] His emphasis was on 'the diversity of American patterns of thought and behavior'. Gone were the 'simple pictures of a stable prerevolutionary America', he wrote, demolished by the 'explosion of research' undertaken since the 1960s. 'Virtue,' according to Kloppenberg, 'was ubiquitous in eighteenth-century American discourse.' It had different meanings in different contexts and it changed over time.[40] It was central to religion and republicanism but its several meanings rendered the first 'ambiguous' and the second 'fuzzy', at least as far as the man of virtue was concerned. Moral philosophy represented a third tradition involving Locke and natural law, and the Scottish realists, ethics and accountability. Americans were able to weave these strands together in their struggle against Britain, argued Kloppenberg, precisely because they did not need to delve too deeply into their meanings. What Americans sought was autonomy, 'not only for the nation, but for individuals as well'. Autonomy and popular sovereignty were 'at the center of the American vision of politics during those years'. In the case of popular sovereignty, 'the location in the people themselves of the ultimate decision-making authority for the new nation', Kloppenberg differed from historians such as Edmund Morgan and Pauline Maier and others who were inclined to dismiss it as a fiction or myth.[41]

While the idea of civic virtue survived the ratification struggle, and that of the common good 'continued to animate the republicanism of at least some Jeffersonians – and some federalists' during the 1790s, what of the third tradition, that of 'liberalism based on responsibility rather than cupidity'?[42] Kloppenberg challenged both Banning's characterization of liberalism and his description of Appleby's characterization of republicanism. Appleby, according to Banning, had exaggerated her portrait of republicanism by presenting it as 'backward-looking and anti-egalitarian'. He may have been correct, commented Kloppenberg, but his own description of liberalism, based on Macpherson's analysis of possessive individualism, 'as a celebration of the "unrestrained pursuit of private interests" [was] also one-sided'. This was only one face of liberal capitalism. 'Laissez-faire liberalism was not present at the creation', he confidently asserted; it emerged 'over the course of the nation's first hundred years'.[43]

Kloppenberg's interpretation 'of the intermingling of religious, republican, and liberal themes' in the political culture of late eighteenth-century America, drew attention 'to the distance between the ethical thrust of such ideas and the flattened discourse of nineteenth-century individualism and democracy'. It was based essentially on his interpretation of what the ideas of autonomy and popular sovereignty actually meant.

> Autonomy meant the combination of personal independence and moral responsibility that was central to the ideas of John Locke and Adam Smith, James Madison and Thomas Jefferson ... Popular

sovereignty meant the commitment to representative government as a form uniquely attractive because of its open-endedness.[44]

Though Americans were happy with fragmentation because the United States Constitution 'reflected the reality and the ideals of a wildly diverse, pluralistic society', they committed themselves 'to a pair of principles that held out a formidable challenge to the new nation'.[45] Thus, he concluded, 'Gordon Wood is surely right that American political debate narrowed in the nineteenth century and Joyce Appleby is also right that the Jeffersonian moment of an equal commitment to material and moral progress was short-lived. But the principles of autonomy and popular sovereignty had been enshrined, and they exerted a powerful hold on the American imagination.'[46]

Looking back over three decades at the achievements of the new intellectual historians, social historian Michael Meranze commented that they had given us, 'a far more complex grasp of the conceptual and linguistic worlds of the late eighteenth century', but this had come at a price: the separation of discourse and ideology from social practice.

> Attention to 'historical languages' and to the constitutive nature of discourse has heightened our awareness of the importance of discursive traditions. But this attention has severed the connections of discourse to actual public policy, social struggles, or everyday use.[47]

When Drew McCoy attempted to bridge the gap, Meranze found the outcome less than successful, claiming that he did not 'fully connect either ideology or policy to extradiscursive effects or location'. 'One would be hard pressed, in reading *The Elusive Republic*,' he observed, 'to recognise either Thomas Jefferson or James Madison as defenders of a slave regime or to understand "expansion across space" as the effective ideology of genocide.'[48]

The bicentennial: a return to normal history?

When James Banner reviewed *Beyond Confederation: Origins of the Constitution and American National Identity* (1987), a multi-authored collection of essays marking the bicentennial of the Constitution, he greeted the volume as a return to 'normal

history'. Not only did the collection of essays reflect 'a disengage-
ment' from the 'overwhelming concern' of historians 'with
ideology and perception', but revealed 'the glimmerings of a fresh
concern for concrete reality, for politics, interests, and institutions'.[49] Yet issues relating to concepts of republicanism,
liberalism and democracy would continue to engage historians in
the years ahead. Banner's comments were somewhat premature
and not a little misleading since idealists had never banished realists despite the unparalleled success of the former over the past
two and a half decades. If 1987 did not mark a discernable watershed in the historiography of the Federal Constitution, it did
witness a profusion of publications. Historians were less than
overwhelmed by the result. Writing in the *New York Review of
Books* in 1988, Gordon Wood claimed that what was most
remarkable about the bicentennial, was the extent to which its
scholarship had been 'colored by the students and followers of
Leo Strauss, the German-born political theorist who taught at the
University of Chicago in the 1950s and 1960s'. Straussian scholarship Wood complained, tended to reinforce fundamentalist
views of the Constitution and diminished 'respect for history'.
What was needed was 'less veneration for the Founding Fathers
and a deeper sense of the historical process'.[50] Peter Onuf,
Professor of History at the University of Virginia, took a more
generous view. Unlike 1976, he pointed out, historians had to
share a crowded stage with political scientists, legal scholars,
lawyers and judges.[51] The legacy of the bicentennial appears to
have dictated the agenda of recent years: the focus on specific
clauses of the Constitution, the Bill of Rights, the character of
anti-Federalism and, of course, original intent.

Unlike the editor of the *Journal of American History* who
invited contributors to a special issue marking the bicentennial to
take the long view of the Constitution on the grounds that 'there
was little that was new or anticipated from further study of its
drafting and ratification', the editor of the *William and Mary
Quarterly* knew better. Not only did the journal launch a reappraisal of Gordon Wood's mighty 1969 tome, but it published a
series of sparkling essays which spilled over into 1988. Despite
the challenge from historians of liberalism, religion and social
class, *The Creation of the American Republic* was still indispens-

able to historians of the Constitution. Critics such as Edward Countryman, Jackson Turner Main and Gary Nash were even less persuaded of its argument than when it first appeared, while others, though fulsome in their praise of Wood's achievement, as in fact were Countryman and Nash, contested the prominence accorded republicanism.[52] Jack Rakove (1947–) took a different tack, identifying 'its uneven integration of the experiences of Revolutionary governance with the transformation of ideas' as its greatest weakness. He recalled that he had always asked Wood to tie the 'intellectual developments he had analysed so brilliantly' to 'the real world of political life, where values and ideology mingle with personal ambitions, imperfect knowledge, and even more imperfect resources to define the choices and produce the decisions that politics is finally about'.[53]

Among the state of the art essays published in the *William and Mary Quarterly* in its bicentennial edition was James H. Hutson's 'Riddles of the Federal Constitutional Convention' which probed existing explanations of what took place on the floor of the Convention and 'out of doors', finding traditional political historians, quantifiers and intellectual approaches all wanting. He criticized the tendency among political scientists and some historians to equate the *Federalist* with the Constitution and identified the question of the integrity of Madison's *Notes* as 'a problem whose solution exceeded all others in significance'. In his view, 'the convention [was] best understood in the traditional way as essentially a practical affair, concerned principally with the distribution of power between contending interests, large states and small, North and South'.[54] There were broad areas of agreement among delegates on principles of government before the sessions began including 'the separation of powers, checks and balances, government by consent, and the rule of law'. Explicitly distancing himself from Beard and his followers, Hutson maintained that 'since the convention delegates shared so many convictions, the area for disagreement on political theories and principles was small'. The ratification process, however, was another matter.[55]

Jack Rakove described 'the prevailing image of the convention as a cumulative process of bargaining and compromise in which a rigid adherence to principle was subordinated to the pragmatic tests of reaching agreement and building a consensus' and, like Hutson, believed that historians still favoured the older view that the convention's success was 'a tribute to the framers' talents, if not for logrolling, then at least for pragmatic accommodation', but sought to move the discussion forward by relating the respective roles of ideas and interests to political behaviour within the convention.[56] While Rakove did not dispute that the vote taken on 16 July, the so-called 'Great Compromise', was a 'breakthrough', he did question whether in fact it was a compromise. 'In the end, of course, reason did not prevail against will.'[57] There was little discussion of the New Jersey plan for its advocates 'had already achieved their point ... The real debate over the thrust of the New Jersey Plan thus began only *after* its rejection.'[58] It had proved impossible to convert the majority against the New Jersey Plan into a coalition in favour of proportional representation in both houses.[59] The small states remained unpersuaded that they had little to fear in the extended republic 'with its multiplicity of interests' that Madison conceived.[60] What the debate over apportionment did was to expose

> the central tension – or even contradiction – that lay at the core of the general theory that Madison labored so hard to develop. For the recognition that there was one overriding issue that threatened to establish a great 'division of interests' between slave and free states could not be easily rendered compatible with the pluralist imagery of the diverse sources of faction.[61]

When 'the specter of sectional conflict' legitimated the appeal of the small states to security, Madison lost confidence in his pre-convention analysis.

But if Madison's concept of the extended republic was the key to what happened in the Convention for Rakove, it was not true of Isaac Kramnick. 'There was a profusion and confusion of political tongues among the founders', he wrote, though, unlike their descendants two hundred years later, it was something they could live with. In 'The "Great National Discussion"' he identified 'the languages of republicanism, of Lockean liberalism, of work-ethic Protestantism, and of state-centered theories of power and sovereignty' as the most significant, though there were others such as 'the language of jurisprudence', 'scientific whiggism' and 'the "moral sentiment" schools of the Scottish Enlightenment', the discussion of which he proposed to leave to others.[62] Precisely because of the restrictions placed by the Constitution on the exercise of power, 'the extent to which the Constitution is a grant of power to a centralized nation-state' has been lost. It was a loss that reflected 'a persistent privileging of Madison over Hamilton in reading the text'. Those who participated in the 'great national discussion' however, regardless of partisanship, 'agreed with Hamilton that the Constitution intended a victory for power, for the "principle of *strength* and *stability* in the organization of our government, and *vigor* in its operations"'.[63] Hamilton's 'achievement', and that of his contemporaries at Philadelphia, was the 'creation of the American state'. In support of his position Kramnick drew on the conclusions of Elkins and McKitrick in their classic 1961 article, 'The Founding Fathers: Young Men of the Revolution', that

> while most of the Antifederalists were states-centered politicians whose heroics took place before 1776, most of the Federalists were shaped by the need to realize the national interest in an international war. Their common bond was an experience that transcended and dissolved state boundaries.[64]

Madison, too, 'was a state builder', but while Hamilton saw the nation-state as 'seeking power in a competitive international system of other power-hungry states, Madison saw the nation-state as necessary only to protect private rights and thus to ensure justice'. Even this was too much for anti-Federalists who saw Madison's state as 'a monstrous betrayal of the Revolution and its spirit'.

> Like most revolutions, the American began as a repudiation of the state, of power, and of authority in the name of liberty. Like most revolutions, it ended with a stronger state, the revival of authority, and the taming of liberty's excesses.[65]

Slavery and the framers

'The word "slavery" was never mentioned in the Constitution [in 1787],' wrote Paul Finkelman in the year that Americans celebrated the bicentennial of their Constitution, 'yet its presence was felt everywhere'. 'Slavery was *there* at the constitutional begin-ning,' noted William Wiecek, 'like an unbidden, malevolent spirit at a festive celebration: the fairy-tale witch who was not invited to the christening but who came anyway and in an act of spite left a curse on the child.' Don Fehrenbacher suggested that the Constitution was bifocal. The Founding Fathers had hedged in slavery, but it was there at their feet though not before their eyes. Frederick Douglass probably caught the anomalies of the Constitution best when he wrote in 1850 that liberty and tyranny were both present in the Constitution.[66] As a theme in the histori-ography of the Constitution, the subject of slavery has moved in and out of focus due more to contemporary politics than the intrinsic merits of its historical relevance. While the importance of abolitionism and the advent of the Civil War ensured that slavery remained central in much of the writing about the Constitution in the middle decades of the nineteenth century, thereafter the subject virtually disappeared from constitutional discourse until the era of Civil Rights in the 1960s.[67] Yet no inter-est at the Convention was more substantial than that of the slaveholding south. As Madison commented 'the real difference of interest lay, not between the large and small but between the Northern and Southern States. The institution of slavery and its consequences formed the line of discrimination'.[68]

While Charles Beard and Frederick Jackson Turner, 'the twin giants of modern American historiography' undoubtedly carried American history in new directions, it was partly because these historians 'systematically minimized its importance' that 'the significance of slavery in American history has been obscured'. 'In their indifference to the Negro,' wrote Staughton Lynd, 'Turner and Beard were typical of Northern liberals at the turn of the last century.'[69] Not until the 1960s when black protest spread to northern cities in the wake of the Civil Rights movement in the South, was there a revival of interest in the relationship between the institution of slavery and the creation of the Constitution. In a series of articles beginning in 1963, radical activist Staughton Lynd not only pointed to the vast lacunae in the progressive *oeuvre* over slavery, but also vindicated the abolitionist view that slavery 'helped to shape the Constitution because slavery was the basis of conflict between North and South, and compromising that conflict was the main work of the Constitutional Convention' and linked the three-fifths compromise to a concealed compromise between the Congress meeting in New York and the Convention sitting in Philadelphia. Drawing on aspects of the work of nineteenth-century historians Richard Hildreth and George Bancroft on population growth and the importance of the west, Lynd challenged Max Farrand's interpretation of the Constitution on a number of telling points. In addition, the emergence of American legal history as a respectable field of study in American law schools in the 1970s attracted the attention of students interested in both history and law. As early as 1963, Paul L. Murphy had urged historians to reclaim legal and constitutional history from lawyers and judges, the practitioners of a dubious 'law office history', and to study the development of law in its historical context.[70]

In 'The Abolitionist Critique of the Constitution' Lynd rejected as misleading Farrand's view that the adoption of the three-fifths ratio was not a compromise reached in the Convention but something 'recommended by Congress in 1783 and adopted by eleven states before the Convention met, and ... part of the original New Jersey Plan'. Lynd asserted that slavery was indeed 'the basis of the great Convention crisis' drawing not only on Madison's views but on statements at the Convention by Pinckney, King, Mason and Gouverneur Morris as well as disputes 'which had been boiling up for years in the Continental Congress'.[71] He also disputed Farrand's attempt 'to disengage the question of the admission of new states at the Constitutional Convention from sectional strife'. Conscious of its minority status, 'the South expected the West to be slave rather than free' in anticipation of which, Lynd reasoned, the South was willing to yield its demand that commercial legislation be passed by a two-thirds majority.[72]

Could the Revolution have abolished slavery asked Lynd rhetorically? 'It came very close' he believed. Rejecting Farrand's conclusion that the majority 'regarded slavery as an accepted institution, as a part of the established order', he countered that 'almost without exception, the Fathers felt that slavery was wrong and almost without exception they failed to act decisively to end it'. Lynd attributed the failure to a number of reasons. First, they could not imagine a society 'in which whites and Negroes would live together as fellow-citizens'. Second was their commitment to private property and third, being economic realists, 'uprooting so substantial a reality as slavery was too much to ask'.

> Unable to summon the moral imagination required to transcend race prejudice, unwilling to contemplate social experiment which impinged on private property, too ready to rationalize their failure by a theory of economic determination, the Fathers, unhappily, ambivalently, confusedly, passed by on the other side ... The abolitionists were right in seeing the American Revolution as a revolution betrayed.[73]

The three-fifths compromise which 'sanctioned slavery more decidedly than any previous action at a national level' was adopted by the Convention in Philadelphia on 12 July 1787. Yet one day later, and with a southern majority, the Continental Congress meeting in New York, some of whose members also served in the Convention, adopted the Northwest Ordinance which barred slavery from the territory.[74]

How to account for these seemingly contradictory actions and 'the impact of the Ordinance on the work of the Constitutional Convention' was explored by Lynd in 'The Compromise of 1787' (1966).[75] Lynd posited that southerners may have supported the Northwest Ordinance for a number of reasons: that 'even without slavery', the area might be expected to support southern policies in Congress; that it was 'a tacit endorsement of slavery in the Southwest' and that with agreement on reducing the size of the population required, new states in the north-west might be admitted more rapidly to the Union. 'Whether or not the Ordinance was consciously intended to resolve problems in the Convention, it may have had that effect,' wrote Lynd.[76] Lynd rejected the notion that the three-fifths compromise was attained by a combination of 'large states'; rather it was the result of a combination of southern states 'aided by now one Northern state, now by another'. He argued that 'section as well as size was involved in the great Compromise' and that by early July, 'the conflict of large and small states had been partially transformed into a conflict of North and South'. Though the three-fifths vote was agreed by a nine–two vote on 11 June as the basis for representation in the lower house, 'it now became once more problematical because it was connected to Western expansion'.[77]

Based on assumptions about population growth (including slaves) in the determination of membership of the House and admitting western states on the basis of equality with the original states, 'were alternative means' of augmenting southern power in Congress. Perceptions of shifts in the direction of population growth gave both regions 'an interest in discarding the existing arrangement of one vote in Congress' and a 'basis for compromise', though its formulation would prove 'excruciatingly difficult to formulate'.[78]

> The Ordinance supplied a *deus ex machina* uncannily appropriate. The beauty of its admission requirements was that they appeared at the time to promote the South's interests in the House while protecting the North's interest in the Senate.[79]

Lynd hypothesized 'that there occurred in early July 1787 a sectional compromise involving Congress and Convention, Ordinance and Constitution, essentially similar to those of 1820 and 1850' and that circumstances make it reasonable to conclude 'that "conference and inter-communication" occurred'. If the antislavery clause was acceptable to the south and the fugitive slave clause reassured any doubters, was it the north rather than the south that made the major concession in drafting the Ordinance? Lynd believed that these details could have become known in Philadelphia in time to influence the voting of 12–14 July. As to the reasons why Congress and Convention acted 'so differently', Lynd concluded

> The evidence suggests that the motives which moved men in making Ordinance and Constitution were essentially the same. The drafters at Philadelphia were troubled about slavery as were the legislators in New York ... In each case the North made the compromises the South demanded, but in Congress, because of the South's mistaken assumptions about the future of the Northwest, an antislavery clause would be included. The fugitive slave clause adopted unanimously by both bodies shows, if not that there was a sectional compromise between Congress and Convention, at least that the makers of both Ordinance and Constitution were ready to compromise the concept

that all men are equal. This was the fundamental compromise of 1787.[80]

Though accepted by James Henderson and by Peter Onuf, Lynd's 'concealed compromise of 1787' has received a mixed reception among other historians.[81] According to Howard Ohline, Lynd's evidence of a 'sectional swap' 'was good, but circumstantial'. The trouble was that his hypothesis did not explain 'what the North received in exchange'. The relationship between slavery and representation was far too complex to be 'understood in a simple North–South frame of reference'.[82] While not rejecting it outright, Paul Finkelman believed that it was weakened by the lack of debate in Congress about the prohibition of slavery in the 1787 Northwest Ordinance and the absence of comments in members' correspondence. Moreover Manassah Cutler could not have conveyed news of the prohibition adopted by the Congress meeting in New York to the convention at Philadelphia because he did not learn of the wording of the ordinance until 19 July. James Hutson claimed that Lynd's hypothesis was flawed, being derived from Cutler's diary which he described as 'an unreliable source'. Since the editors of the Hamilton papers show that Alexander Hamilton was not in Philadelphia during the month of July, he together with Cutler could not have carried compromise proposals from Congress to the Convention between 12 and 14 July. Don Fehrenbacher was also sceptical about the paucity of documentary evidence. 'Lynd's best piece of evidence,' he wrote, was 'a recollection by Madison as recollected in turn by his one-time secretary in the 1850s', but it mentioned only the fugitive slave clauses, not the three-fifths compromise.[83] Gordon Wood found Lynd's argument about the influence of slavery on the making of the Constitution 'anachronistic and overdrawn'.[84]

In 1972, William Freehling provided the classic defence of the framers of the Constitution in an article which stressed the positive changes which the Revolution initiated.[85] Abolition occurred in some northern states, gradual abolition in others, and there were increased levels of manumission in the upper south, all in the face of formidable opposition from settlers. He regarded the ending of the slave trade, and the inclusion of the fugitive clause as a victory against slavery despite the cost, the price to be paid for 'luring' Georgia and South Carolina into the union. In the last analysis, argued Freehling, the founders placed the union before slavery. This argument found widespread support among historians, among whom Bernard Bailyn was pre-eminent, both before and after the bicentennial of the Revolution. In one of the most important collections of essays ushered in by the bicentennial Bailyn exonerated the founders of the Republic 'for having tolerated and perpetuated a society that rested on slavery'. To assume that they could have done anything more was 'to expect them to have been able to transcend altogether the limitations of their own age'.[86]

When Bailyn included this essay in his 1990 collection *Faces of the Revolution*, he cut two telling phrases.[87] The statement that to pursue the subject of slavery further would have been 'to allow the Revolution to slide off into fanaticism' which had appeared in the original, was dropped, as was a quotation from Freehling that the impact of the Revolution on slavery was to reduce it to 'a crippled, restricted and peculiar institution'. In both versions of the essay Bailyn maintained that while most of the Revolutionary leaders 'hated slavery', 'they valued the preservation of the Union more'.[88] In his 1990 study *The Road to Disunion,* Freehling reiterated his position on the extension of the slave trade. 'I believe', he wrote, that 'Carolinians meant their ultimatum' and that the majority of convention delegates believed them, dismissing an alternative view advanced by Finkelman, somewhat bafflingly, as 'too cynical'. However, he discarded the term 'antislavery' which he admitted he had used 'too loosely' in 1972 leading to widespread misunderstanding.[89] Still expressing disquiet at the use of his conclusions, Freehling further shifted his position on slavery and the founders in a subsequent collection of essays, *The Reintegration of American History* (1994). In the essay 'The Founding Fathers, Conditional Antislavery, and the Nonradicalism of the American Revolution', he maintained that rather than the path of antislavery

> The Founding Fathers instead set us on our nonrevolutionary social history. Despite their dismay at slavery ... they both timidly reformed and established towering bulwarks against reform, not least because many of them preferred a monoracial America.[90]

Unlike Freehling, William Wiecek, Professor of Law and History at Syracuse University, gave the Constitution a proslavery character. In *The Sources of Antislavery Constitutionalism in America, 1760–1848* (1977), Wiecek identified ten clauses that 'directly or indirectly accommodated the peculiar institution' and characterized the Constitution as embodying 'a mediation of sectional differences that were based chiefly on slavery'.[91] Though the 'deep South bloc', made up of South Carolina and Georgia delegates, was a minority at Philadelphia, 'slavery was more clearly adopted and explicitly established under the Constitution than it had been under the Articles'.[92] Wiecek described the compromise over the inclusion of slaves for purposes of apportioning representation in the lower house – which early in the Convention nearly destroyed the prospect of a new constitution – as 'carefully wrought'. Even so, it was the 'second major and essential compromise' of the Convention, the slave trade compromise, the one which attracted most adverse comment during the ratification process, which 'demonstrated that, for the framers, the highest good was the national union. For this, they sacrificed all other considerations, including the well-being of black Americans'.[93] Indeed, Wiecek comments that the members of the Convention appeared to be indulging the slaveholders.[94] As debate continued to smoulder among historians over what were the aims of the framers concerning slavery, Wiecek claimed

> three things [might] be said with assurance about the framers' intent. First, the Philadelphia Convention knowingly and deliberately inserted into the Constitution several provisions, distributed among ten clauses, that were intended to enhance the internal security of slavery in the states and to protect two of its extrajurisdictional effects (fugitive slaves and the slave trade). Second, despite somewhat vague and tepid antislavery sentiments of many of the delegates from the states above North Carolina, these proslavery provisions were inserted due to the determination and bluff of the deep-South regional bloc, supported by pleas for compromise from Connecticut and Virginia delegates. Third, and most importantly, the delegates did not intend to disturb the federal consensus. Both Federalist and Antifederalist delegates ... emphasized their dedication to the consensus.[95]

Like Gouverneur Morris in 1787, Wiecek concluded that the compromises of the Constitution attempted 'to blend incompatible things' and, while the consequences of this mismatch could be postponed in the short term, they could not be avoided indefinitely. Thus 'the framers passed on to posterity a document embodying open-ended possibilities, leaving it to them to work out a resolution of new problems as they came up', a line of reasoning taken up by some historians at the time of the bicentennial of the Constitution.[96] By 1988 Wiecek had moved from designating the compromises as attempts 'to blend incompatible things', to aligning slavery with progress: 'In 1787 slavery was wholly compatible with the American constitutional order; indeed was an essential element of it.' Gone also in 1988 was his perception of 'the framers' intent', recharacterized as 'a misleading phrase': 'There were numerous framers and varying intents.'[97] Wiecek also criticized Farrand's interpretation of 'the great dispute' as the struggle between large and small states over representation as 'fundamentally out of focus'.[98] Wiecek did not commit himself on the hypothesis advanced by Lynd that the Confederation Congress and the Constitutional Convention may have coordinated their efforts in resolving the 'slave questions then before the nascent nation' but neither did he dismiss it.[99] He found Freehling's judgement on the Constitution 'a generous estimate' and a valid one, which was not entirely consistent with his following comment, that 'it should not obscure the fact that the framers' generation embedded slavery so firmly in the constitutional order that it required nothing less than a revolution in attitudes followed by the slaughter of some six hundred thousand Americans, to eradicate it'.[100]

Paul Finkelman agreed with Wiecek about the proslavery character of the Constitution. In *Slavery and the Founders* (1996), a collection of previously published and revised essays, Finkelman argued that 'slavery was a central issue of the American founding' (though not *the* central issue that Lynd had made it), and that the Garrisonians 'were correct in their analysis of the Constitution as a slaveholders' compact'.[101] He identified five propositions in the Constitution which dealt directly with slavery and a further seven 'that indirectly guarded slavery'. Other clauses (he lists six), which though not initially relating to slavery, were subsequently invoked by the courts or Congress to protect the institution of slavery. While these latter should not be employed to illustrate the proslavery nature of the Constitution they do 'illustrate the way the Constitution set a proslavery tone, which enabled Congress and the courts to interpret seemingly neutral clauses in favor of slavery'. They also challenged Freehling's argument that the impact of the framers should be seen not in terms of what changed in the late eighteenth century but how the Revolutionary experience influenced antebellum history.[102] David Brion Davis thought the short run perspective was preferable.[103]

Finkelman also rejected Freehling's claim that the slave trade and fugitive slave clauses were adopted 'to lure Georgia and South Carolina into the Union'.[104] In his view, the delegates from the Deep South did not need to be lured into the Union: they were already deeply committed to the Constitution by the time the debate occurred and had already won major concessions on the three-fifths clause and the prohibition on taxing exports. These were permanent features of the Constitution, unlike the slave trade provisions, which would lapse in twenty years. Few states would have risked going it alone over the temporary right of importing slaves, a prospect made even more unlikely because at the time none was actively importing slaves from Africa, a fact that undermined the argument advanced by Earl Maltz that giving Congress the authority to ban imports of new slaves would have been detrimental to their economies. Maltz had concluded that 'even a delayed grant of authority ... must be considered anti-slavery and nationalistic', but, as Finkelman pointed out, the slave trade clause was a specific exception to the general power given Congress to regulate commerce. Moreover, the fugitive slave clause was 'added at the last possible moment, without any serious debate or discussion ... a boon to the South without any quid pro quo for the North'.[105] Like Wiecek, Finkelman also concludes with a lament for the dead of the Civil War. 'Only after a civil war of unparalleled bloodshed,' he wrote, 'and the adoption of three constitutional amendments could the Union be made more perfect, by finally expunging slavery from the Constitution.'[106]

Unlike Wiecek and Finkelman who saw efforts to undermine slavery as weak, timid and ineffectual, Gary Nash regarded them as formidable. Not for the first time he challenged the position taken by Bailyn and others, that to have sought more was unrealistic.[107] Originally a series of lectures given in honour of Merrill Jensen at the University of Wisconsin in 1988, Gary Nash's *Race and Revolution* (1990) is a short, important and impassioned work that not only challenges the traditional line of argument whereby the moral imperatives of antislavery were sacrificed to accommodate the greater needs of the union, but blamed the North for this state of affairs rather than the intransigence of South Carolina and Georgia. Also, Nash sought 'to show how economic and cultural factors intertwined in what was not a judicious decision by the leaders of the new American nation but their most tragic failure'.[108] More than other historians Nash stressed not only the growth of 'the antislavery impulse' during the revolutionary era and for some years after, a development he claimed that nineteenth- and early twentieth-century historians 'from Abiel Holmes and John Gorham Palfrey in the antebellum period to postbellum historians such as Hermann von Holst, George Bancroft, Henry Adams, John Fiske, and Woodrow Wilson' had ignored.[109] Nash identified five 'interlocking factors' that made the revolutionary decades 'the opportune time for abolishing slavery'.

> First, it was the era when the sentiment for ridding American society of the peculiar institution was strongest. Second, it was the moment when the most resistant part of the new nation, the lower South, was most precariously situated and thus manifestly ill-prepared to break away from the rest of the states. Third, it was a period when the system of thought called environmentalism, was in full sway, suggesting that the degraded condition of slaves was a matter of social conditioning, not innate inferiority. Fourth, it was a time when the opening of the vast trans-Appalachian West provided the wherewithal for a compensated emancipation. Lastly, it was the era when the use of this western domain as an instrument for binding the nation together had moved to the forefront of the public mind and when the existence of this vast unsettled territory as part of a national domain provided an area where the free slaves could be colonized if they were not to be permitted to remain in the settled parts of the country.[110]

Central to Nash's study was 'the natural rights tradition of the revolution', self evident in the Declaration of Independence, in revolutionary pamphlets and expounded initially by Bernard Bailyn in *The Ideological Origins of the American Revolution* (1967). Nash refuted Donald Robinson's assertion that no leading politician was seriously engaged with the issue between 1765 and 1780. Antislavery sentiment was strong in New England in the 1770s but was also present in the Chesapeake where it had links to evangelicalism.[111] But, if antislavery sentiment was so strong, why were there compromises over slavery at the Constitutional Convention in 1787 and 'again in the last decade of the eighteenth century'?[112] Nash argued that historians have never considered 'that a national plan for abolishing slavery might have been an integrating rather than a divisive mechanism, helping to create a genuinely national society'.[113] As for South Carolina's and Georgia's threat to leave the union, it had a hollow ring. With the Spanish in Florida and the powerful Creek confederacy at their back, 'no states were more in need of the military power of a federal government in the late 1780s'.[114] Nash tied the apparent unwillingness of historians to question whether South Carolina and Georgia would pull out of the union to the perception of northern-educated and northern-based historians who for more than a century, believed 'that slavery was a southern problem rather than a national problem'.

> In effect northern gradual-abolition laws have gotten the North off the hook ... Northern leaders – political, academic, and clerical – consistently ducked the issue that the Revolutionary leaders had insisted must be solved if the nation was to be united ... Slavery would continue to grow in the South and the problem of slavery would continue to require a national solution.

When it came, it brought five times the American casualty rate of the Second World War.[115]

With the exception of Finkelman's and Maltz's work, studies of slavery and the Constitution, for the most part legalistic and historiographical, gave way in the 1990s to broader works on the American Revolution in which slavery was one issue among others, albeit an important one, or to studies of Antebellum America in which the Constitution served as a prelude to later developments.[116] In *Original Meanings: Politics and Ideas in the Making of the Constitution* (1997) which built on much of his earlier work, Rakove wryly observed that it was hardly surprising that 'compromise' was such a 'staple theme' of most narrative accounts of the Federal Convention since 'in the end, the framers granted concessions to every interest that had a voice'.[117] What was sacrificed, he recognized (like Hildreth) was a moral principle 'to attain a tangible political end'. It was the second compromise on representation, however, that Rakove saw as ultimately the more costly. He shifted attention to the compromise awarding parity of representation to states in the Senate as the more significant of the two compromises over representation.[118] By the time Don Fehrenbacher's *The Slaveholding Republic* was posthumously published in 2001, the issue of slavery's importance at the Convention had to some extent receded. When matters 'touching slavery' arose in the Continental Congress and the Confederation Congress, they 'had been incidental or ancillary to some matter or purpose generally considered of greater immediate importance'. The same was true of the Federal Convention: 'Most delegates agreed they had come for the primary purpose of strengthening the national government by adding to its list of specific *power*s and by investing it with the *power* to govern effectively.'[119]

Original intent

In welcoming the new opportunities offered by the bicentennial to historians, political scientists and lawyers in 1987, Harry Scheiber, Professor of Law at the University of California, Berkeley, linked the acceleration of new constitutional and legal studies to 'the world of contemporary partisan politics and ideological confrontations'.[120] The latter arose with the expansion of constitutional liberties and rights since the 1950s, 'achieved in part through new legislation or executive orders and, of course, in very great part through judicial interpretation of the Fourteenth Amendment and its "incorporation" of the Bill of Rights'. Furthermore, 'the reaction to all this from the Right', he wrote, 'has also had its impact: Reagan-era neoconservatism has adopted a strident doctrine of "original intent" formulated in terms designed to wrap policies of minimalism for the civilian sector of government in the mantle of constitutional imperatives'.[121]

In the following year, Leonard Levy, 'the dean of American constitutional historians', launched a powerful attack on the theory of originalism in *Original Intent and the Framers' Constitution* (1988). Levy posed the question of 'whether a constitutional jurisprudence of original intent, as advocated by Chief Justice William H. Rehnquist, ex Judge Robert H. Bork, and former Attorney General Edwin Meese III' was 'realistic and viable'.[122] Levy related how at the very time when the *Encyclopedia of the American Constitution*, of which he was the editor-in-chief, and in which there was no entry on 'original intent' or 'originalism', closed its editorial doors in 1985

> Edwin Meese III, then attorney general of the United States, casti-gated the Supreme Court in a sensational speech before the American Bar Association for opinions that he disliked and he demanded that the Court abandon decisions based on its views of sound public policy. The Court, Meese declared, should give defer-ence to what the Constitution – its text and intention – may demand. In answer to his question, 'What then, should a constitu-tional jurisprudence actually be?' Meese asserted, 'It should be a Jurisprudence of Original Intention'.[123]

Levy did not challenge the belief that the Supreme Court was 'the official and final interpreter of the Constitution', but observed that recognition of the court's authority had never prevented disputes from raging about how the Constitution should be inter-preted. Moreover, 'the Court has professed to favor a constitutional jurisprudence of original intent since the first decade of its history', or 'more accurately, the Court has invoked the authority or intent of the Framers whenever it suited the Justices'.[124] Furthermore, during the 'formative period of our national history, the High Court, presidents, and Congress construed the Constitution without benefit of a record of the Convention's deliberations'; the best of which – Madison's *Notes* – was not published until fifty years after the Convention had met. What mattered to contemporaries, asserted Levy, was the text of the Constitution, 'construed in the light of conventional rules of interpretation, the ratification debates and other contem-porary expositions'.[125] That the 'founders of the national government and its early officers simply did not think in terms of the original intent at Philadelphia' was apparent in the debates over the Bank Bill in 1791 and Jay's Treaty in 1796.[126] Madison's preference on this issue for the state ratifying conventions was 'extraordinary', even 'inexplicable', in light of the intense partisanship that characterized them and the fact that their proceedings were 'so incompletely and poorly reported'.[127]

Whether the framers originally intended the Supreme Court to exercise the power of judicial review has been regarded as 'the crucial question of constitutional history'.[128] In line with his reading of the creation of the Constitution, Charles Beard asserted confidently in *The Supreme Court and the Constitution* (1912), that the framers must have intended to give the Court this power, that it was part of the system of checks and balances and intended to protect minorities against majorities. When his study was reissued in 1939, Beard claimed that he had 'settled' the great controversy. But if the framers intended the Court to exercise this power, 'why did they not explicitly provide for it?', asked Levy, dismissing the charge that the Supreme Court usurped this power.[129] Rakove took the view that 'the framers did intend judicial review to apply to the realm of national legislation, where it would help maintain boundaries among the branches of national government'. Problems were more likely to arise, however, 'along the unchartered borders where the powers of state and national government would overlap'.[130] Earlier commentators were equally divided and some of the most distinguished such as Edward S. Corwin oscillated between the two.

Levy not only found the historical record deficient and the conduct of the judges contradictory and ill-informed but the text of the Constitution was itself problematic. 'Ambiguity and vagueness crop up in the nonstructural sections ... ambiguous words permit different understandings, while vague words do not allow for much understanding' at all. The reverse was also true. There were parts where the text is 'utterly clear but because of its inappropriate specificity', it did not mean what it said.[131] Levy dismissed as arbitrary both Corwin's distinction between words relating to governing institutions and those relating to power and rights and Justice Frankfurter's distinction between a static Constitution and an evolutionary one. There was no suggestion in Madison's *Notes* that the framers designed either two types of clauses or 'strict definitions' that intended 'to freeze the past rather than allow it to serve as a guide for the future'.[132] Levy made his own position clear.

> When the Framers were ambiguous or vague, the likely reason is that they meant to be. They intended their ambiguity and vagueness to be pregnant with meaning for unborn generations, rather than be restricted to whatever meaning then existed ... Thus, when the Framers left a crucial term wide open, as in 'unreasonable search', 'probable cause', 'freedom of speech', 'excessive bail', and 'cruel and unusual punishment', they probably chose words deliberatively, leaving room for the widest possible interpretation.[133]

Levy defended the Supreme Court justices against the charges levied against them by the originalists: that they exceeded their authority, made decisions in accordance with their personal views, advanced social policies and undermined democracy. He concluded with a ringing attack on Meese, Rehnquist and Bork, reserving his particular distaste for the last of these.[134]

Published in the same year as Levy's work, Mark Tushnet's *Red, White and Blue* (1988) laid out, amongst other things, the problems of an originalist approach to the Constitution from the perspective of historical knowledge.[135] 'Originalist history requires definite answers,' wrote Tushnet, 'and clear ones (because it seeks to constrain judges) [but] where the originalist seeks certainty and clarity, the historian finds ambiguity.'[136] In pursuit of 'unambiguous historical facts', originalists 'embrace what are fundamentally flawed historiographic methods'. They

> presume that they can detach the meanings that the framers gave to the words they used from the entire complex of meanings that the framers gave to their political vocabulary as a whole and from the larger political, economic, and intellectual world in which they lived.[137]

If originalism was to penetrate the framers' meaning, argued Tushnet, 'its method must be hermeneutic' but that would not deliver the ends which the originalists sought. 'In imaginatively entering the world of the past, we not only reconstruct it', but have to use creative imagination 'to bridge the gaps between that world and ours', and this could not provide the certainty which the originalists seek.[138]

Rakove brought together the principal statements of the

'liberal' and 'conservative' positions, together with a number of essays on the history of the Constitution and legal theory in *Interpreting the Constitution* (1990).[139] He credited Attorney General Meese and Associate Justice William J. Brennan with bringing the issue into the public arena, giving it 'a new impetus and importance'. In his view 'many of the most acute assessments of originalism have come from those who reject it on both practical and normative grounds – that is, as both a problem of historical reconstruction and a theory of constitutional interpretation. Yet by doing so, they also suggest that the idea of a jurisprudence of original intention may have a durable life of its own'. Of the four essays in this collection that were explicitly historical in perspective, two examined 'the theories of legal interpretation that were available to framers, ratifiers and the first interpreters of the Constitution'.[140] H. Jefferson Powell, in exploring the 'cultural resources' available to Americans in the late eighteenth century who sought 'to conceptualize the unprecedented task of interpreting a written constitution', identified two contradictory traditions.[141] The first of these was British Protestantism, referred to also as 'British biblicalism', which, together with Enlightenment rationalism, were hostile to the 'interpretation' or 'construction' of written documents. According to Powell, either or both were part of 'the mental furniture of virtually all literate Americans in the half century between the Declaration of Independence and the presidency of John Quincy Adams'. There was also an opposing mental framework, that of 'the rich common law traditions of legal interpretation'.[142] Powell argued that the Constitution, 'a single normative document' was to be understood 'at least in part through the traditional processes of legal interpretation'. The framers 'did not discuss in detail how they intended their end product to be interpreted', but 'they clearly assumed that future interpreters would adhere to then-prevalent methods of statutory construction'.[143] The debate over ratification, however, revealed 'sharp disagreements over which interpretive approach was acceptable'.[144] The 1790s saw the intensification of conflict over 'substantive constitutional doctrine' as political parties took shape during the latter part of Washington's administration, but it was during the presidency of Washington's successor John Adams, that Jefferson and Madison 'formulated the theory of the Constitution, and of its proper interpretation' that held sway for the next quarter century and which was 'the precursor of modern intentionalism'.[145]

Charles A. Lofgren agreed with Powell on a number of points but disputed his interpretation of the historical evidence on constitutional interpretation after 1787.[146] Lofgren shifted attention away from the framers to the ratifiers. Although 'the originators rejected the use of framer intent', he wrote, this did not mean that they excluded the idea of 'intent' from constitutional interpretation. On the contrary, 'they were clearly hospitable to the use of original intent in the sense of ratifier intent, which is *the* original intent in a constitutional sense'.[147] Examining evidence from the 1796 House debate on the treaty-making power, Madison's contribution to it and his later views, Lofgren concluded that '*both* Federalists *and* Republicans accepted use of original intent in the form of ratifier intent', thus dismissing the views of Powell and challenging those of Rakove who queried why it should be assumed 'that those who *merely* ratified the Constitution grasped its meaning better than those who wrote it – or those who have since seen how it works in practice?' This was beside the point, argued Lofgren, since from an 'intentionalist' perspective, 'how the ratifiers understood the Constitution and what they expected from it, *defines* its meaning'.[148]

Hutson and Rakove addressed the issue of the sufficiency of historical knowledge about 'American constitutional and legal theory' when the Constitution was adopted, and later in the 1790s, 'when the first disputes over its interpretation led to the formation of the first political party system of Federalists and Democratic-Republicans'. Rakove observed that 'since all appeals to original intent [were] appeals to the records of history, a jurisprudence of original intent requires a high degree of confidence in the quality of our documentary sources and in the capacity of judges (and other concerned parties) to read them intelligently'.[149] Though Hutson accepted the reliability of Madison's notes on the Federal Convention, regarding them as 'far superior' to the records of state conventions, they were nevertheless incomplete.[150] Rakove's 'Mr Meese, Meet Mr

Madison' which appeared first in the *Atlantic Monthly* (December 1986) questioned whether a few quotations from *Federalist* No. 10 and No. 51 were sufficient to sustain appeals 'to his original intentions at the 1787 Convention or his original understandings'. Nor was it easy to reconcile Madison's view of the vices of republican government with his concern 'to prevent democratic majorities in the states from violating individual and minority rights'.[151]

A significant event in the historiography of the Constitution was the publication in 1996 of Rakove's *Original Meanings*. It was the first full-length interpretative study of the Constitution since Wood's *Creation of the American Republic* almost three decades earlier and, if it did not match that work in terms of its sheer scale and depth of scholarship, it was nonetheless a highly accomplished piece of work linking ideas and experience. *Original Meanings* built on Rakove's earlier work, in particular his 1979 monograph *The Beginnings of National Politics* in which he had paid tribute to the work of both Wood and J. R. Pole, and drew on his own myriad articles and essays which had appeared in leading journals and collections during the previous twenty years, especially 'From One Agenda to Another: The Condition of American Federalism, 1783–1787'.[152] *The Beginnings of National Politics* had received a hostile reception in the pages of the *William and Mary Quarterly* at the hands of James Ferguson for its rejection of the existence of clear party lines in the Continental Congress and its generally nonprogressive approach to its subject.[153] Unlike Jensen and his students, Rakove does not see the Federal Constitution as the outcome of a protracted struggle between conservatives and radicals in which the advocates of a more powerful central authority finally prevailed over the proponents of state sovereignty. To emphasize continuities, Rakove argued, served only to obscure the radical nature of the measures adopted in 1787. It also ignored the enormous intellectual leap that enabled the framers of the Constitution to link the familiar problems of federalism with more complex and open-ended questions about republican government in general.

> Under the Articles of Confederation the division of authority between Congress and the states was straightforward. The conduct

of the war and of foreign policy were the responsibility of Congress while internal affairs fell to the individual states. Problematic during the war when Congress lacked the power to match its responsibilities, this division of authority proved no more satisfactory once the military conflict was over.[154]

Original Meanings addressed 'the politics of constitution-making and the major problems of constitutional theory and institutional design that Americans had to consider when they replaced the Articles of Confederation with a true national government'; and sought to 'evaluate how much authority "original meaning" or "original intention" or "understanding" should enjoy in its ongoing interpretation.'

> The debate over this question can be reduced to two positions. The advocates of *originalism* argue that the meaning of the Constitution (or of its individual clauses) was fixed at the moment of its adoption, and that the task of interpretation is accordingly to ascertain that meaning and apply it to the issue at hand. The critics of *originalism* hold that it is no easy task to discover the original meaning of a clause, and that even if it were, a rigid adherence to the ideas of the framers and ratifiers would convert the Constitution into a brittle shell incapable of adaptation to all the changes that distinguish the present from the past.[155]

Rakove's interest in the latter originated not in the 1980s controversy over the 'jurisprudence of original intention' but rather in his earlier curiosity 'about the role that appeals to historical evidence played in certain controversies of the previous decade. Eschewing the temptation to 'resolve pressing problems of current controversy', Rakove set out 'to present a contextually grounded account of how the Constitution was drafted and ratified that will give those seeking to ascertain original meanings a more informed basis for considering what the entire process of its adoption entailed'.[156]

> Because originalism depends on our knowledge of the past, it raises further questions beyond the normative problem of deciding whether or not it provides a sound theory of Constitutional interpretation. How do we *know* what the constitution originally meant? Do we simply read pertinent snatches of debate from the Federal Convention and salient passages of *The Federalist*, or must we undertake a more complicated inquiry?[157]

Rakove inverted the nineteenth-century view, one still much in vogue during the following century, that national issues led to a recognition of the need for change.[158] It was 'the failings of state governments' that drove the movement for constitutional reform and provided 'the experimental evidence upon which the Convention drew' in seeking 'to fashion an improved model of republican government'. Rakove shifted attention to the activities of state legislatures, making much of complaints about the poor quality of domestic legislation and the 'contentious character' of state politics, both of which he maintained, 'suggested that the promise of the Revolution was somehow being betrayed'.[159] He emphasised the role of Madison who sought (and failed) to win approval for a veto on state laws. Madison was 'the crucial actor' and the Constitution could not be understood unless 'we make sense of Madison'. In Madison's view, neither state legislatures nor their constituents could be relied on to support 'the general interest of the Union, the true public good of their own communities, or the rights of minorities and individuals'. Private rights would be better secured in an extended republic with a multiplicity of interests rather than through the states.[160]

Rakove did not dismiss the allegation that the Constitution was the result of a series of actions that were 'illegal, even revolutionary, in character'. The framers did seize the main chance 'and then developed procedural and conceptual innovations to give their revolutionary act as much legitimacy as they could muster'. They also attempted 'to establish new standards of constitutional legality as well as constitutional legitimacy'. Adopting the precedent established by the ratification of the Massachusetts constitution, 'the resort to popular sovereignty in 1787–88 marked the point where the distinction between a constitution and ordinary law became the fundamental doctrine of American political thinking'. But if establishing the legitimacy of the Constitution was one thing, (the decision to accept or reject), what individual clauses meant, 'a second and far less tidy aspect of the struggle over ratification' related to what the Constitution meant.[161] Since 1789, Rakove concluded, the United States had two constitutions. There was 'the formal document adopted in 1787–88, with its amendments' and 'the working constitution comprising the body of precedents, habits, understandings, and

attitudes that shape how the federal system operates at any historical moment'. He defined the problem of originalism as the
relation between them. Though Powell and Lofgren had made
useful contributions to the debate over originalism, the story was
more complicated than either had supposed. Neither had probed
the political struggles of the 1790s to discern how they shaped
theories of constitutional interpretation.[162] 'The predictions that
both sides offered in 1787–88', wrote Rakove, 'were directed
toward the overriding question of ratification'. 'Their rival claims
sought not to create an evidentiary record ... to guide later interpreters but to advance the arguments most likely to influence the
course of ratification'.[163] Madison himself switched from initial
anxiety about the encroaching powers of the legislature to
support intervention in treaty powers, not because the original
intent of the Constitution was being betrayed but because it
suited the opposition tactics of the 1790s.

Rakove did not have the last word. By 1999 a consensus
seemed to be emerging among constitutional scholars and it was
time to drop 'the baggage of an old and unhelpful debate about
the relationship between original meaning and constitutional
interpretation', observed David Konig, but it was not yet over
among historians. What they still needed to produce was 'the
most accurate, thoroughly documented, and impeccable history'
possible. Konig posed the problem that if human nature was
always the same, how could the cycle of history be changed? But
on investigation he found that ideas about the immutability of
human nature were no more fixed than other ideas of the
period.[164] On the other hand, Gary McDowell, former speech
writer to Edwin Meese and subsequently director of the Institute
of United States Studies at the University of London for a period
of ten years, sought to buttress the claims of original intent in an
article published in 2000.[165] McDowell recovered a tradition
unrecognized by Powell that could also help to establish the
meaning of the Constitution divorced from 'the subjective intentions of those who were involved in its creation', that was
recourse to 'dictionaries or law dictionaries published at the time
of the writing and ratifying of the Constitution.' It was 'part of
an antecedent tradition, both legal and philosophic, that gave rise
to the Constitution itself'.

The belief that the language of the law means something, and that its meaning is intended to bind down those who would interpret it, [is] nothing less than the essence of American constitutionalism.[166]

Notes

1 Caroline Robbins, *The Eighteenth-Century Commonwealthman* (Cambridge, MA; 1959); Douglass G. Adair, '"Experience Must be Our Only Guide": History, Democratic Theory, and the United States Constitution' in Ray A. Billington (ed.), *The Reinterpretation of Early American History: Essays in Honor of John Edwin Pomfret* (San Marino, CA; 1966), pp. 29–48; Douglass G. Adair, '"That Politics May Be Reduced to a Science": David Hume, James Madison and the Tenth Federalist', *Huntington Library Quarterly*, 20 (1957), pp. 343–60; H. Trevor Colbourn, *The Lamp of Experience: Whig History and the Intellectual Origins of the American Revolution* (Chapel Hill, NC; 1965); Clinton Rossiter noted the relatively limited influence of Locke in the political thinking of the revolutionary generation. Clinton Rossiter, *Seedtime of the Republic: The Origin of the American Tradition of Political Liberty* (New York; 1953), p. 141.

2 Jack P. Greene (ed.), *The Reinterpretation of the American Revolution: 1763–1789* (New York; 1968), p. 40.

3 Michael P. Zuckert, *The Natural Rights Republic: Studies in the Foundation of the American Political Tradition* (Notre Dame, IN; 1996), p. 202.

4 Bernard Bailyn, *Pamphlets of the American Revolution, 1750–1776* (Cambridge, MA; 1965), *The Ideological Origins of the American Revolution* (Cambridge, MA; 1967, revised 1992) and *Origins of American Politics* (New York; 1968); Greene, *Reinterpretation of the American Revolution*, pp. 39–40, 55–6; John Howe, 'Gordon S. Wood and the Analysis of Political Culture in the American Revolutionary Era', *WMQ*, 3rd ser., 44 (1987), pp. 569–75, 569.

5 Gordon S. Wood, *The Creation of the American Republic, 1776–1787* (Chapel Hill, NC; 1969, 1998), pp. viii–ix, xvi; Ruth H. Bloch, 'The Constitution and Culture', *WMQ*, 3rd ser., 44 (1987), pp. 550–5, 550–1.

6 Wood, *Creation of the American Republic*, pp. xv–xvi.

7 In a landmark article that traced the emergence of the concept and placed it in the context of a broader historiography, see Robert E. Shalhope, 'Toward a Republican Synthesis: The Emergence of an Understanding of Republicanism in American Historiography', *WMQ*, 3rd ser., 29 (1972), pp. 49–80, 70. For a useful summary of republicanism which takes into account the historiography of the 1970s and 1980s, see Gordon S. Wood, 'Republicanism' in Leonard W. Levy and Kenneth L. Karst (eds), *Encyclopedia of the American Constitution*, 2nd edn (New York; 2000), V, pp. 2211–13. Wood's entry appeared first in the Supplement to the first edition of the *Encyclopedia* published in 1992.

8 Wood, *Creation of the American Republic*, pp. 47–8.

9 Wood, *Creation of the American Republic*, p. 53.

10 Wood, *Creation of the American Republic*, p. 68.

11 Wood, *Creation of the American Republic*, p. 73.
12 Wood, *Creation of the American Republic*, p. 513, and 'Rhetoric and Reality in the American Revolution', *WMQ*, 3rd ser., 23 (1966), pp. 3–32.
13 J. G. A. Pocock, *The Machiavellian Moment: Florentine Political Thought and the Atlantic Republican Tradition* (Princeton, NJ; 1975), pp. 467, 525, 528–9; for an earlier and helpful statement of English developments, see his 'Machiavelli, Harrington and English Political Ideologies in the Eighteenth Century', *WMQ*, 3rd ser., 22 (1965), pp. 549–83 and 'Virtue and Commerce in the Eighteenth Century', *Journal of Interdisciplinary History*, 3 (1972–73), pp. 119–34; Lance Banning, *The Jeffersonian Persuasion: Evolution of a Party Ideology* (Ithaca, NY and London; 1978), pp. 21–69.
14 Pocock, *Machiavellian Moment*, p. 513.
15 Pocock, *Machiavellian Moment*, pp. 521–7 and 'Virtue and Commerce', p. 120.
16 Pocock, *Machiavellian Moment*, pp. 521–7.
17 Pocock, *Machiavellian Moment*, pp. 528–9 and 'Virtue and Commerce', p. 131; Gerald Stourzh, *Alexander Hamilton and the Idea of Republican Government* (Stanford, CA; 1970).
18 Banning, *Jeffersonian Persuasion*, pp. 16–17.
19 Banning, *Jeffersonian Persuasion*, pp. 17–18.
20 Banning, *Jeffersonian Persuasion*, pp. 114–15, 124.
21 Banning, *Jeffersonian Persuasion*, pp. 127–8.
22 Banning, *Jeffersonian Persuasion*, pp. 128–9, 138–9.
23 Banning, *Jeffersonian Persuasion*, pp. 154, 159.
24 Banning, *Jeffersonian Persuasion*, pp. 162–78.
25 Drew R. McCoy, *The Elusive Republic: Political Economy in Jeffersonian America* (Chapel Hill, NC; 1980), pp. 10–11, 48–9.
26 McCoy, *Elusive Republic*, pp. 82–3.
27 McCoy, *Elusive Republic*, p. 121.
28 McCoy, *Elusive Republic*, pp. 106–9; for more extended treatments of Madison, see Lance Banning, *The Sacred Fire of Liberty: James Madison and the Founding of the Federal Republic* (Ithaca, NY; 1995) and Drew R. McCoy, *The Last of the Fathers: James Madison and the Republican Legacy* (New York; 1989).
29 Willi Paul Adams, *The First American Constitutions: Republican Ideology and the Making of the State Constitutions in the Revolutionary Era* (Chapel Hill, NC; 1980).
30 Joyce Appleby, 'Liberalism and the American Revolution', *NEQ*, 49 (1976), pp. 3–26; Joyce Appleby, *Capitalism and a New Social Order: The Republican Vision of the 1790s* (New York; 1984).
31 Joyce Appleby, 'The Social Origins of American Revolutionary Ideology', *Journal of American History* (hereafter *JAH*), 64 (1978), pp. 935–58, 937. This and other articles by Appleby have been published in *Liberalism and Republicanism in the Historical Imagination* (Cambridge, MA; 1992).
32 Joyce Appleby, *Economic Thought and Ideology in Seventeenth-Century England* (Princeton, NJ; 1978).
33 Appleby, 'Social Origins of American Revolutionary Ideology', p. 940.
34 Robert E. Shalhope, 'In Search of the Elusive Republic', *Reviews in American*

History, 19 (1991), pp. 468–73, 468.

35 Isaac Kramnick, *Bolingbroke and his Circle: The Politics of Nostalgia in the Age of Walpole* (Cambridge, MA; 1968).

36 Isaac Kramnick, 'Republican Revisionism Revisited', *AHR*, 87 (1982), pp. 629–64, 631; the article was included in Isaac Kramnick, *Republicanism and Bourgeois Radicalism: Political Ideology in Late Eighteenth-Century England and America* (Ithaca, NY; 1990); for a sweeping overview of the field ten years after his first landmark article, see Robert E. Shalhope, 'Republicanism and Early American Historiography', *WMQ*, 3rd ser., 39 (1982), pp. 334–54.

37 Kramnick, 'Republican Revisionism Revisited', p. 633.

38 Kramnick, 'Republican Revisionism Revisited', p. 658.

39 James T. Kloppenberg, 'The Virtues of Liberalism: Christianity, Republicanism, and Ethics in Early American Political Discourse', *JAH*, 74 (1987), pp. 9–33 and incorporated in *The Virtues of Liberalism* (New York; 1998), pp. 21–37; see also the same author's 'Intellectual History, Democracy and the Culture of Irony', in Melvin Stokes (ed.), *The State of U.S. History* (Oxford and New York; 2002), pp. 199–222, 111–12.

40 Kloppenberg, 'Virtue', in Jack P. Greene and J. R. Pole (eds), *A Companion to the American Revolution* (Oxford; 2000), pp. 696–700, 696.

41 Kloppenberg, 'Virtues of Liberalism', pp. 9–10, 11, 24 and 'Intellectual History, Democracy, and the Culture of Irony', p. 212; Edmund S. Morgan, *Inventing the People: The Rise of Popular Sovereignty in England and America* (New York; 1988); Pauline Maier, *American Scripture: Making the Declaration of Independence* (New York; 1998).

42 Kloppenberg, 'Virtues of Liberalism', pp. 26–7, 29.

43 Kloppenberg, 'Virtues of Liberalism', pp. 28, 29.

44 Kloppenberg, 'Virtues of Liberalism', pp. 30–1, 32.

45 Kloppenberg, 'Virtues of Liberalism', pp. 30–1.

46 Kloppenberg, 'Virtues of Liberalism', pp. 32–3.

47 Michael Meranze, 'Even the Dead Will Not Be Safe: An Ethics of Early American History', *WMQ*, 3rd ser., 50 (1993), pp. 367–78, 371.

48 Meranze, 'Even the Dead Will Not Be Safe', p. 371.

49 James M. Banner Jr, 'Review of *Beyond Confederation*', *WMQ*, 3rd ser., 45 (1988), pp. 355–60.

50 Gordon S. Wood, 'The Fundamentalists and the Constitution', *New York Review of Books*, 18 February 1988, vol. 35, pp. 33–40, 33–4, 40.

51 Peter S. Onuf, 'Reflections on the Founding: Constitutional Historiography in Bicentennial Perspective', *WMQ*, 3rd ser., 46 (1989), pp. 341–75, 342. Onuf's article provides an excellent overview of much of the work accomplished as a consequence of the bicentennial.

52 'Forum: *The Creation of the American Republic, 1776–1787*: A Symposium of Views and Reviews', *WMQ*, 3rd ser., 44 (1987), pp. 549–640. See Edward Countryman, 'Of Republicanism, Capitalism and the "American Mind"', pp. 556–62; Jackson Turner Main, 'An Agenda for Research on the Origins and Nature of the Constitution of 1787–1788', pp. 591–6 and Gary B. Nash, 'Also There at the Creation: Going Beyond Gordon S. Wood', pp. 602–11; for Wood's response, pp. 628–40.

53 Jack N. Rakove, 'Gordon S. Wood, the "Republican Synthesis", and the Path

Not Taken', *WMQ*, 3rd ser., 44 (1987), pp. 617–22, 621–2; *The Creation of the American Republic* was reprinted in 1998.

54 James H. Hutson, 'Riddles of the Federal Constitutional Convention', *WMQ*, 3rd ser., 44 (1987), pp. 411–23, 422; see also Gary Wills, *Explaining America: The Federalist* (Garden City, NY; 1981), p. 267.

55 Hutson, 'Riddles of the Federal Constitutional Convention', pp. 422–3.

56 Jack N. Rakove, 'The Great Compromise: Ideas, Interests, and the Politics of Constitution Making', *WMQ*, 3rd ser., 44 (1987), pp. 424–57, 424–5, fn. 2.

57 Rakove, 'The Great Compromise', p. 427.

58 Rakove, 'The Great Compromise', pp. 442–3.

59 Rakove, 'The Great Compromise', pp. 443–4.

60 Rakove, 'The Great Compromise', p. 445.

61 Rakove, 'The Great Compromise', pp. 453, 456.

62 Isaac Kramnick, 'The "Great National Discussion": The Discourse of Politics in 1787', *WMQ*, 3rd ser., 45 (1988), pp. 3–32, 4.

63 Kramnick, 'The "Great National Discussion"', p. 23.

64 Kramnick, 'The "Great National Discussion"', p. 25; Stanley Elkins and Eric McKitrick, 'The Founding Fathers: Young Men of the Revolution', *Political Science Quarterly* (hereafter *PSQ*), 76 (1961), pp. 181–216.

65 Kramnick, 'The "Great National Discussion"', pp. 30–1.

66 Paul Finkelman, 'Slavery and the Constitutional Convention: Making a Covenant with Death', in Beeman, Botein and Carter, II (eds), *Beyond Confederation*, pp. 188–225, reprinted in Paul Finkelman, *Slavery and the Founders: Race and Liberty in the Age of Jefferson* (Armonk, NY and London; 1996); William M. Wiecek, 'The Witch at the Christening: Slavery and the Constitution's Origins', in Leonard W. Levy and Dennis J. Mahoney (eds), *The Framing and Ratification of the Constitution* (New York and London; 1987), pp. 167–84, 164, 183–4.

67 James H. Hutson, 'The Creation of the Constitution: Scholarship at a Standstill', *Reviews in American History*, 12 (1984), pp. 463–77.

68 Finkelman, *Slavery and the Founders*, p. 18; Edward Countryman, *The American Revolution* (New York; 1985), p. 190.

69 Staughton Lynd, 'On Turner, Beard, and Slavery' in Staughton Lynd, *Class Conflict, Slavery, and the United States Constitution: Ten Essays* (Indianapolis, IN; 1967), pp. 135–52, 135–6, 137.

70 Paul L. Murphy, 'Time to Reclaim: The Current Challenge of American Constitutional History', *AHR*, 69 (1963), pp. 64–79, 77–9.

71 Staughton Lynd, 'The Abolitionist Critique of the Constitution' in Lynd, *Class Conflict, Slavery, and the United States Constitution*, pp. 153–83, 158–62, 162–7.

72 Lynd, 'The Abolitionist Critique of the Constitution', pp. 169, 173–4.

73 Lynd, 'The Abolitionist Critique of the Constitution', pp. 179, 180–3.

74 Staughton Lynd, 'The Compromise of 1787', in Lynd, *Class Conflict, Slavery and the United States Constitution*, pp. 185–213, 185; originally published in *PSQ*, 81 (1966), pp. 225–50; on the lack of interest among historians in the Ordinance of 1787, see Paul Finkelman, 'Slavery and the Northwest Ordinance: A Study in Ambiguity', *Journal of the Early Republic* (hereafter *JER*), 6 (1986), pp. 343–70, 344, fn. 2.

75 Lynd, 'The Compromise of 1787', p. 189.
76 Lynd, 'The Compromise of 1787', pp. 199–200.
77 Lynd, 'The Compromise of 1787', pp. 200, 202–4.
78 Lynd, 'The Compromise of 1787', p. 210.
79 Lynd, 'The Compromise of 1787', p. 210.
80 Lynd, 'The Compromise of 1787', pp. 212–13.
81 H. James Henderson, *Party Politics in the Continental Congress* (New York; 1974), p. 418; Peter S. Onuf, *The Origins of the Federal Republic: Jurisdictional Controversies in the United States, 1775–1787* (Philadelphia; PA 1983), p. 172.
82 Howard A. Ohline, 'Republicanism and Slavery: Origins of the Three-Fifth Clause in the United States Constitution', *WMQ*, 3rd ser., 28 (1971), pp. 563–84, 566–7.
83 Hutson, 'Riddles of the Federal Constitutional Convention', pp. 416–18; Paul Finkelman, 'Slavery and the Northwest Ordinance' pp. 343–70, fn. 23, 354, revised in Finkelman, *Slavery and the Founders*, pp. 34–56, fn. 17, fn. 18, 180, fn. 21, 181; Don E. Fehrenbacher, 'Slavery, the Framers, and the Living Constitution', in Robert A. Goldwin and Art Kaufman (eds), *Slavery and its Consequences: The Constitution, Equality and Race* (Washington, DC; 1988), pp. 1–23, 20–1.
84 Wood, *Creation of the American Republic*, p. 626.
85 William W. Freehling, 'The Founding Fathers and Slavery', *AHR*, 77 (1972), pp. 81–93.
86 For Bailyn's acknowledgement of his debt to Freehling, see Bernard Bailyn, 'The Central Themes of the American Revolution: An Interpretation', in Stephen G. Kurtz and James H. Hutson (eds), *Essays on the American Revolution* (Chapel Hill, NC; 1973), pp. 3–31, 31, fn. 6.
87 Bernard Bailyn, *Faces of the Revolution: Personalities and Themes in the Struggle for American Independence* (New York; 1990), pp. 200–24, 221–4.
88 Bailyn, 'The Central Themes of the Revolution', pp. 3–31.
89 William W. Freehling, *The Road to Disunion,* vol. 1, *Secessionists at Bay 1776–1854* (New York and Oxford; 1990), pp. 122, 583, fn. 2; Finkelman, 'Making a Covenant with Death'.
90 William W. Freehling, 'The Founding Fathers, Conditional Antislavery, and the Nonradicalism of the American Revolution', in William W. Freehling, *The Reintegration of American History: Slavery and the Civil War* (New York and Oxford; 1994), pp. 12–33, 12–13.
91 William M. Wiecek, *The Sources of Antislavery Constitutionalism in America, 1760–1848* (Ithaca, NY, and London; 1977), pp. 62, 64.
92 Wiecek, *Sources of Antislavery Constitutionalism*, pp. 64–5.
93 Wiecek, *Sources of Antislavery Constitutionalism*, pp. 69, 73.
94 Wiecek, *Sources of Antislavery Constitutionalism*, pp. 78–9.
95 Wiecek, *Sources of Antislavery Constitutionalism*, pp. 81–2.
96 Wiecek, *Sources of Antislavery Constitutionalism*, p. 83; Herman Belz, 'Liberty and Equality for Whom? How to Think Inclusively about the Constitution and the Bill of Rights', *The History Teacher*, 25 (1992), pp. 263–77, 267.
97 William M. Wiecek, '"The Blessings of Liberty": Slavery in the American

Constitutional Order' in Goldwin and Kaufman, *Slavery and its Consequences*, pp. 23–44, 23–4, 28; David Brion Davis, *Slavery and Human Progress* (New York; 1985).

98 Wiecek, '"The Blessings of Liberty"', pp. 30–1.

99 Wiecek, '"The Blessings of Liberty"', pp. 33, 43, fn. 38.

100 Wiecek, '"The Blessings of Liberty"', p. 34.

101 Finkelman, *Slavery and the Founders*, pp. x, ix, 2, 171, fn. 19; Finkelman confirms his position in 'Garrison's Constitution: The Covenant with Death and How It Was Made', *Prologue* 32 (2000), pp. 231–45.

102 Finkelman, *Slavery and the Founders*, pp. 3–5; Freehling, 'The Founding Fathers and Slavery', p. 81.

103 David Brion Davis, *The Problem of Slavery in the Age of Revolution* (Ithaca, NY; 1975), p. 169.

104 On the latter, see 'Slavery and the Northwest Ordinance: A Study in Ambiguity', in Finkelman, *Slavery and the Founders*, pp. 34–56, 36.

105 Finkelman, *Slavery and the Founders*, pp. 28–9, 171, fn. 17; Earl M. Maltz, 'Slavery, Federalism, and the Structure of the Constitution', *American Journal of Legal History* (hereafter *AJLH*), 36 (1992), pp. 466–98, 469.

106 Finkelman, *Slavery and the Founders*, pp. 31, 33.

107 For Nash's comments on Bailyn's original essay 'The Central Themes of the American Revolution', pp. 3–31, 28, Bailyn's response to Nash's review and the latter's counter argument, see *WMQ*, 3rd ser., 31 (1974), pp. 311–14 and 32 (1975), pp. 182–5.

108 Gary B. Nash, *Race and Revolution* (Madison, WI; 1990), p. 6.

109 Nash, *Race and Revolution*, p. 3.

110 Nash, *Race and Revolution*, pp. 6–7.

111 Donald L. Robinson, *Slavery in the Structure of American Politics, 1765–1820* (New York; 1971), p. 55; Nash, *Race and Revolution*, pp. 8–11, 14; Winthrop D. Jordan, *White Over Black: American Attitudes Toward the Negro, 1550–1812* (Chapel Hill, NC; 1968), pp. 10, 291, 297–8; David B. Davis, *The Problem of Slavery in Western Culture* (Ithaca, NY; 1966), part III.

112 Nash, *Race and Revolution*, p. 25

113 Nash, *Race and Revolution*, pp. 25–6.

114 Nash, *Race and Revolution*, p. 27.

115 Nash, *Race and Revolution*, pp. 28–30, 50.

116 Finkelman, *Slavery and the Founders*; Earl M. Maltz, 'The Idea of the Proslavery Constitution', *Journal of the Early Republic* (hereafter *JER*), 17 (1997), pp. 37–59; Jack N. Rakove, *Original Meanings: Politics and Ideas in the Making of the Constitution* (New York; 1996); John Ferling, *A Leap in the Dark: The Struggle to Create the American Republic* (New York; 2003); Don E. Fehrenbacher, *The Slaveholding Republic: An Account of the United States Government's Relations to Slavery* (New York; 2001).

117 Rakove, *Original Meanings*, p. 57.

118 Rakove, *Original Meanings*, pp. 58, 92–3.

119 Fehrenbacher, *Slaveholding Republic*, pp. 27–8, 29, 36–7.

120 Harry N. Scheiber, 'Introduction: The Bicentennial and the Rediscovery of American History', *JAH*, 74 (1987), pp. 667–74, 667–8, 670.

121 Scheiber, 'Introduction', pp. 670, 671; Michael Kammen, *A Machine that*

Would Go of Itself: The Constitution in American Culture (New York; 1986), pp. 324–31.

122 Leonard W. Levy, *Original Intent and the Framers' Constitution* (New York; 1988), pp. xvi.

123 Levy, *Original Intent*, p. xii; an entry on 'Original Intent' by Jack N. Rakove was included in the 1992 Supplement to the first edition of the *Encyclopedia* and republished without alteration in the second edition. Leonard W. Levy, Kenneth L. Karst and John G. West Jr, 'Preface' (1992) and Jack N. Rakove, 'Original Intent' in Levy and Karst (eds), *Encyclopedia of the American Constitution*, 2nd edn, 1, pp. xiii–xiv; 4, pp. 1857–9; according to Rakove, '"Original Intent" is a shorthand term for both a familiar topic of Constitutional History and a problematic theory of Constitutional Interpretation', p. 1857.

124 Levy, *Original Intent*, pp. ix–x.

125 Levy, *Original Intent*, pp. 1–2.

126 Levy, *Original Intent*, pp. 6–7, 11–12.

127 Levy, *Original Intent*, p. 14.

128 Levy, *Original Intent*, pp. 89–99; Rakove, *Original Meanings*, p. 175.

129 Levy, *Original Intent*, pp. 100–1.

130 Rakove, *Original Meanings*, pp. 175–6.

131 Levy, *Original Intent*, pp. 334–5, 336.

132 Levy, *Original Intent*, pp. 343–5, 347–8; Corwin's position was set out in Edward S. Corwin, 'Judicial Review in Action', *University of Pennsylvania Law Review*, 124 (1926), pp. 659–60.

133 Levy, *Original Intent*, p. 349.

134 Levy, *Original Intent*, pp. 350–87.

135 Mark Tushnet, *Red, White and Blue: A Critical Analysis of Constitutional Law* (Cambridge, MA and London; 1988), pp. 18–45.

136 Tushnet, *Red, White and Blue*, pp. 36–7.

137 Tushnet, *Red, White and Blue*, pp. 38–9.

138 Tushnet, *Red, White and Blue*, p. 41.

139 Jack N. Rakove (ed.), *Interpreting the Constitution: The Debate over Original Intent* (Boston, MA; 1990), p. 3.

140 Rakove, *Interpreting the Constitution*, Introduction, pp. 5–6; Edwin Meese III, 'Interpreting the Constitution', originally a speech to the American Bar Association in July 1985, reprinted from *USA Today Magazine*, October 1986 and William J. Brennan Jr, 'The Constitution of the United States: Contemporary Ratification', first presented as a speech to the Text and Teaching Symposium at Georgetown University, 12 October 1985, in Rakove, *Interpreting the Constitution*, pp. 13–21, 23–34.

141 H. Jefferson Powell, 'The Original Understanding of Original Intent' in Rakove, *Interpreting the Constitution*, pp. 53–115, 54.

142 Powell, 'The Original Understanding', p. 57–8.

143 Powell, 'The Original Understanding', pp. 62–3.

144 Powell, 'The Original Understanding', p. 68.

145 Powell, 'The Original Understanding', p. 75.

146 Charles A. Lofgren, 'The Original Understanding of Original Intent?', in Rakove, *Interpreting the Constitution*, pp. 117–50.

147 Lofgren, 'The Original Understanding of Original Intent?', p. 118.

148 Lofgren, 'The Original Understanding of Original Intent?', pp. 134, 142–3; Jack Rakove, 'Mr Meese, Meet Mr Madison', *The Atlantic Monthly*, 258 (1986), p. 98, also in Rakove, *Interpreting the Constitution*, pp. 179–94.

149 Rakove, *Interpreting the Constitution*, p. 7.

150 James H. Hutson, 'The Creation of the Constitution: The Integrity of the Documentary Record' was originally published in the *Texas Law Review*, 5, p. 65.

151 Rakove, *Interpreting the Constitution*, p. 7.

152 Wood, *Creation of the American Republic*; J. R. Pole, *Political Representation in England and the Origins of the American Republic* (New York; 1966); Jack N. Rakove, *The Beginnings of National Politics: An Interpretive History of the Continental Congress* (New York; 1979); Jack N. Rakove, 'From One Agenda to Another: The Condition of American Federalism, 1783–1787' in Jack P. Greene (ed.), *The American Revolution: Its Character and Limits* (New York; 1987), pp. 80–103; Jack N. Rakove, 'Solving a Constitutional Puzzle: The Treaty Making Clause as a Case Study', in *Perspectives in American History, New Series*, 1 (1984), pp. 233–81.

153 E. James Ferguson, review of *The Beginnings of National Politics*, WMQ, 3rd ser., 38 (1981), p. 125; John Murrin perceived a widening gap to have opened up between the ideological and neo-progressive schools. 'Each either attacks, or, perhaps more devastatingly, simply ignores the contributions of the other'. John M. Murrin, 'The Great Inversion, or Court Versus Country', in J. G. A. Pocock (ed.), *Three British Revolutions: 1641, 1688, 1776*, (Princeton, NJ; 1980), pp. 368–453; Rakove, 'From One Agenda to Another', p. 94.

154 Rakove, 'From One Agenda to Another', pp. 82–4.

155 Rakove, *Original Meanings*, p. xiii.

156 Rakove, *Original Meanings*, pp. xiii–xvi.

157 Rakove, *Original Meanings*, pp. xiii–xiv.

158 For a collection of essays which seeks to put Shays and all parties to the conflict 'within the confines of their own world' rather than the anachronistic terms in which they have been usually portrayed, see Robert A. Gross (ed.), *In Debt to Shays: The Bicentennial of an Agrarian Rebellion* (Charlottesville, VA, and London; 1993), p. 7.

159 Rakove, *Original Meanings*, pp. 29–30.

160 Rakove, *Original Meanings*, pp. 36–7.

161 Rakove, *Original Meanings*, pp. 128–9, 130.

162 Rakove, *Original Meanings*, pp. 339–42.

163 Rakove, *Original Meanings*, p. 343.

164 David Thomas Konig, 'Constitutional Contexts: The Theory of History and the Process of Constitutional Change in Revolutionary America', in Sandra F. VanBurkleo, Kermit Hall and Robert J. Kczorowiski (eds), *Constitutionalism and American Culture: Writing the New Constitutional History* (Lawrence, KN; 2002), pp. 3–28; on the irrelevance of orginalism to judicial interpretation, see Eric J. Segall, 'A Century Lost: The End of the Originalism Debate', *Constitutional Commentary*, 15 (1998), pp. 411–39.

165 Gary L. McDowell, 'The Politics of Meaning: Law Dictionaries and the Liberal Tradition of Interpretation', *AJLH*, 44 (2000), pp. 257–83.

166 McDowell, 'The Politics of Meaning', pp. 282–3.

5

African Americans: resistance and revolution

In a symposium on the future of early American history Michael Meranze asked how Americans should think about 'the place of slavery in the American Revolution'. It was a legitimate question even in the 1990s because the subject could still be effectively marginalized. In particular, Meranze was critical of Gordon Wood for failing to take into account two decades of scholarship on slavery in his important 1992 study *The Radicalism of the American Revolution*. Part of a growing literature on the consequences of the Revolution, Wood's study focuses exclusively on winners thus ignoring the roles and responses of the enslaved. The impact of the Revolution on the institution of slavery was limited to consideration of the rise of antislavery and premised on the assumption that in a slaveholding society, the concept of 'freedom' became more sharply defined and meaningful when contrasted with the state of 'unfreedom'.[1] At the time of the Revolution, African Americans, nearly all of them slaves, numbered approximately twenty per cent of the population, a larger proportion than at any time before or since.[2] And as Philip Morgan observed in his monumental study *Slave Counterpoint* (1998) 'slavery was no curious abnormality, no aberration, no marginal feature of early America'. Most eighteenth-century Americans found slavery neither embarrassing nor evil; it was quite simply 'a fundamental, acceptable, thoroughly American institution'.[3] Even so, the subject *was* conspicuous by its absence in the early histories of the American Revolution, histories written mostly by northerners for whom the contradiction between liberty and slavery was underscored in the last quarter of the eighteenth century and first decade of the nineteenth century by the progress of gradual emancipation in the former middle colonies, of abolition in New England and the termination of the African slave trade. African Americans proved no more visible to later scholars of early America who, according to one trenchant critic, 'floated for generations on a placid mainstream oriented geographically toward the northeast, ethnically toward the English, and socially toward the colonial elites'.[4] When in 1847 Lorenzo Sabine inadvertently stirred up the issue of southern support for the revolutionary war by questioning the impact of large numbers of slaves in their midst, southern literary figures took up the challenge. At a time when southerners were asserting that slavery was 'the cornerstone of their civilization and contributed to the stability and prosperity of the entire country', they not only insisted on the absolute devotion of their forebears to the patriot cause but that of their slaves too.[5] In the 1840s and 1850s, anything less would have been subversive of the institution of slavery.

The denial of legitimacy to African American history continued well into the second half of the twentieth century until the struggle for equality in American society, which could no longer be ignored, stimulated interest in, and demands for, a useable African American past, while the methodologies and techniques of the new social history were extending the potential for its investigation.[6] But the new interest in black history that developed in the second half of the 1950s, the 1960s and early 1970s, was confined largely to the antebellum period for which evidence was more readily accessible. Neglecting the formative period of American history, it produced an image of slavery as static and unchanging. More often than not the new historiography depicted enslaved people as passive; acted upon rather than as actors. When, during the years of the civil rights struggle, historians did venture back into the seventeenth and eighteenth centuries, they were likely to address issues of 'race' and to come from and speak to 'mainstream white culture'. They were 'less concerned with blacks themselves than with white attitudes and responses toward blacks'. Nevertheless two volumes broke new ground. In *The Problem of Slavery in Western Culture* (1966), David Brion Davis (1927–) not only located American slavery in a historical and global context, but, following Charles Verlinden, made explicable how slavery jumped the Atlantic. This was followed two years later by Winthrop Jordan's *White Over Black,* which enjoyed both academic and commercial success. Published in 1968, described by Senator Eugene McCarthy as 'the hard year' when civil disorder reached a climax and sectors of American society threatened to implode, *White Over Black* departed from the standard explanation of 'race' prejudice by divorcing it from the debased status of the slave. In arguing that prejudice was anterior to African enslavement and a factor contributing to enslavement, not only did Jordan offer a partial explanation of why race prejudice was proving so difficult to eradicate in contemporary America but also marked out the limits of the American Revolution.[7] What finally brought African Americans into view in the colonial and revolutionary era was not so much the revitalization of early American history which preceded the rise of the new social history, but the sense of black entitlement.[8] By the 1970s, black history was both desirable and necessary in schools and universities across the nation. 'The field expanded, as it had come into being, in connection with efforts to protect the rights and to improve the lives of American blacks,' wrote John Hope Franklin, Emeritus Professor of History at Duke University. History was on their side. They had fought and died 'to eradicate racial and religious bigotry in the world' but the beneficiaries of their efforts tended to be 'the former adversaries of the United States, such as Germany and Japan'. 'Since history validated their claims, Afro-Americans felt that their history should be studied more intensely, written about more extensively, and taught more vigorously.'[9]

When the *American Historical Review* published Ira Berlin's landmark article 'Time, Space and the Evolution of Afro-American Society on British Mainland North America' in 1980, the contours of early African American history appeared to have been established. According to Berlin (1941–) the actions of black people during the American Revolution, the Civil War and the long years of bondage between these two cataclysmic events could be understood merely as a function of the dynamics of slavery or the possibilities of liberty, but must be viewed within the specific social circumstances and cultural traditions of black people.[10] Critical of the last generation of historians of slavery for ignoring the boundaries of historical inquiry – time and space – resulting in a static vision of slave culture, Berlin laid out the extent of diversity revealed in recent slave studies of the early American period by identifying three distinct slave systems: the plantation societies of the Chesapeake, the lowcountry and the non-plantation society of the northern colonies.

> Slavery took shape differently in each with important consequences for the growth of black culture and society. The development of these slave societies depended upon the nature of the slave trade and the demographic configurations of blacks and whites as well as upon the diverse character of colonial economy.[11]

Reflecting in 1983 on the long-term failure of scholars to engage with 'the black experience and the seminal role of slavery during the formative period of the American nation', Ronald Hoffman professed his difficulty in explaining their exclusion. 'But one thing is clear,' he wrote. 'For too many years, historians were parties to the compromise of the founding fathers.'[12] Hence, how African Americans participated in the events of the Revolution, influenced its course and experienced its consequences were not the type of questions asked about the Revolution by historians for almost two hundred years.

Insofar as African Americans were discussed at all by the revolutionary generation of historians, it was as a consequence of their status as enslaved workers on southern plantations where they constituted a potential danger to the rest of the population. 'From their long habit of filling their country with foreign slaves', wrote Warren, Virginia, Maryland and the Carolinas 'were threatened with a host of domestic enemies'. Their numbers exceeded those of freemen on 'the sea coast of five of the most southern provinces', noted Ramsay.[13] The threat became a reality when the Virginia Governor, Lord Dunmore, issued a proclamation promising freedom to those slaves, servants and convicts who would join the King's forces in overthrowing the rebels. According to Ramsay, 'it was supposed that the proffer of freedom would detach them from their master's interest, and bind them by strong ties to support the royal standard'. But Dunmore made his move prematurely. Six months elapsed between the threat and its adoption by which time, wrote Ramsay, 'the negroes had in a great measure ceased to believe, and the inhabitants ceased to fear'. But whereas Ramsay implied that slaves calculated the odds and measured their response accordingly, Warren seems to have assumed that those who fled 'were decoyed away from their masters' by the governor's tactics. Despite the difficulties involved in reaching the British position, Ramsay gauged that several hundred people, black and white, joined Dunmore but hunger and disease on land and at sea ravaged their numbers. Ramsay referred to Dunmore's design 'of subduing Virginia by the cooperation of the negroes' as a failure and that 'the unhappy Africans' who had been part of it ' almost universally perished'. In comparison with Ramsay, Warren was far less dispassionate in her handling of these events, denouncing Dunmore for his 'inhumanity' in declaring 'freedom to the blacks', an action which she linked to his encouragement of southern Indians 'to rush from the wilderness, and make inroads on the frontiers'. Visited by pestilence and disease, Warren cast Dunmore's 'little fleet of fugitives and slaves' as 'the wretched victims of his folly and cruelty'.[14]

The danger in South Carolina was greater for the state endured the worst of the 'revolutionary convulsions'. Here again, Warren portrayed slaves as being 'enticed or stolen away' and 'every other species of property wasted in the general pillage'. A resident of Charleston, Ramsay also wrote about the extensive pillaging of the state by the British but there was more to it than that, for Ramsay believed that 'the mischievous effects of slavery' had facilitated 'the conquest of the country'. 'As the slaves had no interest at stake,' he wrote, 'the subjugation of the State was a matter of no consequence to them. Instead of aiding in its defence, they by a variety of means threw the weight of their little influence into the opposite scale.' Though disparaging the slaves, Ramsay recognized that they, too, had made a choice. He claimed that the British seized around 3,000 slaves but 25,000 were 'lost'.[15]

When George Bancroft addressed these same issues in the second half of the nineteenth century, their was little subtlety in his approach. Bancroft made much more of the pillaging of South Carolina by the British whose 'mad eagerness' for plunder, distracted them from the recruitment of slaves and the termination of the slave trade. But for this, the British might have done away with slavery. A cultural climate prevailed in which theories of social, economic and scientific racism and concepts of the dangerous classes moulded the images of southern slaves and northern workers. Bancroft demonized Dunmore for a policy calculated 'to oblige the rebels to disperse to take care of their families and property' in light of the threat facing them. He invested slaves with an animalism which fed on the tensions inherent in slave societies.

> The men to whose passions he [Dunmore] appealed were either criminals, bound to labour in expiation of their misdeeds, or barbarians, some of them freshly imported from Africa, with tropical passions seething in their veins, and frames rendered strong by abundant food and out of door toil; they formed the majority of the population on tide-water, and were distributed among the lonely plantations in clusters around the wives and children of their owners; so that danger lurked in every home.[16]

But Dunmore's cry did not rouse 'a passion for freedom' among the Africans. For slaves, argued Bancroft, 'bondage in Virginia was not a lower condition than their former one': 'they had no regrets for antient privileges'.[17]

The notion of black agency and assertions of black loyalty were kept alive by African American and radical writers, for the most part outside the mainstream of American historical writing. In two volumes compiled in the decade immediately before the Civil War, William C. Nell (1816–1874) emphasized the African American contribution to the Revolution while excluding those who cast their lot with the British.[18] In his substantial two-volume *History of the Negro Race in America from 1619 to 1880* (1883), George Washington Williams (1849–1891) elaborated the theme of black commitment to the American cause despite the reluctance of Congress and the states to recruit black soldiers and seamen. To demonstrate the contentious nature of the issue, Williams reproduced correspondence between Washington and other military officers. In his view, those slaves in Virginia who responded to Governor Dunmore's emancipation proclamation in November 1775 were badly misled, while those in South Carolina who fled to the British army acted out of frustration as the state resisted all calls to recruit slaves into its forces.[19] Nevertheless Williams had no illusions about what the Revolution meant for most of America's enslaved people. The impact was minimal.

> The colonists asked freedom for themselves and children, but forged chains for Negroes and their children. And while a few individual Negro slaves were made a present of their freedom at the close of the war, on account of their gallant service, hundreds of thousands of their brethren were still retained in bondage.[20]

William E. B. Du Bois (1868–1963), the first African American to be awarded a doctorate in history by Harvard University, was the author of *The Suppression of the African Slave-Trade to the United States of America, 1638–1870*, the first volume in a prestigious new series of historical monographs which began publication in 1896. A distinguished scholar and radical who spent much of his life outside the academic mainstream, Du Bois described Toussaint L'Ouverture, leader of the successful slave uprising in Saint Domingue, France's richest Caribbean colony, as a hero.[21] Lorenzo J. Greene's study *The Negro in Colonial New England* (1942), which set a new standard for local and regional studies, made explicit the character of the African American 'as an actor as well as someone acted upon, a doer on his own'.[22] Making use of pension records, Luther P. Jackson (1892–1950) explored the part played by black soldiers and seamen in Virginia as combatants in the Revolution in a detailed article appearing in the *Journal of Negro History* in 1942, one year after the United States joined the allies in the Second World War.[23] Jackson was in no doubt that black Virginians, free and enslaved, made their contribution to the American cause despite legislation barring their recruitment. Relatively few in number, they were recruited in their own right as well as substitutes (that is, replacing their masters) serving in non-segregated units. Like Williams, Jackson was inclined to dismiss those who gave their allegiance to the British.

> Since Dunmore's expedition failed dismally ... this whole event and other minor episodes lose historical interest when compared with the victory the Negro soldiers and seamen helped to achieve in the American cause.[24]

Marxist historian Herbert Aptheker (1915–) took the concept of black agency a stage further by looking beyond military service during the Revolution in his seminal study *American Negro Slave Revolts* (1943). Aptheker maintained that resistance to slavery in North America took many forms, both individual and collective, from 'laziness', 'thievishness', 'irresponsibility', assassination, arson, sabotage of tools and animals, self-injury, infanticide and flight as well as 'rebellion and conspiracy to rebel', but his broad definition of resistance and his emphasis on conspiracy and rebellion were of less interest to the post-war generation of historians working on antebellum slavery than it would be to the next generation of historians, often their students.[25]

Running away

Indicative of new directions in the study of early American slavery in the early 1970s was Gerald W. Mullin's *Flight and Rebellion* (1972). Critical of historians of the 1950s and 1960s who, failing to recognize key cultural changes in the colonial era, sustained 'the ahistorical treatment of antebellum slavery', Mullin, a student of Winthrop Jordan at Berkeley, refuted their assumption 'that slaves were unable to influence the total society in any important non-economic manner'. Thus, they neglected the slaves themselves.[26] In seeking to learn more about the dynamic character of slavery through the use of newspaper advertisements for fugitive slaves, though not the first historian to make use of this data, Mullin pioneered its systematic exploitation in the new computer age.[27] He identified newspaper advertisements as the kind of documents that Marc Bloch once described as 'witnesses in spite of themselves'. They were 'unconscious evidence', not intended for use by the historian, yet 'more appropriate than narrative sources for the study of a people who could not or were not inclined to write things down'.[28] The slaveholders who used them 'were neither explaining nor defending slavery, they simply – in sparse, graphic phrases – listed their runaway's most noticeable physical and psychological characteristics, while commenting on his origin, work, and use of English'.[29]

Influenced by the work of Orlando Patterson and Elsa Goveia on West Indian slavery, Mullin claimed that not only did slaves in eighteenth-century Virginia 'have a life of their own', but that for a time it 'was partially based on African values'.[30] He argued that the fugitive notices supported an interpretation of slave behaviour that linked types of slave resistance to stages in a process of acculturation and assimilation. Slaves responded to their bondage in different ways depending on their origins and place in the work hierarchy. In turn, this was dependent on knowledge of English which governed the rate and extent of acculturation. Mullin divided styles of rebelliousness into two types: inward and outward. As slaves acculturated 'they became outwardly rebellious and more difficult for whites to control'.

> The plantation slave's actions were typically short-range, direct attempts to deal immediately with his material environment: to fill his hunger, ease his fatigue, or to get revenge on an overseer or master ... The skilled slave who frequently worked on and off the plantation, was usually better off. He rebelled to ameliorate his situation, and occasionally, to reject it outright. His resistance, which was seldom violent and directed inward on himself or the plantation, was aimed toward such long-range and intangible goals as more freedom of movement and leisure time than he normally enjoyed. As a runaway passing as a free man, hired by townsmen who asked few questions about his former owner, he often achieved these objectives.[31]

Before the Revolution, whites were 'confident of their ability to control most types of rebellion'; they seldom viewed runaways as 'exceptionally dangerous'. What brought about radical change was Dunmore's November 1775 proclamation and Gabriel's insurrection in September 1800 'by introducing to whites the possibility of organized rebellion by armed Negroes'. For Mullin, Dunmore's proclamation was of less significance than Gabriel's insurrection: Dunmore's Black regiment Mullin claimed, 'was largely a creation of the planters' imagination and their newspaper press'. That slaves did not take greater advantage of the British invasion 'to escape or rise up' was because for the slaves 'the war and the Proclamation were premature'. By contrast

> In the last quarter of the century runaways changed their usual courses, instead of running south to work or visit they ran north to be free in areas where slavery was gradually outlawed. The notices also provide a provocative glimpse of a formidable and bold

runaway rarely seen in the years before the war ... they now displayed an openly militant nature where, previously 'artful' inconspicuousness had been the norm.[32]

Not until the end of the century did the most 'resourceful runaways' – the skilled artisans – 'become insurrectionists'.[33]

Despite criticisms of its conclusions and methodology, *Flight and Rebellion* opened the way for the further exploration of both the character of slavery in early America and its relationship to resistance. Peter Wood (1943–) sounded a note of caution observing that advertisements for fugitive slaves represented 'little more than the top of an ill-defined iceberg' for many runaways were never advertised. The British historian Kenneth Morgan questioned whether skilled slaves in Virginia were in fact distinguished by their superior ability to run away since Mullin did not indicate what proportion of the population as a whole they constituted. Nor was the distinctive pattern of behaviour among 'new negroes' and artisans found in Virginia replicated elsewhere. With four times as many advertised runaways but only half the number of slaves, at least until the end of the eighteenth century, Philip Morgan argued that fugitive slaves in South Carolina, 'the overwhelming majority' of whom 'travelled to plantations and tried to maintain contact with family and friends', were probably more representative than those of Virginia.[34]

Unlike Mullin, Meaders, Kay and Cary, and others, Philip Morgan questioned whether the act of running away should be 'conceived solely in terms of resistance', tentatively suggesting that such an interpretation was politically inspired rather than historical. Though conceding that many but not all runaways were rebels, he maintained that 'such a simple interpretation wrenches the act of running away out of its social context'. More useful was an examination of the social and cultural significance of the phenomenon of running away.[35] The utility of Morgan's perspective is clearly demonstrated by the unique insight his analysis afforded into the nature and extent of African influence in South Carolina's slave community, the strength and range of kinship ties revealed by visiting, and into 'the magnitude of the occupational opportunities [open] to South Carolina slaves'. His data, however, go up to 1782 and show that in the final years there was a rapid expansion in the number of runaways, followed by an equally rapid contraction: some explanation of this pattern seems called for since we know from other sources that slaveholders lost approximately a quarter of their bondspeople during the course of the Revolutionary war. Having made his point, Morgan could perhaps have gone a stage further noting that at the end of his study, running away did, in fact, become resistance.[36]

Billy Smith and Shane White (1955–) added new dimensions to the study of running away and its relationship to the Revolution, examining the phenomenon in the rather different context of the non-plantation north at the latter end of the eighteenth century which witnessed the rise of antislavery and the enactment of gradual emancipation by the legislatures of Pennsylvania and New York. They were particularly interested in black self-help. 'In political terms,' wrote Billy G. Smith, 'running away always was a forceful but highly personal act of rebellion.' In his essay 'Runaway Slaves in the Mid-Atlantic Region during the Revolutionary Era' (1993) Smith argued that what distinguished the action of slaves in Pennsylvania, Delaware, southern New Jersey, and north-eastern Maryland was that they 'aimed permanently to liberate themselves, especially in the decades after 1760'.[37] Like Mullin and Morgan before him, Smith used runaway notices (1,804 drawn from six Philadelphia newspapers) for a dual purpose, to explore both escapees and slavery itself in a specific regional context. From the physical descriptions of runaways, Smith challenged the notion that slavery in the region was milder than farther south. There were indications of whippings, chaining and disfiguration, though later in the century slaveholders were anxious to disassociate themselves from the infliction of injury. Far fewer fugitives in the region sought out family and friends than in the Chesapeake or Lower South.[38] Escape was not a spontaneous act, a response to some unforeseen event, irritant or sudden whim, but rather something carefully planned in advance.[39] As opportunities for escape multiplied with the development of urban centres, so the number of fugitives increased. They exploded during the years of the Revolution, then declined to an average of 53 a year after 1785. In running away, slaves undermined the economic viability of the slave system among individual slaveholders.

Runaways struck at the economic heart of slavery and thereby hastened its demise during the century's final decades ... Many slaveowners must have perceived that the problem of physically holding onto their labor force, especially young males, the most valuable slaves, was growing more acute.[40]

On the relative importance of altruism and economics in advancing emancipation, Smith came down firmly on the side of the latter.

As part of a larger study of black life Shane White examined some 1,232 advertisements for runaway slaves in New York City and its environs between 1771 and 1805 in *Somewhat More Independent* (1991). He too found that only a minority ran away to visit family and friends; as in Pennsylvania, most fugitives sought to escape slavery permanently. They also absconded in larger numbers than farther south and one in five was a woman.[41] The distribution of runaways over the period showed two peaks, one during the Revolution and the other in the late 1790s and early 1800s. White also concluded 'a new mood of assertiveness among blacks, and consequently an increased tension in race relations' had arisen. What was remarkable was the speed with which slavery disintegrated following the passage of the Gradual Manumission Act. To a large extent, 'the details of the demise of slavery were worked out on an individual basis rather than by legislative fiat'. Historians had been too inclined to focus on white opposition to slavery to the exclusion of black self help. 'If black resistance was not strong enough in itself to bring about the end of slavery, it must surely have hastened its demise.'[42]

Conspiracy

Potentially more lethal threats to slaveholders came from 'rebellion or conspiracy to rebel' which Herbert Aptheker defined as 'the highest form of protest', but in the unfavourable political climate of the post-war years, his corpus of work was generally ignored. Though recognizing the pioneering character of *American Negro Slave Revolts*, Winthrop Jordan was still inclined to dismiss Aptheker's findings as late as 1968, on the grounds that he tended 'to inflate every scrap of evidence into an instance of servile conspiracy and rebellion and to identify rumours as revolts'.[43] Younger scholars proved more responsive. They not only took up Aptheker's findings but built on them. Among the disturbances which so clearly alarmed southern whites, Aptheker had found a distinct pattern.

> The uprisings and plots came in waves, as though anger accumulated and vented itself and then a period of rest and recuperation were needed before the next upsurge. Certainly waves were the rule, with clearly defined periods, as: 1710–1722, 1730–1740, 1790–1802, 1819–1823, 1829–1832, 1850–1860. The uprisings were of *slaves*; that is, free Negro participation was uncommon and white participation (except after 1850) was rare.[44]

Peter Wood discerned another wave – one that manifested itself in the 1770s, and one which furthermore 'was cresting in the eventful year before the Declaration of Independence with more force than scholars of black history have acknowledged or than most historians of the American Revolution have imagined'.

> Between 1765 and 1776, a wave of hope and discontent welled among American blacks. While the manifestations of this spirit have been best documented in the North among urban slaves and free Negroes, they were even more important in the South, where blacks made up a major proportion of the total population, especially in the vital coastal regions. Though not universal, this wave of struggle was also not isolated, sporadic, and uninformed. It touched every major slave colony, and it was closely related to – even influential upon – the political unrest gripping many white subjects in these years.[45]

The result was not a 'two-way struggle' between slaves and masters 'but a three-way battle', involving 'merchant-planter revolutionaries, English officer bureaucrats and the black worker', who constituted 'liberators at opposing corners of a triangle'. The existence of a 'significant third dimension' claims Wood, brings 'an added complexity, logic, and meaning' to the study of the Revolutionary conflict.[46]

Wood pushed his ideas further in a second and more ambitious essay 'Liberty is Sweet' (1993) in which he attempted to recover what African Americans thought about freedom. He rejected the notion that ideas about freedom among African American slaves were picked up from the ongoing debates between whigs and tories or that those enslaved contracted 'the contagion of liberty' belatedly. The evidence of black resistance argues 'that they had a long and bitter familiarity with the ideas and issues at hand'. 'It may well be,' Wood hypothesized, 'that during the generations preceding 1776, African Americans thought longer and harder than any other sector of the colonial population about the concept of liberty, both as an abstract ideal and as a tangible reality.' Resistance was not random but calculated to exploit those times when whites were at a disadvantage such as during epidemics, war and natural disasters and the political conflict with Britain presented further opportunities. Between the Stamp Act crisis and the meeting of the First Continental Congress, 'rumours of insurrection' were rife along the Atlantic coast. In the spring of 1775

> the interlocking struggles of Tories, Whigs, and African Americans intensified ... Black activists ... sought to capitalize on white divisions in their plans for freedom fully as much as white factions tried to implicate half a million blacks in their political designs.

Historians' failure to comprehend black sentiments toward freedom, concluded Wood, meant that 'a significant strand in the ideological origins of the American commitment to freedom' had been overlooked.[47]

Woody Holton went a stage further in *Forced Founders* (1999) by inverting the traditional interpretation of Dunmore's November 1775 Proclamation. While students of the American Revolution seldom mentioned enslaved Virginians before November 1775, Holton observed, slaves were active in the weeks and months before this date. In fact, it was 'only after fugitive slaves had proven their skills as soldiers, sailors, and raiders that Dunmore officially offered them freedom'. Slaves had always resisted their bondage but 'in 1774, they began conspiring to exploit the opportunities presented to them by the imperial crisis'.[48] Also (like Peter Wood) concentrating on events in Virginia during the critical days of April 1775, Holton identified a cluster of five rumoured slave plots in the James River watershed which had eluded both Aptheker and Wood. Holton did not claim that these formed a single conspiracy though one was feasible and there were certainly some white Virginians who believed that a slave insurrection was imminent. It is in this context of 'rising aspirations among blacks and mounting fears among whites' that Holton viewed the events surrounding Dunmore's seizure of Virginia's powder magazine on 21 April in the capital Williamsburg. Holton interpreted the sudden about face of Virginia politicians who, initially bent on recovering the ammunition for their own security, on meeting with the governor, dropped their demands and persuaded the armed crowd that had gathered to disperse, fearing the consequences of Dunmore's threat to declare 'freedom to the slaves and reduce the city of Williamsburg to ashes'. Events in Virginia fuelled rumour and speculation elsewhere in the slave south. When Dunmore finally issued his emancipation proclamation, it came as a disappointment to slaves for it offered freedom only to those who fled their masters to join the governor's forces. Nonetheless, Dunmore's small black force, his 'Ethiopian regiment', wearing uniforms proclaiming 'Liberty to Slaves', was too much for some Virginia conservatives like William Beverley, pushing them into the rebel camp.[49] Since slaves predominated among Dunmore's forces, Holton concluded that, unlike the lower south, the conflict 'pitted two classes, slave owners and slaves, against each other'.[50]

The war

The first and for many years the only scholarly study of the relationship between African Americans and the Revolution appeared in 1961 when, under the auspices of the Institute of Early American History and Culture, Williamsburg, Virginia, *The Negro in the American Revolution* was published. Written by Benjamin Quarles (1904–1996), a Wisconsin-trained African-American historian and Professor of History at Morgan State, a predominantly black university in Baltimore, *The Negro in the American Revolution* was ahead of its time even in 1961 and, though subsequently regarded as a classic, it made little impact at the time.[51] Sharply focused and empirically based, Quarles's finely nuanced study was detached from consensus approaches to the Revolution and the debates of historians over slavery in the 1950s and early 1960s.[52] The same sense of disconnectedness attaches to Thad W. Tate Jr, *The Negro in Eighteenth-Century*

Williamsburg. Completed initially in the spring of 1957 as a research report for the Colonial Williamsburg Foundation which, together with the College of William and Mary, funded the Institute of Early American History and Culture, it was not published until 1965.[53] A pioneering study in micro-history long before the term became fashionable *The Negro in Eighteenth-Century Williamsburg* contrasts with Quarles's work. As far as the slave was concerned, wrote Tate, 'the American Revolution offered in Virginia a few years of hope and little more'. Its real importance was not

> the limited opportunity it gave him to participate as a soldier. Rather it was the fact that large numbers of Americans for the first time began to grasp the inconsistency of slavery and the doctrines of natural rights on which they had based their own struggle for political independence.[54]

In reassessing the book in the light of later scholarship, Tate concluded that it measured up well to work on the transformation of the Chesapeake labour system and the development of a distinct Afro-American culture. What needed consideration though, was the 'sense of restlessness' and 'consciousness of the desirability of liberty on the part of blacks'.[55] This was Quarles's point of departure. However, in depicting flight to the British as a rational choice in the pursuit of liberty, Quarles was subversive of traditional historiography.

The role of the African American in the Revolution, Quarles argued, was best understood by recognizing that black loyalty 'was not to a place nor to a people, but to a principle'. Given a choice, 'the African American was likely to join the side that made him the quickest and best offer'. African Americans were infused with the spirit of '76. 'Whoever invoked the image of liberty, be he American or British, could count on a ready response from the blacks.' How slaves and free blacks engaged with the conflict and with what consequences form the principal themes of Quarles's study.[56] The recruitment of blacks to the Patriot cause was dictated by manpower needs, which though not desperate in the first two years of the war, became acute in the third.[57] Black military service was most extensive in New England where it was pioneered in the towns and subsequently adopted by state governments who reversed earlier policies. 'Negro soldiers served in the minutemen companies of Massachusetts in the early weeks of the war, in the state militias of the Northern states, and in the state and Continental forces.' Unlike Maryland, Virginia declined to enlist slaves though it lifted a ban on free blacks. South Carolina and Georgia remained adamant in opposing slave enlistment despite Congressional prompting, the British occupation of Savannah and the opening of a second campaign in the south. 'The Negro in South Carolina and Georgia who sought to bear arms in the American cause,' wrote Quarles, 'may have felt that the war was being waged for white freedom and black slavery', a subject to which Sylvia Frey and Robert Olwell would return many years later.[58] Service on the American side was extensive but unrecognised, as 'anonymous labour':

> Negroes erected fortifications, manufactured cannon and gun carriages, worked in the salt and lead mines, repaired roads, and drove wagons. To procure Negro labor, state governments and Continental military officers resorted to a variety of techniques: impressing, hiring, or purchasing slaves.[59]

Slaves served other purposes too. Those regarded as booty could be taken and sold, or alternatively used to supplement enlistment bounties. In the south, slaves 'were an acceptable form of currency, much preferable to paper money'. The practices of the state of Georgia were probably unsurpassed: 'On one occasion, the state donated a slave to every soldier who had taken part in a successful campaign; in another instance, the state exchanged slaves for provisions for the troops. Enemy slaves were transmitted to public officials in payment of salaries in the fall of 1782.'[60]

Many cast in their lot with the British. 'This game was more perilous, but the chances of freedom were greater.' The British also seized slaves during the war, but many more deserted to them in the hope of gaining their freedom. Slaves had always run away 'but what in peacetime was a rivulet became in wartime a flood'. Quarles put the number of runaways at 'tens of thousands' which, though high, was 'not nearly as high as it might have been' due to rapid countermeasures taken by planters, especially in Virginia, in the wake of Dunmore's Proclamation. Many of those who succeeded fell prey to smallpox. When Dunmore was forced to abandon his Virginia campaign in 1776, 300 of his surviving black recruits sailed with him.[61] In Boston, New York and Philadelphia, 'wherever the British were, there also were their black auxiliaries'. There was greater opportunity to fight as a soldier in the south but numbers were small. As Quarles observed 'the British needed blacks less as soldiers than as military laborers'.[62] Like their American opponents, the British too 'used the Negro not to work or to fight but as a piece of property'. Some slaves were given to loyalists to compensate them for their losses; others were appropriated as spoils of war; some were held in common by army units.[63]

In assessing the consequences of the Revolution for African Americans Quarles marked out the territory for later historians. With the end of the fighting African Americans became part of the loyalist diaspora which carried men, women and children to places as far apart as East Florida, the West Indies, Canada, Britain, continental Europe and West Africa. Others, being returned to slavery or escaped into freedom, remained in the United States. Moreover,

> [t]he feeling that slavery was inconsistent with the ideals of the war cropped out in many quarters, becoming manifest in the attitude of prominent national figures, in the formation of abolitionist societies, in the concern for Negroes displayed in religious sects, and in the anti-slavery activities of state and federal governments.[64]

Citing Du Bois, Quarles observed that by 1790 the African slave trade had come to a virtual halt north of the Potomac, but in the states of the lower south, importations of Africans reached unprecedented numbers. In the contraction of the slave trade, humanitarianism played a role but economic change was also a factor. With the opening up of the China trade, the dependence of north-east merchants on the slave trade diminished while planters in South Carolina and Georgia saw their economic interests solely in terms of replacing slaves lost in the disruption of war. 'Less widespread and less successful' was the abolition movement.[65] There was no hiding the disappointment at the outcome of the war. 'The condition of slaves on the plantations did not change', though many slaves did become free and some free negroes improved their status. The new nation's commitment 'to the principles of liberty and equality', however, was 'irreversible'. African Americans would gain, Quarles concluded, 'ultimately'.[66] With the same sense of irony and ambiguity that he employed over twenty years earlier, Quarles declared that the Revolutionary War could be called 'a black Declaration of Independence in the sense it spurred black Americans to seek freedom and equality'.[67]

Published three decades after *The Negro in the American Revolution*, Sylvia Frey's study *Water from the Rock* (1991) did not revise Quarles's work but rather extended it at both ends. Acknowledging debts to Quarles, Aptheker and Wood, Frey (1935–) came to the subject with a knowledge of British military records which had persuaded her that the scale of slave resistance was still underestimated.[68] Frey departed from Quarles's work in exploring and incorporating African patterns of slave resistance into her study, in her assessment of British strategy in the South and in tracing the emergence of black culture in the aftermath of the war. Frey distinguished two separate but related processes in the decades preceding and following the Revolution. There was the 'actual conflict of the 1760s–1780s' and the continuing unrest after the war was over that led to a second 'or quiet, revolution' lasting until the end of the first quarter of the next century. The first of these showed that 'a black liberation movement was central to the revolutionary struggle in the South' while the second demonstrated that 'the failure of that movement did not dissipate the black revolutionary potential, which reemerged in the postwar period as a struggle for cultural power'.[69] The threat from the slaves 'to the very existence of the plantation colonies of the South', argues Frey, was real not imaginary, not some figment of the planters' imagination nor the product of newspaper reporting. Though African slaves did not have a revolutionary tradition, they did have a military tradition. 'Everywhere in Africa and in many Middle Eastern societies, slaves had a military role: as sailors for ship captains and merchants, as palace guards, as slavers in slave raiding, as soldiers for local rulers, as members of the regular army.'[70] Before the Revolution, resistance 'found its ideology, strategy, and meaning' for the most part, 'in African patterns of resistance and warfare ... where self-reliance and survival strategies prevailed, the shape and degree of slave resistance was roughly proportional to the possibilities inherent in their situations'.[71]

Like Peter Wood, Frey described the revolutionary war in the south as a 'complex triangular process' involving 'two sets of white belligerents and approximately four hundred thousand slaves'. Frey argued that there existed a dialectical relationship between slave resistance and the British military. The presence of British troops 'was not a sufficient cause for massive resistance, but it was a necessary one'. When the British invaded Georgia, 'roughly one third of Georgia's prewar slave population, escaped their bondage'; in South Carolina 'at least twenty thousand slaves' – probably more – were involved in this 'Triagonal War'.[72] 'For the vast majority of slaves who actively participated in the Revolution, the arrival of the British army was a liberating moment.'[73] Slave resistance was a precondition for the evolution of British strategy in the south. British commanders pursued a policy of 'racial manipulation' using the threat of slave revolt to intimidate white southerners.[74] But the British strategy of manipulating racial conflict backfired. Instead of holding southern planters in line, it became 'a rallying cry for white southern unity' that 'impelled the South towards independence'.[75] In seeking to exploit the threat to the whole system of slavery, a policy that had no support at home, British commanders in the field found themselves overwhelmed by the numbers of slaves fleeing to them. In a major interpretive shift, Frey argues that because of the scale of desertion and the way in which the British employed runaways, they deflected the possibility of larger scale resistance and in doing so 'prevented the revolt from becoming a revolution'.[76] The British army attracted into its ranks 'the most courageous slaves, who had the greatest potential for revolutionary leadership'. In a sense, then, the British army acted as both a sword and a shield, challenging and conserving the system at the same time.[77]

A sense of the impact of these 'turbulent years' and the 'chaos of the American Revolution' was captured in Robert Olwell's evocative *Masters, Slaves, and Subjects* (1998). The struggles of the revolutionary years brought changes to the culture of power within which masters and slaves had operated in colonial South Carolina's lowcountry. His focus is 'on extraordinary and contingent events, the "hurricanes" that broke into the tyranny of the routine and enabled everyone to perceive ordinary social structures and social relations in new, and perhaps revolutionary, ways'.[78] From May 1775 to March 1776, 'the struggle was largely a domestic one between masters and slaves' during which masters faced a double challenge: of making a revolution against the king and, more importantly, of suppressing 'any revolutionary designs' among their slaves.[79] Slaves who remained behind when their masters fled before the British advance, in the absence of the normal institutions of power, 'were free to reshape the social order of the plantations according to their own desires'. It was in places such as these, wrote Olwell, that 'we can gain a tantalizing brief and fragmentary glimpse of a world that colonial South Carolina's slaves made by and for themselves'. Even when masters or overseers remained, their authority was likely to be diminished. Yet there were circumstances in which the masters' authority was destroyed for more extended periods as when the British army occupied Charleston between May 1780 and September 1781, civil authority collapsed and 'the slaves on many low-country plantations were effectively left to govern themselves'.[80]

The turning point

The disorders of war left southern society and the southern economy in disarray. Estimates of the numbers of slaves who fled their owners varied from 80,000 to 100,000 and the plantation system was seriously, although not fatally, weakened. Many whites in the southern states believed that recovery was tied to the restoration of slave labour and South Carolina re-opened its doors to the slave trade. Despite these developments, Sylvia Frey described the American Revolution as 'a major turning point in the history of slavery and of the South'.[81] For Jon F. Sensbach, the revolutionary and early national period was 'one of the defining periods in black life'. 'For African Americans,' he writes, 'the founding of a new nation brought hope, possibilities, frustration, and a backlash of oppression by a slaveocracy determined not to let its investment in human chattel be squandered.'[82] In exploring the themes of continuity and change in the early Republic,

African Americans remain firmly in view but much of the evidence relating to their experience is demographic in character. The crucial link between colonial America and the antebellum period was forged by Ira Berlin in his 1976 essay, 'The Revolution in Black Life' in which he argued that 'the events and ideas of the revolutionary years radically altered the structure of black society and the substance of Afro-American culture'. Between 1770 and 1810 three events came together. First, many blacks achieved freedom in the north and substantial manumission occurred in the upper south. Second, there was 'the maturation of a native born Afro-American population after more than a century of American captivity'. Third, was 'a new, if short-lived, flexibility in white racial attitudes'. Together they made these years 'the pivot point in the development of black life in the United States'. Far more than the period of Reconstruction, the revolutionary era 'laid the foundation for modern Afro-American life'.[83] Just how the Revolution 'reshaped the structure of Afro-American society and American race relations' was developed in the 1983 collection of essays *Slavery and Freedom in the Age of the American Revolution*, in the introduction to which Berlin reminded readers that 'if the Revolution marked a new birth of freedom, it also launched a great expansion of slavery'. The latter was a development conveniently overlooked in the celebration of 'Liberty' and obscured by the conventional chronology of American history which defines Early America and Antebellum America as distinct periods.[84]

The expansion of slavery

Following the revolutionary war, with the exception of Maryland, slavery became more entrenched across the south. The conflict propelled forward economic changes, Frey claimed, but it did not launch them. It speeded up changes in agricultural products which required 'the more rapid adaptation of the labor supply'. In Virginia, the practice of 'hiring out' helped to keep slavery viable in the state by making slaves accessible to non-slaveholders, thus cultivating support for the institution among southern whites. By the same token, the sale of surplus slaves stimulated the growth and development of slavery in the Virginia piedmont and the backcountry of Georgia and South Carolina and in the new states of Kentucky and Tennessee.[85] In exploring 'Black Society in the Chesapeake 1776–1810', Richard Dunn concluded that if 'the Revolution was indeed the first big step toward freedom' for some, for most 'there was as yet no revolution at all'.[86] Whereas in 1776, over half the black population in the mainland colonies had lived in Virginia and Maryland, a generation later, 'nearly 90 percent' of the black population of the Chesapeake was still enslaved and by 1810 the size of the slave population in the region had nearly doubled. How then, asked Dunn, could one reconcile the revolutionary challenge to slavery and the extent of manumission in Virginia and Maryland 'with the continuing adherence to slavery by the white leadership and the expansion of Chesapeake slavery in the post-Revolutionary era?' Robert McColley had tackled the same question in a different way two decades earlier. Dunn suggested that one explanation lay in the subsequent and divergent development of the two states – a trend 'toward black freedom in Maryland and toward continued enslavement in Virginia' – though not all historians would agree with Dunn on the uniform character of the colonial Chesapeake.[87] Throughout the Chesapeake 'the largest slaveholders permitted few free blacks to live among their slaves'. Coastal districts offered the best chance of freedom, especially in Maryland. Between the Revolution and the Civil War, the proportion of all Chesapeake slaves living in Maryland fell from thirty per cent to fifteen per cent. However, 'in most of the Chesapeake, especially in central Virginia, where half of the blacks in the region lived, slaveholding became more widespread and more deeply entrenched than before 1776'. Dunn concluded that

> Even if Washington, Jefferson, Madison, and Monroe had devoted all their leadership skills to the single cause of black freedom, they would still have failed utterly, for their society was moving inexorably in the opposite direction.[88]

Philip Morgan also identified 'the growing entrenchment of slavery' in South Carolina and Georgia as a central theme in his essay 'Black Society in the Lowcountry 1776–1810', together with a parallel and seemingly paradoxical development, namely 'the growing autonomy of the black community'. Significant migratory and demographic changes were under way before the Revolution and intensified after it. Whereas before 1760 nine out of every ten slaves lived in the lowcountry, by 1810 almost half of the state's slaves were to be found in the backcountry.[89] African slaves continued to be purchased but slaves were also bought from more northerly regions of the United States. Demographic changes led to increased opportunities for family formation. From around the early 1750s, the slave population began to grow through natural increase, a pattern maintained during the revolutionary era, 'although the massive influx of Africans in the first decade of the nineteenth century temporarily slowed the upward trend'.[90] According to Morgan, in comparison with long-term demographic and economic changes, 'the impact of the Revolution on lowcountry black life was – in one sense – minimal'. Yet in another sense, the impact of the Revolution 'was far-reaching'. While some slaves stayed put, others went off, taking advantage of the civil war raging in the lowcountry and British military occupation 'to widen their own freedom within bondage and, occasionally, outside of it'. This 'sheer loss of black manpower', Morgan argues, 'was the most dramatic consequence of the Revolutionary War upon lowcountry black life' and, though planters subsequently recovered their authority, 'wartime anarchy created a power vacuum in the countryside that allowed slaves to expand their liberty'. Gains won were not 'readily' surrendered.[91] Morgan linked 'the growing creolization of the slave population, the increased size of lowcountry plantations, the continued predominance of rice production, and more widespread white absenteeism' to 'the growing independence of lowcountry blacks'. These long-term changes resulted in widespread black management demonstrated by the increase in the number of black drivers, and was augmented by the traditional task system. It was also reflected in the ability of lowcountry slaves to accumulate small amounts of property and engage in local trade.

> It was the convergence of these long-term trends, subtle changes, and wartime experiences that produced a distinctive lowcountry social world – one in which planters were more deeply committed to slavery and slaves enjoyed a larger degree of autonomy than anywhere else on mainland North America.[92]

Though seemingly and inexplicably reluctant to revisit the revolutionary years in his 1998 monograph, *Slave Counterpoint*, Morgan does offer some further reflections. For one thing, the Revolution served to heighten the divergence between the Chesapeake and the lowcountry already distinguished by crop production and work patterns and, although each passed through similar stages of development – a frontier stage, a period of institution building and a mature stage, the lowcountry still lagged a generation behind the Chesapeake. Furthermore, Virginia slave imports had virtually tapered off before the Revolution and did not resume thereafter while in South Carolina, 'the Revolution interrupted a veritable orgy of African slave trading'. Anxious to repair losses sustained in the 'vicious Revolutionary war', slaveholders imported 10,000 Africans into Charleston in the 1780s and a further 40,000 in a four-year period in the early 1800s, thereby perpetuating the influence of African culture among the state's slaves in contrast to the African American character assumed by slaves in Virginia.[93]

Religion and freedom

The series of religious revivals known as the Great Awakening, which swept across the colonies in the 1740s, continued in the upper south into the 1790s and, while the ideal of Christian equality it preached proved as elusive as that proclaimed in the American Revolution, it spawned the evangelical movement that gave rise 'to an institution over which slaves exercised control and in which they asserted independence'.[94] In 'The Slave Church in the Era of the American Revolution' (1983) Albert J. Raboteau examined the rise of the Baptists and Methodists in the Chesapeake in the late eighteenth century, the challenge they presented to slavery only to retreat in the face of growing and obdurate white hostility. By including 'blacks and whites in close communities of small, voluntary, religious societies', they moved beyond the old Anglican order and, though they accommodated slavery, 'in their attempt to measure life by the rule of gospel order', they had to face 'the disquieting contradiction between Christian fellowship and human bondage', especially in relation to issues of slave control and slave marriage.[95] Despite failure to resolve these tensions, Raboteau argued that slaves were attracted to these denominations, not only in the Chesapeake but also the lowcountry, because of their identification with 'the poorer sort', their experience of persecution, the antislavery views of a few and their willingness to licence black preachers.[96] The importance of black preachers in the development of African American culture was 'difficult to overestimate' for they 'mediated between Christianity and the experience of the slaves, interpreting the stories, symbols, and events of the Bible to fit the day-to-day lives of those held in bondage'. Separate black churches resulted both from the subdivision of previously mixed congregations and the foundation of independent black churches, the latter facilitated by the growth in the number of free blacks in the Chesapeake and the north-east.[97] It was here 'in the church', that African Americans 'kept alive the deferred promises of revolution'.[98] Sylvia Frey made much the same point concerning separate black churches in the south, adding that 'by insisting upon their own ritual patterns and by asserting certain specifically African aspects of moral values separate from the values of the dominant white culture', African Americans 'established a claim to cultural power'.[99]

When freedom came, it transformed black life, but it was a limited kind of freedom: it did not usually mean the immediate release from bondage or the absence of restraints. When Leon T. Litwack demonstrated the extent to which northern and western states restricted the opportunities of free blacks in antebellum America in *North of Slavery: The Negro in the Free States, 1790–1860* (1961), he shed light on the thorny issue of segregation, but the volume did not stimulate interest in the hitherto neglected subject of northern slavery.[100] What freedom meant in a northern context was first explored by Gary Nash in his 1983 essay 'Forging Freedom: The Emancipation Experience in the Northern Seaport Cities 1775–1820', another essay in the Berlin and Hoffman collection. On the eve of the American Revolution, according to Nash, the size of the black population living in Philadelphia, New York and Boston was around '4000 slaves and a few hundred free blacks'. Fifty years later the number of free blacks had increased to 'nearly 22,000' while the number of slaves had fallen to 'about 500'. During this period African

Americans living in the seaports 'constructed the economic, institutional, and social scaffolding of freedom'. The process was slow, uneven and engendered aggressive hostility from whites, but in moving to the city, changing their names, earning a living, forming families and households and creating new institutions, African Americans distanced themselves from slavery and developed 'a new consciousness'.[101]

Several factors such as the nature of the former slave regime, the character of emancipation, the state of the economy and the demographic profile of the city influenced the transition from slavery to freedom, but more important than all of these was the timing of emancipation. By the end of the eighteenth century Boston and Philadelphia were centres of free African Americans, abolition and gradual emancipation having been promoted there before the revolutionary war was over. On the other hand, New York, where the state legislature adopted a gradual emancipation bill only in 1799, experienced an actual increase in slave numbers.[102] Men and women were attracted to urban centres by the prospect of work but emancipation did not lead to major changes in the occupational structure of black society. Labouring and domestic service continued to be the major sources of employment though 'some improved themselves considerably by plying artisan trades or keeping small shops of their own'. Though there is no occupational data for Boston and New York comparable to that for Philadelphia, Nash contends that since later information on Boston and New York corresponds 'roughly' with that for Philadelphia, the situation in all three cities was similar.[103]

Under slavery the opportunities for the creation and preservation of black family life were restricted for in Boston, Philadelphia and New York many slaves lived alone in white households or with one other adult slave. With freedom came the possibility of a more secure family life though the creation of black households was 'a complex multifaceted process'.[104] The appeal of the city was not only economic; the city also offered the prospect of black community life. As patterns of black residential concentration developed, black churches, schools, mutual aid societies and fraternal organizations were created; they were self consciously termed 'African'. By 1813, there were six black churches in Philadelphia and 11 benevolent societies, while in New York there were only two churches and one benevolent society. The success of black institutional life related to distance from slavery. 'Where slavery had been expunged soon after the Revolution, black institutional life thrived: where it lingered, it had a deadening effect even on those blacks who did escape its clutches.'[105]

Nash explores the fate of black Philadelphians during and after the Revolution in greater depth and detail in his full-length monograph *Forging Freedom* (1988). In terms not dissimilar to those used by Quarles, Nash examined the choices and experiences of black Philadelphians but his larger theme, already signalled in his 1983 essay, was the creation of an autonomous black community.[106] Free blacks in Philadelphia quickly came to the realization that 'the only secure foundation upon which to fashion their lives was one constructed of independent organizations', not white benevolence, but while the first generation pursued its objectives in an atmosphere of 'relative racial harmony', the second struggled 'amid mounting white hostility' in a city that was undergoing rapid change.[107] They laid the foundation for an independent existence by their quest, largely successful, for employment.[108]

Free blacks also asserted their collective identity in petitions to the legislature and in the formation of black organizations beginning with the Free African Society in 1787 which may have been the first black organization of its kind in North America.[109] By 1791 Absalom Jones and other activists favoured a black church, a 'union' church drawing together blacks of different religious persuasions. They argued that 'men are more influenced by their moral equals than by their superiors ... and ... are more easily governed by persons chosen for themselves for that purpose, than by persons who are placed over them by accidental circumstances'. Besides, their condition argued for the 'necessity and propriety of separate and exclusive means, and opportunities of worshipping God, of instructing their youth, and of taking care of their poor'.[110] Thus a desire for separation, rather than discrimination in the former inter-racial methodist congregation, led, in Nash's view, to the opening of the African Church of Philadelphia in 1794.[111] Nash attributed the rise in racial tension and outbreak of sporadic violence in early nineteenth-century

Philadelphia primarily to two factors: the growth of the black population and economic competition with working-class whites, native born and immigrant. Black migrants, supplemented by former Haitian slaves, came to the city from the ring of slave states bordering Pennsylvania. From rural backgrounds, they struggled to make a life for themselves in the city as economic conditions worsened and real wages declined, especially in maritime employment. Free blacks were shut out from the new industrial enterprises – textile mills, machine foundries, and boot and shoe manufacturing, which drew on native-born and immigrant white labour. Despite these barriers, 'scores of free blacks created their own work roles and thus provided themselves with decent material rewards and, equally important, space to operate autonomously'.[112] Deteriorating race relations, argued Nash, helps to explain why it was that black leaders such as Richard Allen and James Forten initially supported the schemes of the American Colonization Society. Ordinary free blacks opposed them from the start.[113]

Australian scholar Shane White (1955–), in his study *Somewhat More Independent* (1991), challenged the notion that slavery 'died' after the Revolution and that the conditions of northern urban slaves were superior to those in the South. White, a lecturer at the University of Sydney, with a Ph.D. from the same institution, found that slavery not only took on a new lease of life after the Revolution but survived for many years after the passage of the state's gradual emancipation act in 1799, especially in the rural environs of the city. Nor could slavery New York-style be described as 'mild'. In some areas, 'such as family life and cultural development, New York slaves had fewer opportunities and fared worse than their southern counterparts'.[114] Within the city, White traced the development of a distinctive black subculture among the free and the unfree. 'The story of New York blacks was not simply one of rapid and wholesale assimilation, but more one of creative adaptation to an often hostile world.'[115] In *Slavery and Freedom in the Rural North* (1997), a study of slavery and its aftermath in a rural county in New Jersey, Graham Russell Hodges (1946–) also challenges the notion that slavery outside the south was mild, presenting a portrait of a vicious institution and of slaveholders who clung to slaves to the bitter end. In the months before the outbreak of fighting, tension ran high and '[a]s war approached, blacks fled to the British'. From Staten Island the British launched raids into New Jersey. 'Combining banditry, reprisal, and commissioned assistance to the British army, these raids served the aims of local black rebellion quite intentionally, often being aimed directly at former masters and their friends.'[116] Like other historians Hodges argued that 'economic incentive remained a major factor in the perpetuation of slavery'.[117]

Adopting a different perspective again is Stephen Whitman (1950–) who addresses the question of the relative importance of economic factors and black self help in promoting emancipation in *The Price of Freedom* (2000). Though located in a slave state, by 1830 not only was Baltimore America's third largest city, but four-fifths of its African American population was 'legally free'. The majority of slaves, nearly three-quarters of the total, lived in Maryland's rural counties. To comprehend the process of manumission Whitman argued, it was not sufficient to focus on slaveholders; it was 'equally necessary to appreciate the actions and behaviour of the blacks who were seeking to become free'. In the early national period, slaves in Maryland 'wrested freedom from their masters in a bewildering variety of unequal power struggles. These were balanced by momentary harmonies of interest, mixtures of exploitation and kindness, and long, patient bargaining interspersed with violent episodes'. Compared with New York and Pennsylvania, Maryland demonstrated some distinctive features. For one thing, manumission was strong when slavery 'grew and flourished, especially in Baltimore'. Second, 'many slaveholders acquired more slaves after manumitting slaves'. Why this should be and why far more blacks became free in Baltimore and certain Maryland counties than elsewhere Whitman attributes to 'the ties between Baltimore's growth and the economic stagnation in southern and eastern Maryland'.[118] It was economic self interest, not humanitarian sentiment, that determined the actions of slaveholders. Manumission occurred not to remove the evil of slavery but to reduce the risk of running away and stimulate higher productivity.[119]

Antislavery

Antislavery had shallow roots in the colonial period. When the Revolution came, the existence of slavery among European Americans struggling for their own freedom was an embarrassment to some, an opportunity for others and inconsequential to most. Yet within two generations, slavery in the United States was no longer a national institution but a regional one. How and why this occurred is part of a much wider debate, much of it focusing on the nineteenth century, over ideal and material interpretations of abolition, sparked by Eric Williams' 1944 study *Capitalism and Slavery*. With the growth of the free black population came rising negrophobia and the construction of 'race'.[120] In a broad and still useful overview, *The First Emancipation* (1967), Arthur Zilversmit explored the limits of northern antislavery from the pre-revolutionary period to the growth of radical abolitionism, evaluating whether abolition succeeded in the north because slavery was no longer financially viable. He concluded it did not. Williams had argued that abolition in the West Indies stemmed from the fact that the institution, being no longer profitable, was incompatible with capitalism.[121] Zilversmit attributed the policy of abolition adopted in most northern states to 'revolutionary élan' and accepted the revolutionary generation's 'espousal of the Rights of Man' as genuine. On the other hand, he demonstrated just how long drawn out the process of emancipation was in the north. He linked the progress of abolition during and after the Revolution to the strength of pre-revolutionary antislavery sentiment and Quaker influence. Despite the fact that it made no mention of slavery and there is no evidence that delegates discussed abolition, the 1780 Massachusetts Constitution 'became the means of eliminating slavery in Massachusetts'. T. H. Breen has called this 'the heroic legal narrative'. In a series of freedom suits, the doctrine 'that slavery was no longer legal in Massachusetts' became accepted, but as Zilversmit pointed out, the Walker case in 1781 and the Jennison cases in 1782 and 1783 'went unnoticed in contemporary newspapers' and sales of slaves continued.[122]

Narrower in range but more revealing was Jean Soderlund, *Quakers & Slavery* (1985), a detailed study of the growth of abolitionism among members of Philadelphia Yearly Meeting to which Quakers of Pennsylvania, New Jersey and parts of Delaware and Maryland belonged. Though Quakers were more likely to be hostile to the slave trade because of its violence, the meeting did not punish slave traders until 1758 or prohibit slave-holding until 1776.[123] Why it took them so long was the subject of Soderlund's book. By examining abolitionism at the local level and looking at the place of Quakers in the larger society, it was possible to see 'how religious belief and economic interest inter-acted in the growth of abolitionism among these Friends'.[124] Soderlund found that antislavery sentiment emerged only in certain local meetings and the analysis of this local level

> shows clearly why the Friends deliberated the question of slavery for an entire century ... By moving away from a single focus on the Philadelphia elite, we can see in one meeting after another how Friends struggled to come to grips with the issue. The eighteenth-century Friends were indeed a 'peculiar people' because their drive to eradicate slavery among themselves was a success.[125]

In 1991, Gary Nash and Jean Soderlund collaborated on a much larger study of emancipation, *Freedom by Degrees*, describing their theme as 'the tug of war between ideological commitments and economic interests, between leaders and followers, between slaves and masters that occurred in Pennsylvania in the eighteenth century over the issue of slavery'.[126] Focusing on Philadelphia and rural Chester County, they examined the importance of a range of factors: revolutionary ideology, natural rights, religious affiliation, occupational status, wealth and gender which might have influenced individuals in emancipating slaves. Few slaveholders demonstrated a commitment to abolition by freeing their slaves outright, Quakers apart: Pennsylvanians achieved emancipation for economic reasons and at bargain prices. In the interplay between ideology and economy the latter was far more instrumental than the former. Condemned under the state's gradual emancipation act to spend their most productive years in bondage, freed men and women in Pennsylvania faced restricted opportunities: family life was fragile and the opportunity to acquire property was limited.[127] Such findings show that compared with *Forging Freedom* published three years earlier, *Freedom by Degrees* is a much bleaker book.

While many of these studies discussed slavery and freedom in a state, city or county context, Winthrop Jordan and Gary Nash, adopting a broader perspective, approached the subject as an issue in national politics in the years immediately after the Revolution. Jordan devoted a substantial section of *White Over Black* (1968) to the limits of the American Revolution, to the failure of antislavery and the definition of the Early Republic 'as a white man's country'. For two decades, claims Jordan, slavery was a critical and divisive issue in the Union until 1808 when the ending of the slave trade 'tackled it at its most vulnerable point'.[128] Jordan maintains that antislavery was weakened from within and destroyed from without: there were incompatibilities between religious and secular impulses, and distance from the Revolution diminished its vigour. Furthermore, fear of slave revolt fuelled by events in Saint Domingue (Haiti) and Virginia loomed large.[129] In *Race and Revolution* (1990), Gary Nash, in revisiting some of the ground covered by Jordan, upbraided pro-northern historians for failing to recognize that at the time of the Revolution slavery was a national problem, one which the north might have been expected to take the lead in resolving. He questioned whether the fragility of the Union usually cited by historians, was really 'the key stumbling block'.[130] In examining the 1790 Congressional debate over slavery, Nash found northern delegates bowing to those of the lower south.

> Just as at the Constitutional Convention of 1787, where the desire of northern delegates for investing the federal government with the power to regulate commerce by simple majority vote in Congress had been traded for their acquiescence to the South on the slave trade and fugitive-slave clauses, now the northern representatives were unwilling to jeopardize funding and assumption by offending representatives from the lower South.[131]

Nash lamented the responsibility of historians for neglecting the black freedom struggles of revolutionary and post-revolutionary America which 'turned the African-American fifth of the population into a far more passive group than it actually was'. 'In reality,' he stated, 'the American Revolution represents the largest slave uprising in our history.'[132]

Notes

1 Gordon S. Wood, *The Radicalism of the American Revolution* (New York; 1992), pp. 7, 186–8; Michael Meranze, 'Even the Dead Will Not be Safe: An Ethics of Early American History', *WMQ*, 3rd ser., 50 (1993), pp. 367–78, 373–4. On the definition of 'freedom', see Orlando Patterson, 'Slavery: the Underside of Freedom', *Slavery and Abolition*, 5 (1984), pp. 87–104; on how these ideas worked to integrate white society in colonial Virginia, see Edmund S. Morgan, *American Slavery American Freedom: The Ordeal of Colonial Virgina* (New York; 1975).

2 Benjamin Quarles, 'The Revolutionary War as a Black Declaration of Independence' in Ira Berlin and Ronald Hoffman (eds), *Slavery and Freedom in the Age of the American Revolution* (Charlottesville, VA; 1988), pp. 283–301, 285.

3 Philip D. Morgan, *Slave Counterpoint: Black Culture in the Eighteenth-Century Chesapeake and Lowcountry* (Chapel Hill, NC; 1998), pp. xv–xvi.

4 Peter H. Wood, '"Liberty is Sweet": African-American Freedom Struggles in the Years before White Independence' in Alfred F. Young (ed.), *Beyond the American Revolution: Explorations in the History of American Radicalism* (Dekalb, IL; 1993), pp. 149–84, 150.

5 Lorenzo Sabine, *The American Loyalists or Biographical Sketches of Adherents to the British Crown in the War of the Revolution* (Boston; 1847), pp. 30, 32; on this controversy, see John Hope Franklin, 'The North, the South, and the American Revolution', *JAH*, 62 (1975), pp. 5–23, 9–10.

6 Jon F. Sensbach, 'Charting a Course in Early African-American History', *WMQ*, 3rd ser., 50 (1993), pp. 394–405, 395; Nathan I. Huggins, 'The Deforming Mirror of Truth: Slavery and the Master Narrative of American History', *Radical History Review*, 49 (1991), pp. 25–46; David Brion Davis, 'Slavery and the Post-World War II Historians', in Sidney W. Mintz (ed.), *Slavery, Colonialism, and Racism* (New York; 1974), pp. 1–16.

7 In his 1978 essay Peter Wood classified both books as 'related essays in European-American intellectual history'. Peter H. Wood, '"I Did the Best I Could for My Day": The Study of Early Black History During the Second Reconstruction, 1960 to 1976', *WMQ*, 3rd ser., 35 (1978), pp. 185–225, 188–9, and fn. 8; David B. Davis, *The Problem of Slavery in Western Culture* (Ithaca, NY; 1966); Winthrop D. Jordan, *White Over Black: American Attitudes Toward the Negro 1550–1812* (Chapel Hill, NC; 1968), pp. ix–x. On the origins debate, see Alden T. Vaughan, 'The Origins Debate: Slavery and Racism in Seventeenth-Century Virginia', *Virginia Magazine of History and Biography*, 97 (1989), pp. 311–54; on 1968, see William L. O'Neill, *Coming Apart: An Informal History of America in the 1960s* (New York; 1971), pp. 360–92.

8 On the new social history, see E. J. Hobsbawm' classic article 'From Social History to the History of Society', *Daedalus*, 100 (1971), pp. 20–45.

9 John Hope Franklin, 'Afro-American History: State of the Art', *JAH*, 75 (1988), pp. 162–73, 162.

10 Ira Berlin, 'Time, Space and the Evolution of Afro-American Society on British Mainland North America', *AHR*, 85 (1980), pp. 44–78, 78.

11 Berlin, 'Time, Space and the Evolution of Afro-American Society', p. 45.

12 Ronald Hoffman, 'Preface' in Berlin and Hoffman, *Slavery and Freedom in the Age of the American Revolution*, p. xi.

13 Mercy Otis Warren, *History of the Rise, Progress and Terminaton of the American Revolution*, ed. Lester H. Cohen, 2 vols (Indianapolis, IN; 1988), I, p. 110; David Ramsay, *The History of the American Revolution*, ed. Lester H. Cohen, 2 vols (Indianapolis, IN; 1990), I, p. 233.

14 Ramsay, *American Revolution*, I, pp. 233, 235; Warren, *History*, I, pp. 110–11, 163.

15 Warren, *History*, II, p. 451; Ramsay, *American Revolution*, II, p. 496 and *History of the Revolution of South Carolina, from a British Province to an Independent State*, 2 vols (Trenton, NJ; 1785).

16 George Bancroft, *History of the United States of America, from the Discovery of the Continent*, VIII (Boston; 1878), pp. 223–4, 298.

17 Bancroft, *History*, VIII, p. 298; on the sources of social, economic and scientific racism, see Duncan J. MacLeod, *Slavery, Race and the American Revolution* (London; 1974).

18 William C. Nell, *Services of Colored Americans in the Wars of 1776 and 1812* (Boston; 1851, reprinted in New York; 1976). *The Colored Patriots of the American Revolution* appeared in 1855.

19 George W. Williams, *History of the Negro Race in America from 1619 to 1880: Negroes as Slaves, as Soldiers, and as Citizens*, 2 vols (New York; 1883), I, pp. 351–2, 357–8.

20 Williams, *History of the Negro Race in America*, I, p. 411; John Hope Franklin, *George Washington Williams: A Biography* (Chicago; 1985).

21 W. E. B. Du Bois, *The Suppression of the African Slave-Trade to the United States* (New York; 1896, reprinted New York; 1954); W. E. B. Du Bois, 'The Suppression of the African Slave-Trade' in *Writings*, comp. Nathan I. Huggins (New York; 1968), pp. 74, 1306.

22 Lorenzo J. Greene, *The Negro in Colonial New England* (New York; 1968 [1942]); Wood, '"I Did the Best I Could for My Day"', p. 193.

23 Luther P. Jackson, 'Virginia Negro Soldiers and Seamen in the American Revolution', *Journal of Negro History* (hereafter *JNH*), 27 (1942), pp. 247–87.

24 Jackson, 'Virginia Negro Soldiers and Seamen', p. 249.

25 Herbert Aptheker, *American Negro Slave Revolts* (New York; 1943, reprinted New York; 1969), p. 3. For a discussion of maronage in British North America, see Herbert Aptheker, *To Be Free: Studies in American Negro History* (New York; 1948), pp. 11–30; Eugene D. Genovese, *Roll Jordan Roll: The World the Slaves Made* (New York; 1976) and *From Resistance to Rebellion: Afro-American Slave Revolts in the Making of the Modern World* (Baton Rouge, Lousiana; 1979).

26 Gerald W. Mullin, *Flight and Rebellion: Slave Resistance in Eighteenth-Century Virginia* (New York; 1972), p. ix and note 27.

27 Mullin, *Flight and Rebellion,* p. x. For an earlier attempt to use advertisements to gain access to slaves, see Lorenzo J. Greene, 'The New England Negro as Seen in Advertisements for Runaway Slaves', *JNH*, 29 (1942), pp. 125–46, 125 and the even earlier collection of runaway notices, Carter G. Woodson (ed.), 'Eighteenth Century Slaves as Advertised by their Masters', *JNH*, 1 (1916), pp. 163–216.

28 Mullin, *Flight and Rebellion*, p. x.
29 Mullin, *Flight and Rebellion*, pp. 39–40; for a critique of the use of runaway advertisements, see Jonathan Prude, '"To look upon the lower Sort": Runaway Ads and the Appearance of Unfree Labor in America 1750–1800', *JAH*, 78 (1991–1992), pp. 124–60.
30 Mullin, *Flight and Rebellion*, p. xii; Elsa V. Goveia, *Slave Society in the British Leeward Islands at the End of the Eighteenth Century* (New Haven, CT; 1965) and Orlando H. Paterson, *The Sociology of Slavery: An Analysis of the Origins, Development and Structure of Negro Slave Society in Jamaica* (London; 1967).
31 Mullin, *Flight and Rebellion*, pp. 36–8, 58.
32 Mullin, *Flight and Rebellion*, pp. 124, 128–9.
33 Mullin, *Flight and Rebellion*, p. 82.
34 Peter H. Wood, *Black Majority: Negroes in Colonial South Carolina: From 1670 Through the Stono Rebellion* (New York; 1974), p. 240; Kenneth Morgan, *Slavery and Servitude in North America, 1607–1800* (Edinburgh; 2000), pp. 99–100; Philip D. Morgan, 'Colonial South Carolina Runaways: Their Significance for Slave Culture', *Out of the House of Bondage*, special issue of *Slavery and Abolition*, ed. Gad Heuman, 6 (1985), pp. 57–78, 57, 59, 69.
35 Morgan, 'Colonial South Carolina Runaways', pp. 57, 74; Mullin, *Flight and Rebellion*; Daniel E. Meaders, 'South Carolina Fugitives as Viewed through Local Colonial Newspapers with Emphasis on Runaway Notices 1732–1801', *JNH*, 60 (1975), pp. 288–319; Marvin L. Michael Kay and Lorin Lee Cary, *Slavery in North Carolina 1748–1775* (Chapel Hill, NC and London; 1995), p. 121.
36 Morgan, 'South Carolina Runaways', pp. 73–5, fn. 3. Tables 1–5 include data after 1775. There are citations for 1779, a slave who ran away in 1779 and reference to a trend in the 1790s.
37 Billy G. Smith, 'Runaway Slaves in the Mid-Atlantic Region during the Revolutionary Era' in Ronald Hoffman and Peter J. Albert (eds), *The Transforming Hand of Revolution: Reconsidering the American Revolution as a Social Movement* (Charlottesville, VA, and London; 1996), pp. 199–230, 202; see also Billy G. Smith and Richard Wojtowicz (eds), *Blacks Who Stole Themselves: Advertisements for Runaways in the Pennsylvania Gazette, 1728–1790* (Philadelphia, PA; 1989).
38 Smith, 'Runaway Slaves in the Mid-Atlantic Region', pp. 206, 211–13, 219–22.
39 Smith, 'Runaway Slaves in the Mid-Atlantic Region', pp. 214–19.
40 Smith, 'Runaway Slaves in the Mid-Atlantic Region', pp. 224, 226–7, 228–9.
41 Shane White, *Somewhat More Independent: The End of Slavery in New York City, 1770–1810* (Athens, GA, and London; 1991), pp. 120, 124, 126–7, 139–40.
42 White, *Somewhat More Independent*, pp. 141, 144, 148, 149.
43 Jordan, *White Over Black*, p. 601.
44 Aptheker, *American Negro Slave Revolts*, p. 3.
45 Peter H. Wood, '"The Dream Deferred": Black Freedom Struggles on the Eve of White Independence', in Gary Y. Okihiro (ed.), *In Resistance: Studies in African, Caribbean, and Afro-American History* (Amherst, MA; 1986), pp.

166–87, 168.

46 Wood, "'The Dream Deferred'", pp. 168–9.

47 Wood, "'Liberty is Sweet'", pp. 151–6, 159–60, 162–3, 172.

48 Woody Holton, *Forced Founders: Indians, Debtors, Slaves, and the Making of the American Revolution in Virginia* (Chapel Hill, NC; 1999), p. 160.

49 Holton, *Forced Founders*, pp. 142–8, 152–61.

50 Holton, *Forced Founders*, pp. 153, 161; Jeffrey R. Crow, 'Slave Rebelliousness and Social Conflict in North Carolina, 1775 to 1802', *WMQ*, 3rd ser., 37 (1980), pp. 79–102; Alan D. Watson, 'Impulse Toward Independence: Resistance and Revolution among North Carolina Slaves, 1750–1775', *JNH*, 63 (1980), pp. 317–28; Robert Weir, *Colonial South Carolina* (Millwood, NY; 1983), pp. 200–3; Peter H. Wood, '"Taking Care of Business" in Revolutionary South Carolina: Republicanism and the Slave Society' in Jeffrey R. Crow and Larry E. Tise (eds), *The Southern Experience in the American Revolution* (Chapel Hill, NC; 1978), pp. 268–93, 283.

51 Benjamin Quarles, *The Negro in the American Revolution* (Chapel Hill, NC; 1961).

52 Alfred F. Young, 'American Historians Confront "The Transforming Hand of Revolution"', in Hoffman and Albert (eds), *The Transforming Hand of Revolution*, p. 405.

53 Thad W. Tate Jr, *The Negro in Eighteenth-Century Williamsburg* (Williamsburg, VA; 1965).

54 Tate, *The Negro in Eighteenth-Century Williamsburg*, pp. 120–1.

55 Tate, *The Negro in Eighteenth-Century Williamsburg*, Preface, p. ix.

56 Quarles, *The Negro in the American Revolution*, pp. vii, x, xi.

57 Quarles, *The Negro in the American Revolution*, pp. vii, 7–18, 51–110.

58 Quarles, *The Negro in the American Revolution*, pp. 53, 57, 60, 63, fn. 51, 67.

59 Quarles, *The Negro in the American Revolution*, pp. 198–9.

60 Quarles, *The Negro in the American Revolution*, pp. 108, 110.

61 Quarles, *The Negro in the American Revolution*, pp. 110, 114–15, 119, 123–30.

62 Quarles, *The Negro in the American Revolution*, pp. 118–32, 134–6, 142, 146–52, 199.

63 Quarles, *The Negro in the American Revolution*, pp. 156–7.

64 Quarles, *The Negro in the American Revolution*, pp. 172–81, 185. On loyalism, see W. S. G. Walker, *The Black Loyalists* (New York; 1976); Ellen Wilson, *The Loyal Blacks* (New York; 1976); Graham R. Hodges, *Black Loyalist Directory* (New York; 1996). A recent collection of essays, *Moving On: Black Loyalists in the Afro-Atlantic World,* ed. John W. Pulis (New York and London; 1999) was dedicated to Quarles's memory; Simon Schama, *Rough Crossings: Britain, the Slaves and the American Revolution* (London; 2005); Cassandra Pybus, *Epic Journeys of Freedom: Runaway Slaves of the American Revolution and their Global Quest for Liberty* (Boston; 2006).

65 Quarles, *The Negro in the American Revolution*, p. 200.

66 Du Bois, *Suppression of the African Slave-Trade*, pp. 50–1; Quarles, *The Negro in the American Revolution*, pp. 194–5, 200.

67 Quarles, 'The Revolutionary War as a Black Declaration of Independence'.

68 Sylvia R. Frey, *Water from the Rock: Black Resistance in a Revolutionary Age* (Princeton, NJ; 1991), pp. 3–4.
69 Frey, *Water from the Rock*, p. 4.
70 Frey, *Water from the Rock*, pp. 46, 48.
71 Frey, *Water from the Rock*, p. 51.
72 Frey, *Water from the Rock*, pp. 45–6, 86, 108.
73 Frey, *Water from the Rock*, pp. 118–19, 167; Elizabeth Cometti, 'Depredations in Virginia during the Revolution' in Darrett B. Rutman (ed.), *The Old Dominion: Essays for Thomas Perkins Abernethy* (Charlottesville, VA; 1994), pp. 145, 147.
74 Frey, *Water from the Rocks*, p. 63.
75 Frey, *Water from the Rock*, pp. 45, 108, 114, 141; on the relationship between slave resistance and planter unity, see also Robert A. Olwell, '"Domestick Enemies": Slavery and Political Independence in South Carolina, May 1775–March 1776', *Journal of Southern History* (hereafter *JSH*), 55 (1989), pp. 21–48.
76 Frey, *Water from the Rock*, p. 87.
77 Frey, *Water from the Rock*, pp. 127–8, 141.
78 Robert Olwell, *Masters, Slaves, and Subjects: The Culture of Power in the South Carolina Low Country, 1740–1790* (Ithaca, NY and London; 1998), p. 14.
79 Olwell, *Masters, Slaves, and Subjects*, pp. 225–6.
80 Olwell, *Masters, Slaves and Subjects*, p. 260.
81 Frey, *Water from the Rock*, pp. 326, 211.
82 Sensbach, 'Charting a Course in Early African-American History', p. 400.
83 Ira Berlin, 'The Revolution in Black Life', in Alfred F. Young (ed.), *The American Revolution: Explorations in the History of American Radicalism* (Dekalb, IL; 1976), pp. 349–82, 351.
84 Berlin and Hoffman, *Slavery and Freedom in the Age of the American Revolution*, pp. xv, xvii.
85 Frey, *Water from the Rock*, pp. 222–3; Sarah S. Hughes, 'Slaves for Hire: The Allocation of Black Labor in Elizabeth City County, Virginia, 1782 to 1810', *WMQ*, 3rd ser., 35 (1978), pp. 260–86.
86 Richard S. Dunn, 'Black Society in the Chesapeake 1776–1810' in Berlin and Hoffman, *Slavery and Freedom in the Age of the American Revolution*, pp. 49–82, 81–2.
87 Dunn, 'Black Society in the Chesapeake', pp. 49–52, 63, 65–7; Robert McColley, *Slavery and Jeffersonian Virginia*, 2nd edn (Urbana, IL; 1973 [1964]).
88 Dunn, 'Black Society in the Chesapeake', pp. 63, 81–2.
89 Philip D. Morgan, 'Black Society in the Lowcountry, 1776–1810', in Berlin and Hoffman, *Slavery and Freedom in the Age of the American Revolution*, pp. 83–142, 83–4.
90 Morgan, 'Black Society in the Lowcountry', pp. 84–8.
91 Morgan, 'Black Society in the Lowcountry', pp. 108, 109, 110–11.
92 Morgan, 'Black Society in the Lowcountry', pp. 118–21, 141.
93 Morgan, *Slave Counterpoint*, pp. xix, 62. In footnote 48, p. 62, Morgan refers readers to the essays of Dunn, Morgan and Kulikoff for the 'contrast-

ing wartime experiences of Virginia and South Carolina' in Berlin and Hoffman, *Slavery and Freedom in the Age of the American Revolution*, pp. 49–171. On the process of post-revolutionary movement and forced migration, see Allan Kulikoff, 'Uprooted People: Black Migrants in the Age of the American Revolution, 1790–1820' in the same volume, pp. 143–71, particularly 159–61,166 and on the development of an African American culture in the Chesapeake, Allan Kulikoff, 'The Origins of Afro-American Society in Tidewater Maryland and Virginia, 1700 to 1790', *WMQ*, 3rd ser., 35 (1978), pp. 226–59.

94 Albert J. Raboteau, 'The Slave Church in the Era of the American Revolution' in Berlin and Hoffman, *Slavery and Freedom in the Age of the American Revolution*, pp. 193–213, 193–4.

95 Raboteau, 'The Slave Church', pp. 197–9, 200.

96 Raboteau, 'The Slave Church', pp. 202–3.

97 Raboteau, 'The Slave Church', pp. 203–6, 208–9.

98 Raboteau, 'The Slave Church', pp. 211–13.

99 Frey, *Water from the Rock*, p. 328.

100 Leon T. Litwack, *North of Slavery: The Negro in the Free States, 1790–1860* (Chicago; 1961).

101 Gary B. Nash, 'Forging Freedom: The Emancipation Experience in the Northern Seaport Cities 1775–1820' in Berlin and Hoffman, *Slavery and Freedom in the Age of the American Revolution*, pp. 3–48, 3–4.

102 Nash, 'Forging Freedom', pp. 10–11.

103 Nash, 'Forging Freedom', pp. 18–19, fn. 20.

104 Nash, 'Forging Freedom', pp. 27–8, 38–9.

105 Nash, 'Forging Freedom', pp. 10–11, 45–7.

106 Gary B. Nash, *Forging Freedom: The Formation of Philadelphia's Black Community, 1720–1840* (Cambridge, MA; 1988), p. 2.

107 Nash, *Forging Freedom*, p. 5.

108 Nash, *Forging Freedom*, pp. 80–8.

109 The Free African Union of Providence, Rhode Island may have been founded earlier. Nash, *Forging Freedom*, pp. 98, and 305, fn. 71.

110 Nash, *Forging Freedom*, pp. 12, 113–14.

111 Nash, *Forging Freedom*, pp. 122, 127–30.

112 Nash, *Forging Freedom*, pp. 144–5, 153; on competition with Irish workers, see p. 223.

113 Nash, *Forging Freedom*, pp. 212–45; on Forten, see the excellent biography by Julie Winch, *A Gentleman of Color: The Life of James Forten* (New York; 2002).

114 White, *Somewhat More Independent*, p. 210.

115 White, *Somewhat More Independent*, p. 206.

116 Graham Russell Hodges, *Slavery and Freedom in the Rural North: African Americans in Monmouth County, New Jersey, 1665–1865* (Madison, WI; 1997), pp. 93, 95–6, 98.

117 Hodges, *Slavery and Freedom in the Rural North*, pp. 118, 119, 121, 136.

118 T. Stephen Whitman, *The Price of Freedom: Slavery and Manumission in Baltimore and Early National Maryland* (Lexington, KY; 1997), pp. 1, 4.

119 Whitman, *Price of Freedom*, p. 161.

120 Roger Anstey, *The Atlantic Slave Trade and British Abolition, 1760–1810* (Atlantic Highlands, NJ; 1975); Christine Bolt and Seymour Dresher (eds), *Anti-Slavery, Religion and Reform* (London; 1980); Joyce E. Chaplin, 'Slavery and the Principle of Humanity: A Modern Idea in the Early Lower South', *JSH*, 24 (1991), pp. 299–315; David Brion Davis, *The Problem of Slavery in the Age of Revolution, 1770–1823* (Ithaca, NY; 1966); Davis, *The Problem of Slavery in Western Culture*; Howard Temperley, 'Capitalism, Slavery and Ideology', *Past and Present*, 75 (1977), pp.94–118; Eric Williams, *Capitalism and Slavery: The Caribbean* (Chapel Hill, NC; 1944); for further refinements to the controversy, see David Brion Davis, 'Reflections on Abolitionism and Ideological Hegemony', *AHR*, 92 (1987), pp. 797–812; John Ashworth, 'The Relationship between Capitalism and Humanitarianism', *AHR*, 92 (1987), pp. 813–28; Thomas L. Haskell, 'Convention and Hegemonic Interest in the Debate over Antislavery: A Reply to Davis and Ashworth', *AHR*, 92 (1987), pp. 829–78. On the rise of negrophobia, see James Brewer Stewart, 'The Emergence of Racial Modernity and the Rise of the White North, 1790–1840', *JER*, 18 (1998), pp. 181–217.

121 Arthur Zilversmit, *The First Emancipation: The Abolition of Slavery in the North* (Chicago and London; 1967), pp. vii–viii; Williams, *Capitalism and Slavery*.

122 Zilversmit, *The First Emancipation*, pp. 112–15, 137–8; T. H. Breen, 'Making History: The Force of Public Opinion and the Last Years of Slavery in Revolutionary Massachusetts' in Ronald Hoffman, Mechal Sobel and Fredrika J. Teute (eds), *Through a Glass Darkly: Reflections on Personal Identity in Early America* (Chapel Hill, NC; 1997), pp. 67–95, 72.

123 Jean R. Soderlund, *Quakers and Slavery: A Divided Spirit* (Princeton, NJ; 1985), p. 4.

124 Soderlund, *Quakers and Slavery*, pp. 4–5.

125 Soderlund, *Quakers and Slavery*, p. 12.

126 Gary B. Nash and Jean R. Soderlund, *Freedom by Degrees: Emancipation in Pennsylvania and its Aftermath* (New York and Oxford; 1991), p. xiv.

127 Gwenda Morgan, 'Emancipation Studies: The Demise of Slavery in Pennsylvania and New York', *Slavery and Abolition*, 13 (1992), pp. 207–12, 208.

128 Jordan, *White Over Black*, p. 292.

129 Jordan, *White Over Black*, pp. 342–9, 374, 375–80.

130 Gary B. Nash, *Race and Revolution* (Madison, WI; 1990), pp. 27–30.

131 Nash, *Race and Revolution*, pp. 41–2.

132 Nash, *Race and Revolution*, pp. 57–8.

6

'A new era in female history'

When Ray Raphael wrote that 'there were few ladies of leisure in late colonial America', that 'most women worked, and worked hard', and that resistance to British policy and the revolutionary war required them to work even harder, he was expressing a view that would have been unintelligible before the late twentieth century.[1] Yet the role of women in the American Revolution, unlike that of Native Americans, went largely unrecognized by the revolutionary generation of historians as well as those who came after them.[2] Women were not wholly absent from contemporary histories but as a subject of serious scholarly inquiry, the history of women 'is less than four decades old'.[3] Writing in the now classic anthology, *Women in the Age of the American Revolution* (1989), Linda Kerber (1940–) defined the problem with the revolutionary historians as both conceptual and linguistic; they 'literally lacked a language' to describe what was going on in front of their very eyes.[4] Mary Beth Norton's essay in the same volume explored the question of why women remained in the shadows once history developed as a professional discipline. Male historians of the Revolution, it seems, 'simply ignored the experience of women altogether', while women writers, lacking the educational opportunities and professional training long open to men, were more interested in the history of the family and broader questions about women's role in the past.[5] The gender division persisted and only in the last quarter of the twentieth century did the history of women and the history of the Revolution intersect. Finally in 1989, Linda Kerber could write 'the ingredients – both material and theoretical – for an analysis that recognizes the role of gender in the revolutionary war are now available. We know better than to discount the female experience as inherently marginal or trivial'.[6]

The revolutionary generation

The discourse of history was masculine. As dependent beings, subject to the authority of fathers, brothers and husbands, women were deemed to have no status independent of men and no political identity of their own. Thus, lacking the means to influence the course of events, they played no role in history and since history 'was largely the story of war and politics', women 'were not fit to be readers, writers or even the subjects of history'. While women's writings on 'religion, manners, marriage and even education' were gaining some level of acceptance in the eighteenth century, the same was not true of the 'traditionally male preserve' of history. Perceived as physically and mentally inferior to men, identified more closely with emotion than reason, Enlightenment theory, writes Kerber, questioned whether women were even capable of patriotism.[7] Yet female patriotism was not doubted by David Ramsay or Mercy Otis Warren, the foremost contemporary historians of the Revolution or the authors of the declarations of sentiments of the women of Philadelphia and New Jersey whom Norton and Kerber write about in *Liberty's Daughters* and *Women of the Republic* (1980). Judith Sargent Murray declared that 'history proved ... women "were as patriotic" as men'.[8]

It was not women's patriotism that led to their inclusion in the history books but their victimhood. Women gained admission to patriot histories as innocent victims of a sliding scale of perpetrators made up of Indians, mercenaries, loyalists and British troops. In loyalist accounts, the perpetrators and victims changed places.[9] Accounts of atrocities appropriated women's bodies and those of their children but whether patriot or loyalist, paid little regard to their hearts and minds.[10] Accounts of atrocities served a double purpose. On the one hand, they were effective in establishing the inhuman, savage and cruel behaviour of the enemy; on the other, they projected idealized images of female innocence and virtue that were surely hard to sustain during normal times let alone during the disorders of war.

216

There is nothing in David Ramsay's *History of the American Revolution* (1789) to suggest that women stepped outside their domestic roles during the resistance campaigns against British policies though their activism was widely reported and encouraged in the colonial press, discussed in private correspondence, visible on the streets and in American homes. When war came, Ramsay had no doubts about women's patriotism and was unusual in devoting a lengthy paragraph to the wartime experiences of women in South Carolina, drawing mostly on the activities of well-to-do Charleston women. Ramsay paid fulsome tribute to female patriotism but cast the women in familiar caring and supportive roles and as social beings. Only the context had changed. Women bolstered their husbands' resolve when they were tempted to throw in their lot with the British.

> The patriotism of the ladies contributed much to this firmness. They crowded on board prison ships, and other places of confinement, to solace their suffering countrymen. While the conquerors were regaling themselves at concerts and assemblies, they could obtain very few of the fair sex to associate with them ... On other occasions the ladies in great measure retired from the public eye, wept over the distresses of their country, and gave every proof of the warmest attachment to its suffering cause ... When, in the progress of the war, they were also comprehended under a general sentence of banishment, with equal resolution they parted with their native country, and the many endearments of home – followed their husbands into prison-ships and distant lands, where they were reduced to the necessity of receiving charity.[11]

Writing in the immediate aftermath of the American Revolution, David Ramsay provided the model for later histories of the conflict in this as in other aspects of the Revolution.[12] Women in Ramsay's *History of the American Revolution* were most likely to be the victims of Native American attacks. He wrote of women widowed and children left fatherless. In one engagement in the Wyoming Valley, 'near 200 women were made widows, and a much greater number of children were left fatherless'. In the retreat from the area, 'some women were delivered of children in the woods, and many suffered from want of provisions'. Following the retaliatory campaign led by Colonel Zebulon Butler, there was further Indian retribution, this time in Cherry

Valley when thirty-two of the inhabitants were killed and scalped, the victims of which were 'mostly women and children'. Tory atrocities also occurred in frontier areas where 'American refugees' as Ramsay called them, fought alongside Native Americans in the north-east. The explicit omission of some details which, if related 'would be sufficient to freeze every breast with horror' served to heighten the sense of repulsion.[13] Yet Ramsay's discussion of these encounters was in some ways very modern. He struggled to find an explanation of tory behaviour that was not simply dependent on the 'selfish passions of human nature'. He gave it a sociological dimension in the breakdown of social ties among the displaced Americans.[14]

In dealing with cases of rape, Ramsay displayed the same reticence as he had in dealing with frontier violence and for the same reason. 'The rapes and brutalities committed on women, and even on very young girls, would shock the ears of modesty, if particularly recited.' New Jersey was the scene of the most publicised cases of rape; the men involved were British and Hessian soldiers belonging to the royal army. As in the cases of frontier violence, Ramsay searched for explanations that would make the commission of such brutal acts comprehensible. He located them in the very successes of the British which loosed their troops upon the inhabitants, 'unrestrained by the terrors of civil law, uncontrolled by the severity of discipline, and elated with their success'. The violence committed against women took place in their own homes where they had remained having received 'printed protections, signed by order of the commander in chief'. In vain did they produce these protections. 'The Hessians could not read them, and the British soldiers thought they were entitled to a share of the booty, equally with their foreign associates.' To deter soldiers from such 'flagrant enormities', wrote Ramsay, 'immediate and severe punishments' were essential 'without which an army is a band of armed plunderers'. The British response proved feeble and inadequate.[15]

Despite her own celebrity and myriad activities in support of the Revolution, there is little in Mercy Otis Warren's *History* to suggest that women were a force in the revolutionary struggle.[16] In fact, women hardly figure at all in this work. Her husband James described her as possessing a 'Masculine Genius' coupled with that 'Weakness which is the Consequence of the Exquisite delicacy and softness of her Sex'. From her behaviour, her correspondence and her plays, she might well be considered a feminist, but as Rosemarie Zagarri (1956–) argues, Warren did not subscribe to such beliefs: 'She accepted subordination of women to men, believed in separate spheres for each sex, and supported the division of occupations based on gender. She never advocated a public role for women, either in the professions or in politics. Women, she suggested, should exercise influence through "the soft whisper of private friendship" rather than in public forums.' Warren did not challenge existing gender roles but worked within them, 'affirming patriarchy at the same time she circumvented its most confining limitations'. It was her dilemma, Zagarri concludes, 'to be a feminist without feminism'.[17] This view of Warren has been challenged by Kate Davies (1973–) who argues that Catharine Macaulay and Mercy Otis Warren, who enjoyed a lengthy correspondence,

> felt that as women of learning they had a particular role to play in such debates. They were confident ... they might intervene, writing letters and pamphlets, treatises and poems, which achieved different kinds of public circulation and acclaim. They also argued that their gender itself qualified them to produce what both described ... as the definitive republican histories of their respective nations. In their different ways, using a language of sentiment or affection, of learning or profession, both argued, in an era when public history was regarded as a definitively 'masculine' genre, that women made the best historians. Warren and Macaulay saw themselves as women and as writers, at the intellectual heart of Atlantic political culture.[18]

Women in Warren's history of the Revolution were variously perceived and described as 'the feebler sex', without experience, delicate, tender and obedient. The first mention of women recorded the terror and consternation of the inhabitants of Boston, who fearful for themselves 'and trembling for their friends' engaged in the fighting going on around them, were affected 'by the hideous shrieks of the women and children connected with the king's troops, who beheld their husbands, their friends, and relations, wounded, mangled, and slain, ferried over the river in boat-loads, from the field of carnage'.[19] The next mention of women is of the consorts of the commander in chief and his officers when the Continental army was encamped for the winter at Valley Forge, some miles from Philadelphia where a British army under Sir William Howe was ensconced in far more desirable winter quarters. Washington and some of his officers, 'in defiance of danger, either to themselves or to such tender connexions, sent for their ladies from the different states to which they belonged, to pass the remainder of the winter, and by their presence to enliven the gloomy appearance of a hutted village in the woods, inhabited only by an hungry and half-naked soldiery'. Warren interpreted this episode as a challenge by the Americans to their adversaries but was not entirely convinced of its merits, adding in a footnote, that 'nothing but the inexperience of the American ladies, and their confidence in the judgement of their husbands, could justify this hazard to their persons, and to their feelings of delicacy'.[20] With sympathy and admiration Warren dealt with the wives of enemy officers accompanying Burgoyne's forces on their march from Canada, who tended their wounded husbands when, in 1777, the British were defeated at Saratoga. Singled out for particular mention was the story of Lady Ackland whose 'sufferings exhibit a story so affecting to the mind of sensibility', especially as it included 'the most interesting detail of military transactions', a comment that could be interpreted as Warren's affirmation of the norms of male-centred history. Her emphasis shifted from admiration for the bravery of the several German and one English women, 'this little group of distressed females', to the humanity and civility demonstrated by their American captors who showed themselves the equal of the British in recognizing the claims of gender, class and deference.[21]

In dealing with the incidence of rape in New Jersey Warren was more explicit than Ramsay but expressed the same reticence on the subject, but unlike him, made no attempt to contextualize it. 'The historian would willingly draw a veil over the wanton outrages committed on the wretched inhabitants left in the town, most of them of the feebler sex', who had stayed in an attempt to save their property.

> The principal ladies of Fairfield, who from their little knowledge of the world, of the usages of armies, or the general conduct of men, when circumstances combine to render them savage, could not escape the brutality of the soldiery, by shewing their protections

from governor Tryon. Their houses were rifled, their persons abused, and after the general pillage and burning of every thing valuable in the town, some of these miserable victims of sorrow were found half distracted in the swamps and in the fields, whither they had fled in the agonies of despair.[22]

The modern writer Ray Raphael claims that rape was a common practice and that historians have been negligent in saying so little 'about women being looted, raped, widowed, and left homeless'.[23]

Both David Ramsay and Mercy Otis Warren related the brutal murders of Jane McCrea and Hannah Caldwell who were destined to become female martyrs of the American Revolution and whose deaths have haunted the histories of the revolutionary war ever since.[24] The killings of McCrea, the fiancée of a young loyalist officer in Burgoyne's forces, and of Caldwell, wife of the Rev. James Caldwell, a leading protagonist of the Revolution in New Jersey – the former allegedly scalped by treacherous Indians in 1777, the latter shot in 1780 by marauding British troops – were notorious.[25] An examination of how each writer dealt with these stories tells us something about the way they constructed their narratives and why some incidents take on a life of their own regardless of their historical importance. In both histories, the women were presented as victims but while Ramsay dealt with the killings in a somewhat perfunctory manner, Warren's accounts were laden with emotion and heavy with imagery. As Jane McCrea journeyed to meet her lover, Warren wrote, 'her heart glowed in expectation of a speedy union with the beloved object of her affections'. When a quarrel ensued among her escort, 'the blooming beauty, shivering in the distress of innocence, youth and despair', became 'the victim of their fury'. In depicting Hannah Caldwell's death, Warren placed her carefully at the centre 'of her little domestic circle' with a baby in her arms, 'unapprehensive of danger, shrouded by the consciousness of her own innocence and virtue' when she was shot. No respect was paid to the women's bodies. 'The bleeding corpse' of Jane McCrea was 'left in the woods, to excite the tear of every beholder' while in the case of Hannah Caldwell, 'a hole was dug' and 'the body thrown in'.[26]

Both historians attributed the same consequences to these

atrocities. The butchering of Jane McCrea brought the reputation of the British army to a new low, for the Indians who killed her were their allies. The death of Hannah Caldwell, shot by a British soldier through a window in her own home during one of the British incursions into New Jersey, violated all the known laws of warfare between civilized nations. These incidents handed the Americans two of their biggest propaganda coups of the entire war and they knew how to exploit them, as Burgoyne and others acknowledged.[27] But of more immediate importance was the fact that they boosted recruitment into the American armed forces among local inhabitants, thus, in McCrea's case, contributing to the defeat of the British at Saratoga a few weeks later and in Caldwell's case reviving the fortunes of the New Jersey militia, so lamentable in 1776.[28] And if Ramsay handled the consequences of these atrocities rather better than Warren, it was because he made extensive, unacknowledged and almost verbatim use of reports from the British *Annual Register*. Warren, for her part, referenced her use of the Earl of Harrington's evidence given before the parliamentary enquiry into Burgoyne's conduct and published by Burgoyne in his own account of the proceedings.[29]

Among contemporary writers, it is the loyalist Peter Oliver to whom we must turn for some recognition of the role of women as active agents in the revolutionary conflict, even though his account, limited to Massachusetts, was written not in praise of women, but to bury the Revolution. In identifying the various activities undertaken by women, Oliver's purpose was to belittle, demean and ridicule American resistance to British policy. He wrote in a satirical vein, making no claims to objectivity. He had a story to tell but because he was not trying to write history within the generally accepted meaning of the term, he was able to break out of the narrow limits within which it was confined in a way that Mercy Otis Warren could not. Oliver mocked female participation in public protests, the inclusion of women's names on petitions, and the activities they undertook in support of the American cause. It was 'highly diverting', he wrote, 'to see the names & marks, to the Subscription, of Porters & Washing Women' who agreed not to import '*Silks, Velvets, Clocks, Watches, Coaches & Chariots*'.[30] The following commentary on the attempt to curtail funeral extravagance, however, reveals as much about the author's bitterness as it does about organizing resistance to British policy in Massachusetts Bay.

> Under Pretence of OEconomy [sic], the Faction undertook to regulate Funerals, that there might be less Demand for English Manufactures. It is true indeed that the Custom of wearing expensive Mourning at Funerals, had, for many Years past, been noticed for Extravagance, & had ruined some Families of moderate Fortune; but there had been no Exertions to prevent it; 'till now, the Demagogues & their Mirmidons had taken the Government into their Hands. But what at another Time would have been deemed oeconomical, was at this Time Spite & Malevolence. One Extreme was exchanged for another. A Funeral now seemed more like a Procession to a *May Fair*; and Processions were lengthened, especially by the Ladies, who figured a way, in order to exhibit their Share of Spite, & their Silk Gowns. In short, it was unhumanizing the Mind, by destroying the Solemnity of a funeral Obsequy, & substituting the Gaiety of Parade in its Stead. The vulgar Maxim, *that there is no Inconvenience without a Convenience*, now took place; for whereas, formerly, a Widow, who had been well rid of a bad Companion, could conceal her Joy under a long black Vail, she was now obliged to use what Female Arts she was mistress of, in order to transform her Joy into the Appearance of a more decent Passion, to impose upon the Croud of numerous Spectators.[31]

Another scheme intended to keep up the opposition to British policy was the encouragement of manufacturing in which the production of wool was much favoured. As Oliver wrote:

> Mr *Otis's* black Regiment, the dissenting Clergy, were also set to Work, to preach up Manufactures instead of [the] Gospel. They preached about it & about it; untill the Women & Children, both within Doors & without, set their Spinning Wheels a whirling in Defiance of *Great Britain*. The female Spinners kept on spinning for 6 Days of the Week; & on the seventh, the Parsons took their Turns, & spun out their Prayers & Sermons to a long Thread of Politicks, & to much better Profit than the other Spinners; for they generally cloathed the Parson and his Family with the Produce of their Labor. This was a new Species of Enthusiasm, & might be justly termed, the Enthusiasm of the Spinning Wheel.[32]

When it came to the ban on tea, 'the Ladies' played their part here too, being so zealous for the Good of their Country, that they agreed to drink no Tea, except the Stock of it which they had by them; or in Case of Sickness. Indeed, they were cautious enough to lay in large Stocks before they promised; & they could be sick just as suited their Convenience or Inclination. Chocolate & Coffee were to be substituted for Tea; & it was really diverting, to see a Circle of Ladies about a Tea Table, & a Chocolate or Coffee Pot in the midst of it filled with Tea, one chusing a Dish of Chocolate, & another a Cup of Coffee. Such a Finesse would not only be a laughable Scene to a Spectator, but it must be a Fund of Mirth to theirselves, who framed such an evasive Conceit.[33]

Oliver continued with this mockery, going on to describe how the many women who could not afford to keep a quantity of tea in stock 'were forced to take Turns to be sick, & invite their Acquaintances to visit them; & so the Sickness went on by Rotation'. It was all madness of course, but it worked, at least in part, since Parliament partially rescinded the act.[34]

Much to his chagrin, the women in Oliver's account were assuming roles inconsistent with accepted patterns of female behaviour. Individual and collective behaviour were equally distasteful to him. Whether the individuals were real or metaphorical is less important than the purpose to which Oliver was putting them: that was to depict the downward spiral on which women embarked when, beginning with self-assertion, they moved on to participation in violent protest and from this to taking up arms. When British forces arrived from Halifax and passed through the streets of Boston, 'It happened, that a Lady was standing at her Door to enjoy her Share of it'. A man who had declared that the troops should never land and that 'he would fight up to his Knees in Blood to prevent it' challenged her, 'What do you stand there for? I would not look at them,' to which she replied, 'You are a very pretty Fellow! You said that you would fight up to your Knees in Blood, to destroy them, & you are now afraid to *look* at them'.[35] In a second example, Oliver claimed that the 'fair Sex' had thrown off 'their Delicacy' and adopted the new fashion of tarring and feathering, but 'it was a great Pity that they did not consult their own Characters, before they adopted it. The Feather Part indeed suited the Softness of the Sex'; but the idea of feathers, united with tar, was 'rather disgustfull – yet one of those Ladys of Fashion was so complaisant; as to throw her Pillows out of [the] Window, as the Mob passed by with their Criminal, in Order to help forwards the Diversion'.[36] What this could lead to was demonstrated in the third of Oliver's illustrations, the case of

> a remarkable Heroine, who stood at an House Door firing at the Kings Troops; there being Men within who loaded Guns for her to fire. She was desired to withdraw, but she answered only by Insults from her own Mouth, & by Balls from the Mouths of her Muskets. This brought on her own Death, & the Deaths of those who were within Doors.[37]

While the meaning of the first of these encounters is somewhat ambiguous, there is no mistaking the meaning of Oliver's final message, that aberrant female behaviour led to death and destruction.

Nineteenth-century histories

In the work of nineteenth-century historians women sank further into obscurity, with the singular exception of the writings of Elizabeth Ellet (1818–1877). Bancroft and Hildreth contented themselves with retelling the stories of the deaths of Jane McCrea and Hannah Caldwell.[38] In addition Bancroft made a brief but unappreciative reference to the 'women of America' who 'never grew weary of yielding up articles necessary for the comfort of their own households, to relieve the distresses of the soldiers' and a slightly more extended one to the 'women of Philadelphia' who

> rallying round the amiable Esther Reed, wife of the president of Pennsylvania, now made a more earnest effort: they brought together large donations of clothing, and invited the ladies of other states to adopt a like plan. They thus assisted to keep alive the spirit of patriotism in the army, but their gifts could not meet its ever-recurring wants.[39]

Ellet, who had been born in New York state and spent her early married life in South Carolina where her husband taught at the South Carolina College in Columbia, having already established her reputation as a poet, critic and translator, turned to history. In 1848 she published a two-volume work entitled *Women of the*

American Revolution adding a third volume, *Domestic History of the United States*, in 1850 in the light of the popular success of the earlier volumes. While the former comprised biographical sketches of over eighty American women gleaned from surviving records and oral testimonies, the latter attempted something quite different – to place gender 'at the narrative center of the Revolutionary experience' and 'to tell the history of the American Revolution from the perspective of both men and women'.[40]

In the preface to the 1848 edition of *Women of the American Revolution*, Ellet emphasized the 'extreme difficulty' of obtaining reliable sources. 'Inasmuch as political history says but little – and that vaguely and incidentally – of the women who bore their part in the Revolution, the materials for a work treating of them and their actions and sufferings must be derived in great part from private sources'.[41]

> While much that might have illustrated the influence of women and the domestic character and feeling of those days had been lost or obscured by time, it appeared yet possible, by a persevering effort, to recover something worthy of an enduring record. With the view of eliciting information for this purpose, application was made severally to the surviving relatives of women remarkable for position or influence, or whose zeal, sacrifice, or heroic acts had contributed to promoting the establishment of American independence.[42]

Ellet stressed the authenticity of her accounts, refuting suspicion that she might have supplied any deficiencies in her material 'by fanciful embellishment', though modern historians such as Alfred Young have questioned her reliability.[43] The final paragraph in which she claimed to have consulted 'nearly all the books upon the Revolution' and gratefully acknowledged the advice of the librarian of the New York Historical Society who afforded her access to the Society's books and manuscripts, has a modern resonance. So do her thanks to those who afforded her 'the opportunity of examining family papers' and 'to those numerous friends' who encouraged her 'by their sympathy and kind wishes in this arduous but interesting task'.[44] According to Kerber whose 1989 essay did much to bring Ellet to the notice of modern historians, her work having been summarily dismissed when reprinted in 1900, she 'really does do a measure of justice to the women whose life experiences she had uncovered'.[45]

While Kerber describes Ellet as 'the first historian to address extensively the relationship of women to the American Revolution', Scott Casper goes a stage further, arguing that 'she self-consciously placed her work at the border between the emerging profession of history and the sentimental tradition that celebrated "women's place" in Victorian America'.[46] He identifies Ellet as the first woman to be recognized as 'a scholarly historian of American women' who, challenging 'the male understanding of history from within', employed 'the methods and ideology of historical scholarship from the vantage point of the domestic'. Other women had written history before the Civil War but their work was confined to the school house and the parlour. When Ellet moved into history, she 'stepped upon a public stage dominated and defined by male historians and critics'.[47] In keeping with her role as a serious historian and an historian of women, Ellet required two languages:

> One, associated with male historical writing, was a language of 'fact', 'authenticity', and 'documents' that took the past as a subject for scholarship, emotionally as well as temporarily distant from the historian. The other, associated with female sentimental writing, was a language of 'heart' in which the Revolutionary women were dear foremothers whose loss to history would be a personal as well as a national one.[48]

Prior to publication, extracts from *Women of the American Revolution* appeared in *Godey's Lady's Book*, 'perhaps the most powerful disseminator of ideas about women's roles in this period', and subsequently was favourably reviewed in *The North American Review*, one of the leading periodicals of the day.[49]

What is most distinctive about *Women of the American Revolution*, argues Nina Byam, is that although it is a collection of 'goodwife biographies', Ellet did not deny women agency or limit herself to the study of exceptional women. It is in these features of her work that Ellet comes close to anticipating twentieth-century social history.[50] The third volume, *Domestic History of the American Revolution*, differed from the previous volumes in that Ellet claimed it was based on previously unpublished sources and included those who were neither famous nor wealthy. In this volume 'Ellet attempts to plant the Revolution on every square foot of American soil'. Ellet finds another defender in Carol Berkin, the author of *Revolutionary Mothers* (2005) who argues that when the writing of history attained the status of a profession by the 1880s, a 'gendered amnesia befell the study of the nation's war for independence'. In the new history, there was no place for 'the small heroisms' depicted by Ellett. Yet Berkin argues that the stories of female participation in the struggle did not fade away; they were preserved by other means.

> What might be called an 'Ellett underground' continued to thrive among the organizations of descendants of the Revolutionary gener-ation and among amateur local historians in towns, villages, and counties along the east coast. These women and men kept alive the stories of heroines – those who performed feats of bravery and those who preserved the farms and shops and families that soldiers dreamed of returning to when independence was won. Because of the efforts of these unabashed antiquarians, statues were erected to honour local heroines and medals were struck with the women's likenesses upon them.[51]

'A new era in female history'

Modern women's history has its roots in the new social history and upheavals of the 1960s when old barriers came down, fresh vistas opened up, and the affinity of the social sciences with history was recognized. The rise of modern feminism and its debates contributed key concepts. Virginia's Woolf's essay 'A Room of Her Own', Doris Lessing's *The Golden Notebook* and Simone De Beauvoir's *The Second Sex* found new readers and Betty Friedan's *The Feminine Mystique* spoke to many more. As students flooded into the universities, a new generation was hungry for new knowledge and a better understanding of its past.[52]

The first significant modern statement about the relationship between women and the American Revolution was the pioneering 1976 essay by Joan Hoff (1937–), but it was not until 1980 that the first full-length monographs by Mary Beth Norton and Linda Kerber appeared.[53] Richard Beeman greeted the arrival of *Liberty's Daughters* and *Women of the Republic* as presaging not only 'a new era in female history', a phrase first used by Judith Sargent Murray (1751–1820), 'the chief theorist of republican womanhood', but 'the beginnings of a new field of historical inquiry'.[54] It was still possible to question the value of recovering women's history, as happened at the 1981 conference on the state of Colonial British American history held at the University of Oxford. Although the organizers had encouraged participants to incorporate women and minorities into their papers, the results were disappointing and at least one participant hotly disputed the legitimacy of the subject.[55] Though women's history was slower to take off than either African American or Native American, it has stayed the course and its vitality shows no sign of abating. Its early practitioners, who included Joan Hoff Wilson (now Hoff), Linda Kerber, Mary Beth Norton and Elaine Crane were formidable women not so easy to dismiss. They were already well established in other fields before turning to women's history. But the field of women's history also attracted independent scholars and those outside the ranks of academia. The creation of the Berkshire conference on women's history provided a focus for feminist scholarship. At this stage of its development, American women's history was firmly focused on the experience of American women. Only to a limited extent did it seek to connect to other periods or cultures. Joan Hoff Wilson used the French Revolution as a measure of change but it did not figure significantly in her famous essay. Mary Beth Norton considered work on the English Civil War, the French Revolution, the American Civil War and the Second World War as well as insights from anthropology. Crane, perhaps, is the most explicitly comparative of this generation of historians, with a framework going back to the middle ages.

A foundation had already been laid in the 1970s by Lois Carr and Lorena Walsh, two outstanding early American historians whose careers have not followed the traditional academic path. In studying white women in the early Chesapeake, they argued that the planter's wife enjoyed an economic partnership with her husband which gave women significant authority within the family, but demographic factors subsequently diminished female opportunities. As the gender ratio equalized, women lost their advantages and, as sons grew to maturity, women's influence and power receded.[56] Their situation was further transformed, especially among middle- and upper-class women, by the importation of large numbers of African slaves. Daniel Blake Smith described the process. 'Gradually stripped of economic and familial authority in the household, the eighteenth-century planter's wife increasingly served as an ornament to her husband and family.' Girls in eighteenth-century Virginia and Maryland came to accept a more limited role in family and economic life than seventeenth-century women, but 'in the process deepened their ties to other women and became more self consciously genteel in an increasingly male-dominated world'.[57]

Historians Lois Carr and Lorena Walsh were not concerned with the implications of their study for the era of the American Revolution, but the question of what the American Revolution meant for women was the question that the first generation of women's historians wanted to answer. It remains unresolved, however. Progress was measured in terms of overall benefits and in relation to men. Although references were made to the experience of women in the middle ages, seventeenth- century England and France, American historians' interest in comparative work is limited.

The title of Joan Hoff Wilson's 1976 essay 'The Illusion of Change' was as much a commentary on the 1960s as it was on the Revolution. Already the author of three books, Hoff Wilson combined an interest in American foreign policy with an interest in women's history. Combining theories of feminism and modernization, Hoff Wilson argued that women lacked the consciousness necessary to comprehend their place in society. Their education, such as it was, ill prepared them to understand the rhetoric of Revolution, Mercy Otis Warren notwithstanding. Even more disabling was women's marginalization in an economic system which denied them the experience and skills necessary to take advantage of the expanding economy of the post-revolutionary era. Hoff Wilson claims that 'certain types of female functions, leading either to the well-known exploitation of working women or to the ornamental middle-class housewife of the nineteenth century, were abetted by the American Revolution, although not caused by it'. Women simply had too few opportunities between 1700 and 1800 'to allow them to make the transition in attitudes necessary to insure high status performance in the newly emerging nation.' 'Women of the post-revolutionary generation had little choice but to fill those low status functions prescribed by the small minority of American males who *were* prepared for modernization by enough diverse activities and experiences'.[58]

For Hoff Wilson, women's role and status in society had declined over the colonial period due largely to reasons of demography and economy. Women were also made scapegoats by a besieged clergy.[59] Though promoting autonomy and individualism, the Second Great Awakening increased opportunity for education among men but among women, demands for virtue were internalized and oppressive. The rate of female literacy remained stagnant while that of men forged ahead.[60] There was also a decline in women's legal status after the war and increased reliance on Blackstone, whose commentaries on the English common law circulated widely in the early republic.[61] Those few women who did advocate the rights of women – among whom Hoff Wilson singled out Abigail Adams, Judith Sargent Murray, Elizabeth Southgate Bowne, Elizabeth Drinker, and Mercy Otis Warren – operated within narrow ideological parameters. But they were not feminists.

> Like most of the better organized, but no less unsuccessful Républicaines of France, they seldom, if ever, aspired to complete equality with men except in terms of education. Moreover, none challenged the institution of marriage or defined themselves 'as other than mothers and potential mothers.' They simply could not conceive of a society whose standards were not set by male, patriarchal institutions, nor should they be expected to have done so. Instead of demanding equal rights, the most articulate and politically conscious American women of this generation asked at most for privileges and at least for favors – not for an absolute expansion of their legal or political functions, which they considered beyond their proper womenly sphere. Man was indeed the measure of equality to these women, and given their societal conditioning, such status was beyond their conception of themselves as individuals.[62]

Unsurprisingly Hoff Wilson concludes that 'for women, the American Revolution was over before it ever began'.

Mary Beth Norton takes a different view. Professor of History at Cornell University where she has taught since 1971, Norton rejects Hoff Wilson's contention that the Revolution was 'a step forward' for men, and 'a step backward' for women, but applauds her willingness to question whether categories applicable to men were appropriate to women.[63] Norton reaches a more positive assessment of the impact of the Revolution on women. In *Liberty's Daughters* she argues that the link to republicanism, though initially positive, 'grew ever more restrictive' so that its legacy for women was ambiguous.[64] *Liberty's Daughters* grew out of research initially undertaken for her first book *The British Americans* (1972).[65] In Norton's view, 'the Revolution had an indelible effect upon American women' but it was to be found not 'in the public world of law and politics', but 'in an analysis of women's private writings'.[66] Based on the examination of family papers, Norton acknowledges that her sources privilege literate women, but her assumption that there was more than enough shared experience among women of different classes that the literate could speak for the non-literate, was overly optimistic.[67]

Norton argues that 'the decade of turbulence that preceded the Revolution touched the lives of colonial women as well as men' in a number of ways. Firstly, the intensification of legislative and popular protest against British policies, the observation of days of fasting and prayer, and mob actions impinged upon women's consciousness. Though women in the 1760s might still apologize when they engaged in political discussions, by the 1780s they were 'reading widely in political literature, publishing their own sentiments, engaging in heated debates over public policy, and avidly supporting the war effort in a variety of ways', thus expanding 'the boundaries of the feminine sphere'. Secondly, women were incorporated into the resistance movement when their 'small circle of domestic concerns' took on political significance. As consumers and producers, their cooperation was essential to the success of economic boycotts, a tactic adopted by the colonists in an attempt to force the British government to rescind offending legislation. 'The chosen tactics could succeed only if white housewives and their daughters refused to purchase imported goods and simultaneously increased their production of homespun. Even the work assignments of female slaves would have to be changed if the colonial policy was to be fully effective.' Recognition by political figures of the importance of women's role and 'the realm of the household' enhanced women's status but 'the re-evaluation of domesticity that began during the revolutionary years would eventually culminate in nineteenth-century culture's glorification of woman's household role'.[68]

Norton provides the fullest examination of the Ladies Association which was organized in Philadelphia in 1780 and promoted in other states by means of the press and in circular letters. It proposed an innovative and elaborate scheme of fundraising for the benefit of the soldiers of the Continental army. This campaign was inaugurated by the publication of a broadside entitled *The Sentiments of an American Woman*, whose author was Esther DeBerdt Reed. An appeal to American women for action, it was an assertion of female patriotism. It justified women's intrusion into revolutionary affairs by citing biblical, classical and historical precedents and challenged those men who disapproved of the initiative to contemplate the sorry state of the army. 'In financial terms', Norton concludes, it was 'a smashing success'. Women in Trenton, New Jersey also issued a declaration of sentiments.[69]

Republican motherhood

Linda Kerber's *Women of the Republic* originated in an essay written in memory of Richard Hofstader who died in 1970.[70] Professor of Liberal Arts at the University of Iowa, like Norton Kerber had already made her name with the publication of her first book, *Federalists in Dissent* (1970). But what began as an essay on the passage of ideas from Europe to America, in her case, the impact of Mary Wollstonecraft's *Vindication of the Rights of Woman*, developed into a much broader and more significant study.[71] In *Women of the Republic*, Kerber argues 'that women's work and women's words did make a difference'. The Revolution expanded the range of work undertaken by women.

> The Revolutionary army turns out to have been dependent on women for nursing, cooking, and cleanliness. Both patriot and tory forces could recruit men not because cheerful women waved them off to war, but because those same women bravely stayed on alone, keeping family farms and mills in operation, fending off squatters, and protecting the family property by their heavy labor, often at grave physical risk.[72]

Furthermore, if women's experiences were to be assessed as carefully as those of men, then the 'general contours' of American history might look different too. 'Political theory appears less radical and more conservative when measured against the conscious refusal of constitution makers to recognize women's presence in the Republic and to change women's status.' In addition 'the catalog of significant American literature is enriched by the addition of essays, memoirs, and fiction written by women that have awaited careful evaluation'.[73]

'If American women were to count themselves as the daughters of Liberty,' declares Kerber 'they would have to invent their own ideology.' As the Revolution unfolded, women 'had few theoretical analyses ... on which they might draw for sustenance', but much which told them 'that they were peripheral to the world of politics and decision making'. There was little guidance to be derived from Enlightenment thinkers and even less from the radical whigs.[74] Women's patriotism was doubted as was their capacity for independent thought, women being first subject to the authority of fathers and then husbands. They also lacked property, deemed essential among men.

> Despite anecdotal evidence of the economic and physical sacrifice of individual women, a folklore persisted that discounted women's political behavior, assumed that women were incapable of making reasoned and unbiased political judgements, and emphasized the hesitancy of women to sacrifice their creature comforts for higher national purposes. The popular press shrilly insisted both before and after the war that American women were excessive in their consumption of British goods and books; the critics held that by indulging in British products, American women were undercutting the efforts of American men to develop a fully independent national culture.[75]

Some women who belonged to patriot circles were deferential in their attitudes and disclaimed knowledge of politics, unlike Abigail Adams and Mercy Otis Warren, but even they did not advocate a public political role for women. Kerber dismisses the idea that their reticence was some kind of false consciousness as Lawrence Friedman and Arthur Shaffer implied. 'Their culture had pointedly established that politics was not a female province. The daily lives of women in a preindustrial society *were* largely spent in a domestic circle, a confinement impossible to ignore.' Yet during wartime and in the period of the Confederation, 'politics did intrude into the women's world' and 'women acknowledged its presence and responded to it'.[76]

The role that women devised for themselves was that of 'republican motherhood', the training of sons to be virtuous citizens of the young Republic. Such a role required the expansion of women's educational opportunities and although domesticity and religion were the ultimate legacy of the Revolution, republican motherhood was established on the foundation of the expansion of women's educational opportunity. Kerber's argument draws heavily on the views of Benjamin Rush, the activities of the Philadelphia Female Academy and the orations delivered by its pupils. The creation of an American republic placed an enormous burden on its citizenry to defend it against the cancer of corruption without which it would fail as others had done in the past. 'Maintaining the Republic,' writes Kerber, 'was an educational challenge as well as a political one.'[77]

> Motherhood was discussed almost as if it were a fourth branch of government, a device that ensured social control in the gentlest possible way. If the Republic indeed rested on responsible motherhood, prospective mothers needed to be well informed and decently educated. The industrial revolution, occurring at the same time, reinforced the need for improved education. As the post-war world became more print-orientated, and as it became harder to function in it as an illiterate, interest in the improvement of girls' schooling increased.[78]

Kerber notes that Nancy Cott has previously linked developments such as these to changes in the domestic economy but does not imbue them with any political significance until the advent of the Grimké sisters, Elizabeth Cady Stanton and the emergence of an explicit feminist ideology in the 1830s and 1840s.[79] Whereas in the past, the education of girls was intended to prepare them for marriage, now they were to serve a new purpose, to produce the model republican woman.

> The model republican woman was to be self-reliant (within limits), literate, untempted by the frivolities of fashion. She had a responsibility to the political scene, though was not active in it … A woman's competence was not assumed to extend to the making of

political decisions. Her political task was accomplished within the confines of her family. The model republican woman was a mother ... The Republican Mother's life was dedicated to the service of civic virtue: she educated her sons for it, she condemned and corrected her husband's lapses from it.[80]

How the Revolution impinged on one woman's life is vividly portrayed through a study of Mary Fish, much of it based on correspondence with her second husband Gold Sellek Silliman in Joy Day Buel and Richard Buel Jr's, *The Way of Duty* (1984).[81] Mary Fish's life is portrayed as both typical and atypical, but what makes it distinctive is the sheer volume of material relating to her that survived in the possession of her family.[82]

In telling their story we have found the nature of the material required us to juxtapose the great public events of the period – the religious revival known as the Great Awakening, the trials and perplexities of the revolutionary struggle, the growing secularization of society, the westward migration, the rise of Jeffersonian democracy, and the advent of the Industrial Revolution – with the persistent patterns and daily routines of family and community life.[83]

The authors seek to present Mary's story 'in popular, narrative form' within the context of recent scholarship in social and political history and 'to show how public and private spheres impinged on one another'.[84] Before her second marriage Mary Fish Noyes, a well-educated Connecticut widow, had been in comfortable circumstances but when her husband became an active militia officer his promising career came to an end and thereafter financial difficulties beset the family. Mary struggled to maintain their property even before Silliman was kidnapped by British/Loyalist forces. She lived until 1818 yet 'remained to the end of her life', conclude the Buels, 'less a daughter of the Revolution' than 'a child of the Puritans'.[85] Mary's preoccupation with religion in later life was indeed the dominant legacy bequeathed by the Revolution to many of America's middle-class women.

Women in the seaports

Much closer in interpretation to Hoff Wilson than Norton or Kerber is Elaine Crane's essay 'Dependence in the Era of Independence' (1987). Crane finds implausible the notion that the Revolution represented a kind of watershed. The colonies would gain their independence from Britain, but women would remain 'in a state of submissive dependence'.[86] Little attention was paid to the role and status of women due to two factors. First, there is no evidence to suggest that women 'were conscious of common problems', and those who were, were 'foreclosed from action by the broadly shared agreement about the position of women within late eighteenth-century American society'. Second, 'the Revolution had little meaning for women as women ... insofar as women participated in the Revolution, they did so not on behalf of themselves as women but on behalf of the families, communities, and societies of which they were a part'. Following the Revolution, declares Crane, women 'were as dependent as ever' for 'their role in the new nation had already been determined by their declining position in colonial society'.[87]

As the eighteenth century advanced, women 'were less likely to manage estates or control property'. They were less frequently appointed as sole executrix of their husbands' estates, were less likely to receive an interest in land and, when they did, it was more likely to be limited to a life interest which circumscribed their independence as widows. Moreover, in the late eighteenth and early nineteenth centuries, this dependence was further accentuated by the likelihood of children receiving a higher proportion of the estate than formerly and of daughters inheriting personal property rather than real property. By examining changes in custom, law, economy and religion between 1607 and 1783, Crane demonstrates how the status of women deteriorated, a trend which the Revolution enhanced rather than reversed. As the economy became increasingly commercial and industrial, women's opportunities for economic independence further diminished.[88] Crane finds the concept of republican motherhood unpersuasive. It did not ask any more of women than in the colonial period but 'without the lofty ideology of republican motherhood'.[89] Most likely, stated Crane, the Revolution's legacy was 'to reinforce and justify the idea of separate spheres for women and men' adding that developments in education and religion in the early republic had the same effect.[90]

In *Ebb Tide in New England* (1998) Crane examines the 'feminization of poverty' in four New England seaport towns: Boston, Newport, Rhode Island, Portsmouth, New Hampshire and Salem, Massachusetts. She reiterates her view that 'because of the ways in which American society evolved during the colonial period, the Revolution could not have been a liberating experience for American women'.[91] Crane challenges the concept of republican motherhood as an outgrowth of the revolution, locating its origins not in revolutionary America but in seventeenth-century Europe. Neither republican motherhood nor companionate marriage challenged male dominance or held out the prospect of equality. There was no small irony in the fact that the Revolution was an 'effort to devise a political theory that effectively dismantled the paternalistic, patriarchal, hierarchical, and dependent relationship between Great Britain and the colonies without disturbing the paternalistic, patriarchal, hierarchical, and dependent relationship between husband and wife'. Republican motherhood was the solution.[92] The failure of urban New England women to 'demand rights in the revolutionary era [was] because unlike European women, they had no militant tradition to call upon'.[93]

Critics

Laurel Thatcher Ulrich and Jan Lewis raised different issues in relation to *Liberty's Daughters* and *Women of the Republic*. In *Good Wives* (1982), Ulrich challenges Norton's view that women's roles were constrained by perceptions of separate spheres and that the revolutionary war dissolved traditional boundaries altering a 'line between male and female behavior, once apparently so impenetrable'. On the basis of evidence from New England, she disputes the rigid demarcation of women's roles in mid-eighteenth-century America.[94] Before the Revolution 'almost any task was suitable for a woman as long as it furthered the good of her family and was acceptable to her husband'. Ideology was permissive rather than restrictive. 'Under the right conditions any wife *could* not only double as a husband, she had the responsibility to do so.'[95] In a later essay 'Daughters of Liberty' (1989), Ulrich broadened her criticisms of both Norton and Kerber, questioning the secular approach they had adopted to the study of women and the intellectual vacuum in which Kerber located women during the revolutionary era. Ulrich claims

> that a providential interpretation of history framed the contributions of New England women during the Revolutionary era, that the weekly sermons through which most people in the region interpreted political events included rather than excluded women, and that far from representing an ideological discontinuity in women's lives the Revolution enlarged and reaffirmed the terms of public participation that had prevailed during the inter-colonial wars.[96]

Ulrich then takes two well-known incidents and reinterprets them. The first deals with newspaper stories about spinning meetings in the 1760s, the second concerned a woodcut of a female soldier on a broadside published in 1779. Ulrich rejects the view that spinning meetings were 'a visible manifestation of a much larger politicization of private duties' as Norton had claimed, or that the image of the female soldier was 'a flamboyant emblem of a widespread (though temporary) bending of gender roles'. Rather the spinning meetings were 'as much artefacts of Congregationalism as of revolution and ... the female soldier was not an American women at all but a mid-eighteenth-century English heroine affixed to a broadside that was fundamentally religious'.

> This is not to argue that women's culture in early New England was merely an extension of Congregational theology. Beneath the Revolutionary rhetoric of the Boston newspapers and the celebratory words of Congregational ministers lay a female world sustained by neighborliness, personal piety, and petty trade. The spinning bees were a visible but by no means comprehensive manifestation of that world. The doggerel verses that appeared with the woodcut of the female soldier were another. Religious women helped to shape their own identities through support of Congregational churches. They used the language of war to question the male culture that it nourished, overcoming their own dependence to instruct and chasten their neighbors.[97]

In 'The Republican Wife: Virtue and Seduction in the Early Republic' (1987), Jan Lewis challenges the focus on women as mothers in a republican polity to the neglect of their role as wives.[98] Though the concept of the family as 'the society in miniature' remained central, Lewis argues that among eighteenth-century writers, there was a shift in emphasis away from 'the child–parent nexus to the husband–wife bond' which raised women 'to a new moral and political stature'. When the father–son relationship 'or ruler and subject' predominated, she observes, 'women may conveniently be ignored'. But

> when the most important relationship is between conjugal equals, and when the family is still seen as the correlative of the larger society, then women can no longer be overlooked. If the affectionate union between a man and his wife, freely entered into, without tyrannical interference, is the model for all the relationships in the society and the polity, then the wife, as an indispensable half of the marital union, is a political creature.[99]

In the reformation of manners to which the new nation aspired, women had a central role. Women were both a moral force and an influence over men. Moreover, women were 'to play their moral role not by denying their sexuality, by being "passionless" but by using it to tempt men to be good'. Women's influence was strongest during 'love and courtship'. And 'once she had seduced him into virtue', it was the lot of the married woman 'to preserve her husband in the exalted state to which her influence had raised him', thus inverting 'how earlier Americans had viewed women's sexuality'. No longer held responsible for the fall of man, woman's 'seductiveness is here transformed into her capacity for virtue'.[100]

How women in eighteenth-century America actually experienced the Revolution depended on a range of factors including age, marital status, race or ethnicity, social class and region, political affinity, the movement of armies, the proximity of their homes to the frontier or the coast, and whether they lived in towns or in the countryside, to mention the most obvious.

'Race'

The failure to deal with the subject of 'race' and the impact of the Revolution on black women was another weakness of the new historiography, though Kerber herself raised the issue in an influential article in 1988 in which she explored the use and misuse of the concept of 'separate spheres' in the history of women.[101] 'The language of separate spheres,' observed Kerber, 'was vulnerable to sloppy use. Above all, it was loosely metaphorical.' When historians made use of the metaphor of separate spheres, they often referred 'interchangeably, to an ideology *imposed on* women, a culture *created by* women, [and] a set of boundaries *expected to be observed* by women'. Recognizing that until recently most work 'had been about white middle class women', Kerber criticized it for helping historians to avoid 'thinking about race', not that black women had been wholly absent from the writings of both Norton and Crane.[102]

Jacqueline Jones's essay 'Race, Sex, and Self-Evident Truths: The Status of Slave Women during the Era of the American Revolution' (1989) recalled historians to the fact that the status of black women during the revolutionary era was fundamentally different from that of white women.

> Together, slave women and men endured the agony of bondage, and together blacks, both enslaved and free, struggled to form families that eventually served as the foundation of a distinctive Afro-American culture. The military conflict between loyalists and rebels intensified physical hardship among blacks, while the ensuing social and economic turmoil afforded some of their race the opportunities for a basic kind of freedom that white women and men – for all their rhetoric about the evils of tyranny – already enjoyed. Therefore, any discussion of the war's impact on American women must first highlight racial factors before dealing with issues related to class, regional, ethnic, and religious diversity in the late eighteenth-century population.[103]

In explaining the near invisibility of black women in the historical literature, Jones argues that black women in the latter half of the eighteenth century fell 'between the cracks that divide the study of women from the study of slaves'. While slave women might share certain domestic responsibilities with white women, they lived in bondage with black men. Generalizing about their experience was extremely difficult.[104]

Nonetheless in the period from 1750 to 1800, both within the system of slavery and inside their own homes and communities, women' burdens, Jones argues, set them apart from enslaved men. Gender considerations largely determined work allocations though a range of additional factors such as: 'whether a woman was African- or American-born; whether she lived in the North or South, in a town or rural area; whether she toiled in the swampy South Carolina lowcountry or on a Virginia wheat farm' would influence 'the nature and extent of these burdens'. Developments relating to the revolutionary war brought about the intensification of racial divisions in the young republic 'as large-scale cotton cultivation introduced a new and brutal chapter in the history of slavery' and an 'explicit sexual division of labour emerged within the private and public lives of free blacks'.[105]

The experience of Native American women was also initially ignored. As more extensive work on Native American peoples was undertaken by the new Indian historians (see Chapter 7), it became possible to glimpse the impact of the revolutionary war on Native American women whose communities were frequently uprooted and destroyed. Theda Perdue's book *Cherokee Women* (1998), however, stands alone. A matrilineal society in which 'men and women lived remarkably separate lives', Perdue (1949–), Professor of History at the University of North Carolina, challenges William McLoughlin's interpretation of Cherokee history 'in terms of anomie and renascence'. She argues that eighteenth-century women might have become more rather than less secure in some roles – 'as farmers and as socializers of children, for example'. Focusing 'on gender in the process of cultural change' Perdue argues that most Cherokee women experienced not 'cultural transformation' as a result of trade and war, 'but remarkable cultural persistence'.[106]

Diversity

Joan Gunderson describes her book *To Be Useful to the World* (1996) as a synthesis rather than a work of historical scholarship, but in trying to bring together the experiences of women who were divided by race, class, region and ethnicity, her study was unique. In focusing on the lives of four such different women, she achieves a perspective on the Revolution which conveys the complexity of its outcome in ways that have eluded others. The outcome of the Revolution, she writes, 'appears as a series of trade-offs. Women both gained and lost, but not equally, and one woman's gain might be intimately tied to another's loss'.[107] Elizabeth Dutoy Porter was the wife of a small planter in the Virginia Piedmont who lived out her life within a small compass but whose parents had been Huguenot refugees who had fled France as children and migrated to the colonies from England. Elizabeth lived in a largely French community in the foothills of Virginia where she lived as a widow for a number of decades with control of her property. Her slave Peg, another of Gunderson's subjects, was probably African-born. Deborah Read Franklin was representative of the urban artisanal class though she was the common law wife of Benjamin Franklin, while Margaret Brant was a Mohawk woman of eastern New York whose life saw many twists and turns and reversals. These women were atypical. For Elizabeth, the Revolution probably made little difference except that it enabled her descendents to move west to relieve their land hunger. For Peg it probably led to the loss of family members to the west and the south-west, to Deborah Read Franklin it brought fame and distinction, and to Margaret Brant devastation. The women shared common experiences of marriage, childbirth, household responsibilities, and work roles but race and class were of paramount importance. Though Gunderson characterized late eighteenth-century society as 'in constant motion', neither Elizabeth, Deborah nor Peg were travellers.[108]

> The trade-offs of the Revolutionary era are starkly evident for women. If moving west helped relieve land pressures reducing eastern women's options, it came at a direct cost to American Indian women, who were displaced by the settlement, and to the African-American women whose families were divided to provide the labor in new areas. If the replacement of indentured servants with paid, day labor offered women more control over their lives and working conditions, the women who worked in this way were part of a growing, marginalized class of the poor. If visiting helped sustain ties of kin and friendship, it did so along inceasingly stratified lines of race and class. Women's Revolutionary-era mobility produced

clear winners and losers, sharply divided by lines of race and class.[109]

Class

Not until the 1990s did radical historians take up the issue of class when historians such as Alfred Young and Barbara Clark Smith looked more closely at the forms of popular protest. Ray Raphael published *A People's History of the American Revolution* in 2001.[110] Women's participation in popular politics is explored by Alfred Young in his essay 'The Women of Boston: "Persons of Consequence" in the Making of the American Revolution, 1745–76'.[111] This essay had its origins in an international conference that 'was designed to connect the insights of new scholarship to an ongoing post-war inquiry into the origins, strengths, weaknesses, and prospects of modern democracy'.[112] More than other cities, Boston was home to a disproportionate number of women, among whom were large numbers of widows. Inequality was the norm 'and a large proportion of the town was either impoverished or bordered on the brink of poverty'.[113] Though dependent, a large class of Boston women 'held fast to values of a moral economy and to aspirations for personal independence'.[114] Of the institutions that provided the foundation of the resistance movement – the town meeting, the Congregational meetinghouse, the militia, and the public schools – only one was useful to female resisters.

> Women who participated in activities that ended in Revolution could draw on only one of these institutions: the church. But they could also draw on roles that were by custom theirs in the domestic sphere, their roles as consumers and producers in the household economy and rituals of community punishment and shaming. And, they were heirs to traditions of war.[115]

Women were swept up in the Great Awakening, more so than men. They were less active in the traditions of holiday rituals, and took a more equal part with men in rituals associated with public punishments. They participated in purposeful public riots and in regular wars they exhorted men to patriotism and shamed those deemed cowards.[116] In looking anew at major events in Boston's revolutionary history Young identifies women in several distinct (although overlapping) roles. These were (1) as spectators, (2) as enforcers of consumer boycotts, (3) as manufacturers, (4) as rioters, (5) as mourners in politicized funeral processions and memorial meetings, and (6) as exhorters of men to direct action. Then, in 1775 and 1776, as resistance turned to armed rebellion, women can be found (7) as military supporters and (8) as political refugees. The trend of women's activities is from the genteel to the militant, from small private decisions to large-scale public activities, and from the more moderate to the more radical.[117]

Food riots

Barbara Clark Smith, Curator in the Division of Social History at the National Museum of American History, Smithsonian Institution, explores the food and price riots which took place between 1776 and 1779 in Massachusetts, Rhode Island, Connecticut, New York, Pennsylvania, Maryland and possibly Virginia.[118] A form of 'common people's politics', women featured prominently in them. They offer 'possibilities for political action that resistance and revolution opened for women, not as republican wives or mothers but as social and economic actors within household, neighbourhood, and marketplace'. The war, marked by 'dislocations of supply and redoubling of demand, reliance on depreciating paper currency, and rampant inflation formed the necessary economic context for these riots' occurrence'.[119] It was perceived by those who participated in them and those who wrote about them in the press that these events were related to the patriot cause: 'In a variety of ways, rioters and their allies claimed that confronting merchants in their shops was a patriotic action, much like facing redcoats on the battlefield.' Smith argues that her essay offers 'a new reading of the resistance movement, tracing its relationship to the local world of exchange and market place ethics'. Her account of popular participation in the war effort explores one context 'within which the ideas disseminated by patriot writers and spokesmen in pamphlets, sermons, and the like were received and interpreted'.[120]

The Association

In a subsequent essay, 'Social Visions of the American Resistance Movement' (1997), Barbara Clark Smith looks at how the Association formed to enforce the trade embargo drew women into action in support of the Association. By this Smith did not mean that women merely participated in trade boycotts, a role recognized by Norton and Kerber, and well over a hundred years earlier by Ellet, but that they participated, at least 'to some degree, as political actors'. The women in question were widows. This role was far removed from that of victim and symbol. In other areas, women were victims of armies and irregulars and symbols of liberty and wisdom.

> As the Continental Congress itself realized, women's participation mattered. Although few women were involved in importing and exporting goods, they did own retail shops and taverns, where they often marketed items besides the basics of food and alcohol. Urban women shopped for their families' home consumption, and women were as able and as likely to consume foreign goods as were men. Women had the power to break the provisions of the Association. As a result, the success of nonimportation and nonconsumption required female participation to an unprecedented degree.[121]

Within the context of distinctive streams in American culture – genteel, plebian, artisinal republicanism and evangelical religion, the technique was not new. These were agreements among people, outside formal political structures and distinct from crowd actions:

> All these pacts conferred political significance on ordinary events and mundane parts of life; a patriot was one who did not import, consume, or raise prices on scarce imported goods or the domestic products that replaced them. A patriot, then, clearly fulfilled neighborly ideals, privileging bonds with fellows over immediate, narrow self-interest.[122]

It fell to committees to gather signatures of heads of households to ensure compliance. This meant that widows were drawn into the association. Unlike their roles as victims of armies and irregulars, symbols of liberty and wisdom, in trade boycotts they emerge 'as participants'. In this essay Smith challenges Jameson's contention that the Revolution was social in its *consequences*. She perceives it as social 'from the first years of resistance'.[123]

Camp followers

There were also those women who travelled with the army, for whom the term 'camp followers' is generally employed, although Linda Grant De Pauw contests its usage on the grounds that it should be applied only to those who literally followed the army selling goods and services including prostitution but played no part in military actions.[124] Relatively little was published on this topic before Walter H. Blumenthal's *Women Camp Followers of the American Revolution* (1974)[125] which was followed over twenty years later by Holly A. Mayer's *Belonging to the Army* (1996). Women 'served the army as cooks, washerwomen, and nurses; during battles they carried messages and supplies and assisted with the artillery'. They performed the services which women always performed. How they were supported, whether they were paid or not, fed or not, carried or not, was up to local commanders. They provided necessary services 'in return for minimal support'. John Shy, one of the first of the new military historians, considered that the Americans were disadvantaged by the fact that they had fewer female support staff than the British, but Washington thought there were too many and that they put a strain on scarce resources.[126] 'Women camp followers during the American Revolution lived on the edge, lower in status than the teenage boys and poor men who themselves hovered on the brink of starvation. They performed whatever services were in demand and took whatever they could get in payment. They fended for themselves as best they could.' Some served with the British army.[127]

The Revolution was only one of the forces affecting women's situation. Alterations in American society were under way well before the beginning of hostilities, and the revolutionary period itself was too brief to allow any thorough social transformation. As Gunderson concludes, analysis of white, Native American, and African American women demonstrates that events not only had a different impact on women of different 'races' and classes but also that their impact was not merely positive or negative. If migration to the frontier offered opportunities to white women, it was at the expense of Native American women. New standards of respectability constricted all white women's activities, conferred on some the mantle of moral authority and on others (poor white women and women of colour) the label of deviancy. When upper- and middle-class women became consumers instead of producers, they traded the gender-integrated world of work and family for a more confined gender-segregated world of domesticity, privacy, and dependency. Although collectively 'women found no great improvement in their status' by 1790, Gunderson writes 'the Revolution brought both promise and new restraints' into their lives.[128] While Gunderson sought to capture the diversity of women's experienced through the lives of four very different women, Carol Berkin, using a variety of original records, sought to explore its meaning for many different types of women, often using their own words. The distance between these two books indicates how rich the resources for women's history have become.[129]

Notes

1 Ray Raphael, *A People's History of the American Revolution: How Common People Shaped the Fight for Independence* (New York; 2001), p. 135; Elizabeth Cometti, 'Women in the American Revolution', *NEQ*, 20 (1947), pp. 329–46.

2 Mary Beth Norton, 'Reflections on Women in the Age of the American Revolution' in Ronald Hoffman and Peter J. Albert (eds), *Women in the Age of the American Revolution* (Charlottesville, VA; 1989), pp. 479–93, 479.

3 Mary Beth Norton and Ruth M. Alexander (eds), *Modern Problems in American Women's History*, 3rd edn (Boston and New York; 2003), p. xiii.

4 Linda Kerber, '"History Can Do It No Justice": Women and the Reinterpretation of the American Revolution', in Hoffman and Albert, *Women in the Age of the American Revolution*, pp. 3–42, 17.

5 Norton, 'Reflections on Women in the Age of the American Revolution', pp. 479–80. In the preface to *Women in the Age of the American Revolution*, Ronald Hoffman, one of the volume's editors, paid tribute to such pioneers as Elizabeth Ellet and those of the next generation such as May King Rensselaer (1848–1925) and Alice Morse Earle (1851–1911) each of whose output was prodigious. Ronald Hoffman, 'Preface' in Hoffman and Albert, *Women in the Age of the American Revolution*, pp. vii–ix.

6 Kerber, '"History Can Do It No Justice"', pp. 3–44, 10, 17.

7 Philip Hicks, 'Portia and Marcia: Female Political Identity and the Historical Imagination, 1770–1800', *WMQ*, 3rd ser., 62 (2005), pp. 265–94, 272; Linda K. Kerber, *Women of the Republic: Intellect and Ideology in Revolutionary America* (Chapel Hill, NC; 1980), pp. 35–6; Mary Beth Norton, *Liberty's Daughters: The Revolutionary Experience of American Women, 1750–1800* (Boston; 1980), pp. 177–88; Sheila L. Skemp, *Judith*

Sargent Murray: A Brief Biography with Documents (Boston and New York; 1998), pp. 15–16.

8 Hicks (quoting Murray), 'Portia and Marcia', p. 272.

9 See the contrasting accounts of the battles of Lexington and Concord, 1775 in Richard D. Brown (ed.), *Major Problems in the Era of the American Revolution, 1760–1791*, 2nd edn (Boston, MA; 2000), pp. 145–8; for loyalist accusations of New England savagery at Lexington and Concord, see Douglass Adair and John A. Schutz (eds), *Peter Oliver's Origin and Progress of the American Rebellion: A Tory View* (Stanford, CA; 1967), pp. 120–1; Kerber, *Women of the Republic*, pp. 46–7; Carol Berkin, *Revolutionary Mothers: Women in the Struggle for America's Independence* (New York; 2005), p. 39.

10 On the cultural uses of the female body – as 'a highly visible index to the advance of luxury' and 'a battleground of imperial politics' – see T. H. Breen, *The Marketplace of Revolution: How Consumer Politics Shaped American Independence* (Oxford; 2004), pp. 272–6, 280–1; and on the culture wars in occupied Philadelphia, Kate Haulman, 'Fashion and the Culture Wars of Revolutionary Philadelphia', *WMQ*, 3rd. ser., 62 (2005), pp. 625–62.

11 David Ramsay, *The History of the American Revolution*, ed. Lester H. Cohen, 2 vols (Indianapolis, IN; 1990), II, p. 496; Ramsay was probably responsible for the letter from St Augustine dated 25 June that appeared in the *Pennsylvania Packet*, 21 August 1781, which contains an almost identical account.

12 For coverage similar to Ramsay's, see William Gordon, *History of the Rise, Progress, and Establishment of the Independence of the United States of America*, 3rd edn, 4 vols (New York; 1801), II, pp. 245–7, 386–91.

13 Ramsay, *American Revolution*, II, pp. 468, 469, 470–1.

14 Ramsay, *American Revolution*, II, p. 470.

15 Ramsay, *American Revolution*, I, p. 304.

16 Kerber, *Women of the Republic*, p. 258.

17 Rosemarie Zagarri, *A Woman's Dilemma: Mercy Otis Warren and the American Revolution* (Wheeling, IL; 1995), pp. 162–4; see also Jeffrey H. Richards, *Mercy Otis Warren* (New York; 1995).

18 Kate Davies, *Catharine Macaulay and Mercy Otis Warren: The Revolutionary Atlantic and the Politics of Gender* (Oxford; 2005), p. 3.

19 Mercy Otis Warren, *History of the Rise, Progress and Termination of the American Revolution*, ed. Lester H. Cohen, 2 vols (Indianapolis, IN; 1988), I, pp. 120–1.

20 Warren, *History*, I, pp. 210–11, see fn. on page 211.

21 Warren, *History*, I, pp. 235–8.

22 Warren, *History*, I, pp. 297–8; Alfred F. Young, *Masquerade: The Life and Times of Deborah Sampson, Continental Soldier* (New York; 2004), p. 49.

23 Raphael, *A People's History*, pp. 164, 167–70, 439, fn. 94 but see also Joan Gunderson, *To Be Useful to the World: Women in Revolutionary America, 1740–1790* (New York; 1996), pp. 31–2. Norton, *Liberty's Daughters*, pp. 202–4; Kerber, *Women of the Republic*, p. 46 and fn. 17; Berkin, *Revolutionary Mothers*, pp. 39–41.

24 For the fullest treatment of this subject, see June Namias, *White Captives: Gender and Ethnicity on the American Frontier* (Chapel Hill, NC; 1993), ch. 4.

25 Ramsay, *American Revolution*, II, pp. 370–1, 505.

26 Warren, *History*, I, pp. 233–4, 327–8.

27 Linda Colley, *Captives: Britain, Empire and the World 1600–1850* (London; 2002), pp. 228–30; the front cover of this book is taken from the 1804 painting 'The Murder of Jane McCrea' by John Vanderlyn.

28 Warren, *History*, I, pp. 327–8.

29 Warren, *History*, I, p. 236.

30 *Peter Oliver's Origin*, p. 61.

31 *Peter Oliver's Origin*, pp. 62–3. The quotation 'There's no inconvenience but has its convenience' was taken from Samuel Richardson's novel *Clarissa, or the History of a Young Lady* (London; 1748), II, p. 106.

32 *Peter Oliver's Origin*, pp. 63–4.

33 *Peter Oliver's Origin*, pp. 73–4.

34 *Peter Oliver's Origin*, pp. 73–4.

35 *Peter Oliver's Origin*, pp. 70–1.

36 *Peter Oliver's Origin*, pp. 97–8.

37 *Peter Oliver's Origin*, p. 120.

38 George Bancroft, *The American Revolution* (London and Boston; 1866), III, pp. 371–2; death of Hannah Caldwell, IV (London and Boston; 1874), pp. 372–3.

39 Bancroft, *The American Revolution*, IV, pp. 405–6.

40 Kerber, '"History Can Do It No Justice"', p. 5.

41 Elizabeth Ellet, *Revolutionary Women in the War for American Independence: A One-Volume Revised Edition of Elizabeth Ellet's 1848 Landmark Series*, edited and annotated by Lincoln Diamant (Westport, CT; 1998), p. 15.

42 Ellet, *Revolutionary Women*, p. 16.

43 Young, *Masquerade*, pp. 280–4.

44 Ellet, *Revolutionary Women*, pp. 16–17.

45 Kerber, '"History Can Do It No Justice"', pp. 5–6.

46 Kerber, '"History Can Do It No Justice"', p. 3; Scott E. Casper, 'The Uneasy Marriage of Sentiment and Scholarship: Elizabeth F. Ellet and the Domestic Origins of American Women's History', *Journal of Women's History*, 4 (1992), pp. 10–35, 11.

47 Casper, 'The Uneasy Marriage of Sentiment and Scholarship', p. 12.

48 Casper, 'The Uneasy Marriage of Sentiment and Scholarship', p. 14.

49 Casper, 'The Uneasy Marriage of Sentiment and Scholarship', p. 21.

50 Nina Byam, *American Women Writers and the Work of History, 1790–1860* (Brunswick, NJ; 1995), pp. 233–4.

51 Berkin, *Revolutionary Mothers*, p. xiv.

52 Manuela Thurner, 'Issues and Paradigms in U.S. Feminist History' and Gisela Bock, 'Challenging Dichotomies in Women's History', in Norton and Alexander (eds), *Major Problems in American Women's History*, pp. 2–8 and 8–14.

53 Joan Hoff Wilson, 'The Illusion of Change: Women and the American Revolution' in Alfred F. Young (ed.), *The American Revolution: Explorations*

in the History of American Radicalism (Dekalb, IL; 1976), pp. 383–445; Norton, *Liberty's Daughter*; Kerber, *Women of the Republic*.

54 Richard R. Beeman, 'A New Era in Female History', *Reviews in American History*, 9 (1981), pp. 336–41; Skemp, *Judith Sargent Murray*, p. 108; Kerber, *Women of the Republic*, pp. 189, 287; Norton, *Liberty's Daughters*, p. 238.

55 Jack P. Greene and J. R. Pole (eds), *Colonial British America* (Baltimore, MD; 1984), p. 8.

56 Lois Green Carr and Lorena S. Walsh, 'The Planter's Wife: The Experience of White Women in Seventeenth-Century Maryland', *WMQ*, 3rd ser., 34 (1977), pp. 542–71, 561–71. This article was voted one of the most important articles to be published in the *William and Mary Quarterly* over a fifty-year period.

57 Daniel Blake Smith, *Inside the Great House: Planter Family Life in Eighteenth-Century Chesapeake Society* (Ithaca, NY; 1980), pp. 80–1.

58 Hoff Wilson, 'Illusion of Change', pp. 386–7, 390, 391–3.

59 Hoff Wilson, 'Illusion of Change', p. 406.

60 Hoff Wilson, 'Illusion of Change', p. 409.

61 Hoff Wilson, 'Illusion of Change', pp. 414–15; for the declining legal position of colonial American women, see Cornelia Hughes Dayton, *Women before the Bar: Gender, Law and Society in Connecticut, 1639–1789* (Chapel Hill, NC and London; 1995).

62 Hoff Wilson, 'Illusion of Change', pp. 426–7, 431.

63 Norton, 'Reflections on Women in the Age of the American Revolution', pp. 481–3.

64 Norton, *Liberty's Daughters*, pp. 298–9.

65 Mary Beth Norton, 'Eighteenth-Century American Women in Peace and War: The Case of the Loyalists', *WMQ*, 3rd ser., 33 (1976), pp. 386–409.

66 Norton, *Liberty's Daughters*, p. xix.

67 Norton, *Liberty's Daughters*, pp. xvii, xx; see Raphael's comments, *People's History*, pp. 147, fn. 33, 433.

68 Norton, *Liberty's Daughters*, pp. 155–6.

69 Norton, *Liberty's Daughters*, pp. 177–88.

70 Kerber, *Women of the Republic*, p. xi; Linda Kerber, 'Daughters of Columbia: Educating Women for the Republic, 1787–1805' in Stanley Elkins and Eric McKitrick (eds), *The Hofstadter Aegis: A Memorial* (New York; 1974), pp. 36–59; Linda Kerber, 'The Republican Mother: Women and the Enlightenment – An American Perspective', *AQ*, 28 (1976), pp. 187–205.

71 Kerber, *Women of the Republic*, p. 231.

72 Kerber, *Women of the Republic*, pp. xi–xii.

73 Kerber, *Women of the Republic*, pp. xi–xii. Similar conclusions have emerged in respect of the English Revolution: see Alison Plowden, *Women All on Fire: The Women of the English Civil War* (Stroud; 1998).

74 Kerber, *Women of the Republic*, pp. 27–32.

75 Kerber, *Women of the Republic*, pp. 35–6.

76 Kerber, *Women of the Republic*, pp. 76–9, 80–5; Lawrence J. Friedman and Arthur H. Shaffer, 'Mercy Otis Warren and the Politics of Historical Nationalism', *NEQ*, 48 (1975), pp. 194–215, 206–15; on Abigail Adams, see

Elaine F. Crane, 'Political Dialogue and the Spring of Abigail's Discontent', WMQ, 3rd ser., 56 (1999), pp. 745–74; on petitioning, the only political action open to women, see Cynthia A. Kierner, *Southern Women in Revolution, 1776–1800: Personal and Political Narratives* (Columbia, SC; 1998), p. xx.

77 Kerber, *Women of the Republic*, p. 189.

78 Kerber, *Women of the Republic*, p. 200.

79 Kerber, *Women of the Republic*, p. 200; Nancy F. Cott, *The Bonds of Womanhood: Woman's Sphere in New England 1780–1835* (New Haven, CT; 1977, 2nd edn 1997), ch. 3.

80 Kerber, *Women of the Republic*, pp. 228, 229.

81 Joy Day Buel and Richard Buel Jr, *The Way of Duty: A Woman and Her Family in Revolutionary America* (New York; 1984).

82 Buel and Buel Jr, *Way of Duty*, p. xiii.

83 Buel and Buel Jr, *Way of Duty*, p. xiv.

84 Buel and Buel Jr, *Way of Duty*, p. xiv.

85 Buel and Buel Jr, *The Way of Duty*, p. 281.

86 Elaine F. Crane, 'Dependence in the Era of Independence: The Role of Women in a Republican Society' in J. P. Greene (ed.), *The American Revolution: Its Character and Limits* (New York and London; 1987), pp. 253–75, 257; similar conclusions had been reached much earlier about seventeenth-century English women by Alice Clark, *Working Life of Women in the Seventeenth Century* (London; 1919).

87 Crane, 'Dependence in the era of Independence', pp. 257–8.

88 Crane, 'Dependence in the Era of Independence', pp. 260–1.

89 Crane, 'Dependence in the Era of Independence', pp. 266–8.

90 Crane, 'Dependence in the Era of Independence', pp. 268–9, 270.

91 Elaine F. Crane, *Ebb Tide in New England: Women, Seaports, and Social Change 1630–1800* (Boston; 1998), p. 207.

92 Crane, *Ebb Tide in New England*, pp. 207–9.

93 Crane, *Ebb Tide in New England*, p. 243.

94 Laurel Thatcher Ulrich, *Good Wives: Image and Reality in the Lives of Women in Northern New England, 1650–1750* (New York; 1982), p. 49.

95 Ulrich, *Good Wives*, pp. 37–8.

96 Laurel Thatcher Ulrich, '"Daughters of Liberty": Religious Women in Revolutionary New England' in Hoffman and Albert, *Women in the Age of the American Revolution* , pp. 211–43, 213.

97 Ulrich, 'Religious Women in Revolutionary New England', pp. 213, 214.

98 Jan Lewis, 'The Republican Wife: Virtue and Seduction in the Early Republic', WMQ, 3rd ser., 44 (1987), pp. 689–721.

99 Lewis, 'The Republican Wife', p. 699.

100 Lewis, 'The Republican Wife', pp. 700–1; see also Ruth Bloch, 'American Feminine Ideals in Transition: the Rise of the Moral Mother, 1785–1815', *Feminist Studies*, 4 (1978), pp. 100–26 and Rosemarie Zagarri, 'Morals, Manners, and the Republican Mother', AQ, 44 (1992), pp. 192–215.

101 Linda Kerber, 'Separate Spheres, Female Worlds, Woman's Place: The Rhetoric of Women's History', JAH, 75 (1988), pp. 9–39.

102 Kerber, 'Separate Spheres', p. 17; on slave marriage, Norton, *Liberty's*

Daughters, pp. 65–70; on the Revolution in the south, Mary Beth Norton, '"What an Alarming Crisis Is This": Southern Women and the American Revolution', in Jeffrey J. Crow and Larry E. Tise (eds), *The Southern Experience in the American Revolution* (Chapel Hill; 1978), pp. 203–34, 210–14.

103 Jacqueline Jones, 'Race, Sex, and Self-Evident Truths: the Status of Slave Women during the Era of the American Revolution', in Hoffman and Albert, *Women in the Age of the American Revolution*, pp. 293–337, 296.

104 Jones, 'Race, Sex , and Self-Evident Truths', pp. 298, 323.

105 Jones, 'Race, Sex, and Self-Evident Truths', pp. 296–7.

106 Theda Perdue, *Cherokee Women: Gender and Culture Change, 1700–1835* (Lincoln and London; 1998), pp. 4, 9–10, 63.

107 Gunderson, *To Be Useful to the World*, pp. xi, xii.

108 Gunderson, *To Be Useful to the World*, p. 16.

109 Gunderson, *To Be Useful to the World*, p. 37.

110 Raphael, *A People's History*.

111 Alfred F. Young, 'The Women of Boston: "Persons of Consequence" in the Making of the American Revolution, 1745–76' in Harriet B. Applewhite and Darline G. Levy (eds), *Women and Politics in the Age of the Democratic Revolution* (Ann Arbor, MI; 1990), pp. 181–226.

112 Applewhite and Levy, *Women and Politics in the Age of the Democratic Revolution*, p. 2.

113 Young, 'Women of Boston', p. 183.

114 Young, 'Women of Boston', p. 187.

115 Young, 'Women of Boston', p. 188.

116 Young, 'Women of Boston', pp. 191–2.

117 Young, 'Women of Boston', p. 194.

118 Barbara Clark Smith, 'Food Rioters and the American Revolution', *WMQ*, 3rd ser., 51 (1994), pp. 3–38, 3.

119 Clark Smith, 'Food Rioters and the American Revolution', pp. 5–6.

120 Clark Smith, 'Food Rioters and the American Revolution', p. 6; for similar patterns of participation in Revolutionary France, see Olwen Huften, 'Women in Revolution, 1789–1796', *Past and Present*, 53 (1971).

121 Barbara Clark Smith, 'Social Visions of the American Resistance Movement' in Ronald Hoffman and Peter J. Albert (eds), *The Transforming Hand of Revolution: Reconsidering the American Revolution as a Social Movement* (Charlottesville, VA, and London; 1996), pp. 27–57, 40, 27.

122 Clark Smith, 'Social Visions', p. 38.

123 Clark Smith, 'Food Rioters and the American Revolution', pp. 38, 40, 28.

124 Raphael, *People's History*, pp. 434–5, fn. 45.

125 Walter H. Blumenthal, *Women Camp Followers of the American Revolution* (New York; 1974); Holly A. Mayer, *Belonging to the Army: Camp Followers and Community during the American Revolution* (Columbia, SC; 1996).

126 Raphael, *People's History*, pp. 151–3.

127 Raphael, *People's History*, pp. 155–6.

128 Gunderson, *To Be Useful to the World*.

129 Berkin, *Revolutionary Mothers*.

7

The Indians, the west and the Revolution

Native Americans have long languished at the margins of revolutionary historiography and, more than other American peoples, have suffered from isolation and compartmentalization.[1] Trapped within the false dichotomy of civilized versus savage, Native Americans were almost invariably depicted as cruel and vengeful.[2] Commenting in 1784, Jeremy Belknap was critical of earlier writers for having done less than justice to the aboriginal population:

> Our historians have generally represented the Indians in a most odious light, especially when recounting the effects of their ferocity. Dogs, caitiffs, miscreants and hell-hounds, are the politest names which have been given them by some writers, who seem to be in a passion at the mentioning their cruelties, and at other times speak of them with contempt. Whatever indulgence may be allowed to those who wrote in times when the mind was vexed with their recent depredations and inhumanities, it ill becomes us to cherish an inveterate hatred of the unhappy natives.[3]

Seventeenth-century colonists anxious to assert their identity as Christian, civilized, law-abiding and English, differentiated themselves sharply from those they perceived to lack these qualities; Slotkin described the process as 'definition by repudiation'.[4] In the Declaration of Independence Native Americans are still labelled 'merciless Indian savages whose known rule of warfare is an undistinguished destruction of all ages, sexes, and conditions'.[5]

The revolutionary generation

As colonial resistance gave way to armed struggle, Native Americans, living along an extensive frontier stretching over 1,500 miles, were courted assiduously by the British and their American opponents. As David Ramsay put it, each side recognized that the Indians made 'desirable friends and formidable enemies'. The revolutionary generation of historians were familiar with the Enlightenment view 'that human nature was fundamentally the same in all times and places'.[6] As Arthur Shaffer reminds us, they were also environmentalists. 'Americans could be regarded as Englishmen who had been transformed by the distinctive physical and social environment of the New World [and] if human nature was the same in all times and places, Americans were different by virtue of their unique civil and natural environment.'[7] American historians followed Montesquieu and the Scottish philosophers in conceiving the environment as involving not only geography but also a wide range of social factors.

Among historians of the revolutionary generation, Samuel Williams embraced most enthusiastically Enlightenment theories about 'the condition of man'.[8] While 'men of different countries and nations, appear to be very different from one another', he wrote, 'the constitution of man appears to be the same, in every part of the globe. Nature has given to him the same physical and moral powers, capable of different degrees of improvement, according to the state of society in which he shall be placed'.[9] Williams traced parallels between developments in certain parts of the Americas, such as the role and character of the nobility among the Aztecs, with similar developments in Europe and Asia.[10] But while once there had been indications that native peoples were changing progressively, the coming of the Europeans had had a pernicious impact on their societies. 'The vices we have taught them, the diseases we have spread among them, the intemperance they have learnt of us, and the destruction of their game', appeared irreversible evils. Their minds had become filled 'with prejudices against our arts and improvements' on account of their contempt 'of our morals', 'horrour at the knavery' of our commerce with them, and 'the constant advances we have made into their country'. This, added to the 'frequency and bitterness of their wars, to their constant hardships and sufferings, and to a defective population', signalled their 'total destruction'. In two or three centuries they would be extinct. Appealing to the United States to prevent this catastrophe, Williams observed that it was the practice of 'arbitrary governments to sport with the liberties, and lives of men'. 'A government of reason and nature,' he urged, 'ought to attempt to conciliate the affections of a free, brave, independent and generous people.'[11]

In his *History of the American Revolution* (1789), David Ramsay took an ambivalent view of the Native American, sharing the general assumption that Indians lived in a state of nature and were governed by passion rather than reason. He attributed to them an innate 'passion for rapine' and an 'appetite for depredation', but in describing them also as 'untutored', 'uninformed' and 'unfortunate misled savages', Ramsay employed a vocabulary which suggested that he did not view their character as indelibly fixed.[12] Europeans, whose behaviour towards the indigenous population was reprehensible from the outset, were largely accountable for the dramatic decline in their numbers.[13] Nevertheless, his assessment of their recruitment by the British in the revolutionary war was forthright: it was not simply a matter of cruelty, but a deliberate policy of terror to force the colonies into submission.[14] War was carried into Indian country in the south-east, argued Ramsay, 'not so much to punish what was past, as to prevent all future co-operation between the Indians and British in that quarter'.[15]

In identifying three zones of conflict, the northern, southern and middle, Ramsay established a model for writing about Indian participation in the revolutionary war which has been adopted by many later historians. He dealt with that bordering the south-east in a rather cursory fashion presumably because he had already covered the subject in greater detail in his earlier *History of the Revolution in South Carolina* (1785).[16] When faced with the prospect of a two-prong attack on the state – in the backcountry and on the coast, South Carolina's pre-emptive strike against the Cherokees was vindicated. No previous expedition had enjoyed such success 'as this first effort of the new-born commonwealth', declared Ramsay. In less than three months, 'the Cherokees were so far subdued as to be incapable of annoying the settlements', which would remain untroubled until 1780. American losses were small at around fifty.[17] British strategy, it appeared, had back-fired. Moreover, before the Indian war, 'some well-meaning people could not see the justice or propriety of contending with their formerly protecting parent-state; but Indian cruelties, excited by royal artifices, soon extinguished all their predilection for the country of their forefathers'.[18]

Ramsay rather ignored the middle zone and reserved the greater part of his attention in the *History of the American Revolution* for the northern zone where, due to the vastness of the frontier and the remoteness of the settlements, together with the familiarity of the country enjoyed by refugee Americans and hostile Indians, it was practicable 'for even small marauding parties to do extensive mischief'. Unlike many later accounts, Ramsay's treatment of the atrocities committed in the Wyoming Valley was sober and analytical. A 'new and flourishing settle-ment ... on the eastern branch of the Susquehanna', Wyoming Valley was located in contested country.

> Unfortunately for the security of the inhabitants, the soil was claimed both by Connecticut and Pennsylvania. From the collision of contradictory claims, founded on royal charters, the laws of neither were steadily enforced. In this remote settlement, where government was feeble, the tories were under less control, and could easily assemble undiscovered.[19]

Here 'a storm of Indian and tory vengeance burst with particular violence'. The cycle of mutual destruction culminated in General Sullivan's 1779 expedition into the Indian country with a sizeable force of carefully selected Continental troops, targeting the Senecas, one of the Six Nations, who, as Ramsay reminded his readers, had broken their promise of neutrality. 'Many settle-ments in the form of towns were destroyed,' he wrote. 'Scarce any thing in the form of a house was left standing, nor was an Indian to be seen.'[20] As was the case with the Cherokees, Ramsay believed that the Indians learned their lesson from such demon-strations of American power; they 'became cautious and timid' and 'the ardour of their warriors' was dampened, but in reality, the raids continued. Ramsay recognized that frontier warfare was more savage and devastating than engagements elsewhere. The contests of Indians against Americans and Americans against Indians 'were sufficient to excite compassion in the most obdurate hearts'. What he saw in this conflict was not only a deeper humanitarian issue at stake, but a different type of warfare – the phenomenon of total war. Not only the men and warriors, but the women and children, and whole settlements were involved in the promiscuous desolations.[21]

That Native American actions were prompted by British overtures became a consistent trope of histories of the Revolution well into the twentieth century. That Indian warfare broke all the rules of civilized nations was another; the Indians put to death 'the smiling infant and the defenceless female' as well as 'the resisting armed man'. They were motivated by the 'desire for plunder' and their legacy was one of 'slaughter and devastation'. There were also two set pieces, two recurring stories – the murder of Jane McCrea and the massacre of Christian Moravian Indians. The first of these, discussed in Chapter 6, involved the death of a young woman. According to Ramsay, the episode served as further proof of British perfidy and swelled the ranks of the American army as New Englanders rallied to the American cause to save their wives and daughters from a similar fate.[22] The murder of pacifist Moravian Indians by Americans served a different purpose. It was a massacre by American forces in 1782, but it was a singular event in which the fate of the victims was determined on a vote by members of the local militia.[23] It did not resonate with American audiences in the same way as McCrea's death. It was an aberration. By including both in their histories, historians could signal their objectivity as the best historical writing demanded, but could nonetheless damn the British without damning the Americans. American accusations of the misuse of Indian auxiliaries met with some success in England, being taken up by the parliamentary opposition. The name of Jane McCrea was invoked by Burke, Fox and Wilkes even before Burgoyne made his appearance before the House of Commons in the wake of the Canada fiasco. In fact, Burke's speech was regarded as one of his best, if not his finest.[24]

Author of the *History of the Rise, Progress and Termination of the American Revolution* (1805) Mercy Otis Warren was less restrained in her use of language than Ramsay.[25] Though influenced by the intellectual currents of the Enlightenment, Warren's perspective on the Native Americans was also affected by the fact that they were allies of the British whom she held responsible for the mental and physical deterioration of her brother. Lester Cohen, editor of the modern edition of Warren's *History*, sees the work as a moral tract in which so much was portrayed in stark contrasts of black and white.[26] Warren deemed the Indians 'savages', members of 'ferocious nations' whom the British encouraged to breach America's frontiers.[27] Elsewhere in the text, she described Native Americans as 'the fierce and numerous *hordes* of the wilderness', 'tribes of copper-colored savages', 'native barbarians', 'native savages', 'rude and barbarous nations' and 'fierce and blood-thirsty warriors'.[28] On the nature of Indian warfare, she replicated Edward Gibbon's sentiments 'that the introduction of barbarians and savages into the contests of civilized nations, is a measure pregnant with shame and mischief, which the interest of a moment may impel, but which is reprobated by the best principles of humanity and reason'.[29] Following the death of General Montgomery, Warren maintained that Governor Guy Carleton's exemplary treatment of his American prisoners was due to the fact that he needed 'to mitigate the odium of the disgraceful design of subduing America by the aid of savages'.[30]

Unlike Ramsay, Warren integrated her treatment of Native Americans into a chronological narrative as events unfolded. Thus she noted how 'when the flower of the British troops then in America were shut up in Boston' and the governors of the southern provinces were fleeing to his Majesty's ships, 'a respectable delegation was sent to Montreal, to treat with the white inhabitants, and as far as possible to conciliate or secure the copper-colored nations'. Warren recognized the strategic importance of Canada for whoever possessed it 'will in a great measure command the numerous tribes beyond the lakes'.[31]

Yet for all her emphasis on their proclivity for war, it is Warren, not Ramsay, who is more reflective about the Indians' place in the universal order of things. Like Ramsay, she recognized the baneful influence of the European on the Indian but unlike him, perceived the Indian's way of life as 'but the road to a more improved, and exalted state of existence'. She dismissed as 'absurd and unfounded' the views of those European and American writers who argued that 'the rude tribes of savages' could not be civilized. What, after all, 'were once the ancestors of the most refined and polite modern nations, but rude, ignorant savages?'. Nature had equally endowed 'the whole human species'.

> There is no difference in the moral or intellectual capacity of nations, but what arises from adventitious circumstances, that give some a more early and rapid improvement in civilization than others. This gradual rise from the rude stages of nature to the highest pitch of refinement, may be traced by the historian, the philosopher, and the naturalist, sufficiently to obviate all objections against the strongest efforts, to instruct and civilize the swarms of men in the American wilds, whose only natural apparent distinction, is a copper-colored skin.[32]

Warren viewed the war against Indians as 'a defensive war' and therefore justifiable on moral and political grounds, but the same was not true of 'attempts to penetrate distant countries, and spread slaughter and bloodshed among innocent and unoffending tribes'.[33] Warren, who carried her *History* into the 1790s, was no advocate of western expansion. Reflecting on the 'horrid war' in the 1790s in which she lost a son, she commented 'Happy might it have been for the Atlantic states had they been contented within these boundaries of nature'.[34]

Published in the same year as Warren's account was *American Annals*, compiled by Abiel Holmes (1763–1837) and described in the 1932 *Dictionary of American Biography*, perhaps somewhat generously, as a 'first attempt at an extensive orderly history of the country as a whole' and thus 'an important step in American historiography'. It was in fact largely 'a chronological recital of facts, amassed with a scholar's care from a great variety of sources, manuscript and printed'.[35] A New England Congregationalist clergyman, founding member of the Massachusetts Historical Society and its secretary from 1813 to 1833, Holmes was a chronicler rather than a historian. Although many of the entries in the *Annals* were short, those on Indian affairs were treated at some length. Holmes described British operations in the north as 'predatory rather than military'.[36] The narrative drew heavily on Ramsay's without the latter's breadth and ambivalence. Holmes portrayed the Indians as the dupes of British agents whose 'promises and presents', together 'with the desire for plunder, induced them to invade the frontiers' with predictable results. What makes Holmes's account distinct, is the litany of detail it supplies: the numbers of homes burnt, settlements wiped out, acres of corn destroyed, distances travelled; the number of warriors, tories, militia men and soldiers involved; men killed and those taken prisoner. Reports of activities in the south and west were only marginally less detailed in this respect than those in the north.[37]

Less intimately involved in the making of the Revolution and the military conflict than either Ramsay or Warren, Jeremy Belknap took a longer view of the role of Native Americans in the eighteenth century. Despite his chastisement of an earlier generation of colonial historians for their treatment of the Indians, Belknap himself was not free from the faults he attributed to others. Belknap highlighted the Indians' use of stealth and subterfuge, the torture of prisoners, the horrors of captivity, cruelty towards children, the aged and infirm and the fate of pregnant women who, having been taken prisoner, met their deaths when they could no longer keep up with the moving columns. Famine stalked these marches for Indians gorged themselves when game was plentiful, and went hungry when none was to be found.[38] Belknap made some attempt to balance this appraisal with recognition of their kindnesses and tenderness to some of their victims. And there was one offence which could not be charged against them though it was common enough among 'more civilized' nations, namely rape. How to explain this Belknap was unsure; possibly it was attributable to the Indians' physiognomy, a subject usually of more interest to European than American writers.[39] Having accorded the Indians a prominent role in the colonial wars in his first volume and much of the second volume, it is difficult to account for their virtual disappearance from Belknap's consideration of the revolutionary conflict. He only referred to two incidents, the attack on Bennington and Sullivan's expedition.

Strikingly different in tone from these patriot histories was that of loyalist Peter Oliver who, in his account of the breakdown of British authority in North America, challenged the concept of the Indian as a savage.[40] It was a relative matter according to Oliver. In his defence of the Indian way of war Oliver appeared to be responding to those American critics who denounced the British use of Indian allies. 'Every Nation hath something Peculiar in its Mode of War,' wrote Oliver. 'An Indian prefers the Mode of fighting behind a Tree, or of skulking in Bushes. He prefers the Hatchet, the scalping Knife & the Tomahawk, to the Bayonet, the Sword & the Cutlass. His Weapons give, at least, as sudden, if not a less painfull Death, than the Englishman's Weapons.' Perhaps less easy to defend was scalping, but Oliver rejected criticism on this score too: 'it is of no more Consequence than taking off the Shirt of his Garment'. Besides, scalping had been encouraged in the colonies with the offer of bounties 'for more than a Century past'. As for employing the Indians 'in the present Contest', it should be remembered that they had been employed in former wars. Oliver also pointed out that when solicited, the Indians had resisted American overtures. In their view, the conflict was a domestic dispute, one between parents and children in which they would not meddle.[41] Whether Oliver believed what he was writing or was mischievously inverting the sentiments expressed by the revolutionary historians is difficult to tell, though the pen portraits he drew of his enemies suggests the latter.[42]

The nineteenth century: the middle decades

The 'most marked feature of the American landscape in the 1780s', according to James Merrell (1953–), 'was not that the vast center of the continent remained Indian Country. Rather it was the ubiquity of the Indian presence everywhere in America'. By 1840, however, the era of 'widespread face-to-face contacts between Natives and whites were a thing of the past; never again would Indians occupy so central a place in American life'.[43] The extent to which Native Americans slipped from the consciousness of historians of the revolutionary era can be seen in the work of Timothy Pitkin. When Pitkin's *Political and Civil History of the United States of America 1763–1797* appeared in 1828, it contained barely a reference to them. The title of the book precluded the need for any extensive discussion, but their almost total absence from the text is indicative of their irrelevance to the post-revolutionary generation. General Montgomery's expedition to Canada was deemed worthy of brief mention but the Indians not at all. Only in the context of Anglo-French rivalry in North America did the existence of Native Americans receive any acknowledgement, and, even then, they were bound to the French so that qualities ascribed to the latter were shared equally with the former.[44] On the other hand, Pitkin's examination of the diplomacy of the Revolution emphasized the uncertainty of the future of the lands between the Alleghanies and the Mississippi to which Spain laid claim. There was nothing inevitable about western expansion. Indeed, Pitkin paid tribute to John Jay who was still alive when the *History* was published, whose labours 'in a great measure' secured the western country for the United States which was now inhabited 'by millions of his fellow citizens'.[45] For Americans writing in the middle decades of the nineteenth century, the phenomenal rise of the west was of much greater significance and interest than the defeat of the Native Americans in the revolutionary war and the forfeiture of their lands.

As the revolutionary generation of historians gave way to the romantic, 'Native Americans', according to Steven Conn, 'had no place in the romance of America'.[46] It is not that Native Americans were wholly missing from contemporary histories. Parkman, Prescott and Bancroft all wrote about Indians – but they were perpetually outside *the* narrative of the new nation that was being constructed. Elements of this scenario were present in colonial times and can be found to some extent in the writings of the revolutionary generation. During the War for Independence, Crèvecoeur predicted that the Indians were 'doomed to recede and disappear before the superior genius of the Europeans', while John Lendrum was even more convinced of this as can be seen in the 1795 and 1836 editions of his history of the Revolution. 'They waste, they moulder away and, as Charlevoix says of the Indians of Canada, they disappear.' Few Indians died as a consequence of war, declared Lendrum. Rather famine, pestilence and spirituous liquors 'were the usual killers'.[47] Despite appeals by men and women such as Samuel Williams and Mercy Otis

Warren, by the mid-nineteenth century, the fate of Native Americans was no longer viewed as man-made but determined by nature. The decline was inevitable; there was therefore no one to blame and nothing to apologize for.[48]

Both Bancroft and Parkman found fault with James Fenimore Cooper's fictional Indian – often a sentimentalized romantic savage – and while this image was to be found in early nineteenth-century American literature, it was not to be found in the histories of Bancroft and Parkman.[49] Both Parkman and Bancroft depicted the Indian as inferior and, in David Levin's view, the difference between them was merely a matter of degree.[50] In the first of the three volumes written on the American Revolution, Bancroft devoted a weighty chapter to 'The Aborigines East of the Mississippi' in which he discussed their languages, customs, government, religion, character and origins. Roy Harvey Pearce found this 'analysis of savagism' relatively complex and sophisticated but neither Bancroft nor his contemporaries had moved beyond the conclusions reached by their antiquarian forebears.[51] The content and structure of this chapter was retained as late as the 1875 edition, but in volume two of 'The Author's Last Revision' (1888), the writing became sharper, the text shorter, the structure broken up into separate chapters, and the references deleted. Bancroft also substituted the past tense for the present used in all previous editions, and the term 'Red Men' replaced 'Aborigines' in the chapter title though Bancroft had used the former term freely in the text of earlier editions.[52] Alden Vaughan has argued that the colour 'red' was not usually associated with American Indians before the middle of the nineteenth century when pseudo-scientific theories of 'race' and 'color' were gaining credibility, and served as justification for the continuing expropriation of black labour under slavery and the appropriation of Indian lands. In earlier centuries, there was an assumption, however vaguely defined, that Native Americans would one day be absorbed into the settler societies.[53]

When Bancroft initially discussed the 'natural endowments of the Indians', it appeared that he held them in (almost) equal esteem with 'their more cultivated conquerors'. There were even some aspects of European society from which the Indians were free – the extraction of information or confession by various forms of torture such as the thumb-screw, the rack, the boot and the wheel and modes of official punishment that made use of the gallows, the block and fire. There was not a quality which the white man possessed 'which did not also belong to the American savage.... the map of the faculties is for both identical'. The fact that Indians belonged to the human race, however, did not mean that they were a part of American society. The Americans were an improving people, the Indians were not. Bancroft offered 'proofs'.[54] Despite strenuous efforts to 'ameliorate' the condition of the Indian, 'above all, to educate the young', the effort had been 'in vain'. Whether it was the Jesuits, Franciscans, Puritans, Church of England, Moravians, and in Bancroft's own day, women, the results varied little. 'The copper-colored men are characterized by a moral inflexibility, a rigidity of attachment to their hereditary customs and manners', a state of affairs Bancroft believed was reflected in the sameness of their physiognomy and limited range of facial expression.[55] Compared with the 1875 edition, Bancroft's final statement on the character of the Indians was briefer, more direct, hard edged and racialized.

> The red man has aptitude at imitation rather than invention; he learns easily; his natural logic is correct and discriminating, and he seizes on the nicest distinctions in comparing objects; but he is deficient in the power of imagination and abstraction. Equalling the white man in the sagacity of the senses and in judgements resting on them, he was inferior in reason and in ethics. Nor was this inferiority attached to the individual: it was connected with organization, and was the characteristic of the race.[56]

When Bancroft moved from this generalized picture of Native Americans to address the American Revolution, the result is nonetheless startling. The image projected of Indians in the revolutionary war was one of snarling dogs at the end of a leash, a powerful metaphor that serves the narrative well. There was no precedent Bancroft claimed for the British deployment of Indians in the revolutionary war. In a previous war, the Seven Years War, the British had bought off the Indians to ensure their neutrality. 'No war-party of savages' was ever sent to hound Canadian villages, he wrote. Learning from the French who enjoyed better relations with the Indians and had greater need of their support, the British king and his ministers adopted former French policy and 'against their own colonies and kindred, loosed from the leash these terrible auxiliaries'.[57] Whereas Mercy Otis Warren had had no difficulty in accepting bravery in war as a characteristic trait of Native Americans, Bancroft took the opposite view, namely that the Indian way of waging war precluded any acceptance of their valour. Their tactics were cowardly and despicable.

> The cannibal Indian was a deadly foe only as he skulked in ambush, or prowled on the frontier, or burned the defenceless farm-house, or struck the laborer in the field, or smote the mother at her household task, or crashed the infant's head against a rock or a tree, or tortured the prisoner on whose flesh he was to gorge ... Yet Gage, without much compunction, gave directions to propitiate and inflame the Indians by gifts, and to subsidize their war-parties.[58]

If Bancroft's treatment of the American Indian lacked the immediacy and ambivalence of Ramsay and Warren, still less the occasional insights of Belknap and the sensibility of Williams, his access to a wider range of sources, especially European, enabled him to reconnect the history of the western edge of the rebellious colonies to both British colonial policy and international diplomacy. And he was the first historian to make historic heroes out of Daniel Boone and George Rogers Clark. The ambitions of European powers to perpetuate their influence in North America at the expense of their rivals and the fledgling young republic opened up new perspectives on the last years of the colonial era, on wartime events, diplomacy and how the west was won or, from a Native American perspective, how it was lost. Into this legal and military quagmire, Bancroft introduced a new character, the archetypal 'hardy backwoodsman'.

> With the love of wandering that formed a part of their nature, the hardy backwoodsman, clad in a hunting-shirt and deerskin leggings, armed with a rifle, a powderhorn, and a pouch for shot and bullets, a hatchet and a hunter's knife, descended the mountains in quest of more distant lands, which he forever imagined to be richer and lovelier than those which he knew. Wherever he fixed his halt, the hatchet hewed logs for his cabin, and blazed trees of the forest kept the record of his title-deeds; nor did he conceive that a British government had any right to forbid the occupation of lands which were either uninhabited or only broken by a few scattered clans of savages.[59]

Bancroft tied the emergence of the backwoodsman not only to the advance of the frontier but to concepts of self-sufficiency and self-defence. 'The adventurer in search of a new home on the banks of the Mississippi risked his life at every step; so that a system of independent defence and private war became the custom of the backwoods.' Undeterred by fear, the settler depended for his security on 'perpetual readiness' to defend himself for 'not a twelve-month passed away without a massacre of pioneers'. Daniel Boone's eldest son was one victim.[60]

With some justification and probably the benefit of hindsight, Bancroft invested the lands between the Alleghanies and the Mississippi River with the power to bind America together: the river was 'the guardian and the pledge of the union of the states of America'. Had Americans 'been confined to the eastern slope of the Alleghanies, there would have been no geographical unity between them, and the thread of connection between states that merely fringed the Atlantic must soon have been sundered'.[61] This outcome was not, however, inevitable, for Spain had its own ambitions in North America. With support from Britain and France, Spain sought to recover Florida and 'shut out' the United States not only from the lands west of the Mississippi but 'even on its eastern side'.[62] Somewhat melodramatically, Bancroft attributed their failure at this time to George Rogers Clark. 'While the absolute monarch of the Spanish dominions and his minister thought to exclude the republic from the valley of the Mississippi, a power emerged from its forests to bring their puny policy to nought.'[63]

If Bancroft's writings did much to shape the dominant view of Native Americans in the mid-nineteenth century, Hildreth was the antithesis. Avoiding Bancroft's moral judgements and rhetorical flourishes, Hildreth generally refrained from using the terms 'savage' and 'barbarian' to depict the Indians, and though he recognized the inadequacy of sources, like Bancroft and others, made sweeping generalizations about their character. Whereas Bancroft emphasized similarities which enabled him to incorporate the Indians into a single family of man, Hildreth's emphasis was on difference. For him, difference was exemplified in the first instance by the vast number of languages spoken by Native Americans. Also distinct was their form of government and law.

'Strictly speaking, according to our notions', he wrote, 'the Indians could hardly be said to have either government or laws', but such a notion was erroneous.[64] The structure of authority in Indian society derived from three sources: respect for the elderly; the wisdom of the chiefs; and what Hildreth termed 'the supernatural'. When matters of public interest arose, whole tribes came together to discuss the issues. Nor were Indians acquisitive: they held their lands in common and they had little idea of accumulation. As long as circumstances permitted, they were generous.[65]

Hildreth gave Indian warfare a rationale and legitimacy that was rare among writers in the nineteenth century. War was held in the highest esteem in Indian society, Hildreth recognized, and he rejected the notion that it was undertaken in the hope of plunder and conquest. Rather 'it was the fury of hatred and revenge, the restless spirit of enterprise, still more, the desire for honor and distinction, that stirred up the warriors to deeds of blood'. Since Indian war parties were generally small because of the problem of supplies, especially on long journeys when 'they endured the utmost extremes of hunger and fatigue', the pitched battles and general engagements of European warfare were ill-suited to their resources. 'Surprise was the great point of their tactics' and 'their ardor was great'. To some extent Hildreth's recognition of the structures and value systems of Native Americans set him apart from other historians, but even he fell back on the concepts of civilization and savagery, even infantilization, in the course of his analysis. 'Bursts of passionate activity were followed by long intervals of indolence,' he wrote. The Indians lacked 'the pertinacity', 'perseverance' and 'fixed purposes' of 'civilized life': they were 'children of impulse'.[66] Even so, Hildreth provided plausible answers to the question of why Native Americans were so hostile to European newcomers. Murder, kidnapping and enslavement had been the hallmarks of early encounters.[67]

In describing the course of events between Native Americans and the rebel colonists, Hildreth covered much the same ground as Bancroft and earlier historians but with an admirable concision and clarity that generally escaped the older man. He skilfully integrated zones of conflict into his historical narrative, both those in the interior beyond the mountains where Native Americans sought to avert the advance of settlers, and those where they already intermingled as in western New York which witnessed the fiercest encounters.[68] In dealing with Indian and tory incursions into Wyoming and Cherry Valley, which Bancroft had milked for all they were worth, Hildreth declared 'these barbarities, greatly exaggerated by reports embodied since in poetry and history, excited every where a lively indignation', but he did not deny the miserable fate of some taken prisoner.[69] He also provided a fuller picture of how settlers followed in the wake of successful American operations in the west and his treatment of Spanish diplomacy, territorial claims and military activity stood in sharp contrast to Bancroft's theatrical juxtaposition of Spanish monarch and American backwoodsman.[70] Hildreth also recognized the scale and significance of the huge land grants that had been secured from the Indians as a consequence of their partisanship during the war.[71] It was the responsibility of the newly appointed superintendents, 'to see that the regulations of Congress were enforced; to keep the Indians quiet by doing them justice'. The chances of this were slim since, as Hildreth recognized, Indian hostilities were 'generally provoked' by the 'encroachments' and 'misconduct' of frontier settlers and state authorities worked to undermine the exclusive control of Indian affairs that Congress possessed under the Articles of Confederation.[72]

Professionalization, the west and the vanishing Indian

Though contemporaries, John B. McMaster (1852–1932) and Edward Channing (1856–1931) stood on opposite sides of the professional divide. Described by Ellen Fitzpatrick in her study of historical writing as an 'amateur social historian' with no advanced degree in history, McMaster became Professor of History at the University of Pennsylvania after publishing the first volume of his eight volume *History of the People of the United States*.[73] A man of broad interests and experience, McMaster aspired to write a social and cultural history of the American people. He accumulated vast quantities of material on subjects new and old, much of it gleaned from newspapers, but did not really know what to do with it. Though his work was initially welcomed by historians such as J. Franklin Jameson as an attempt to move beyond the realm of political history, McMaster subsequently attracted criticism for his lack of conceptualization, direction and interpretation. It was said of him that he 'skilfully regiments his facts upon parade, but they do not march'.[74] Edward Channing, on the other hand, was a New England-born, Harvard-educated historian who, within three years of gaining his Ph.D. (1880), obtained a position at Harvard where he remained until his retirement in 1929, devoting himself to the production of what became known as the 'Great Work', a multi-volume, prize-winning history of the United States.[75] Described by John Higham as 'a crusty little man at Harvard', he 'methodically work[ed] his way through the whole sweep of American history on the basis of original sources'. His *History of the United States* (1905–1925) was 'the most ambitious, and in some ways the crowning result of the conservative evolutionist approach to American history'. Channing believed in the idea of progress and singled out the victory of the forces of union over those of particularism as the central theme of American history.[76] While McMaster and Channing approached the writing of American history from different standpoints, both were pioneers in their fashion, yet their treatment of Native Americans was retrograde, McMaster defining them in terms of violence and cruelty and Channing as people apparently without will or purpose of their own. As a subject of investigation, Native Americans were of even less interest to historians at the turn of the twentieth century than they had been previously, superseded in part by a fascination with the speculative ambitions of the revolutionary generation, the diplomatic manoeuvring of European powers and the pioneering exploits of those who 'won' the west.[77]

McMaster dated his *History of the People of the United States* from the year 1784 but began this work with a sketch of the aboriginal population. At the time of writing, he claimed that less than 5 million out of 50 million Americans had ever seen an Indian and their image had been 'softened' by the passage of time and the shrinkage of numbers. McMaster claimed that Indians were viewed with a 'singular mixture of truth and romance' derived from the stories of James Fenimore Cooper and the lives of Red Jacket and Brant, but his claim that 'an Indian in his paint and feathers is now a much rarer show than a Bengal tiger or a white bear from the Polar sea' invokes images of Indians as museum exhibits or show tent performers. In order to 'recover' their former character, he drew on examples of Indian cruelty from the revolutionary war. These related only to the Iroquois, and demonized Joseph Brant if not Red Jacket. McMaster's characterization was much influenced by that of Bancroft with an added taint of racism. The Indian had skill in hunting, daring in combat and courage under the most gruesome of tortures.[78] Indian warfare was 'given to the dark and crooked ways which are the resort of the cowardly and the weak'. His 'mental attainments' matched his character. 'His squaw was his slave ... His imagination was singularly strong, his reason singularly weak. He was as superstitious as a Hottentot negro and as unreasonable as a child.'[79] At the time of the Revolution

> There were to be found, from Cape Ann to Georgia, few men who had not many times in their lives seen numbers of Indians, while thousands could be found scattered through every State, whose cattle had been driven off, and whose homes had been laid in ashes by the braves of the Six Nations, who had fought with them from behind trees and rocks, and carried the scars of wounds received in hand-to-hand encounters. In every city were to be seen women who had fled at the dead of night from their burning cabins; who had, perhaps, witnessed the destruction of Schenectady; or were by a merciful Providence spared in the massacre of the Minisink; whose husbands had gone down in the universal slaughter of Wyoming.[80]

The Indian, concluded McMaster, was essentially 'a child of nature', engaged in a constant struggle for survival, but decidedly not a 'noble savage'. If his victimization of the border population was one sided and his failure to recognize the agricultural character of the indigenous people east of the Mississippi flawed, McMaster was right about one thing. Native Americans were still to be found everywhere in American society at the end of the revolutionary war.[81]

Channing devoted the third volume of his *History of the United States* (1912) to the American Revolution. Somewhat inexplicably, he divided Native Americans into 'the Iroquois and the Indians', then subdivided them into 'those under British influence and those favorable to the French'. When the French were defeated, the 'French' tribes were brought within the sphere of

British influence, 'greatly to their disgust and dismay'.[82] But if Channing had no real interest in Native Americans in their own right, he was concerned with the fate of those western lands within the charters of the older colonies into which emigrants were already flooding regardless of the Proclamation Line, and he paid particular attention to the economic interests of both the British and Americans in the west. The Seven Years War had encouraged British officers and soldiers 'to try their luck in America' and many stayed, among whom were men who became leading figures in the American armed forces: Horatio Gates and Charles Lee, who settled in the Valley of Virginia, and Arthur St Clair and Richard Montgomery too, but interest in western lands went beyond these men.[83] 'The greed of Englishmen for wild lands,' wrote Channing, 'and for lands already partly adapted to the uses of civilization was not confined to military men or to those who actually emigrated. Noblemen and speculators were constantly applying to the royal government for western lands and for valuable tracts east of the Alleghanies.' Proposals put forward by a syndicate of Englishmen and Americans, including Benjamin Franklin and Joseph Galloway, for the establishment of a new colony called Vandalia on huge tracts of western land was promoted by Thomas Walpole, an Englishman. Had not the Revolution intervened, it was possible a new series of colonies might have been created west of the Alleghanies. It was in the west that Channing saw the beginnings of the revolutionary movement 'because the political and commercial interests of the westerners were necessarily often unlike those of the Atlantic colonies'.[84]

Between the publication of McMaster's first volume in 1883 and Channing's third volume in 1912, significant shifts took place in the organization, teaching and writing of American history. Not only was the writing of American history substantially institutionalized and professionalized but new initiatives carried it in different directions. Not the least of these had its impetus in the paper presented by Frederick Jackson Turner (1861–1932) at the Columbian exhibition in Chicago in 1893 entitled 'The significance of the frontier in American history'. It was, writes Allan Bogue, 'the most celebrated paper in American historiography'.[85] A mid-westerner and former student of Herbert Baxter Adams at

The Johns Hopkins University, the institution which pioneered graduate education in the United States, Turner, then Assistant Professor of History at the University of Wisconsin, urged historians to look away from the Atlantic coast, the distant shores of Europe and the German forests for the forces that shaped American society and politics and instead into their own backyard. There, the convergence of a number of factors, 'the existence of an area of free land, its continuous recession and the advance of American settlement westward explained American development'. But Turner's image of the frontier was strangely devoid of Native Americans as if, when the first Englishmen settled in North America, it was to all intents and purposes virgin soil and unoccupied land. The irony of embracing the frontier but excluding its indigenous population was one that eluded Turner's generation, who as Gordon Wood observes, 'preoccupied with the roots of the United States and its institutions scarcely acknowledged the existence of the native American peoples'. Moreover, when Turner made his mark in the 1890s, Indians 'were on their way to oblivion'.[86] Influenced by the work of Richard White, Patricia Limerick, one of the 'new' western historians, has tied Turner's rigidity in defending the frontier thesis less to his environmentalism than to his role as a founding member of the historical profession and the pressures incumbent upon him as a young scholar in its earliest years. The luxury of revision was not open to him though among his writings, suggests Limerick, are pieces which hint that Turner could have constructed an alternative history of the west based on contingency rather than determinism.[87]

Not that university teachers obtained total dominance over the production of scholarly publications at this time, as the work of men such as Justin Winsor and George Beer testify. Harvard educated man of letters, Justin Winsor (1831–1897), one time director of the Boston Public Library and later chief librarian at Harvard, not only brought a large number of scholarly essays together in the highly regarded eight-volume *Narrative and Critical History of America* (1884–89), but also wrote a number of full-length monographs. Among these was *The Westward Movement* (1897) in which, writing before Channing and expressing himself somewhat inelegantly, he tied western developments to the American Revolution.[88] On the imposition of the Proclamation Line (1763) confining settlement to the eastern side of the Alleghanies, he wrote, 'there were signs of discontent which were easily linked with the resentment that defeated the Stamp Act. So the demand for a western existence was a part of the first pulsation of resistance to the mother country, and harbingered the American Revolution'.[89] What makes his work more valuable and its neglect unjustified, is the coverage given to western lands between 1782 and 1798 in which Native Americans, neither belittled nor patronized, were cast as major players seeking to recover something from the disastrous war.

Native Americans were equally excluded in the writing of American History between 1900 and 1960 as they had been in the late nineteenth century.[90] Two significant studies on the west followed some twenty years apart. In the first of these, *The Mississippi Valley in British Politics* (1916), Clarence V. Alvord (1868–1928), sought to refocus the attention of historians on the west rather than the east, and on British policies regarding the vast areas west of the Alleghanies rather than the unrest in the seaports. 'Whenever the British ministers soberly and seriously discussed the American problem,' he claimed, 'the vital phase to them was not the disturbances of the "madding crowd" of Boston and New York but the development of that vast transmontane region that was acquired in 1763 by the Treaty of Paris.'[91] Thomas P. Abernathy's *Western Lands and the American Revolution* (1937) presented a more detailed examination of the rival claims of speculators, state governments and the movement of population into the region. He examined the various theatres of conflict concluding with a chapter on the struggle with the Shawnees over Kentucky. Abernathy defended Dunmore's military activities in the backcountry, but following the removal of the powder from the magazine in Williamsburg, noted reports of the governor's threats to stir up the 'red men to oppose the colonies'.[92] He put a positive spin on the activities of George Rogers Clark in the Illinois country.[93]

The term 'savage' was still synonymous with the Native American. When Evarts B. Greene, Professor of History at Columbia University and a former student of Channing, published *The Revolutionary Generation, 1763–1790* in 1943, the fourth volume in the prestigious *History of American Life* series which sought to set new standards in the writing of American social history, he used the term freely, though his work was revisionist in some respects.[94] Native Americans were subsumed in a conflict between whigs and tories which on the frontiers was played out between 'provincial conservatives and impatient frontiersmen'. Influenced more by Turner (on democracy) than by Bancroft (heroic individuals and pioneering families, individualism and self defence), but battling against both, Greene struggled to offer a more balanced perspective on frontier warfare and the revolutionary war, but could not break free from the still dominant perception of unrestrained brutality as the salient characteristic of the Native American. Though Indians needed 'careful handling', Greene shifted the greater share of responsibility for border warfare to disreputable traders.[95] He was not disputing 'the heroism of the eighteenth-century pioneers who built the new commonwealths – their courage, self-reliance and democratic spirit', but he hardly romanticized, still less idealized, frontier life. Lest he should be misunderstood he added that 'brutal treatment of the red man was partly the work of normally decent men outraged by the killing of wives, children and friends'. No evidence was used to support this particular claim but Greene did provide numerous examples of the frontier's more vicious characters.[96] Like many historians in the last two centuries, in dealing with the role of Native Americans in the revolutionary war, Greene examined the areas of conflict in the north-east, north-west and south-east where 'the blows of war' fell with different weight. In his view, it was the rural population of the south that was the worst affected. Greene also perpetuated the idea that Native Americans on the frontier were 'frequently directed by British agents', who were also held accountable for encouraging attacks on isolated settlements beyond the mountains.[97]

Transformations: 1965–

It was not until the latter part of the 1960s and the 1970s that attitudes towards the history of Native Americans underwent significant change.[98] Scholars seeking to write a new kind of history, one that was inclusive rather than exclusive, faced two big problems: how to write the history of Native Americans previously characterized only as stereotypes, and how to rewrite the history of America previously focused narrowly on elites. Francis Jennings (1918–) grappled with both these conundrums and, if he did not ultimately resolve them, we should admire the passion and effort he devoted to pursuing them during the thirty years of his professional career. The first issue revolved around the question of whether historians possessed or could acquire the means to understand the cultures and actions of Native Americans, who in the colonial and revolutionary era 'usually lived entirely outside the colonial social and institutional order'.[99] Nor did Native Americans fit easily into the conventional categories of historical analysis. 'Theories of history based on class conflict,' Jennings observed, 'whether of socialist or capitalist orientation, do not provide for the hybrid relationships that occur when societies with different systems of social organization adjust to each other on terms other than quick assimilation of the one by the other.' Furthermore,

> the romantic theory of revolution, in which all the lowly unite to rise against their oppressors, is embarrassed by the American Revolution's multiplicity of variously oppressed and exploited peoples who preyed upon each other; what most aggrieved the poor frontiersman was his sovereign's ban on robbing the even poorer native, and the first target of the Indian's hatchet was the frontiersman's skull.[100]

The new Indian history of the last three decades which 'puts Indian peoples at the center of the scene and seeks to understand the reasons for their actions' owes much of its inspiration to the same impulses that shaped the new social history and can be seen as part of a broad front made up of those who, conscious of American pluralism, diversity and division in the heady atmosphere of the 1960s, sought to recover the histories of the neglected and excluded with a view to rewriting the master narrative. It was an effort that resembled E. P. Thompson's determination to rescue the English working class from the 'enormous condescension of posterity'.[101] Some of the new Indian historians have been attracted to the concept of 'the inarticulate', a term first popularized in the United States by Jesse Lemisch, and their work remains embedded in concepts of class, race and latterly, gender. Others found wider opportunities in ethnohistory, sometimes referred to rather simplistically as the marriage of history and anthropology. Seeking a 'consensual definition' of the term, James Axtell offered the following in 1978: 'the use of historical methods and materials to gain knowledge of the nature and causes of change in a culture defined by ethnological concepts and categories'.[102] Theda Perdue defined these as 'anthropological models of kinship, political organization, economic systems, and worldview'. These enable historians 'to distinguish what is useful and what is not among traditional sources and a value-free context or at least a less value-laden one in which to interpret these sources' though, as Perdue points out, ethnohistory could not afford historians access to women's lives when traditional sources had not taken cognizance of them.[103]

The chronology of the Indians' revolution only partially overlapped with that of European colonists. According to Jennings, it extended from the diplomatic negotiations of mid-century and the appearance of Christopher Gist, agent for the Ohio Company, on the Ohio River in 1751, to the Treaty of Greenville in 1795 that followed Tecumseh's defeat at the Battle of Fallen Timbers. Colin Calloway, author of *The American Revolution in Indian Country* (1995), described the period from 1775 to 1795 as the 'Twenty Years' War'.[104] Much earlier, Justin Winsor and Mercy Otis Warren also recognized that the revolutionary phase of the Indians' struggle against the former colonists persisted to the end of the eighteenth century and into the next century.

Like other essays in Alfred Young's now classic 1976 volume *The American Revolution,* Jennings's pioneering essay 'The Indians' Revolution' is concerned with agency. What Jennings did in this essay is restore to Native Americans what generations of historians had denied them, namely, the ability to think and act for themselves. Focusing on the Ohio country where, for over a period of fifty years, Native Americans sought to defend their territorial integrity against the intrusion of newcomers, Jennings explored how they forged large scale confederations of a new and distinctive kind. The most important of these was the Covenant Chain which bound together in alliance and friendship the

British, Iroquois and Ohio Indians (the Delawares, the Shawnees, and the 'Mingo' Iroquois). Yet drawing on the work of Jack Sosin, Jennings was more successful in demonstrating the importance of the west, especially the Quebec Act, in the coming of the Revolution than in reconceptualizing the role of Native Americans. In the end the colonial side of Jennings's analysis tended to overshadow the Indian and his account was only partially successful in breaking out of the traditional framework of more conventional narratives. 'The gentry cried out passionately for liberty in general,' Jennings concluded, 'but itemized it as rights for themselves to hold slaves and attack Indians.'[105] Even so Jennings's essay anticipated the major shift in perspective towards the study of larger units of analysis, intertribal relations and diplomatic activity.[106]

Diplomacy and military strategy were the subject of two studies that preceded Jennings's landmark essay, indicating both the direction of change and its limitations. James O'Donnell (1937–) – whose monograph *Southern Indians in the American Revolution* (1973) focused on British and American policies towards the four major southern tribes: the Cherokees, Choctaws, Chickasaws and Creeks – attributed the failure of earlier historians to assess Indian influence on the revolutionary war, not to the fact that the subject had become virtually detached from American history, but to its complexity. Even when viewed from an essentially Eurocentric perspective, so many variables had to be taken into account. There were 'two central governments, thirteen individual state governments, two military commands, thousands of warriors and frontiersmen, and dozens of officials in the British and American Indian departments', as well as 'the sweep of events from North to South'.[107] Yet O'Donnell stressed the continuity of American Indian history. 'The story unfolded in this study', he writes, is in many ways 'the repetition of an oft-told tale'. In seeking to protect their interests, once again American Indians inadvertently chose the losing side, leaving themselves exposed to further land seizures.[108]

In *Southern Indians in the American Revolution*, O'Donnell does not present Native Americans as pawns or dupes nor as cruel or vengeful, but acting in their own interests and, in the war in the west, they were fighting 'for their very survival'.[109] Yet the

Indians remain shadowy figures. O'Donnell does not examine the structure of Native American societies or the nature of their cultures despite the fact that one of his original aims was to examine the impact of the war on Indian society. He downplays both the tensions within the respective nations as well as between them and, while recognizing the importance of gift-giving, neglects the significance of trade.[110]

More indicative of new directions in Native American history is Barbara Graymont's *The Iroquois in the American Revolution* (1972), the first full-length study of 'the most powerful group on the continent'. Strategically located on the borders of European settlement in New York and Pennsylvania, the Iroquois played 'an immensely important role in the European power struggle'.[111] As in the south, the belligerents sought to preserve the friendship 'or at least the neutrality' of the Six Nations who made up the Confederacy, but geographical proximity and economic dependency made it impossible for the Iroquois to stand apart from the conflict.[112] Under pressure from the British and the Americans, the Iroquois Confederacy fragmented. Unlike O'Donnell, Graymont insists that 'a full understanding of Iroquois history can be achieved only through a comprehension of the cultural foundations of the Iroquois people'. What Graymont wants to understand is 'how and why their kinship state ... broke apart as a result of the white man's conflict and thrust the Iroquois into civil war'.[113]

Rarely did historians discuss the problem of sources in writing about Native Americans but Graymont addresses the issue head-on. Her study 'is confined almost wholly to documents written by whites and from the white point of view'. Indian history was oral. It depended 'for the most part 'upon such mnemonic devices as pictographs, notched reeds, and wampu, strings and belts, as well as the memory of the elders'. The few personal Indian documents that survived 'though sparse, are immensely rewarding and help to give a new perspective to the story'. It was a matter of regret, she states, that 'the brilliant and literate Joseph Brant was never inspired to write his autobiography, or that Sayenqueraghta or Skenandon or Colonel Louis Atayataghroghta never had an amanuensis'.[114] When the Revolution came, it tore the Iroquois confederacy apart. 'It was the tragic paradox of the Iroquois,' writes Graymont, 'that they could no longer do without the presence of the white man, but in this dependence lay the seeds of their destruction.'[115] More so than any other historian, Graymont demonstrates just how persistent the British and Americans were in applying pressure to the Iroquois: 'the whites would not leave them alone'.[116] In seeking to explain why Iroquois options were so limited, Graymont explores the impact of their encounter with Europeans in an ethnographic opening chapter. Before the Revolution, Iroquois peoples had became increasingly dependent on European goods, which over time were transformed from luxuries into necessities. Here the British had the advantage over the Americans. When the Americans aspired to replace the British, they found that Indian friendship was costly. When the British finally won over the Iroquois, Graymont credits the arrival of a ship 'laden with trinkets' at Irondequoit with helping to seal the agreement.[117]

In addition to their economic dependency and strategic location, there were other reasons why the League of the Iroquois was prone to division on the eve of the Revolution. Missionary activity among them and the loss of power by traditional leaders, the sachems, were other factors. Graymont identifies religion as a key indicator of future loyalties. New England missionaries had won over the Oneida and Tuscarora nations to the American cause.[118] In addition, even before the outbreak of fighting, the sachems were losing power to the younger warriors. The authority of the former was based on consensus and they had no means of enforcing their views except by persuasion.[119] As the war between the British and their erstwhile colonists intensified, some of the warriors joined the belligerents regardless of the views of the sachems.[120] The successes of the British, though minor, breached the unity of the League and the pro-American Oneidas and Tuscaroras reconsidered their neutrality.[121] Graymont does not ignore Indian atrocities as at Cobleskill and examines the conflict in the Wyoming Valley in some detail, but pointedly prefaces her remarks with the comment that 'whites have always been prone to label any overwhelming Indian victory a massacre and to call any of their own battle triumphs over the Indians a great victory'. The Indians resented the accusations.[122] When the war ended, the Iroquois 'were undefeated on the battlefield', writes Graymont:

they would be finally 'conquered by treaty'.[123] Like other Native Americans who saw themselves as independent peoples, the Iroquois were not represented at the peace treaty where the British ceded all their claims south of Canada and east of the Mississippi to the Americans. Though some of the Iroquois were to find sanctuary in Canada, treaties with the Americans forced them to surrender large tracts of land.[124] The Oneida and the Tuscarora nations who had fought with the Americans, though guaranteed their lands under the 1784 Fort Stanwix Treaty, were the first to lose them. Within one generation their lands were gone and, moving west, they struggled 'to build a new community in Wisconsin Territory'.[125]

In the three decades since the publication of *The Iroquois in the American Revolution*, there have been numerous studies of Indian nations who participated in the revolutionary war, but there is still no comprehensive analysis of their role in the Revolution despite the methodological breakthrough provided by ethnohistory which addressed some of the problems identified by Jennings.[126] While ethnohistory has met with criticism, not least among Native Americans whose concept of history is based on myth and memory and who question the ability of non-Natives to write their history, it nonetheless influenced the work of a new generation of scholars who came to prominence in the 1980s and dominated the 1990s.[127] This generation of scholars, both American and international, contributed to the popularization of a range of innovative concepts, some of which derived from studies of the initial encounter between Europeans and the indigenous peoples of the Americas being commemorated (or not) in the early 1990s. In addition to 'encounter', there was 'exchange', 'contact' and 'Indians' new world', each of which has interaction between peoples at its core.[128] A second category of concepts such as 'borderlands', 'paths', and 'the middle ground', reify locations as well as serving as metaphors for certain ideas.[129] The categories were not mutually exclusive nor did they make older theoretical frameworks redundant. Concepts of class, race and gender preserve their utility because by applying the same categories of analysis to all Americans, they retain the potential to incorporate Native Americans into the history of the Revolution and much else besides.

The 'new' Indian history requires scholars to make adjustments to periodization and geographical scope. The problem with regional studies and those of individual colonies and states, argues Gregory Dowd (1956–), is that their boundaries, defined by Anglo-American usages, were less meaningful to Native Americans than to colonists and modern historians.[130] A major shift in perspective towards larger units of analysis and intertribal activity was anticipated by Jennings in his study of the Covenant Chain, and was most fully realized in Dowd's own work, *A Spirited Resistance* (1992).[131] 'Historians have begun to realize,' writes Dowd, 'that Native Americans acted in a world beyond the locality, that they explored ranges of possibilities and traveled widely to do so, and that they taught, learned from, and argued with each other in the process.'[132] The late eighteenth century witnessed the greatest amount of intertribal activity until the present day.[133]

Peter C. Mancall's *Valley of Opportunity* (1991), is a work of a very different type from that of Barbara Graymont in that it does not focus exclusively on Native Americans but 'seeks to reconstruct the economic world of valley residents', Native American, colonial and post-revolutionary, who despite their differences 'came to define their lives in relation to the market economy of eastern North America'.[134] The adoption of the term 'borderland' to describe the region emerges relatively late in the book which, beginning with a description of the regional environment, traces the establishment of the Indian population, the development of intercultural trade between Indians and colonists, the emergence of the colonial economy, the destruction of existing valley communities during the revolutionary war and the creation of the post-war economy.[135] Mancall points to the 'vastly different meanings' that the war had for Indians and colonists. Since most of the colonists supported the American cause, neutrality ceased to be an option for Native Americans. Neither people anticipated the nature of the conflict which followed.[136] Apart from one pitched battle, the combatants 'fought an unconventional war' waging 'intentionally destructive campaigns'.[137] 'The war put an end to the Indians' agriculture and hunting and at its end epidemics such as dysentery, measles and smallpox ravaged the refugee communities.'[138] Mancall argues that the scale of mortality among the Iroquois, estimated by Anthony Wallace at fifty per cent, made the prospect of economic recovery unlikely. He believes that many of the former valley residents ended up in what Wallace termed 'slums in the wilderness'. Mancall rejects the long-term perspective on the impact of the Revolution on Indian communities favoured by historians such as O'Donnell. For the Indians of the Upper Susquehanna Valley, the impact of the war was sudden and devastating. Though Indian communities had been weakened by the expansion of the commercial market before the war, the revolutionary war was nonetheless 'a stunning assault on interracial relations'. Prior to the war, colonists and Indians had lived together peacefully but 'after the Revolution few settlers in the valley wanted Indian neighbours' and, with 'government support for private economic development ... the region was lost to the Indians'.[139]

The ability of Native Americans and colonists to live and deal with each other in pre-revolutionary America is one of the major themes of much of the new work. Richard White defines the process somewhat differently from Mancall. The 'middle ground' was a conceptual framework, 'quickly and widely imitated' because it 'offered a coherent and intelligible interpretive tool to replace the traditional linear model of frontier history'.[140] It also recognized that Native Americans spent less time at war with colonial societies than time at peace with them. *The Middle Ground* (1991) relates how Europeans and Indians who initially 'met and regarded each other as alien, as other, as virtually nonhuman', constructed over a period of two centuries 'a common, mutually comprehensible world' in the region around the Great Lakes, called by the French, the *pays d'en haut*. Here the 'older worlds of the Algonquians and of various Europeans overlapped, and their mixture created new systems of meaning and of exchange'. Accommodation did not mean acculturation, nor was it limited to the *pays d'en haut*. The process described by White involved cultural change of a different sort. It was dependent on the inability of either side to achieve their ends by force and to succeed required one party to understand enough of 'the world and reasoning' of the other, 'to put it to their own purposes'. It took place *on the middle ground*, 'the place in between' – 'in between cultures and peoples and in between empires and the non-state world of villages'.[141] When these accommodations too broke down, the Indians were again reconstructed 'as alien, as exotic, as other'.[142]

Events in the west during the American Revolution, writes Richard White, were far removed from the ideological conflict that was being waged along the eastern seaboard. It was a small world where village interests, power struggles between villages and factions within villages determined loyalties and where the British military presence was limited.[143] White depicts a generational gap between village leaders – who 'loaded village interests onto imperial or revolutionary wagons and rode them as far they could go' – and the former alliance chiefs. Village leaders were either elderly men whom the Europeans had long ignored or a new generation, 'more parochial and less sophisticated' than their predecessors. 'Once familiar with Quebec, Montreal, Philadelphia, and New Orleans, and practised in negotiations with all the peoples between the Mississippi and the Atlantic, they now dealt only with their immediate neighbours.' During the course of the war, most of these Indians remained 'localistic' and 'independent'; 'few', claims White, 'acted as tribal units'.[144] Fighting revived again in 1784 when 'the chronic murders, horse thefts, and raids typical of relations between Anglo-American and Indian villagers before the Revolution resumed once more'.[145]

Among recent studies, interest in the nations in the south-east is marked. Here many traders intermarried with Cherokees, Creeks, Choctaws and Chikasaws, developing what some historians have claimed was a new social system. Many changes began before the outbreak of fighting and continued long after it had ceased. They were the consequences of intensive diplomacy, trade, advancing white settlement, Indian adjustments, state and government policies and missionary activity. 'The class system also became a significant source of conflict and factionalism within the society.' As a result of the emergence of a property-owning class among Native Americans, a plantation economy, slave labour, poverty and the spread of racial attitudes reminiscent of the slave-owning societies of the south developed. When the United States emerged the dominant power, and in some areas the only power, Indian peoples lost the ability to manoeuvre they had once enjoyed by playing one power off against another, which ultimately led to their removal.[146]

Tom Hatley introduces the term 'paths' into the discourse of relations between newcomers and natives. A study of changing relationships between 1670 and 1785, *The Dividing Paths* (1992), invokes both 'village rhetoric' and 'an actual trail' leading from Charlestown to the Cherokee Lower Towns.

> From the earliest days, intersections of commerce and diplomacy moved across both a metaphorical and literal path between the two peoples. After the 1730s, the main path between Charlestown and the Cherokee villages was called the Dividing Paths, after a fork in the trail near the fall line, where one fork proceeded into the Cherokee town of Keowee while the other passed west toward the Creek settlements of the upper Flint and Chattahoochee.[147]

At the beginning of the eighteenth century, contact between Carolinians and Cherokees was relatively open, but during the course of the century, though trade and communication continued, 'the branch of the trail leading toward increasing openness was shunned' by people on both sides. As the relationship became increasingly strained, choices were made but the possibility once existed of their alternatives – 'toward racial and cultural openness, toward a loosening rather than a tightening of routines of dependency, toward economic diversity', despite the fact that 'there were few regions of North America where the contrast between colonist and native was as sharp or as sustained'. Hatley employs the same terms in discussing Cherokee and colonial culture and makes gender central to his analysis. One society was patriarchal, the other matriarchal, and differences in gender roles led to 'distinctive patterns of authority, myth, and economy'.[148]

Dealing with white Carolinians became increasingly difficult as racial lines hardened in the later colonial period.

> Up into the mid-1770s Cherokee leading men continued to respond, though less hopefully, to demands for land or other concessions with specific actions as well as with talks. The issue now confronted by the village leadership was much more complex than access to land. Instead the Cherokee leading men faced the difficult task of negotiating with a people whose cultural limits were becoming more rigid.[149]

Hatley argues that 'the extreme pressures of the Revolutionary decade' led to the breakdown of the 'processes of accommodation and compromise within tribal councils' that held the Cherokees together.[150]

> As they grew into leadership during the 1760s, Cherokee men of the Revolutionary generation found their status threatened by anti-tribal incidents and the difficulties of their hunting economy. At the same time, they witnessed the adaptive innovations of tribal women and may have felt their pride equally challenged from within the village. And economic change within the village economy would provide the basis of differing strategies during the 1770s to achieve a shared cultural objective: survival.[151]

Hatley associates the further concessions granted in 1777 with another split inside Cherokee society created by the opposition of women to the war.[152]

Daniel Usner's study *Indians, Settlers, and Slaves in a Frontier Exchange Economy* (1992) posits more favourable relations between the diverse peoples of the Lower Mississippi Valley before the American Revolution than might have been predicted. Claimed by France, Louisiana was an area relatively neglected by metropolitan authorities when compared with the more economically promising Caribbean and Canada. Though tobacco, rice, indigo, timber and deerskins were exported, commercial relations developed independently between the peoples of the region. Usner describes this economy which sustained the inhabitants as 'a frontier exchange economy'. Europeans bought food, handicrafts and deerskins from the Indians who traded for European goods and firearms. Africans slave and free became pedlars and craftsmen. Europeans enslaved Indians and Africans but, claims Usner, race relations were relatively fluid. Demographic and economic changes between 1763 and 1783 led to the decline of the frontier exchange economy and the rise of the plantation economy. Frontier exchange activities, 'the farming, herding, hunting, and trading practices devised over the eighteenth century', never totally disappeared from the landscape. They survived 'in the interstices of the expanding plantation society' of the Lower Mississippi Valley. 'Indeed, customary means of production and exchange would prove to be strong roots for popular livelihood and everyday resistance well into the nineteenth century.'[153]

Claudio Saunt and Greg O'Brien have also charted patterns of change among the Creeks and the Choctaws but carry their analysis further into the nineteenth century than either Hatley or Usner. Claudio Saunt's *A New Order of Things* (1999) in which class is central to the analysis, traces how 'Creek mestizos had a profound and disruptive impact on Creek society'.[154] The sons of British fathers and Creek mothers, they 'introduced notions of private property and centralized authority into a society that had valued communal ownership and shared power. The true test of Creek identity, according to Saunt, lies not so much in the accident of birth, even into a prestigious clan, but in resistance to change'.[155]

The Indians' Revolution takes an ideological turn in the work of Greg O'Brien. In *Choctaws in a Revolutionary Age, 1750–1830* (2002) he examines how power and authority – Indian concepts that pose difficult interpretive problems for historians of Native America – were reconstituted among the Choctaws as a result of contact with Europeans. The Europeans provided access to gifts and trading opportunities which transformed wealth and power in ways that supplemented and superseded the more traditional avenues through spiritual power, access to which was controlled by the chiefs. Throughout the eighteenth century, Choctaws played competing European powers off against each other. As the American Revolution developed in the mid-1770s, Choctaws sided primarily with the British, although a significant contingent from the Sixtowns Division assisted Spain in the conquest of Mobile and Pensacola. Only after the Revolution did the Americans replace the British in competition with the Spanish. After the treaty of San Lorenzo in 1795, the United States maintained an increasingly pervasive presence in what in 1798 became the Mississippi Territory. Though Spain retained nominal control over the Gulf Coast area, 'the United States dominated relations with the southern Indian groups from that time'. Choctaw men fought in the revolutionary war, but they also experienced an ideological revolution within their society. Their true revolution was

> only tenuously connected to the revolutionary war. The ideological revolution within their society began to surface before the war and continued for decades afterward. When Choctaw elites altered their concepts about where power came from and what having authority meant, they initiated an era of revolutionary change every bit as powerful as that unleashed along the Atlantic Coast.[156]

As regional and tribal studies multiply, Colin Calloway's carefully titled monograph *The American Revolution in Indian Country* (1995), a study of eight towns dispersed across eastern North America, still offers the broadest analysis of Native American experiences during the course of the revolutionary war. Calloway makes no claims to be comprehensive, in fact he repudiates the idea, describing the towns as 'small patches of a huge tapestry'. Although he does not address Native American critics explicitly, he states categorically that he is not trying to tell 'the Indian side of the story'. His is 'a non-Indian view of Indian history, and a non-American view of American history'. He writes as 'an expatriate Briton who holds no brief for British colonialism but who believes that distance and objectivity can be as valuable as "inside information" in writing good history'.[157] His preference for towns is determined by the fact that they not only provide a better insight into the divisions within Indian societies but also demonstrate more graphically the impact of the Revolution on the lives of individuals.

Adopting James Merrell's concept of the 'Indians' new world', created as a consequence of the changes wrought in Indian societies by the arrival of Europeans and Africans, Colin Calloway offers an excellent overview of the state of Indian America in 1775. He brings to this analysis an emphasis on demographic change on the frontiers of Euro-America and the descent into violence which preceded the outbreak of the Revolution. By 1775, economic dependence upon Europeans, though varying in degree, was the norm. 'Cherokees in the mountains of the interior were no more willing or able to do without European trade goods than were coastal groups surrounded by European settlers.'[158] But if trade promoted interaction between natives and newcomers, land issues were what drove them apart.

> As the eighteenth century wore on, Indian people and Indian cultures were being engulfed by an ocean of European and African people ... The population of North Carolina shot from 45,000 in 1750 to 275,000 in 1775. Five thousand Scots migrated to North Carolina alone in the decade before the Revolution ... Products of cultures of violence and much else that was undesirable besides, they made 'hard neighbours' to the Indians.[159]

On the eve of the Revolution, 'murder and revenge, not mediation and accommodation, typified relations'.[160]

The American Revolution was 'one of the darkest periods in American Indian history'.[161] Determining 'Indian dispositions and allegiances' during the military conflict, however, is 'difficult and hazardous'. Native Americans were initially confused and divided over their responses. Drawing on the work of Gregory Dowd and Richard White among others, Calloway argues that, backed by supplies from the British and promoted by attempts to create a pan-Indian alliance, militants saw the conflict as an opportunity to recover lost ground. However, most people fluctuated in their sentiments, and participation in the fighting was often relatively brief. Indian leaders 'displayed considerable statecraft in steering their people through the treacherous diplomatic waters churned up by the revolution'.[162] 'By the end of the Revolution, Indian country was pockmarked with ruined villages from the Mohawk Valley to the Tennessee.' Survivors 'faced an uncertain future as they set about rebuilding war-torn lives. Many of them also had bitter scores to settle with fellow Indians as well as with white adversaries'.[163] The real disaster lay in the Revolution's outcome.[164]

The peace

The Peace of Paris not only ignored the indigenous population but deprived it of potential allies and diplomatic weight. The news that they had been abandoned by their erstwhile allies and their lands ceded to the Euro-Americans and the Spanish was met with anger and disbelief.[165] 'The end of the Revolution produced a new phase of conflict between Indians and Americans in the Ohio country.' The final defeat of the Indians came at the Battle of Fallen Timbers in 1794: 'Defeated in battle and abandoned by the British, the Indians could only watch as Wayne's troops put the area to the torch. A dozen years after the end of the Revolution, the American strategy of burning Indian food supplies finally ended the Indians' war for independence.'[166]

Notes

1 James H. Merrell, 'Some Thoughts on Colonial Historians and American Indians', *WMQ*, 3rd ser., 46 (1989), pp. 94–119; Colin G. Calloway, *New Worlds for All: Indians, Europeans, and the Remaking of Early America* (Baltimore, MD and London; 1997), p. 198; Gregory Evans Dowd, *A Spirited Resistance: The North American Indian Struggle for Unity, 1745–1815* (Baltimore, MD and London; 1992), p. xii.

2 Douglas Greenberg, 'The Middle Colonies in Recent American Historiography', *WMQ*, 3rd ser., 36 (1979), pp. 396–427, 415–16.

3 Jeremy Belknap, *History of New-Hampshire*, I, (Philadelphia; 1784), p. 103; Sidney Kaplan, 'The History of New-Hampshire: Jeremy Belknap as Literary Craftsman', *WMQ*, 3rd ser., 21(1) (1964), p. 33.

4 Winthrop D. Jordan, *White Over Black: American Attitudes Toward the Negro, 1550–1812* (Chapel Hill, NC; 1968), p. xiv; Gwenda Morgan, *The Hegemony of the Law: Richmond County, Virginia, 1692–1776* (New York and London; 1989), pp. 4–5; Richard Slotkin, *Regeneration through Violence: The Mythology of the American Frontier, 1600–1860* (Middletown, CT; 1973), p. 22; Kenneth M. Morrison, 'Native Americans and the American Revolution: Historic Stories and Shifting Frontier Conflict' in Frederick E. Hoxie (ed.), *Indians in American History* (Arlington Heights, IL; 1988), pp. 95–115, 113.

5 Richard D. Brown (ed.), *Major Problems in the Era of the American Revolution, 1760–1791*, 2nd edn (Boston, MA; 2000), p. 172.

6 Lester H. Cohen, *The Revolutionary Histories: Contemporary Narratives of the American Revolution* (Ithaca, NY and London; 1980), p. 121.

7 Cohen, *Revolutionary Histories*, p. 122; Arthur H. Shaffer, *The Politics of History: Writing the History of the American Revolution, 1783–1815* (Chicago; 1975), pp. 170, 171.

8 Clifford K. Shipton, 'Samuel Williams', Biographical sketches of those who attended Harvard College in the Classes 1761–1763, *Sibley's Harvard Graduates*, XV (Boston, MA; 1970), pp. 134–46.

9 Samuel Williams, *The Natural and Civil History of Vermont* (Walpole, NH; 1794), pp. 133, 196; Shaffer, *Politics of History*, p. 72.

10 Williams, *Natural and Civil History*, pp. 203–4.

11 Williams, *Natural and Civil History*, p. 208.

12 David Ramsay, *The History of the American Revolution*, ed. Lester H. Cohen, 2 vols (Indianapolis, IN; 1990), II, pp. 463, 465, 467, 470–1.

13 Ramsay, *American Revolution*, II, pp. 463–4.

14 Ramsay, *American Revolution*, II, pp. 464–5.

15 Ramsay, *American Revolution*, II, pp. 466–7.

16 David Ramsay, *History of the Revolution in South-Carolina from a British Province to an Independent State*, 2 vols (Trenton, NJ; 1785), I, pp. 155–60; see also David Ramsay, *History of South Carolina from the first Settlement in 1670 to the Year 1808*, 2 vols. (Charleston, SC; 1809), I, pp. 209, 259–60, 277, 279–82.

17 Ramsay, *Revolution in South-Carolina*, I, p. 159.

18 Ramsay, *Revolution in South-Carolina*, I, pp. 160–1.

19 Ramsay, *American Revolution*, II, p. 467.

20 Ramsay, *American Revolution*, II, pp. 471–2.

21 Ramsay, *American Revolution*, II, pp. 473–5.

22 Ramsay, *American Revolution*, II, pp. 370–1; William Gordon, *The History of the Rise, Progress and Establishment of the Independence of the United States of America*, 4 vols (London; 1788), II, pp. 544–5; Mercy Otis Warren, *History of the Rise, Progress and Termination of the American Revolution*, ed. Lester H. Cohen, 2 vols (Indianapolis, IN; 1988), I, pp. 233–4; Barbara Graymont, *The Iroquois in the American Revolution* (Syracuse, NY; 1972), pp. 151–2; Richard Hildreth, *The History of the United States, from the Discovery of the Continent to the Organization of Government under the Federal Constitution 1492–1789*, 3 vols (1849), III, pp. 204–5; Armstrong Starkey, *European and Native American Warfare, 1675–1815* (London; 1998), pp. 111–12; Colin Calloway, 'The Continuing Revolution in Indian Country', in Frederick E. Hoxie, Ronald Hoffman and Peter J. Albert (eds), *Native Americans and the Early Republic* (Charlottesville, VA and London; 1999), pp. 3–33, 31; Elise Marienstras, 'The Common Man's Indian: The Image of the Indian as a Promoter of National Identity in the Early National Era' in Hoxie et al., *Native Americans and the Early Republic*, pp. 261–96, 279.

23 Ramsay, *American Revolution*, II, pp. 74–5; Warren, *History*, I, pp. 285–6, Hildreth, *History*, III, pp. 422–3.

24 *A State of the Expedition from Canada as Laid Before the House of Commons, by Lieutenant-General Burgoyne*, 2nd edn (London; 1780; reprinted, 1969), pp. 65–7; Troy Bickham, *Savages within the Empire: Representations of American Indians in Eighteenth-century Britain* (Oxford; 2006), pp. 264–71.

25 Warren, *History, passim*.

26 Warren, *History*, I, p. xxii.

27 Warren, *History*, p. 114.

28 Warren, *History*, I, pp. 138, 222, 279, 285; II, pp. 633–4.

29 Cohen failed to find the exact quotation in Gibbon's *History of the Decline and Fall of the Roman Empire* but the sentiment expressed in Warren's quotation accords with similar sentiments in his work, see Warren, *History*, I, fn. p.137.

30 Warren, *History*, p. 186.

31 Warren, *History*, pp. 140–1, 207, 222–3 and 227.

32 Warren, *History*, I, pp. 284–5.

33 Warren, *History*, p. 285.

34 Warren, *History*, p. 187.

35 Abiel Holmes, *American Annals*, 2 vols (Cambridge, MA; 1805); M. A. DeW. H., *Dictionary of American Biography*, ed. Dumas Malone, IX (New York; 1932), pp. 160–1.

36 Holmes, *American Annals*, II, p. 341.

37 Holmes, *American Annals*, II, pp. 345–6, 376.

38 Belknap, *History of New-Hampshire*, I, pp. 282–5; on Belknap's changing views on education, conversion and antislavery, see George B. Kirsch, 'Jeremy Belknap and the Problem of Blacks and Indians in Early America', *Historical New Hampshire*, 34 (1979), pp. 202–22.

39 Belknap, *History of New-Hampshire*, I, pp. 286–7.

40 *Peter Oliver's Origin*, p. 132.

41 *Peter Oliver's Origin*, pp. 132–4.

42 *Peter Oliver's Origin*, pp. 29–45.

43 James H. Merrell, 'American Nations, Old and New: Reflections on Indians and the Early Republic', in Hoxie et al., *Native Americans and the Early Republic*, pp. 333–53, 333.

44 Timothy Pitkin, *A Political and Civil History of the United States of America from the Year 1763 to the Close of the Administration of President Washington, in March, 1797*, 2 vols (New Haven, CT; 1828), I, p. 139.

45 Pitkin, *Political and Civil History*, I, p. 5.

46 Steven Conn, *History's Shadow: Native America and Historical Consciousness in the Nineteenth Century* (Chicago and London; 2004), pp. 200–1.

47 J. Hector St John de Crevecoeur, *Letters from an American Farmer, and, Sketches of Eighteenth-Century America*, ed. Albert E. Stone (New York; 1981), p. 122, cited in Merrell, 'American Nations', p. 335; John Lendrum, *A Concise and Impartial History of the American Revolution to Which is Prefixed A General History of North and South America* (Boston, MA; 1795), I, p. 220.

48 Gary B. Nash, 'The Concept of Inevitability in the History of European-Indian Relations' in Carla Gardina Pestana and Sharon V. Salinger (eds), *Inequality in Early America* (Hanover, NH, and London; 1999), pp. 267–91; Merrell, 'American Nations', p. 333.

49 Conn, *History's Shadow*, p. 204; Robert F. Berkhofer Jr, *The White Man's Indian: Images of the American Indian from Columbus to the Present* (New York; 1978), pp. 93–5.

50 David Levin, *History as Romantic Art: Bancroft, Prescott, Motley and Parkman* (Stanford, CA; 1959), pp. 129–33.

51 Roy Harvey Pearce, *Savagism and Civilization: A Study of the Indian and the American Mind* (Baltimore, MD; 1967), p. 162; originally published in 1953 and entitled *The Savages of America*.

52 George Bancroft, *History of the United States of America: The Author's Last Revision* (New York; 1888), II, pp. 86–136.

53 Alden T. Vaughan, 'From White Man to Redskin' in 'Changing Anglo-American Perceptions of the American Indian', *AHR*, 87 (1982), pp. 917–53. Duncan J. MacLeod, *Slavery, Race and the American Revolution* (London and New York; 1974); William R. Stanton, *The Leopard's Spots: Scientific Attitudes toward Race in America, 1815–1859* (Chicago; 1960); Nancy Shoemaker, however, observed that the colour 'red' was in use among south-eastern Indians in the mid-1720s; Nancy Shoemaker, 'How Indians Got to be Red', *AHR*, 102 (1997), pp. 625–44, 627–37 and *A Strange Likeness: Becoming Red and White in Eighteenth-Century North America* (New York; 2004), pp. 125–40.

54 Bancroft, *History of the United States*, III, pp. 300, 301–2.

55 Bancroft, *History of the United States*, III, pp. 302–3, 304–5.

56 Bancroft, *History of the United States*, II, p. 126.

57 Bancroft, *History of the United States*, IV, p. 58; on popular images and prej-

udices towards Indians in the early Republic, see Daniel R. Mandell, 'The Indian's Pedigree (1794): Indians, Folklore, and Race in Southern New England', *WMQ*, 3rd ser., 61 (2004), pp. 521–38; Marienstras, 'The Common Man's Indian', pp. 261–96; on massacre, Ian K. Steele, *Betrayals: Fort William Henry and the 'Massacre'* (New York and Oxford; 1990); Belknap, *History of New-Hampshire*, pp. 298–9.

58 Bancroft, *History of the United States*, (1889), IV, pp. 58–9.

59 Bancroft, *History of the United States,* (1889), IV, pp. 78–89.

60 Bancroft, *History of the United States*, (1889), IV, p. 84.

61 Bancroft, *History of the United States,* (1888–9), IV, p. 308.

62 Bancroft, *History of the United States*, (1889), IV, pp. 308–9; for a fuller treatment of this issue, see Hildreth, *History*, III, pp. 289–92; on the diplomatic wrangling during the war and after, see Pitkin, *Political and Civil History*, II, pp. 88–116, 434–7.

63 Bancroft, *History of the United States* (1889), IV, pp. 309–15.

64 Hildreth, *History,* I, p. 52.

65 Hildreth, *History*, I, pp. 54–5.

66 Hildreth, History, I, pp. 58–9.

67 Hildreth, *History*, I, pp. 69–70.

68 Hildreth, *History*, III, pp. 287–9.

69 Hildreth, *History*, III, pp. 262–3.

70 Hildreth, *History*, III, pp. 162, 260–1, 284–6, 289–92.

71 Hildreth, *History*, III, p. 425.

72 Hildreth, *History*, III, pp. 461–62.

73 Ellen Fitzpatrick, *History's Memory: Writing America's Past, 1880–1980* (Cambridge, MA and London; 2002), p. 29; John B. McMaster, *A History of the People of the United States: From the Revolution to the Civil War*, 8 vols (New York; 1883–1913).

74 Fitzpatrick, *History's Memory*, pp. 30–1, quotation page 31.

75 Edward Channing, *History of the United States*, 6 vols (New York; 1905–25); Fitzpatrick, *History's Memory*, p. 268, fn. 20.

76 John Higham, *History: Historical Scholarship in America* (Baltimore, MD; 1983), p. 168.

77 R. David Edmunds, 'Native Americans, New Voices: American Indian History, 1895–1995', *AHR*, 100 (1995), pp. 717–40, 720.

78 John B. McMaster, *A History of the People of the United States* (New York and London; 1931), I, pp. 6–7.

79 McMaster, *People of the United States*, I, pp. 7–8.

80 McMaster, *People of the United States*, I, pp. 5, 6.

81 Merrell, 'American Nations', pp. 336–7.

82 Channing, *History of the United States*, III, p. 15.

83 Channing, *History of the United States*, III, pp. 17–22.

84 Channing, *History of the United States*, III, pp. 23–4.

85 Allan G. Bogue 'Frederick Jackson Turner', *ANB*, vol. 22, pp. 18–21.

86 Gordon S. Wood, 'A Century of Writing Early American History: Then and Now Compared', *AHR*, 100 (1995), pp. 678–96, 694–5; Edmunds, 'Native Americans, New Voices', p. 717; Richard Hofstadter, *The Progressive Historians: Turner, Beard and Parrington* (New York; 1968), pp. 104–5.

87 Patricia Nelson Limerick, 'Turnerians All: The Dream of a Helpful History in an Intelligible World', *AHR*, 100 (1995), pp. 697–716, 701–2. On Turner and professionalism, Limerick draws on the work of Richard White.

88 Justin Winsor, *The Westward Movement: The Colonies and the Republic: West of the Alleghanies, 1763–1798* (Boston and New York; 1897).

89 Winsor, *Westward Movement*, p. 2.

90 Edmunds, 'Native Americans, New Voices', pp. 721–2; Nash, 'The Concept of Inevitability', pp. 267–91.

91 Clarence V. Alvord, *The Mississippi Valley in British Politics: A Study of the Trade, Land Speculation, and Experiments in Imperialism Culminating in the American Revolution*, 2 vols (New York; 1959 [1916]), p. 13.

92 Thomas P. Abernathy, *Western Lands and the American Revolution* (New York; 1959 [1937]), pp. 137, 141.

93 Abernathy, *Western Lands*, p. 247.

94 Evarts B. Greene, *The Revolutionary Generation, 1763–1790* (New York; 1943) (vol. 4 of the series *A History of American Life*), pp. 174, 178, 238, 256.

95 Greene, *Revolutionary Generation*, p. 174.

96 Greene, *Revolutonary Generation*, pp. 178–9.

97 Greene, *Revolutionary Generation*, pp. 238–9.

98 Edmunds, 'Native Americans, New Voices', p. 723.

99 Greenberg, 'The Middle Colonies in Recent American Historiography', p. 415.

100 Francis Jennings, 'The Indians' Revolution' in Young (ed.), *American Revolution*, pp. 319–48, 344; see also Francis Jennings, *The Invasion of America: Indians, Colonialism, and the Cant of Conquest* (Chapel Hill, NC; 1975).

101 Richard D. White, *The Middle Ground: Indians, Empire, and Republics in the Great Lakes Region, 1650–1815* (New York; 1991), p. xi; E. P. Thompson, *The Making of the English Working Class* (London; 1963), p. 13.

102 James Axtell, 'The Ethnohistory of Early America: A Review Essay', *WMQ*, 3rd ser., 35 (1978), pp. 110–44, 113.

103 Theda Perdue, *Cherokee Women: Gender and Culture Change, 1700–1835* (Lincoln, NB, and London; 1998), pp. 3–4.

104 Jennings, 'Indians' Revolution', p. 323; Colin G. Calloway, *The American Revolution in Indian Country: Crisis and Diversity in Native American Communities* (New York; 1995), p. 293.

105 Jennings, 'Indians' Revolution', p. 344; Jack M. Sosin, *The Revolutionary Frontier, 1763–1783* (New York; 1967); Jack M. Sosin, *Whitehall and the Wilderness: The Middle West in British Colonial Policy, 1760–1775* (Lincoln, NB; 1968).

106 Francis Jennings, *The Ambiguous Iroquois Empire: The Covenant Chain: Confederation of Indian Tribes with the English Colonies from its Beginnings to the Lancaster Treaty of 1744* (New York and London; 1984); Daniel K. Richter and James H. Merrell (eds), *Beyond the Covenant Chain: The Iroquois and their Neighbors in Indian North America, 1600–1800* (Syracuse, NY; 1987).

107 James H. O'Donnell III, *Southern Indians in the American Revolution*

(Knoxville, TN; 1973), p. x.
108 O'Donnell, *Southern Indians*, pp. 52–3.
109 O'Donnell, *Southern Indians*, pp. vii, viii.
110 O'Donnell, *Southern Indians*, p. 137.
111 Graymont, *Iroquois*, pp. vii, 25.
112 Graymont, *Iroquois*, p. 1.
113 Graymont, *Iroquois*, pp. vii–viii.
114 Graymont, *Iroquois*, p. ix.
115 Graymont, *Iroquois*, p. 25.
116 Graymont, *Iroquois*, p. 1.
117 Graymont, *Iroquois*, pp. 91–2, 122–3.
118 Graymont, *Iroquois*, p. 33.
119 Graymont, *Iroquois*, pp. 85, 163.
120 Graymont, *Iroquois*, pp. 97, 102.
121 Graymont, *Iroquois*, p. 101.
122 Graymont, *Iroquois*, pp. 166, 174.
123 Graymont, *Iroquois*, p. 276.
124 Graymont, *Iroquois*, pp. 272, 282–3.
125 Graymont, *Iroquois*, pp. 286, 288.
126 Axtell, 'The Ethnohistory of Early America', pp. 110–44; Jennings, 'Indians' Revolution', pp. 319–48.
127 Joy Porter, 'Imagining Indians: Differing Perspectives on Native American History', in Melvin Stokes (ed.), *The State of U.S. History* (Oxford and New York; 2002), pp. 347–66; see also Daniel K, Richter, 'Whose Indian History?', *WMQ*, 3rd ser., 50 (1993), pp. 379–93, 380–2.
128 Alfred W. Crosby, *The Columbian Exchange: Biological and Cultural Consequences of 1492* (Westport, CT; 1972); James H. Merrell, *The Indians' New World: Catawbas and their Neighbors from European Contact through the Era of Removal* (Chapel Hill, NC; 1989); Daniel H. Unser Jr., *Indians, Settlers, and Slaves in a Frontier Exchange Economy: The Lower Mississippi Valley before 1783* (Chapel Hill, NC, and London; 1992), pp. 8–9; Calloway, *New Worlds for All*; Andrew R. L. Cayton and Frederika J. Teute (eds), *Contact Points: American Frontiers from the Mohawk Valley to the Mississippi, 1750–1830* (Chapel Hill, NC; 1998).
129 Cayton and Teute, *Contact Points*; Tom Hatley, *The Dividing Paths: Cherokees and South Carolinians through the Era of Revolution* (New York and Oxford; 1992); Richard D. White, *The Middle Ground: Indians, Empire, and Republics in the Great Lakes, 1650–1815* (New York; 1991).
130 Dowd, *Spirited Resistance*, pp. xi–xii.
131 Jennings, *Ambiguous Iroquois Empire*; Dowd, *Spirited Resistance*, p. xiii.
132 Dowd, *Spirited Resistance*, p. xiii.
133 Dowd, *Spirited Resistance*, p. xix.
134 Peter C. Mancall, *Valley of Opportunity: Economic Culture along the Upper Susquehanna, 1700–1800* (Ithaca and New York; 1991), pp. xi, 7.
135 Mancall, *Valley of Opportunity*, p. xii.
136 Mancall, *Valley of Opportunity*, p. 131.
137 Mancall, *Valley of Opportunity*, pp. 135–9.
138 Mancall, *Valley of Opportunity*, pp. 194–6.

139 Mancall, *Valley of Opportunity*, p. 232.
140 Cayton and Teute, *Contact Points*, pp. vi–vii.
141 White, *Middle Ground*, pp. ix–x, 52–3.
142 White, *Middle Ground*, p. x.
143 White, *Middle Ground*, pp. 367–8, 378.
144 White, *Middle Ground*, p. 398.
145 White, *Middle Ground*, p. 411.
146 Claudio Saunt, *A New Order of Things: Property, Power, and the Transformation of the Creek Indians, 1733–1816* (New York; 1999), p. 304.
147 Hatley, *Dividing Paths*, p. xiv.
148 Hatley, *Dividing Paths*, pp. xii–xiii, xiv–xv.
149 Hatley, *Dividing Paths*, pp. 210–11.
150 Hatley, *Dividing Paths*, pp. 217–18.
151 Hatley, *Dividing Paths*, p. 226.
152 Hatley, *Dividing Paths*, pp. 220–1.
153 Usner, *Indians, Settlers, and Slaves*, pp. 8–9.
154 Saunt, *New Order of Things*, p. 2.
155 Edward J. Cashin, 'Review of Claudio Saunt, *A New Order of Things*', WMQ, 3rd ser., 57 (1999), pp. 859–60.
156 Greg B. O'Brien, *Choctaws in a Revolutionary Age, 1750–1830* (Lincoln, NB; 2002), p. 11.
157 Calloway, *American Revolution*, pp. xv, xvi.
158 Calloway, *American Revolution*, p. 11.
159 Calloway, *American Revolution*, pp. 19–20.
160 Calloway, *American Revolution*, pp. 21, 23.
161 Calloway, *American Revolution*, p. 290.
162 Calloway, *American Revolution*, pp. 26, 32, 290; Dowd, *Spirited Resistance*, ch. 3; White, *Middle Ground*, pp. 367, 398.
163 Calloway, *American Revolution*, p. 64.
164 Calloway, *American Revolution*, p. 272.
165 Calloway, *American Revolution*, pp. 272–3.
166 Calloway, *American Revolution*, pp. 280, 289.

CONCLUSION

When David Ramsay, Jeremy Belknap and Samuel Williams produced their histories, they wrote for specific purposes, addressed specific audiences (national, state or both), and strove to write within the currently accepted boundaries of historical writing. When they stepped outside these parameters, as did Belknap and more especially Lendrum who was honest enough to call himself a compiler, they informed their readers of what they were doing. They sought to recover the truth and to write about it objectively. The best of them consulted written sources and interviewed participants in the events they described but as late as Timothy Pitkin, they regretted their lack of British sources, the *Annual Register* always excepted. For the most part, Mercy Otis Warren and Thomas Hutchinson also observed the rules but they also wrote themselves into their histories. Yet it could be argued that it is Peter Oliver, a participant observer like the others, observing no rules at all, who affords us entry into the heart of the Revolution and identifies, African Americans excepted, the many actors engaged in the conflict. George Bancroft, who dominated the nineteenth century almost to the exclusion of everyone else, except perhaps Richard Hildreth, rectified the matter of sources, but reintroduced providence – largely but not wholly absent from the revolutionary histories – into the affairs of men, but cast Native Americans, African Americans and women as passive figures, that is when he included them at all. With the rise of professional training in the nation's expanding educational institutions, two schools of interpretation emerged – the imperial and the progressive – the influence of which is still apparent today. The former viewed the Revolution from the perspective of empire, the latter focussed on internal divisions and the consequences of revolutionary upheaval. In these histories, the roles of women, Native Americans and African Americans were almost wholly excluded. It was not until the turbulent 1960s and the rise of the new social history that those who had played a part in the momentous events of the Revolution re-entered the history books though the process was slow and is still ongoing. New work on

297

the American Revolution can still be identified with these divergent approaches.

Woody Holton's *Forced Founders* (1999) is provocative, lively and iconoclastic.[1] Writing from a neo-progressive standpoint Holton maintains that rather than being at the forefront of the Revolution, Virginia's gentry leaders were forced to act by their social inferiors. Its heroes are the smallholders, tenants, and poor whites whose decision to withhold tobacco from sale in 1773 initiated the non-exportation movement and whose demands for independence brought forward the final break with Britain. Michael McDonnell's work takes off where Holton's ends though his article on 'Popular Mobilization and Political Culture in Revolutionary Virginia', based on his doctoral dissertation at the University of Oxford, appeared in the *Journal of American History* the year before Holton's book was published. Holton and McDonnell have cooperated on a number of projects. Ray Raphael's *People's History of the American Revolution* (2001), though written by someone outside the academy, manages to be both scholarly and popular. Holton and Raphael succeed in incorporating African Americans and Native Americans into their narratives and in the case of Raphael also women. Rhys Isaac's sequel to *The Transformation of Virginia* (1983) is not so easy to pigeonhole. While the earlier monograph was assigned to the progressive camp, his *Landon Carter's Uneasy Kingdom* (2004) is a work of a very different stamp in which he seeks to tell 'the story of the coming of the American Revolution as experienced by an apprehensive Virginia planter patriarch, based on his well known diary'. The diary allows Isaac not only to tell Carter's story but those 'of the African Americans, the women and the young persons' who appear in it.[2] The radical historian Alfred Young has also produced two innovative histories which are difficult to categorize. They could be called micro-histories but they are also dissertations on historical memory and on how history is written. In *The Shoemaker and the Tea Party* (1999) and *Masquerade* (2004) Young seeks to recover the lives of George Hewes and Deborah Sampson by separating so far as he could the reality from the myth. While both books make fascinating reading, they have been criticized for the use of conjecture.[3] If Young, Raphael and Holton have reinvented progressivism for the twenty-first century, it may not be too far fetched to argue that the Atlanticists are the lineal descendants of the imperialists.

The Debate on the American Revolution set out unashamedly to examine the American side of the story. It was a choice consciously made and reflected the limitations imposed on a book of this size by so large a topic and herein lies the irony, for at the end of the twentieth century and the beginning of the twenty-first, a 'new' British history has taken shape, one reconceptualized within an Atlantic world, and latterly an imperial one. While John Brewer is most closely identified with the former, Peter Marshall, formerly Professor of Imperial History at King's College, London, has reinvented the latter. In *The Making and Unmaking of Empires* (2005), Marshall demonstrates how in North America 'imperial reform was frustrated and rule of any kind eventually proved to be impossible over people for the most part self-consciously English'. At the same time, however, the British government succeeded in creating 'an imperial structure' in Bengal which met the aims they had sought to realize in North America: a structure of local government that ensured 'that British territories were effectively defended and that the wealth of the empire was properly husbanded through a system of trade regulation'.[4]

Among works linking the concept of the Atlantic world to the American Revolution are T. H. Breen's *The Marketplace of Revolution* (2004) and Gwenda Morgan and Peter Rushton's *Eighteenth-Century Criminal Transportation: The Formation of the Criminal Atlantic* (2004). In the former Breen uses the twin concepts of consumer revolution and an empire of goods, not to argue that these caused the American Revolution, but that they promoted unity among the colonists and provided instruments whereby colonial resistance was to prove effective. In *Eighteenth-Century Criminal Transportation: The Formation of the Criminal Atlantic*, Morgan and Rushton have linked criminal transportation to changing perspectives of Britain and the American colonies in a discourse of difference arguing that once Americans realized that their Britishness was second class, then criminality became a key characteristic of the overmighty 'other' – in effect, they saw themselves as victims of a criminal empire.[5]

While eighteenth-century British history has been reinvigorated, if not reinvented, new work appeared in the United States at the turn of the century on popular politics in the aftermath of the Revolution. Drawing on popular rituals and print culture, Simon Newman, David Waldstreicher, Len Travers and Jeffrey Pasley extended the boundaries of revolutionary studies into the early national period.[6] Yet the history of the American Revolution has also taken a curious turn. The mood has become defensive and biography is once again fashionable, not to mention lucrative. This appears to be a reaction of sorts against forty years of social history during which the founding fathers allegedly languished in obscurity or met with contempt. According to Gordon Wood, attitudes towards the founding fathers among historians had changed profoundly. Not so long ago 'few Americans could look back at these revolutionaries and constitu-tionmakers without being overawed by their brilliance ... but not anymore, at least in the eyes of some professional historians'.[7] He wrote much the same thing in the introduction to his book *The American Revolution*. In the past historians 'rarely, if ever, ques-tioned the worth of the Revolution. At present ... it has become fashionable to deny that anything substantially progressive came out of the Revolution'.[8]

In *Setting the World Ablaze: Washington, Adams, Jefferson, and the American Revolution* (2000), John Ferling (1940–) claims that 'if Adams and Jefferson could read much that has been written in recent years about early American history, they would be more bewildered than exasperated'. Committed to social history, and shaped by political correctness and multiculturalism, professional historians during the past quarter century by and large have neglected the role played by leaders in important events.[9] Citing David Hackett Fischer, Ferling claims the 'only creature less fashionable in academe than the stereotypical "dead white male is a dead white male on horseback"'. In his book, 'a study of personality, character, aspirations, drives, choices, ideas, visions, leadership, and courage', Ferling uses comparative biog-raphy in an attempt 'to link personal and impersonal elements in the contours of the American Revolution and the war that accom-panied it'. It is a study of three leading figures in the American Revolution whom he wants to put 'back into the crosshairs of history'.[10] In many ways this is an admirable study but it does neglect forty years of modern historiography. And politics aside, it does point up what is perhaps the key problem in writing about the American Revolution for professional historians. When John Adams raised the question of who would write the history of the American Revolution, he was concerned about his own reputation and fearful that Franklin and Jefferson would run away with the glory. He fretted over bias, 'political correctness', and the damage historians might cause to the rising nation's reputation. He doubted whether anyone would ever be able to write the history of the Revolution. The problem that confronts the modern historian of the Revolution is how to incorporate the vast array of actors who participated in it into a single narrative. The leaders have never been absent from the history books, but the participants who were legion and to some extent recognized at the time, tended to vanish from nineteenth- and twentieth-century history, not least from the pages of professional practitioners. To associate the most innovative decades in the writing of American history with 'political correctness' and 'multiculturalism', seems to miss the point.[11] The gains were enormous but there was a price – the fragmentation of the history of the Revolution is one of them. The challenge is to create a new synthesis.

Notes

1 Woody Holton, *Forced Founders: Indians, Debtors, Slaves, and the Making of the American Revolution in Virginia* (Chapel Hill, NC; 1999); Michael McDonnell, 'Popular Mobilization and Political Culture in Revolutionary Virginia: The Failure of the Minutemen and the Revolution from Below', *JAH*, 85 (1998), pp. 946–8.

2 Rhys Isaac, *Landon Carter's Uneasy Kingdom: Revolution and Rebellion on a Virginia Plantation* (Oxford and New York; 2004), p. xi.

3 Alfred F. Young, *The Shoemaker and the Tea Party: Memory and the American Revolution* (Boston, MA; 1999) and the same author's *Masquerade: The Life and Times of Deborah Sampson: Continental Soldier* (New York; 2004).

4 John Brewer, *The Sinews of Power: War, Money and the English State 1688–1793* (London; 1989); P. J. Marshall, *The Making and Unmaking of Empires: Britain, India and America c. 1750–1783* (Oxford; 2005), p. 12. See also David Armitage and Michael J. Braddick (eds), *The British Atlantic World* (Basingstoke; 2002); Linda Colley, *Captives: Britain, Empire and the World* (London; 2004); Stephen Conway, *The War of American*

Independence (London; 1995) and *The British Isles and the War of American Independence* (Oxford; 2000); Eliga H. Gould, *The Persistence of Empire: British Political Culture in the Age of the American Revolution* (Chapel Hill, NC and London; 2000); Andrew J. O'Shaughnessy, *An Empire Divided: The American Revolution and the British Caribbean* (Philadelphia, PA; 2000); Kathleen Wilson, *The Sense of the People: Politics, Culture and Imperialism in England 1715–1785* (Cambridge; 1995).

5 T. H. Breen, *The Market Place of Revolution: How Consumer Politics Shaped American Independence* (New York; 2004); Gwenda Morgan and Peter Rushton, *Eighteenth-Century Criminal Transportation: The Formation of the Criminal Atlantic* (Basingstoke; 2004), ch. 6.

6 Simon P. Newman, *Parades and the Politics of the Street: Festive Culture in the early American Republic* (Philadelphia, PA; 1997); Len Travers, *Celebrating the Fourth: Independence Day and the Rites of Nationalism in the Early Republic* (Amherst, MA; 1997); David Waldstreicher, *In the Midst of Perpetual Fetes: The Making of American Nationalism 1776–1820* (Chapel Hill, NC; 1997); Jürgen Heideking, Geneviève Fabre and Kai Dreisbach (eds), *Celebrating Ethnicity and Nation: American Festive Culture from the Revolution to the Early 20th Century* (New York and Oxford; 2001); Jeffrey L. Pasley, *'The Tyranny of Printers': Newspaper Politics in the Early American Republic* (Charlottesville, VA; 2003).

7 Gordon S. Wood, 'The Great Generation', *New York Review of Books,* 29 March 2001, pp. 17–22, 17.

8 Gordon S. Wood, *The American Revolution: A History* (New York; 2002), p. xxiv.

9 John Ferling, *Setting the World Ablaze: Washington, Adams, Jefferson, and the American Revolution* (Oxford and New York; 2000), p. ix.; David H. Fischer, *Paul Revere's Ride* (New York; 1994), p. xiv.

10 Ferling, *Setting the World Ablaze,* p. xi.

11 On the origins of the new social history, see Jack P. Greene and J. R. Pole, *Colonial British America: Essays in the New History of the Early Modern Era* (Baltimore, MD and London; 1984), pp. 4–7.

FURTHER READING

Overviews

Higham, John, *History: Professional Scholarship in America* (Baltimore, MD; 1983)

Kraus, Michael and Davis D. Joyce, *The Writing of American History*, revised edn (Norman, OK; 1985)

Newman, Simon P., 'Writing the History of the American Revolution' in Melvyn Stokes (ed.), *The State of U.S. History* (Oxford; 2002), pp. 23–44

The first hundred years: late eighteenth century to late nineteenth century

Cohen, Lester H., *The Revolutionary Histories: Contemporary Narratives of the American Revolution* (Ithaca, NY; 1980)

Hoffer, Peter Charles, *Liberty and Order: Two Views of American History from the Revolutionary Years to the Early Work of George Bancroft and Wendell Phillips* (New York and London; 1988)

Shaffer, Arthur, *The Politics of History: Writing the History of the American Revolution, 1783–1815* (Chicago; 1975)

Van Tassel, David D., *Recording America's Past: An Interpretation of the Development of Historical Studies in America 1607–1884* (Chicago; 1960)

Vitzhuam, Richard, *The American Compromise: Theme and Method in the Histories of Bancroft, Parkman, and Adams* (Norman, OK; 1974)

The professional era

Breen, T. H., 'Ideology and Nationalism on the Eve of the American Revolution: Revisions Once More in Need of Revising', *JAH*, 84 (1997), pp. 13–39

Dickinson, H. T. (ed.), *Britain and the American Revolution* (London; 1998)

Ekirch, Roger, 'Sometimes an Art, Never a Science, Always a Craft: A Conversation with Bernard Bailyn', *WMQ*, 3rd ser., 51 (1994), pp. 625–58

Greene, Jack P., 'The Flight from Determinism: A Review of Recent Literature on the Coming of the Revolution', *SAQ*, 61 (1962), pp. 235–59

Greene, Jack P. (ed.), *The Reinterpretation of the American Revolution 1763–1789* (New York; 1968)

Higham, John, 'The Cult of the "American Consensus": Homogenizing our History', *Commentary*, 27 (1959), pp. 93–100.

Hoffman, Ronald and Peter Albert (eds), *The Transforming Hand of Revolution: Reconsidering the American Revolution as a Social Movement* (Charlottesville, VA and London; 1996)

Hofstadter, Richard, *The Progressive Historians: Turner, Beard, Parrington* (New York; 1968)

Hutchinson, William T. (ed.), *The Marcus W. Jernegan Essays in American Historiography. By his Former Students at the University of Chicago* (Chicago; 1937)

Morgan, Edmund S., 'The American Revolution: Revisions in Need of Revising', *WMQ*, 3rd ser., 14 (1957), pp. 3–15

Morgan, Gwenda, 'Community and Authority in the Eighteenth-Century South: Tidewater, Southside and Backcountry', *JAS*, 20 (1986), pp. 435–48

Novick, Peter, *That Noble Dream: The 'Objectivity Question' and the American Historical Profession* (Cambridge, MA and New York; 1988)

Pole, J. R., 'Historians and the Problem of Early American Democracy', *AHR*, 63 (1962), pp. 626–46

Wood, Gordon S., 'Rhetoric and Reality in the American Revolution', *WMQ*, 3rd ser., 23 (1966), pp. 3–32

African Americans, bond and free

Davis, David Brion, 'Slavery and the Post-World War II Historians', in Sidney W. Mintz (ed.), *Slavery, Colonialism, and Racism* (New York; 1974)

Franklin, John Hope, 'Afro-American History: State of the Art', *JAH*, 75 (1988), pp. 162–73

Huggins, Nathan I., 'The Deforming Mirror of Truth: Slavery and the Master Narrative of American History', *Radical History Review*, 49 (1991), pp. 25–46

Wood, Peter H., '"I Did the Best I Could for My Day": The Study of Early Black History during the Second Reconstruction, 1960 to 1976', *WMQ*, 3rd ser., 35 (1978), pp. 185–225

Women, gender, patriarchy

Brooks Higginbottam, Evelyn, 'African-American Women's History and the Metalanguage of Race', *Signs*, 17 (1992), pp. 251–74

Fletcher, Anthony, *Gender, Sex, and Subordination in England, 1500–1800* (New Haven, CT; 1995)

Knott, Sarah and Barbara Taylor (eds), *Women, Gender and Enlightenment* (Basingstoke; 2005)

Norton, Mary Beth, 'The Evolution of White Women's Experience in Early America', *AHR*, 89 (1984), pp. 593–619

Scott, Joan W., 'Gender: A Useful Category of Historical Analysis', *AHR*, 91 (1986), pp. 1053–75

Native Americans, borderlands, the west

Conn, Steven, *History's Shadow: Native America and Historical Consciousness in the Nineteenth Century* (Chicago; 2004)

Forum: 'The Middle Ground Revisited', *WMQ*, 3rd ser., 63 (2006), pp. 3–96

Nobles, Gregory H. 'Breaking into the Backcountry: New Approaches to the Early American Frontier, 1750–1800', *WMQ*, 3rd ser., 46 (1989), pp. 641–70

Wallace, Anthony F. C., *The Death and Rebirth of the Seneca* (New York; 1970)

History and memory

Cray, Robert E. Jr, 'Major John André and the three Captors: Class Dynamics and Revolutionary Memory Wars in the Early Republic, 1780–1831', *JER*, 17 (1997), pp. 371–97

Fitzpatrick, Ellen F., *History's Memory: Writing America's Past,*

1880–1980 (Cambridge, MA, and London; 2002)

Nash, Gary B., *First City: Philadelphia and the Forging of Historical Memory* (Philadelphia, PA; 2002)

Purcell, Sarah, *Sealed with Blood: War, Sacrifice and Memory in Revolutionary America* (Philadelphia, PA; 2002)

Young, Alfred F., *The Shoemaker and the Tea Party: Memory and the American Revolution* (Boston, MA; 1999)

New American history, New American political history

Beneke, Chris, 'The New New Political History', *Reviews in American History*, 33 (2005), pp. 314–24

Cogliano, Francis D., 'Founders Chic', *History,* 90 (2005), pp. 412–19

Pasley, Jeffrey L., Andrew W. Robertson and David Waldstreicher (eds), *Beyond the Founders: New Approaches to the Political History of the Early American Republic* (Chapel Hill, NC; 2004)

Thompson, Peter, *Rum Punch and Revolution: Taverngoing and Public Life in Eighteenth-Century Philadelphia* (Philadelphia; 1998)

Tuck, Stephen, 'The New American Histories', *Historical Journal*, 48 (2005), pp. 811–32

.

INDEX